W9-BKJ-706

"Revolution" is a powerful, violent word. But it is scarcely powerful or violent enough to describe the changes created by the process known as the industrial revolution. That radical upheaval, which began in England two centuries ago and spread around the globe, completely remade human society. In his introduction to this volume, historian Peter N. Stearns calls the industrial revolution "one of those rare occasions in world history when the human species has altered its framework of existence."

In this unique volume, Stearns and coauthor John Hinshaw examine this process of fundamental change, both from a global vantage point and close-up. They chronicle the progress of industrialization from 1760 to the present in all developed countries worldwide. Their goal is to create a portrait of the industrial revolution that reflects both its tremendous scope and its varied forms.

The volume focuses on the transformation of industry itself—the impact on work, factories, inventions, and government involvement in the workplace. But it also examines the revolution's enormous social impacts, such as alienation, consumerism, communism, unemployment, and the altered roles of women and black workers. It offers readers an in-depth understanding of the upheaval that has affected our lives more profoundly than any event since the invention of agriculture.

(Continued on back flap)

THE
ABC-CLIO
WORLD HISTORY
COMPANION TO

The Industrial Revolution

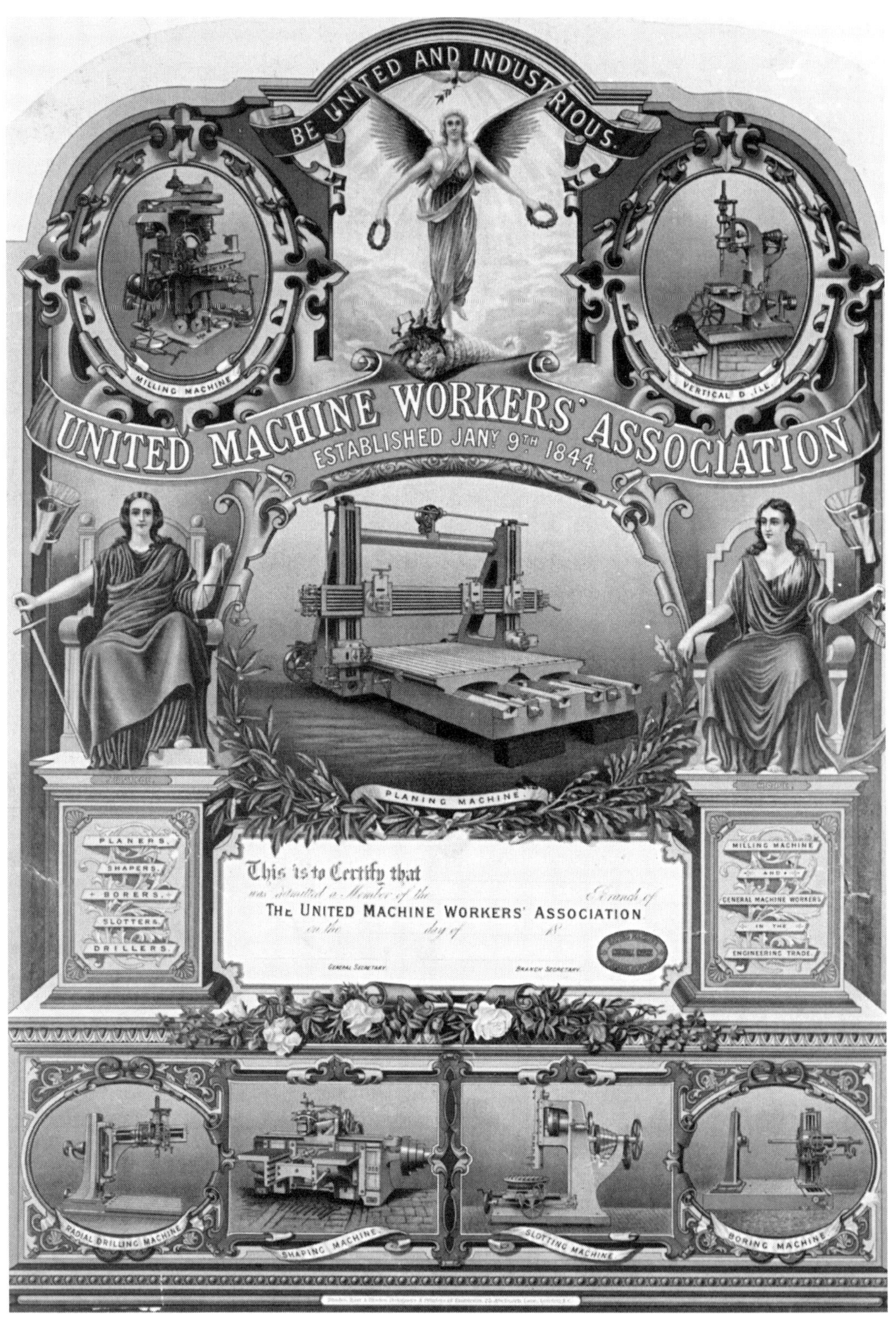

Established in England in 1844, the United Machine Workers' Association displays the instruments of the industry on its membership certificate.

THE
ABC-CLIO
WORLD HISTORY
COMPANION TO

The Industrial Revolution

Peter N. Stearns
John H. Hinshaw

WINGATE UNIVERSITY LIBRARY

Copyright © 1996 by Peter N. Stearns and John H. Hinshaw

All rights reserved. No part of this publication may be reproduced, stored in a retrieval system, or transmitted, in any form or by any means, electronic, mechanical, photocopying, recording, or otherwise, except for the inclusion of brief quotations in a review, without prior permission in writing from the publishers.

Library of Congress Cataloging-in-Publication Data

Stearns, Peter N.
The ABC-CLIO world history companion to the industrial revolution / Peter N. Stearns, John H. Hinshaw.
p. cm.
Includes bibliographical references and index.
ISBN 0-87436-824-3 (alk. paper)
1. History, Modern—19th century. 2. Industrial revolution. 3. Economic history. I. Hinshaw, John H., 1963– . II. ABC-Clio Information Services. III. Title.
D359.7.S74 1996 96-19326

02 01 00 99 98 97 10 9 8 7 6 5 4 3

ABC-CLIO, Inc.
130 Cremona Drive, P.O. Box 1911
Santa Barbara, California 93116-1911

This book is printed on acid-free paper ♾.
Manufactured in the United States of America

Contents

Introduction: Defining the Industrial Revolution

The industrial revolution began in Great Britain almost 250 years ago, in the 1760s. Within a half century it started to spread, first to northwestern Europe and the newly formed United States. Early industrialization in Belgium, France, and the American Northeast dates from the 1820s. By the 1880s industrial revolutions had begun in Russia and Japan as well as in several parts of southern and east-central Europe, such as Catalonia, Poland, and the Czech area around Prague. Canada, Australia, and parts of South Africa also undertook serious industrial development around this time. A third wave of industrial revolutions had been launched by the 1960s in South Korea and other parts of the Pacific Rim and, more tentatively, in Turkey, Mexico, and Brazil.

The term *industrial revolution* did not arise immediately. Some French writers spoke of a *révolution industrielle* early in the nineteenth century, emphasizing the importance of the mechanization of the French cotton industry. The philosopher and economist John Stuart Mill first used the term in English in 1848, and it began to spread. But the term became common only after the publication in 1884 of *Lectures on the Industrial Revolution in England* by the sociologist Arnold Toynbee. Toynbee used the phrase to dramatize what he thought was the moral decay of the British working classes. His lectures, published posthumously, sold well, and the term began to enter usage in textbook histories, although many scholars have objected to the term as an oversimplification of the process of industrialization in the nineteenth century. Unquestionably, the term needs careful definition, lest it sound too much like a literal revolution of a political sort, toppling existing institutions in the space of a decade or less. Most definitions focus on the experience of Europe and the United States, but more recent industrialization follows the same general principles.

Industrial revolutions constitute those rare occasions in world history when the human species alters its framework of existence. Indeed, the only previous development comparable in terms of sheer magnitude was the Neolithic revolution—the conversion from hunting and gathering to agriculture as the basic form of production for survival. Like the Neolithic revolution, industrial revolutions bring fundamental changes in the ways people work, where they live (settled communities rather than nomadic bands, then cities instead of rural communities and farms), the potential economic surplus available, and the numbers of people who can be supported around the world. These changes inevitably have ramifications reaching into almost every aspect of human experience—into the habits of thought and the relations between men and women as well as into systems of production and exchange. The full story of industrial revolution is precisely the examination of these multiple impacts.

The essence of industrial revolution, however, is fairly simple. Stripped to its bare bones, an industrial revolution consists of the application of new sources of power to the production process, achieved with transmission equipment necessary to apply this power to manufacturing. And it involves an increased scale of human organization that facilitates specialization and coordination at levels preindustrial groupings rarely contemplated.

The industrial revolution progressively has replaced humans and animals as the power sources of production with motors powered by fossil fuels, supplemented by water power and, very recently, by nuclear power. The key invention in Europe's industrial revolution was the steam engine, which harnessed the energy potential of coal. Later industrial revolutions also used electric and internal combustion motors (developed by the 1870s) and petroleum as well as coal. Before the industrial revolution almost all production in manufacturing and agriculture relied on equipment powered by people or draft animals, with some small assistance from waterwheels. Except for waterwheels, used mainly to mill grain, almost all tools were designed for manual use. Looms for weaving cloth were powered by foot pedals, and the fibers were strung by hand. The industrial revolution progressively introduced steam or other power to the production process and steadily increased the proportion of the process accomplished by equipment without direct human guidance. Power looms thus not only replaced foot pedals but also crossed threads automatically after a worker had attached them to the frame. Machine tending involved making sure the thread supply remained constant and dealing with snapped threads or other breakdowns; the cloth itself did not have to be touched by hand until it was gathered. Dramatic new sources of power—far more powerful than what people and animals could provide and transmitted to the product by semiautomatic machinery—were the technological core of the industrial revolution.

The organizational facet of the industrial revolution was initially symbolized by the factory, but the organizational principles spread beyond the factory itself. Most production operations before the late eighteenth century centered on the household, with collaboration and specialization among ten or fewer people. Even though many early industrial factories were small, they promoted the grouping of greater numbers of people for the production process. They also increased the amount of specialization; tasks were subdivided, which increased the total production even aside from new technology. Even most large work gangs before the industrial revolution, such as slaves in the mines and agricultural plantations of the Americas, had been relatively unspecialized. Finally, industrial-style organization involved more conscious management of workers toward a faster as well as a more fully coordinated work pace—again, a contrast with the more relaxed work styles characteristic of much preindustrial labor, including much slave labor. Thus, redefined work discipline and specialization, along with growth in the size of the work unit, constituted the organizational core of the industrial revolution. Labor systems that could not match these organizational characteristics, including slavery and purely household production, declined or even disappeared during industrialization.

The two central features of industrialization—revolutions in technology and in the organization of production—yielded one clear result: a great increase in the total output of goods and in individual worker output. Per capita productivity went up, in some cases massively. In specific industries, like cotton spinning, this effect showed by the early nineteenth century. A French or British spinning worker in 1820 France or Britain using steam-driven spindles instead of a manual spinning wheel could produce literally a hundred times the thread of a preindustrial counterpart. This productivity gain was unusual—the doubling of per capita output possible with early mechanical looms was a more typical result, as in Western European weaving by the 1820s and 1830s, but even this level could begin to transform the material framework of the society involved. Whole economies—including nonindustrial as well as industrial sections—grew between 2 percent (early industrial Britain) and 10 percent (contemporary China) per year. Increased output could be and often was used in various ways: to increase inequality in the standard of living, to support higher tax revenues, to provide for rapidly growing populations, or to change and possibly improve material conditions for the masses. These varied results and the balance among them form vital topics to explore in dealing with the impact of industrialization on individuals and societies.

An industrial revolution is unquestionably an odd type of revolution, which is one reason some economic historians object to the terms. The kinds of revolutions easiest to define are political upheavals, like the French Revolution of 1789 or the Russian Revolution of 1917, which seem to have defined beginnings and endings. The industrial revolution of Europe is another matter, for it clearly spread over many decades and countries and had no tidy beginning or end. For example, steam-powered factories began to be opened in Great Britain in the 1780s. The change quickly swept through a few important industries—cotton spinning was almost entirely mechanized within a decade—but the economy as a whole changed far more slowly. By 1850 there were still as many craft workers as factory workers and as many rural people as urban. Industrialization had changed the work lives as well as the prospects and outlook of the nonfactory majority, but it had not yet revolutionized them. And although productivity had exploded in a few sectors, again as in cotton spinning, overall per capita output grew only gradually (about 2 percent per year) because so much of the population still worked in traditional settings.

Industrialization, in fact, frequently gains momentum several decades after the first serious introductions of new equipment and factories. Some societies experimented with a few factories and had no subsequent industrial revolution at all. But even many regions that did industrialize in some manufacturing sectors saw a greater wave of change forty or fifty years after their initial engagement. The "second industrial revolution" in western Europe, late in the nineteenth century, thus perhaps brought more changes to more people than the first revolution did. Both Japan and Russia redefined and accelerated their industrialization processes in the 1920s and 1930s, a half century after these processes began. Industrial revolutions, clearly, are long, recurrent, and hard to pinpoint.

Debates about the concept of industrial revolution properly remind us of its complexity, but they need not distract from the fundamental alterations the process generates over time. The huge differences between the Britain of 1880 and that of 1780, the United States of 1900 and that of 1820, or the Japan of 1960 and that of 1880 took shape gradually and unevenly—but they unquestionably occurred.

The revolutionary quality of industrialization is particularly obvious in the world context. British and even French industrialization proceeded from earlier patterns of economic and social change. The introduction of steam-driven equipment denoted a real shift, but one that occurred within an already dynamic context. These countries had been developing capitalism for several centuries; many businesses invested in long-term projects (particularly in foreign trade) and sought high profits long before industrialization began. Growing interest in science, rising popular literacy, and increased consumer interests were other changes in western Europe that predated and prepared the industrial revolution there. Later industrial revolutions, largely imitative of earlier developments elsewhere, had revolutionary implications more quickly. Russia began to form a factory labor force within the same generation as it abolished rural serfdom and began to spread literacy; Japan produced a new entrepreneurial class only a generation after abolishing feudalism; South Korea launched industrialization only a generation after the economic and political oppression of Japanese occupation. In these cases, change moved with bewildering speed, and the industrial revolution formed a central part of massive social and political transformations.

Finally, the industrial revolution, albeit a special kind of revolution, does have chronological coherence. It begins (though often in societies already changing rapidly) with the widespread adoption of new equipment and the factory form in several key industries. But when does it end? Because many industrial forms spread gradually, the process does not have a neat termination point. French peasants, for example, began widespread use of tractors only after World War II; their commitment to mechanization in the production process came surprisingly late. The unevenness of industrialization means that fundamental changes may continue for well over a century after the process identifiably began. Furthermore, industrial revolution generates recurrent change even in the sectors it first affects. Many British cotton workers, faced in the 1890s with new American-devised machines that allowed a single worker to tend eight to sixteen mechanical looms rather than the two to four of early industrialization, judged that their work lives were changing in a far more radical fashion than those of their predecessors. They were probably wrong, but they had an arguable case. Whether they like it or not, industrial societies accept a commitment to recurrent cycles of technical and organizational innovation, and thus a periodic renewal of a sense of unsettled upheaval.

The most revolutionary period of the industrialization process ends, however, when most workers and managers (whether in factories or smaller workshops) use some powered equipment and operate according to some of the principles of industrial organization. At this point, the larger society has gained an ability to apply industrial procedures to most branches of the economy, and although it may not fully have done so (as with the somewhat laggard French peasants), virtually every major group has faced some serious adjustment to the impact of the industrial revolution. Historically, this point has been reached seventy to a hundred years after serious technological innovation first begins. It is legitimate, for example, to peg the end of the U.S. industrial revolution at about 1920, when factory production overwhelmingly dominated other forms in manufacturing and when half the population lived in cities. Vast economic changes were to occur after 1920, extending the transformations the industrial revolution had wrought, but the industrial context was set.

The definition of the industrial revolution, thus, includes a massive set of changes that begin when radical innovations in technologies and organizational forms are extensively introduced in key manufacturing sectors and that end, in the truly revolutionary phase, when these innovations are widely, though not necessarily universally, established in the economy at large. Subsequent changes, often quite unsettling, are virtually assured, but they arise within the contours of an industrial society.

The industrial revolution has had massive worldwide impact, even in regions that did not fully industrialize, from the late nineteenth century onward. Growing needs for markets and raw materials, plus new transport systems, organizational forms and weaponry, have altered world relationships and individual lives on every continent. Here is another, wider facet of industrialization essential to any definition.

The *ABC-CLIO World History Companion to the Industrial Revolution* focuses on central developments in the process of change from the eighteenth century to present-day industrialization. Thus it defines the major new machines, the new work processes, and many of the individuals and trade union groups directly involved. The international dimensions of the industrial revolution receive great emphasis. Too often, industrial history texts deal with the British process (unquestionably the first, and so in some senses the most important) but underplay other industrial revolutions. The debate over the term industrial revolution has suffered from undue focus on Britain; it is not surprising that the first experience was particularly gradual and in some ways hard to define. But industrial revolution has occurred in many places, and this book deals with various national patterns and uses a variety of national illustrations for key terms and events. Further, some treatment of the industrial revolution's impact on the world at large, even regions that have not yet industrialized fully, is essential, for the power of the transformation quickly altered economic and diplomatic patterns well beyond the industrial centers. This means that a variety of different industrial revolutions must be covered, including developments in East Asia and parts of Latin America quite recently. Further, the role of still other areas, such as India and Africa, in supplying and facing the impact of industrialization demands attention as part of the basic treatment of the subject.

Finally, while concentrating on developments most directly involved in the industrial revolution, the *Companion* pays serious attention to ramifications in other aspects of life. One of the great innovations in research on the industrial revolution in the past two decades has focused on its larger social impact. Industrial revolution is not just a technical or economic change. It affects women's experience and the treatment of older people; it alters the nature of war (and is often shaped by war in turn). Without trying to cover the whole of the last two centuries of world history, the *Companion* addresses the major effects of this fundamental modern transformation.

References On criticisms of the industrial revolution concept, Cameron, Rondo. "The Industrial Revolution: A Misnomer," *History Teacher* 15 (1982); "The Industrial Revolution: Fact or Fiction?" *Contention* 4 (1994). On key aspects of the process, Berg, Maxine. *The Age of Manufactures, 1700–1820.* Totowa, NJ: Barnes and Noble, 1985; Landes, David S. *The Unbound Prometheus: Technological Change and Industrial Development in Western Europe from 1750 to the Present.* Cambridge, UK: Cambridge University Press,1970; Stearns, Peter N. *The Industrial Revolution in World History*. Boulder, CO: Westview, 1993.

THE
ABC-CLIO
WORLD HISTORY
COMPANION TO

The Industrial Revolution

Abolitionism

Abolitionists advocated that slavery be restricted or abolished. During the eighteenth and nineteenth centuries, these activists in England and the United States helped to end the "peculiar institution." Many scholars argue that the success of abolitionism had more to do with the economic and political changes that the industrial revolution wrought on European and U.S. societies and economies than with the moral suasion of abolitionists.

In the early eighteenth century, many social groups in England benefited from and supported the lucrative trade in slaves between Africa and the Caribbean and the sugar produced on Caribbean plantations by unfree laborers. Support for slavery came not only from the planters (many of whom lived in England) but also from the merchants who outfitted slave expeditions and the workers who built the slave ships. The importance of sugar gave planters enormous political and economic power, and many invested their financial surplus in early manufacturing concerns. However, the planters' enormous political influence gradually atrophied in the early nineteenth century as the price of their sugar rose relative to sugar produced in non-English colonies. In response to the increasing costs of a sugar monopoly, merchants, workers and the growing class of industrialists advocated laissez-faire economic policies and questioned the mercantilist trade policies favored by planters. (Cheaper imports of foodstuffs would allow industrialists to effectively raise workers' standards of living without requiring a rise in wages.) The restriction of the slave trade was not a rejection of white supremacy so much as an expression of faith in laissez-faire economic policy. Antislavery campaigns may have influenced some workers' sense of the woes facing "free" industrial wage labor.

By the 1830s Britain had banned the international trade in slaves, but slave societies continued in the United States South until 1865 and in much of the Caribbean and Brazil until the 1880s. Although English abolitionists had boycotted sugar made with slave labor in English colonies, they did not argue that manufacturers should refuse to buy cotton or other goods made with unfree labor in other parts of the world.

During the late eighteenth and early nineteenth centuries in the United States, many white abolitionists opposed slavery partly out of belief in the superiority of wage labor and partly because slavery had "polluted" the racial purity of the country. These abolitionists advocated forcing slaves and free blacks to emigrate to the Caribbean or Africa. Gradually, black abolitionists succeeded in shifting the terms of debate, and by the 1830s an increasing number of white abolitionists favored the immediate emancipation of slaves without expatriation. However, many black abolitionists and radical whites questioned the usefulness of nonviolent tactics, such as petitions, because Congress (at the urging of southern planters) had passed a rule that forbade that body from debating the petitions of abolitionists. Abolitionists' agitation and the vehement reaction to it in the South nonetheless brought the question of slavery to the top of the political agenda and helped to precipitate the growing divisions that led to the American Civil War.

The most consistent advocates of abolition were, of course, black slaves and freedmen themselves. Blacks' resistance to slavery took many forms, from "passive" strategies such as feigning sickness or stealing food to the social revolution of "black Jacobins" in Haiti in the 1790s. Although slave revolts in the southern United States (such as that of Nat Turner in 1830) caused widespread panic among white southerners, they were relatively rare, for slaves were greatly outnumbered by whites. However, many slaves escaped to freedom, and a few, notably Harriet Tubman and Frederick Douglass, became famous speakers and writers for the abolitionist cause. Although abolitionists eventually succeeded in destroying the system of slavery, they were unable to overcome the institutionalized racism that turned freed slaves into sharecroppers—toiling in conditions little better than slavery.

See also Corn Laws; Emancipation; Racism.

References Blackburn, Robin. *The Overthrow of Colonial Slavery, 1776–1848* (1988); Williams, Eric. *Capitalism and Slavery* (1944).

Accidents

The industrial revolution unquestionably increased the rate and severity of accidents at work. Preindustrial work could cause accidents, in falls, cuts, and problems with draft animals. More commonly, certain jobs caused endemic health problems—printers and painters with lead poisoning, some weavers with chest deformities due to activating hand looms with their upper bodies. Industrial power equipment actually reduced the risk of some deformities, but it greatly heightened accidents and work-related illnesses of other sorts. Use of chemicals increased, causing various risks of poisoning. High-speed power equipment created new opportunities for loss of fingers and limbs. Boilers could and sometimes did explode. The expansion of metallurgical furnaces could cause burning or scalding. The tremendous growth of the labor force in coal mines and the need to dig mines ever deeper accounted for a series of major disasters.

Workers worried greatly about accident dangers. In early industrialization, employers seemed to take few precautions. Child workers on textile machinery, often required to repair thread while the machine was operating, frequently lost fingers. Many observers in virtually every new industrialization—including those occurring in places like Mexico today—claimed that employers refused to go to the modest expense of screening off exposed machine parts in a period when investment funds were stretched. Proper timbering in coal mines might be neglected. Of course it was not in employers' interests to ignore safety altogether; quite apart from worker reactions, accidents could damage equipment and delay production. Nevertheless, machinery became steadily more complicated, raising the risks. Growing use of power equipment in craft work—for example, machine-powered lathes in woodworking shops and on construction sites—increased the range of accidents in the later nineteenth century. The introduction of internal combustion engines for cranes and, soon, trucks and automobiles created further risks. Unquestionably, the rate of death by work accident rose dramatically in industrial societies during the nineteenth century.

Largely at the urging of unions, governments of industrial countries began to step up factory safety requirements and inspections from about 1870 onward. Some countries, including Germany, had a tradition of government inspection of mines that went back even earlier. Workers' concern about growing accident rates, particularly as the pace of work stepped up around 1900, prompted trade unions to press for more control, and major strikes often followed mine disasters. Better safety measures almost certainly reduced accident rates, though not necessarily worker anxiety, by 1900. Mining fatalities in Belgium fell by about 10 percent in the first decade of the twentieth century, for example. Many U.S. states, as well as several European countries, began to introduce workman's compensation laws, which required employers to pay workers injured on the job. Dominant thinking shifted from the assumptions of the early industrial period—when employers typically blamed workers for "imprudence" as the cause of accidents—to the notion that owners were accountable for working conditions.

Nevertheless, safety regulations remained a contentious area. In the interest of maintaining war output during World War I, the United States increased federal regulation, forming a Working Conditions Service in the Department of Labor. This regulation slackened during the 1920s, however, as union power declined and greater reliance was placed on voluntary employer efforts. New Deal legislation, in addition to providing disability payments under Social Security, again encouraged more attention to industrial hygiene.

Industrialization continued to promote more work accidents in the twentieth century, particularly in countries where the process was just beginning. Safety regulations often seemed lax, as governments worked to increase output and foreign investors looked to economize on their investments. Major disasters, such as the 1984 explosion in an U.S.-owned chemical plant in Bhopal, India, (over 200 people killed, over 20,000 maimed), were simply one indication of an ongoing problem. Even in advanced industrial societies the effectiveness of regulations varied; early in the 1990s many workers claimed that U.S. packing houses were causing increasing accidents by speeding up their cutting machines. Moreover, new equipment could pose unexpected problems; excessive computer use caused a growing incidence of carpal tunnel syndrome among office workers, for example. Finally, even as some of the most overt safety problems were brought under partial control, more insidious health problems, like stress and fatigue, seemed to increase in the twentieth century—one source of the increasing tendency among U.S. workers to retire at an earlier age.

See also Environment; State, Role of the.

References Rosner, David, and Gerald Markowitz, eds. *Dying for Work: Workers' Health and Safety in Twentieth-Century America* (1986); Stearns, Peter N. *Lives of Labor: Work in Maturing Industrial Society* (1975).

Advertising

Because the industrial revolution depended on growing consumer interest and generated a massive level of goods, advertising was inevitably bound up in the process. Specific industrial inventions, initially in printing and photography, also facilitated advertising by cutting the cost of newspapers and flyers and, ultimately, adding pictorial illustrations and film as well as radio outlets.

Advertising began in the eighteenth century. The growing number of store owners in England and other countries used eye-catching displays and signs to attract customers. Early newspapers routinely carried notices of products for sale, often intermingled with regular articles to blur the distinction between commerce and objective reporting. As industrialization advanced and the need to sell goods increased, advertising changed; in the West, the 1870s form a fairly clear dividing line. After this point, advertising was increasingly geared toward the masses as well as toward middle- and upper-class consumers. The growing mass press, like the London *Daily Mail*, depended on lots of advertising, which supported its cheap purchase price; in turn, flashy headlines and a gripping style helped lure working-class readers who would, of course, also see the ads. The tone of advertising changed as well. Most early advertising was informational, stressing availability, price, and quality. By the late nineteenth century, advertising took on a more emotional cast. Silk goods, for example, were described in terms of utility and price in U.S. newspaper lists even in the 1890s, but after 1900 they began to be touted as "alluring," "bewitching"—"to feel young and carefree, buy our silk." Similar transformations occurred for other products. Automobiles, for instance, were initially advertised largely in terms of economy, good mechanics, and sometimes speed. But by the 1930s advertising increasingly stressed cars' appearance and fashionability, in order to appeal to a wider market that included women.

By the early twentieth century, a substantial advertising business was beginning to develop; it came into its own in the United States by the 1920s. Modern advertisers clearly gained the capacity to create demand for goods. Famous cases have demonstrated that clever advertising,

By the 1920s, manufacturers encouraged the purchase of their products through advertisements that asked consumers to identify themselves with the product.

rather than product quality, have boosted one brand of cigarettes over another. Advertisers were also constrained by public beliefs, however, and they worked within the culture, advertising products in terms of existing family values, ideas about gender, and so on.

See also Consumerism.

References Ewen, Elizabeth, and Stuart Ewen. *Captains of Consciousness: Mass Images and the Shaping of American Consumers* (1982); Marchand, Roland. *Advertising the American Dream: Making Way for Modernity* (1985).

AFL

See American Federation of Labor.

African-American Workers

See Black Workers.

Agriculture

The industrial revolution unquestionably diminishes and transforms agriculture in terms of the relative importance of its product and the proportion of the labor force it engages. Social classes based in agriculture, notably the peasantry and the aristocracy, decline, and urban workers and businessmen rise, though the process is usually gradual. Changes in agriculture are absolutely essential for industrialization, for greater productivity in food must precede any massive growth in the urban labor force.

Significant changes in European agriculture began in the late seventeenth century, initially unconnected to industrialization proper. Led by the Dutch, many farmers and estate owners began to drain marshes, expanding the land available for farming. New farming principles were introduced, such as the use of nitrogen-fixing crops such as the turnip. Many groups discussed better methods, and individual promoters, like "Turnip" Townshend in England, spread the gospel of innovation. By periodically planting turnips or peas, land could be used annually, and many areas gradually moved away from the traditional three-field system in which one-third of the land had to be left fallow every year. Some new equipment was introduced, such as the seed drill, and estate owners, particularly in England, experimented with better methods of stock breeding. In other words, some of the same innovative ideas that were affecting manufacturing entered agriculture, particularly where large estate owners were eager for new profits (as in England). Peasant farming, typically, changed more slowly, though here, too, tools improved, as the more efficient scythe replaced sickles for harvesting. Most important was the increasing use of New World crops such as the potato, which produced a greater abundance of cheap foods, spurring population growth and releasing more starch products for sale in urban markets. Collectively, these changes, sometimes called an "agricultural revolution," constituted the first big improvements in European farming since the Middle Ages. They sustained both growing populations and increased urbanization.

Advances in agricultural productivity accompanied the early stages of industrialization almost everywhere. The Japanese government promoted more efficient farming in the 1870s and 1880s. Russia's emancipation of the serfs in 1861, though complicated, did generate increased market production, and under the Soviet government the collectivization program strove to produce more food with fewer workers, if only with mixed success. Governments (for example, Japan) also began requiring tax payments in cash, which helped provide industrial capital but also forced peasants to sell more food to meet the tax payments.

Once in motion, industrial revolutions further encourage agricultural change. Growing urban markets help motivate increasing commercial specialization on the farms. Science and the growing chemical industry are enlisted to produce new fertilizers—a major development in Germany from the 1830s onward. New equipment becomes available as the principles of mechanization are applied to agriculture.

Thus the harvesters and other devices introduced by the mid-nineteenth century helped convert vast lands in North America to efficient commercial grain farming to feed not only North American cities but also industrial centers in Europe. By 1850 Britain had begun to reduce any effort to maintain adequate agriculture, realizing that it was more productive to concentrate on industry, including industrial exports, while importing foods from eastern Europe, Australia, New Zealand, and North America. Although the British pattern was unique—no other major industrial country let agriculture slide to such an extent—world trade in foods supplemented industrialization efforts in many parts of western Europe. Thanks to agricultural change and, sometimes, new imports, rural populations began to fall rapidly, dropping to under 50 percent of the total in England by 1850 and continuing to plummet. By the twentieth century not only the relative size but also the absolute number of the farming population had plunged in every industrial area, thanks to the steadily increasing efficiency of industrial agriculture.

See also Chemical Industry; Collectivization; Green Revolution; McCormick; Plantations; Potato.

References Horn, Pamela. *The Rural World, 1780–1850: Social Change in the English Countryside* (1981); Stearns, Peter N., and Herrick Chapman. *European Society in Upheaval: Social History since 1750* (1992).

Air Conditioning

In 1922 Willis Carrier made it possible not only to cool air (through ice or mechanical fans) but to remove humidity from hot, sticky air, and thus was air conditioning born. Carrier used coils filled with highly volatile refrigerants, such as freon, to draw heat and moisture from inside rooms and transfer it outside; as the refrigerants cooled, air was pumped back to the inside where the process began again. This technological innovation helped to speed the spread of corporate headquarters from the North to such southern cities as Houston, Dallas, and Atlanta. Air conditioning has accompanied the spread of multinational corporations throughout the world in the twentieth century. Initially used in movie theaters, hotels, and corporate headquarters, room and home air-conditioners were quickly adopted by the upper and middle classes. An industry in its own right, air conditioning was increasingly installed in office buildings, public facilities, homes, and even automobiles throughout the entire world. Although they create a physical climate many find more conducive to concentrated, sustained physical or mental labor, the chemical ingredients in air conditioning, ironically, have helped to deplete the ozone, hastening the greenhouse effect that is warming the planet.

See also Dupont de Nemours; Environment.

Alger, Horatio

See Self-Help Literature.

Ali, Muhammed (1769–1849)

This Ottoman governor seized Egypt from the Ottoman Empire in 1805, ruling it until the 1840s. Ali was the first Muslim leader to understand the significance of Western industrialization, which had been brought home to Egypt by a successful French invasion in 1798 and then by subsequent British intervention. Ali sought to establish an Egyptian state that could catch up with the West by imitating its economy. He expanded education and updated the tax code to promote business. He sent many Egyptian students to Europe to learn the principles of the new technology. By the 1830s he was importing English equipment and workers to build textile factories, sugar refineries, paper mills, and armaments shops. He also promoted cash crops like cotton to give Egypt new earnings on the world markets. His industrialization effort failed, however, for the Egyptian factories could not compete with their European counterparts. Britain wanted no strong power in the region, and it therefore aided the Ottoman government in blocking Ali's efforts at military expansion.

Ali's promotion of more commercial agriculture was, however, a lasting success, making Egypt a supplier of raw materials in the growing world market while also enriching a new group of landowners and merchants. His efforts, then, display the mixed results of one of the first efforts to react to industrialization outside Europe itself.

Alienation

The concept of alienation is frequently used by social historians dealing with industrial work and the working class. The word means hostility to or estrangement from some activity or experience. Karl Marx, in *Capital*, applied the term particularly to the work processes of industrial capitalism. Because workers no longer owned producing property and because their formal training often declined, Marx argued that they were alienated from the products of their work, with no real stake or identity in the manufacturing process. His claim made good theoretical sense, though historians and social scientists have had problems coming up with practical measures of alienation that would show how and to what degree workers lost a sense of meaning. Labor protest articulated many grievances concerning work—but can the most alienated workers even advance clear goals? Certainly some workers, at various stages of industrialization, have seemed alienated. In the early stages of the industrial experience some workers simply left the factories, even though they had no clear options, simply because they could not stand the strangeness and the lack of meaning. Later, some workers—for example, the German miner Max Lotz, whose letters were published by a social scientist soon after 1900—articulated what must be judged alienation. They spoke of their work as a daily struggle, not so much because of physical toil but because the supervision was so severe, the significance so unclear, the process so nerve-racking. Lotz was a sincere socialist who hoped an ultimate socialist victory would change the framework of labor; he had no faith in stopgap reforms, for the problems ran too deep.

Most workers were probably not profoundly alienated, for many did make partial accommodation, such as instrumentalism, that is, reducing expectations of work in favor of higher pay. But a degree of alienation has dogged the experience of industrial work for many people, particularly assembly-line workers.

The concept of alienation has been extended in the twentieth century to include white-collar workers whose careers do not meet their expectations of middle-class success. These workers encounter alienation in midcareer and express it by working less hard and often seeking early retirement. Alienation, blue- and white-collar, may also be expressed by frequent illness. In sum, alienation is an important if somewhat elusive aspect of the impact of industrialization.

References Koditschek, Theodore. *Class Formation and Urban Industrial Society: Bradford, 1750–1850* (1990); Shepard, Jon. *Automation and Alienation* (1971).

Alternating Current

Initial transmission of electricity used direct current, which flows evenly through a wire but requires a complex commutator to transmit successfully to a motor. Direct current is still used in batteries, as in automobiles, but it requires a switching arrangement—the commutator—to connect one after another to the coils on a rotating armature to act with the poles and cause the motor to rotate. This complexity inspired the search for an alternating current that would reverse flows at rapid intervals, or cycles, connecting with motors through slip rings. Alternating current, used for home appliances, simplifies both the generators and the electric motors. Moreover, it can easily be transformed to high voltages, which greatly increases efficiency over long-distance power lines. Electric transformers can step up the voltage for transmission, then step it down for use in actual motors.

Though developed by the work of several researchers, alternating current was first utilized by Nikola Tesla (1856–1943), an electrical engineer born in Austria-Hungary. Trained in a technical school and at the University of Prague, Tesla then moved to the United States, where he invented a motor with coils arranged so that when alternating current energized them, the resulting magnetic field rotated at a predetermined speed. He patented his motor in 1888 and then sold it to George Westinghouse transportation equipment.

See also Electronics.

Amalgamated Society of Engineers

This great British union of skilled factory workers—the British term for machine tools workers is engineers—was formed in 1851 from a variety of strong local organizations. The union, with 11,000 initial members, was formed on craft union principles, emphasizing the valuable skills of its members and attempting to bargain carefully rather than dissipate resources in frequent strikes. Like other British "New Model" unions in the 1850s, the ASE placed a premium on respectability and self-improvement for its members, while also providing solid financial benefits such as assistance in illness and unemployment. The union also pressed for political gains and helped induce the grant of suffrage to male workers in 1867 and the legalization of unions in 1871 and 1875. Direct bargaining with employers helped do away with nonmonetary payments and long delays between paydays. The success of this kind of union was reduced by the deep depression of the 1870s. In later decades the union, though still strong, lost a number of bitter strikes against employers who sought to introduce piece-rate payments as a means of more fully controlling worker productivity. This more difficult context prompted the ASE to cooperate more fully with new industrial unions and to provide some of the resources and leadership for general movements such as the Trades Union Congress, though the union remained relatively moderate.

American (U.S.) Civil War (1861–1865)

This war pitted the North, the region of the United States most committed to industrial production and wage labor, against the South, the region most closely tied to plantation-style agricultural exports based on slave labor. The North had an overwhelming superiority in railroads, iron mills, and machine production; the South had some industrial facilities, but believed that Britain, the chief consumer of Southern cotton, would eventually intervene to end the war. The North's military strategy destroyed the economy of the South by blockading its exports and Britain quickly turned India and Egypt into suppliers of cotton. The South, like many Third World countries, learned that the production of agricultural commodities rarely provides economic leverage on industrial countries. The South's defeat was ensured when the North encouraged the defection of Southern slaves, many of whom formed a crucial part of the North's army.

The economic impact of the war was enormous. Together, the North and South had expended 5 billion 1860 dollars in the struggle and sustained 700,000 deaths and several hundred thousand wounded. Many fortunes were made by those who had supplied the Northern army. In one case, J. P. Morgan bought several thousand defective rifles for $3.50 apiece and sold them to a general for $22 each. Much Southern industry, crops, and livestock were destroyed. As a result of the emancipation of slaves, Southern planters lost most of their capital; the South's economic development lagged far behind the North for many years. Although historians disagree whether the war accelerated industrialization in the North, the North definitely passed several laws during the war that stimulated national economic growth, such as the Homestead Act, banking legislation, and land grants for universities and railroads. Use of railroads and factory-produced goods made this the first "industrial" war, and it was studied as such by outside observers, including German generals.

See also Emancipation; Plantation.
Reference Andreano, Ralph. *The Economic Impact of the American Civil War* (1962).

American Federation of Labor (AFL)
The American Federation of Labor was formed in 1886 to coordinate the activities of national craft unions. After the failure of the Knights of Labor to organize industrial unions or to establish production cooperatives, the AFL advocated the view that unions should focus primarily on economic issues, using the leverage that their occupations gave them with employers. This approach favored highly skilled workers, and the mainstays of the AFL were the building trades (carpenters, plumbers, etc.). By 1904 the AFL had about 1.5 million members.

Unlike most European unions that affiliated with social democratic or labor parties, the AFL's brand of pragmatism led it to downplay political issues and avoid direct affiliation with political parties. Instead, the U.S. union followed the advice of Samuel Gompers, the AFL's leader, of "rewarding your friends and punishing your enemies." Nevertheless, a large number of AFL members were indeed socialists, and a resolution in 1894 calling for the nationalization of all the means of production was only narrowly defeated. Instead, the AFL called for the eight-hour day, selective nationalization of utilities and the railroads, and other legislative reforms. Another leftist insurgency in 1903 was beaten back, and shortly thereafter Gompers entered a short-lived alliance with some manufacturers via the National Civic Federation. By the 1940s the AFL's policy of political neutrality was weakening and the AFL began to acknowledge its de facto endorsement of the Democratic Party.

The AFL had a somewhat antagonistic relationship to the unskilled, black, female, and immigrant parts of the U.S. working class. During the 1910s the AFL opposed unemployment insurance because it felt workers should simply be paid enough to take care of themselves during layoffs and feared that the benefit would make workers dependent upon the government. The AFL supported the exclusion of the Chinese from the United States, a view that most white workers shared. Although in the 1880s the AFL attempted to forbid its members from barring black workers, it had little power over its member unions; by the early 1900s the federation allowed unions either to exclude blacks outright, or to organize them into separate locals.

The AFL was largely unsuccessful in organizing workers in mass production industries such as steel or auto, partly because of unionists' views of the unskilled but also because unions invariably confronted not only employers but also the police, state militia, or even federal troops. As the industrial sector of the economy grew throughout the twentieth century, the AFL came to represent a proportionally smaller part of the working class (although the federation's membership actually was slowly expanding). The Great Depression ravaged the AFL, reducing its membership by about one-third. The federation proved unwilling or unable to organize industrial workers, and the AFL expelled the more radical CIO unions in 1938. The two federations merged in 1955.

See also Industrial Workers; Knights of Labor.
Reference Philip Taft. *The A.F. of L. in the Time of Gompers* (1957).

Anarchism
See Syndicalism.

Argentina
In the nineteenth century Argentina's economy was dominated by the exports of hides, beef, and wheat from its rich pampas. Although the country made few manufactured goods, its volume of agricultural goods made it one of the ten largest participants in the world market by 1900. By 1920 Argentina "possessed" over 20,000 miles of railroad, most of it owned by British banks, and half of its population was urbanized. Unlike most of Latin America, nearly all of Argentina relied on

wages for their survival. World Wars I and II, as well as the Great Depression of the 1930s, hampered Argentina's exports and hindered its imports of manufactured goods. Argentina responded by following a policy of import substitution of manufactured products; by the 1930s half a million Argentineans worked in industry. Industrial production soared in the 1940s and 1950s under the government of populist Juan Perón, who relied not only on the military but the trade unions for his political survival. Perón tried to diversify Argentina's economy by diverting profits from its agricultural exports into industry as well as social welfare schemes. Argentina's industrial economy slowly expanded until 1976, when it was decimated by the open-market policies of the military junta that ruled the country from 1976 to 1983.

See also Perónism; World Systems Theory.

Reference Lewis, Paul H. *The Crisis of Argentinean Capitalism* (1990).

Aristocracy

The most significant relationship between the aristocracy and the industrial revolution was a negative one. In the long run, though often very gradually, industrialization reduced the importance of the aristocracy. By promoting new ways to generate and collect wealth and encouraging a social system in which money began to replace traditional status and legal privilege as the chief criterion for success, industrialization promoted a new elite of big businessmen, who dominated the traditional aristocracy. This process took many decades. Many businessmen remained impressed by aristocratic prestige and sought to imitate their traditional betters by buying landed estates, marrying their daughters to aristocratic heirs, and cooperating with the aristocracy politically (as in compromise tariff legislation). At the end of the nineteenth century a mixed upper class of businessmen and aristocrats dominated much of Europe. The full collapse of the aristocracy came only by the mid-twentieth century. A similar, perhaps even more durable, aristocratic-entrepreneur collaboration developed during the Meiji restoration in Japan.

Aristocrats had difficulty adapting to the principles of an industrial economy, and not only because agriculture was their primary base. Their class traditions argued against too much devotion to money-grubbing and specialized training. Many aristocrats attacked industrialization by fighting for protection for agriculture. Individual aristocrats played an important role in advocating labor reforms—to safeguard workers against the worst industrial hardships but also to counterbalance upstart factory owners. This latter motivation was a major source of early reform laws in Britain and, with Bismarck, in Germany. Countries without an aristocratic tradition, like the United States, were slower to moderate some of the harsh conditions of industrialization.

Individual aristocrats, finally, played a significant role in outright industrialization, even though their class as a whole might suffer. British aristocrats, less suspicious of commerce than their counterparts on the Continent, helped set a context for the first industrial revolution. Several major landowners in Britain and some Prussian estate owners (the Junkers) expanded mining operations or even established factories as part of the early industrial process. Their capital and influence helped launch industrialization in many European countries and in Japan.

See also Feudalism.

Reference Spring, David. *European Landed Elites in the Nineteenth Century* (1977).

Arkwright, Richard (1732–1792)

This English inventor advanced the transition from hand spinning to power spinning in factories by inventing the water frame, patented in 1769. The water frame used rollers, revolving at different speeds, to stretch out fiber, which then was twisted into thread by flyers and bobbins operating continuously. Arkwright did not invent roller spinning, but he perfected it and made it commercially profitable. His machinery was first run by water power, but the steam engine was soon used successfully. Arkwright's thread was twisted so hard that it was mainly used for calico (cotton) wraps. Arkwright also patented improvements in accessory processes, such as carding of fiber, in 1775. He was one of the rare early industrial inventors who also succeeded in business, in contrast to most of his colleagues who saw their ideas exploited by other entrepreneurs.

See also Crompton, Samuel; Hargreaves, James; Textiles.

References Derry, Kingston, and T. I. Williams. *A Short History of Technology* (1961); Mathias, Peter. *The Transformation of England* (1979).

Armour, Philip Danforth (1832–1901)

Philip Armour was one of the "robber barons" of the late nineteenth century. After making a fortune providing meat to the Union army during the American Civil War, he formed Armour and Company (1870), which by the 1890s was one of the largest meatpacking companies in the U.S. He helped to develop the centralized slaughtering of cows and pigs that turned butchering from a localized craft into a mass production industry. Instead of one man killing, skinning, and turning a hog's carcass into food, workers repeatedly did one stage of the work along continuously moving "disassembly lines." Armour also helped to develop modern marketing and distribution of meat by using, for example, refrigerated railroad cars to transport fresh meat to distant markets. Armour's philosophy was to "use everything from the hog but the squeal," and what couldn't be made into bacon or sausage was turned into lard, soap, or glue.

See also Refrigeration.

Artificial Silk Company (Russia)

This company is an example of the role of foreign entrepreneurship in the early stages of Russian industrialization. It was founded in Myszkov in 1911 by Belgian entrepreneurs linked to a Brussels concern. The company developed an improved process for treating cellulose and producing rayon. The company did fairly well, but, like many foreign firms, reported problems with Russian workers: the workers were hostile to non-Russian direction and seemed slow to pick up the necessary new skills. Strikes not only disrupted production but sometimes threatened the lives of the foreign managers and the skilled workers brought in to train local personnel. In this context the need to recruit Russian management emerged quickly. Foreign firms like the Artificial Silk Company were swallowed up in the wake of the 1917 revolution.

See also Russia; Synthetic Fabrics.

Artisans

Artisans were one of the most important classes of workers in the industrialization process, but their role was unusually complex. All preindustrial economies had large groups of artisans, both urban and rural, responsible for all kinds of manufacturing, from textiles and food processing to traditional metallurgy. Artisans are workers who manufacture products using relatively simple tools while relying on considerable skills. Typically, they undergo an extensive training period as apprentices. Then they serve a stint as journeymen, working in a small artisan shop alongside the owner-master, often living and dining there in conditions of considerable familiarity if not equality. Many journeymen aspire to become masters in their own right, and although the real opportunities vary, some mobility within one's lifetime is common. Many urban artisans form organizations, or guilds, that protect artisanal conditions and try to prevent undue change. Artisans and their guilds are proud of their products and seek to maintain quality.

The industrial revolution operated on principles different from those of the artisanal economy. Innovation replaced reliance on traditional methods; powered equipment cut into skills and artistry; mass production displaced emphasis on artistic quality; a gap between employer and worker replaced the more collaborative customs of artisans. Guild controls over technique and firm size had to be weakened before serious industrialization could take place. In the long run, industrialization reduced the size of the artisanry, while undermining its conditions of work. This was true in England after 1850 and in Japan after 1920. In Japan, artisan traditions of abundant leisure were particularly attacked during industrialization.

Individual artisans, however, were vital to the industrialization process. Many crucial inventions came from artisans eager to improve methods of production; this ingenuity was a particularly vital resource in eighteenth-century Britain, where a traditionalist guild system was less significant. Larger numbers of artisans took skilled factory jobs, where they could parlay their skills into higher earnings. This shift was essential in metallurgy and machine building, for it created an important bond between artisans and the "aristocracy of labor" in the factories and inhibited unity of action with unskilled and skilled workers. Many artisan masters expanded operations to become factory entrepreneurs, another important connection between craft experience and industrial innovation.

Artisans also sought to resist industrialization or develop new organizations to defend their position. Because of their skills and tradition, artisans were in a better position to organize than were most early factory workers. Some artisans opposed the industrial economy outright, converting to early forms of socialism or fighting in revolutions such as 1848. Other artisans formed unions to bargain for better wages and hours. Almost everywhere, artisans formed the initial trade unions, even in Russia, where artisans in newly growing cities like St. Petersburg imported goals and organizational capacity from central Europe in the 1860s. Although artisan (craft) unions often stood aloof from factory workers, seeking to bargain respectably and to rely on scarce skills, the artisanal lead helped guide larger trade union movements during the nineteenth century in Europe and North America. Artisans also provided leadership for many socialist movements and for various labor reforms and educational gains.

The number of artisans increased in most early industrial revolutions, for growing cities needed more carpenters, bakers, and jewelers. Only a few artisanal crafts, such as weaving, were substantially displaced by the new factories. Gradually, however, additional inventions, like the sewing machine or new shoe manufacturing equipment, began to reduce the number of outright artisans. Moreover, after 1850 artisanal conditions themselves began to be affected by new equipment and a more industrial pace. Much labor strife in the later nineteenth century involved artisans (construction workers, for instance) fighting to retain some control over their jobs. On the whole, the distinction between artisans and other kinds of manufacturing workers became less important as a result of these trends, though some differentiation persisted through the twentieth century.

See also Discipline; Revolutions of 1848; Work; Working Class.

References Rock, Howard P. *Artisans of the New Republic: The Tradesmen of New York City in the Age of Jefferson* (1979); Stearns, Peter, and Herrick Chapman. *European Society in Upheaval: Social History since 1750* (1992); Zdatny, Steven. *The Politics of Survival: Artisans in Twentieth-Century France* (1990).

Assembly Line

The creation of a continuous flow of production was the goal or reality in a number of late nineteenth century industries, including oil refining, meatpacking, and steel. However, the moving assembly line was most inextricably linked to the rise of the mass-produced automobile. Like the development of the automobile itself, the development of the assembly line occurred in stages and arose from the effort of a number of different persons and companies.

In the early twentieth century, most car production was done in batches by small groups of skilled workers. Henry Ford recognized the possibilities of the assembly line, which allowed continuous production of cars by semi-skilled workers. Between 1908 and 1913 Ford installed assembly lines in his factories. Although Ford recognized the value of the concept, teams of engineers worked out the details. Other auto companies quickly adopted the practice, and by 1912, Buick, for instance, was producing the chassis of their cars on assembly lines, though its chassis were simply pushed from one work site to another on lines of two-by-fours. Ford, however, led the industry, putting his cars on chain-driven assembly lines that were combined with scientific management techniques, and production increased dramatically. Semi-skilled workers performed repetitive motions on small parts of the process as each unit moved by.

Ford's new factories were built in order to take full advantage of the assembly line. Instead of working in cramped quarters, new facilities allowed moving assembly lines to converge at the appropriate moment. By 1914 Ford's Highland Park factory had 14,000 workers and 15,000 machines. His new River Rouge plant was even more advanced: "In conveyers alone it was a wonderland of devices. Gracy, belt, buckle, spiral, pendulum gravity roller, overhead monorail, 'scenic railway' and 'merry-go-round,' elevating flight—the list was long both in range and in adaptation to special purpose." Ford's strategy was to radically lower the price of his product and build a "car for the great multitude." The strategy worked. Between 1909 and 1914 the price of the Model T fell from $900 to $440, and by 1923 Ford had gained 55 percent of the world market in automobiles.

The constant, brisk pace made the work difficult, and Ford had great difficulty in maintaining a work force. At certain points, turnover in his factories was 1,000 percent a year. Because Ford had a very popular product, he was able to dramatically raise wages and institute a series of social welfare programs. Workers' adaptation to the assembly line was never complete, however, and their dissatisfaction contributed to the rise of industrial unionism in the 1930s.

See also Fordism.

References Flink, James J. *The Automobile Age* (1988); Meyer, Stephen. *The Five Dollar Day: Labor, Management, and Social Control in the Ford Motor Company, 1890–1921* (1981).

Australia

Since the nineteenth century the Australian economy has been based in large part on exports to other industrial areas. Both agricultural products—meat and wool—and minerals were shipped, first particularly to Britain, then elsewhere; by the late twentieth century Australia had become Japan's primary provider of all raw materials except fuel. Like Canada, Australian production was based on advanced technology, which permitted high wages and industrial living standards. Britain and (after 1950) the United States supported extensive investments. Australia also generated large industries, mainly for its own consumption. A huge steel mill was set up in 1915. By the 1950s 28 percent of the labor force was in manufacturing. An active labor movement also developed in Australia, and the country pioneered in considerable welfare legislation.

Reference Wilson, Charles. *Australia, 1788–1988: The Creation of a Nation* (1987).

Automation

Automation is the mechanization of the work process and one of the classic stratagems by which employers can gain increases in productivity as well as enhance their control over the work process itself. Since industrialization is by definition a replacement of human or animal power by mechanical power, the development of automation is an intrinsic, though controversial, aspect of the industrialization process. Although automation was a constantly evolving process throughout the nineteenth century, it definitely surged in the latter nineteenth and the early twentieth centuries when such industries as machine building, automobiles, and shipbuilding tried to supply a rapidly expanding market and then again after World War II in industries such as automobiles, electronics, and petrochemicals.

Viscose rayon manufacture at a Courtaulds Fibers plant in Mobile, Alabama, in 1995. Automated textile production replaced the manual labor of traditional workers during the early nineteenth century.

In early nineteenth-century Britain, after the putting-out system had initiated the subdivision of the process of making cloth, industrialists began to consolidate the work force into factories. Using steam and water power, mill owners began to use new machinery to help deskill the craft of certain workers, such as hand-loom weavers or wool croppers. Some of these workers argued that the new system, although economical in the monetary sense, upset what historians have come to call workers' "moral economy" because it dehumanized their work and lowered their standard of living. Some workers petitioned mill owners, threatening retribution from "General Ludd"; in some cases, Luddite workers destroyed the machinery that threatened their livelihood.

Whether out of a shared belief in progress or because overt machine wrecking was futile, workers generally sought to restrict rather than oppose outright the imposition of new machinery. Throughout the nineteenth century, skilled textile workers, some of their crafts created by new technology, sought to limit the number of machines that a person could operate. Whenever possible, skilled workers, such as machinists, sought to restrict the entry of new workers, for employers often hired younger workers to use new machines to perform tasks prohibited by the work rules.

Battling new technology and opposing the dilution of work rules was frequently a frustrating task. Puddlers, glass blowers, and machinists were frequently successful in slowing down the pace of automation throughout the length of the nineteenth century, but most workers, including textile workers and cobblers, met with little success. Even extremely highly skilled work could be automated and jobs eliminated within a short period of time. In the 1920s and 1930s tens of thousands of rollers of steel sheets were replaced by mechanized rolling mills as steel companies attempted to supply the burgeoning mass market for automobiles. Displaced workers referred to the new mills as "big morgues" since they eliminated so many jobs. Beginning in the 1910s U.S. auto companies such as Ford and General Motors became leaders in automation.

New technology did not always simply deskill workers: the jobs of highly skilled machinists and open-hearth workers, for example, were both made possible by advances in workplace technology. However, the accelerating pace of automation in the twentieth century eroded much of the craft-like control that machinists and open-hearth workers once held over the workplace. Many of the building trades experienced a fair degree of new technology but were still considered skilled. Carpentry, a preindustrial craft, began to use mass-produced windows in the mid-nineteenth century, and by the mid-twentieth century carpenters were using power saws and mechanical nail drivers. By contrast, the skills of plasterers were almost totally undermined by the advent of mass-produced "sheet rock" in the mid-twentieth century.

Although automation is frequently perceived as economically inevitable, governments have generally played a key role in developing automation. In the early nineteenth century, the U.S. government funded Eli Whitney's development of interchangeable parts and helped to train many of the men who would later lead the machine tool and armaments industries. Similarly, throughout the twentieth century, the U.S. military has funded defense corporations' attempts to create completely automated factories. The automation efforts of General Electric were satirized in the mid-1950s by Kurt Vonnegut in *Player Piano*. Indeed, some historians have argued that the ideal of the workerless factory captivated employers who confronted militant unions of machinists not because automation was more efficient (it often was more expensive) but because it gave the illusion of total control, free of operator error.

After World War II, the pace of automation greatly accelerated as Fordist employers sought to supply mass markets while holding down overall labor costs. At least in Europe and the United States, most unions have acquiesced to automation as long as the remaining workers shared in the productivity gains of employers. One of the classic examples is the United Mine Workers, which in the late 1940s allowed the mechanization of mining in order to stabilize the profitability of the industry (which was losing markets to oil) and to guarantee the remaining miners decent wages. Similarly, dockworkers' unions agreed to containerization programs, in which cargo was loaded via crane in large containers (often directly onto trains or trucks) in exchange for large wage gains. However, many workers express concern about being subordinated to the needs of machinery—a concern enhanced by the recognition that continuing technological advances may eliminate their jobs.

Since the 1960s the increasing sophistication of computers has allowed employers to closely supervise, deskill, and automate jobs as diverse as fast-food cook, airline receptionist, social worker, and real estate agent. For instance, airline receptionists are electronically monitored to make sure they are not spending too much time with their customers and that they are meeting a quota of sales for their shift. Data-entry work is often done on computer terminals in poorer countries or regions and then transferred by satellite to companies. The accelerating pace of automation and the increase in unemployment since the 1970s have weakened the union movement throughout the world, removing an important barrier to this process.

References Garson, Barbara. *Electronic Sweatshop: How Computers Are Transforming the Office of Tomorrow into the Factory of the Past* (1988); Noble, David F. *Forces of Production: A Social History of Automation* (1984).

Automobile

The development of the internal combustion automobile resulted from the cumulative accumulation of technical knowledge among European and U.S. entrepreneurs. Gasoline-powered engines triumphed over steam, electric, or diesel (which inventors had experimented with to make road vehicles) largely because gasoline engines were smaller, more reliable, and more powerful and because by the late nineteenth century gasoline had become a cheap and readily available commodity. In the late nineteenth century, European car makers such as Carl Benz produced more advanced machines (and, equally important, cars that were more commercially successful) than their U.S. counterparts. By the early twentieth century, however, U.S. car producers were closing the technical gap and were producing cars for a mass market rather than for the higher-priced European "class market."

By the 1910s Henry Ford's cheap and sturdy Model T had become the most common automobile in the world. Ford was able to lower the production costs of his Model T by applying the time management strategies of Frederick Winslow Taylor, which allowed Ford to use large numbers of semi-skilled workers on moving assembly lines. Ford dramatically raised workers' wages, in part to compensate for the brutal pace of work and in part to retain a stable work force. Beginning in the 1920s General Motors, led by Alfred P. Sloan, began to market somewhat more expensive cars with a much wider range of consumer options than Ford offered. Sloan also extended credit to his customers so they could pay for their purchases over time.

The automobile has arguably transformed everyday life in industrialized countries more than any other machine in the twentieth century. The car's impact was initially most profound on rural life. Many farmers were attracted to the Model T because of its low cost and reliability. It also had a high clearance that allowed it to negotiate poor roads. Ford's cars, trucks, and tractors allowed farmers to produce more crops and to transport them to urban markets, and they facilitated socializing, thus relieving some of the isolation of rural life.

Automobiles quickly had an enormous impact on cities as well. By the 1920s the middle class in the United States had begun to move into the cheaper land on the edges of cities, although many of them still worked in the center city. Although suburbanization was interrupted by the Great Depression, the trend greatly accelerated after World War II, as the national grid of "super" highways was developed in the 1950s. As early as the 1920s, businesses began to be able to move goods via trucks (instead of rail), which helped to decentralize the location of factories and warehouses and accelerated the movement toward suburbs. After World War II many blue-collar workers began to move into the cheaper land on the edges of cities—a benefit made available by mass "automobility." The federal government subsidized the suburban boom through highway construction and by giving cheap loans for suburban (but not urban) construction. As businesses and people moved to the edges of cities, the inner cities were increasingly stripped of their population, fiscal viability, and previous social functions.

Although the social and economic impact of the automobile was most extreme in the United States, many other nations attempted to manufacture cars, and even less-industrialized countries were extensively influenced by cars, trucks, and busses. European countries experienced mass automobile ownership somewhat later than the United States, and their governments succeeded in ensuring that their large cities were not so adversely affected by suburbanization. Car production in less developed regions such as Mexico, Brazil, Turkey, and Eastern Europe has also greatly expanded since World War II. Although poorer countries such as India and China, which were struggling to industrialize in the twentieth century, have produced few cars for individuals, trucks and buses are widespread and have greatly changed the transportation of people and commodities. India and China provide examples of import substitution—industrializing countries developed manufacturing capabilities that reduced dependence on imports, though they did not become major automobile exporters.

Since World War II the most dramatic new player in car production has been Japan. Japan began to produce cars and especially trucks for military purposes in the 1930s, but the industry was relatively small. After World War II the U.S. military bought numerous Japanese trucks, but only in the 1950s did car makers begin producing large numbers of automobiles. By the late 1960s Japanese car makers, with the active support of their government, had begun to export large numbers of cars to the United States and Asia—by the 1980s Japan had become the world's largest producer of cars. Beginning in the 1970s South Korea attempted to emulate Japan's success, although the rising technological requirements of car production, including the introduction of microcomputers in cars and on the production line, and the oversaturation of European and U.S. markets has hampered Korea's effort. In the 1970s and 1980s the entry of lower-wage countries such as Japan and then Korea have placed great pressure on European and U.S. companies; in response, U.S. companies have shifted production to maquiladora factories in Mexico or elsewhere. By the 1980s automobile production was becoming a world phenomenon, as established companies coordinated production between established and "offshore" factories.

See also Fordism; Oil.

Reference Flink, James J. *The Automobile Age* (1988).

Banking, Investment

Banking has played an important role in shaping the course of industrialization throughout the world. Although bankers were not extensively involved in industrialization until the 1830s, they played a crucial role thereafter by channeling savings into railroads, new banks, or governmental borrowing for infrastructure projects or wars. Many investment bankers were originally merchants, such as the Barings brothers, who were slave merchants before becoming financiers and establishing the Barings Brothers & Co. of England.

The expansion of railroads and industries such as iron and steel required massive amounts of capital for machinery, raw materials, and labor costs. Andrew Carnegie remarked: "It is astonishing the amount of working capital you must have in a great concern, it is far more than the cost of the works." After 1880 investment bankers both in England and the United States began to take an active interest in running the industries that they had financed. J. P. Morgan and other bankers justified their increasing control by arguing that they were able to supply money only as long as they maintained the trust of other investors. As a result, bankers tended to discourage their corporations from risk taking or innovation, although they were instrumental in shifting operations from the original entrepreneur or his family to more bureaucratic forms of organization. Operating in the "regulatory vacuum" of the laissez-faire state, bankers often encouraged the formation of monopolies or cartels in order to limit risk and maximize profit.

Since the 1930s, however, the U.S. government has sought to limit the control of individual banks over industry by prohibiting banks from owning stock in industrial companies, which they were allowed to do in Europe or Japan. Critics of this regulation argue that it has discouraged U.S. banks from lending to industry, which often earns a lower return than real estate, and thus has contributed to deindustrialization and an oversupply of commercial real estate.

See also Banking System; Finance Capital; Gold Standard; Mellon, Andrew C.; Money; Westinghouse, George.

References Carosso, Vincent P. *Investment Banking in America* (1970); Davis, Lance Edwin. "The Capital Markets and Industrial Concentration: The U.S. and U.K., A Comparative Study." (1966).

Banking System

The banking system is composed of the various institutions that help to facilitate or regulate the circulation of money and capital. It includes private or public banks and government agencies like the U.S. Federal Reserve. Before the industrial revolution, individuals or firms acquired loans from private banks, but in the eighteenth century national banks were established in England, the United States, and other countries to stimulate industries and economic growth. National banks also facilitated national and international commerce, permitting deposits and exchanges associated with growing change. Supplying individuals and firms with sufficient capital to keep the economy expanding (without triggering inflation or depression) has proved to be an extraordinarily difficult task.

Many bankers were leery of industrial firms until the 1830s, when they began to play an increasingly important role in developing manufacturing. In the 1850s the French bank Crédit Mobilier facilitated the growth of railroad networks and other industries by pooling the capital of thousands of individuals. However, there were few effective regulations on banks or investments to prevent unscrupulous individuals like

Jay Gould (or even established banks like Crédit Mobilier) from cheating investors by "watering" stock or otherwise manipulating their finances.

By the late nineteenth century, bankers were not only loaning money to firms but increasingly helping to open up new industries. For instance, the Mellon family helped to develop the aluminum industry in the United States, and the French Rothschild family initiated and then controlled the Russian oil industry prior to the 1917 Russian Revolution. By the late nineteenth century, many European and Japanese banks had developed close relationships with industrial concerns and often acquired enough stock to exercise monopolistic or oligarchic control. In Japan, these zaibatsus were termed "monopolies of capital."

Although the government was always an important part of the banking system, the philosophy of laissez-faire limited governmental activity until the twentieth century. For instance, the charter for the National Bank of the United States (established in 1790) was allowed to lapse in the 1830s. Without a national bank, the federal government had few tools to intervene in depressions or financial panics—or even to regulate the circulation of currency. (Economies generally entered a crisis after financial speculations or manipulations caused investors to sell their currency in favor of gold, causing a short-term capital shortage.) Federal control over the currency was briefly reestablished in the 1860s and 1870s and then abandoned once again until the establishment of the Federal Reserve in 1913. The "Fed" attempted to ensure that the currency was elastic enough (and strong enough) to facilitate economic growth.

In the 1920s and 1930s, the role of government underwent a significant transformation. With great reluctance, most countries abandoned the gold standard in favor of paper currencies. However, the inability of most countries to regulate their economies and currencies disrupted the international system of trade—some governments arbitrarily devalued their currencies to encourage exports—and these factors greatly contributed to the Great Depression and World War II. During the 1930s in the United States, laissez-faire principles gave way to a more interventionist role for government. Faced with a crisis in the banking system, the New Deal government increased its power to regulate the fiscal solvency of banks and the stock market.

In the 1940s most of the world's governments agreed to greater control over international trade, and the United States dollar (backed by gold reserves) became the accepted standard against which other currencies were measured. This period of international banking and economic stability began to break down in the late 1960s as changes in the international economy outpaced the institutional controls placed on it; in 1971 the United States devalued its dollar and no longer converted its currency into gold. In the 1970s and 1980s banks followed their corporate clients and became increasingly international. National governments have found it more and more difficult to control their currencies—largely because of the significant amounts of money held by international investors and banks.

See also Banking, Investment; Bretton Woods Agreement; Finance Capital; Keynesianism; Morgan, John Pierpont; New Deal.

References Brett, E. A. *International Money and Capitalist Crisis: The Anatomy of Global Disintegration* (1983); James, John A. *Money and Capital Markets in Postbellum America* (1978); Kindleberger, Charles P. *A Financial History of Western Europe* (1984).

Bank of England

European banking evolved considerably from the Middle Ages, allowing transactions in different cities by exchanging promissory notes. But a large central bank emerged only with a charter of 1694 that grouped prominent financiers in London under government backing. The new bank loaned the government over a million pounds, and in return was allowed to issue paper money. Other experiments in paper money occurred at the same time, but most failed. The Bank of England alone succeeded, and for more than a century it held a unique place in public and private finance. The existence of a strong central bank encouraged private banking activity and facilitated commercial activity throughout the nation. Local banks needed to hold only small reserves, because they could draw on accounts with the Bank of England in case of sudden demand for money; this capability facilitated not only commercial transactions but loans for investment purposes. Clearly, a strong central banking system of the sort that took shape in England during the eighteenth century was a key ingredient in early industrialization, and it was widely copied by other countries.

Belgium

Belgium was the second country to industrialize (Britain was first). Belgium had been a major center of urban commerce and domestic manufacturing, particularly in textiles, since the Middle Ages. The area also had extremely rich coal resources, the basis for a rapidly growing mining industry. Just across the English Channel from Britain, Belgium was an obvious target for expansion efforts by British entrepreneurs, like the influential Cockerill family. Mechanization began in Belgian textiles in the 1820s, though, as in many areas where complex hand weaving prevailed, factories gained ground only slowly. By 1846 less than half of all textile workers were in large factories. Metal crafts also survived well, even as modern metallurgical operations developed. The massive expansion of coal mines, however, quickly added to the factory labor force. Railways developed rapidly, initially under private ownership; the state began taking control after 1870. A substantial machine-building and armaments industry arose, supplying other parts of Europe, including France, as well as Belgium itself. Belgian industrial leadership played an active role in spreading the industrial revolution, notably to Russia, and Belgium also became a major colonial power with the acquisition of the Congo in Africa. The revolution of 1830 that established Belgian independence set up a regime dominated by middle-class interests; Belgium was slow to grant the working class the vote or to introduce some of the common late nineteenth-century labor reforms, and a substantial socialist movement arose by 1900 in this context.

Reference Mokyr, Joel. *Industrialization in the Low Countries* (1978).

Bell, Alexander Graham (1847–1922)

Alexander Graham Bell invented the telephone in 1876. Bell was interested in human speech and, like his father and grandfather before him, taught deaf students. In the mid-1870s, Bell worked on a multiplexing system that would allow overburdened telegraph systems to simultaneously send more than one signal. Competing against other inventors, Bell developed the telephone system. Bell reproduced the variations in human speech via variations in electricity, transmitted it, and then translated the electrical signals into sound. Numerous technical hurdles had to be overcome before the system was commercially viable, but Bell extended the communications revolution, which facilitated the development of large corporate bureaucracies. Most major inventions after Bell were developed by systems of university-trained engineers and scientists; he was one of the last of the breed of lone brilliant inventors.

See also Bell Laboratories; Inventions; Technology.

Reference Bruce, Robert V. *Alexander Graham Bell and the Conquest of Solitude* (1990).

Bell Laboratories

As industrialization has accelerated, the scale of economic activity has increased and technology has grown more complex. Bell Labs represents the shift of invention from lone inventors, like its namesake, Alexander Graham Bell, to systems or institutions that are sponsored by corporations or even consortiums of companies in conjunction with the government. Bell

Inventor Alexander Graham Bell speaks to the crowd before conducting an aerial experiment.

Laboratories was set up by American Telephone and Telegraph in 1925. It is an enormous conglomeration of university-trained engineers and scientists whose mission is to carry out primary and applied research for the telephone system. Many important scientific advances have come out of Bell Labs, including lasers, the transistor, microwave radio relay, and solar-powered battery cells.

See also Invention; National Aeronautics and Space Administration; Technology.

Reference Reich, Leonard S. *The Making of American Industrial Research: Science and Business at GE and Bell, 1876–1926* (1985).

Bessemer, Henry (1813–1898)

Henry Bessemer was an Englishman who in 1856 "invented" and, more importantly, helped to perfect a process for transforming iron into steel. (An American, William Kelly, had independently invented the same process in 1856.) The Bessemer converter (so called because it converted iron to steel) blew air through molten pig iron, which removed its carbon, making it more malleable. The heat generated by the interaction of oxygen and carbon also increased the temperature of the molten iron, allowing steelmakers to avoid using additional fuel. Robert Mushet introduced a crucial chemical intervention when he discovered that manganese added to molten steel removed excess oxygen and sulfur, thus allowing the steel to be more uniform in quality. Although it had been possible to make steel before the Bessemer process, the new process was cheaper and allowed the metal to be made in larger quantities and steel began to replace iron. By the 1870s the process was widely used in the United States, allowing industrialists to circumvent puddlers and use cheaper labor.

See also Open Hearth.

Reference Krause, Paul. *The Battle for Homestead, 1880–1892: Politics, Culture, and Steel* (1992).

Black Workers

Since the rise of racialized slavery in the Americas in the sixteenth century, the labor of black workers has been an important (if unacknowledged) part of global industrialization. Slave labor created many of the raw materials (notably cotton) for Europe's factories and many of the foodstuffs (sugar, for example) for its increasingly urbanized population. The capital surplus from the slave trade and plantation production helped to underwrite industrialization in Europe and the United States. Even when slaves were freed, black workers suffered the burden of racism, for most industrialists and workers barred blacks from factory employment. Nonetheless, black workers were a crucial part of the working class in the United States, Latin America, and Africa.

Africans brought with them many important skills that helped build the emerging slave societies in North and Latin America. Many of the blacksmiths on Brazil's slave plantations had gained their expertise in Africa. West Africans from the "Grain Coast" were skilled agriculturists, and Africans' skill with rice growing was absolutely central to the development of that crop in the Americas. After the development of plantation crops (sugar, cotton, and rice), most slaves were used on labor gangs, although by the mid-nineteenth century in the southern United States, slaves were used as coal miners and as factory workers in textile mills or iron foundries.

After their emancipation, most black workers were economically marginalized as sharecroppers and many jobs or economic sectors were closed to them. In the United States, most factory owners asserted that blacks were too inherently lazy to adapt to industrial production, and most trade unions prohibited blacks from membership. Andrew Carnegie recruited most of his unskilled laborers from eastern and southern Europe, although he did hire a small number of skilled black furnacemen from Virginia—a signal to his white workers not to take their privileges for granted. During the period of the Great Migration, when European immigrants became unavailable (due to World War I and changes in immigration laws), industrialists suddenly discovered the virtues of black workers, and a sizable black industrial working class developed. With the rise of social history since 1970, historians have begun to describe the impact of the black working class on the black community and the rest of the working class. Black industrial workers formed the basis for markets for black entrepreneurs and political or union movements. Because blacks were still blocked from many white-collar jobs, deindustrialization in the 1970s and 1980s hit the black working class particularly hard.

Black workers were an important source of labor throughout the world. In Africa, colonial governments displaced black peasants from the land (generally through taxation) in order to create a local working class to work on plantations, in mines, or in emerging cities. Though not industrial workers per se, black labor produced many of the raw materials (rubber, copper, tea, and coffee) necessary for industrial production (or consumption) in the "cosmopolitan" center. After World War II many formerly colonized black workers migrated to Europe or North America, where most of them work in low-paid positions in the service economy. In South Africa the black working class played a crucial role in that country's exploitation of its mineral resources and, more recently, in the transition to a democratic government.

See also Dual Labor Markets; Emancipation; Underclass.

References Harris, William Hamilton. *The Harder We Run: Black Workers since the Civil War* (1982); Trotter, Joe William. *Coal, Class, and Color: Blacks in Southern West Virginia, 1915–32* (1990).

Bobbin Boys

See Child Labor.

Bōren (All-Japan Cotton-Spinners Trade Association)

This Japanese association, formed in the 1880s and operating over the subsequent fifty years, demonstrated the high level of cooperation among Japanese manufacturers. Private enterprise dominated the industrialization of Japanese textiles, but it did not preclude extensive exchange of information. Bōren helped coordinate policies with the government. It also issued trade publications to promote technological modernization and even arranged to loan engineers from one company to another to facilitate technical advance. Bōren went even farther than most Japanese collaborative arrangements, arranging reduced rates on raw cotton with Japanese shippers and setting production quotas for each member to limit competition. Entry to Bōren was easy, but almost all producers had to belong. The cartel's successful management helps account for Japan's rapidity in replacing imports of British cottons and in beginning to export by the 1920s.

See also Cartels.

Reference Patrick, Hugh, ed. *Japanese Industrialization and Its Social Consequences* (1976).

Boring Engines

These engines are vital components in making precision metal products. Boring machines powered by horse-drawn windlasses had been developed between the fifteenth and seventeenth centuries in Europe to bore cannon from bronze or cast iron. Cannon were suspended over a drill and held against it by their own weight as the drill was turned by the horses. These engines were used to make cylinders for the Newcomen steam engines, but they were very imprecise because the diameter of the cylinders was so large. John Wilkinson (1728–1808) developed greater accuracy, and further improvements were introduced in the 1790s. Drill heads were now carried on heavy rods running completely through the cylinder; the power was still supplied by horses turning a shaft. Accurate boring machines, to which new sources of power were later applied, were a vital component of the early machine tools industry, making the equipment essential for steam engines and for textile operations.

See also Machine Building; Wilkinson, John.

Boulton, Matthew (1728–1809)
Boulton was a pioneer in building the steam engine. When James Watt had exhausted his financial resources in experimental work on a usable engine, Boulton came to his aid with the mechanical and financial resources of his factory near Birmingham, England. The first successful engine was built in 1776. Boulton, no technical genius, was one of the English businessmen profoundly influenced by the eighteenth-century Enlightenment ideas of progress and material improvement. He played a significant role in forming groups to promote technical advances, arguing that such developments would promote general well-being.

Bourses du Travail
The Bourses du Travail was a movement of French workers in the 1880s and 1890s to build federations of local and regional unions. In the wake of the Paris Commune of 1871, the French government banned unions, but by 1884, it legalized them again. The government subsidized *bourses* that were supposed to operate as employment agencies, but they were quickly taken over by syndicalists who sought to use strikes and unions to bring about a revolutionary society—preferably a stateless one (anarchism). The *bourses* helped to strengthen the syndicalist tradition in France, and by 1902 the local and regional *bourses* had merged with the national organization of the Confédération Générale du Travail.

References Geary, Dick, ed. *Labour and Socialist Movements in Europe before 1914* (1989); Stearns, Peter N. *Revolutionary Syndicalism and French Labor: A Cause without Rebels* (1971).

Boycott
A boycott is a ban on conducting business with an individual or employer. Captain C. C. Boycott (1832–1897), an agent for a landlord in Ireland, was the first to be boycotted after his tenants refused to have any dealings with him (even social interactions) because they felt he was a rude, arrogant symbol of British colonial rule and exploitation. The boycott was brought to the United States by Irish immigrants and adopted by trade unionists seeking to punish an employer. A boycott was potentially more effective than a strike because unionists not employed by the offending industrialist could also participate in the action. In 1894, for example, the employees of George Pullman struck, and unionized railroad workers enforced a boycott against Pullman by refusing to connect sleeper cars (which Pullman owned and operated) to trains. The boycott spread to any railroad that attempted to operate using Pullman cars. With the aid of the federal government, Pullman and the railroad companies won that battle, but boycotts remained a formidable weapon in labor's arsenal. So formidable did the practice prove that in the 1890s a group of employers established the American Anti-Boycott Association, which prosecuted the United Hatters of North America for a consumer product boycott under the Sherman Anti-Trust Act. Their action resulted in liens being placed on several workers' homes to pay for damages. Secondary boycotts, aimed against employers other than one's own, continued to be practiced by unionized transportation workers (dockworkers, railroads, truckers, and airlines) until banned by the Taft Hartley Act in 1947.

Trade unions still enforce consumer product boycotts, particularly if a company has locked out its employees or is breaking a strike by using permanent replacement workers (scabs). Since the 1960s, unions in the United States have attempted to use these consumer boycotts to isolate and punish particular companies through "corporate campaigns." They have succeeded in forcing employers to rehire fired employees or to open factories that have been closed. However, corporate campaigns are time consuming and the outcome far from certain. For instance, in the mid-1980s unionists at a Hormel meatpacking plant in Austin, Minnesota, were engaged in a particularly brutal strike and urged other unionists not to buy Hormel products.

The strikers then attempted to isolate Hormel from its traditional source of capital by encouraging members of the community to withdraw their savings from a particular bank until the strike was settled. Although this form of boycott can be embarrassing (or even costly) to employers, it is generally less effective than secondary boycotts: despite their thorough efforts, the Hormel strikers lost their campaign.

Boycotts have also played a role on the international scene. Indian boycotts of British goods were part of the independence movement in the early twentieth century. The boycotts also encouraged the growth of Indian industry.

See also Industrial Unions.

Reference Tomlins, Christopher L., and Andrew J. King, eds. *Labor Law in America: Historical and Critical Essays* (1992).

Brazil

Brazil won its independence from Portugal in 1822 and was ruled by an emperor until 1889. Although by 1871 the children of slaves were declared freed, slavery itself was not abolished in Brazil until 1888. Until well after World War II, Brazil's economy remained dominated by its precolonial exports: coffee, cotton, and sugar. There was a small industrial working class in cities such as Sao Paulo, which had large numbers of women in its textile mills because industrialists sought to restrict black workers from industry.

During and after World War II, authoritarian governments took an increasingly interventionist role, seeking to promote industry by building infrastructure projects such as highways and hydroelectric dams. The military also intervened to prevent social reforms in the style of Argentina's Juan Perón. Active government sponsorship developed in reaction to Brazil's vulnerability during the Great Depression of the 1930s. During World War II the government helped to construct a major steel mill and later organized a highly competitive computer industry. Brazil borrowed heavily from abroad to finance the development of steel mills, trucks, mining, and other heavy industry. Development was rapid: in 1957 the country did not make any automobiles; by the 1980s it exported large numbers of cars, as well as military equipment and computers.

Reference Wolfe, Joel. *Working Women, Working Men: Sao Paulo and the Rise of Brazil's Industrial Working Class, 1900–1955* (1993).

Bread Riots

These riots were one of the most common forms of preindustrial urban protest (there were also rural grain riots). Bad harvests caused rising food prices; these price hikes not only hit urban workers directly but also reduced the sale of manufactured goods, thus causing unemployment. Workers often rioted against bakers for unfair prices, asking also that the state intervene to provide affordable food. Women and men alike were active in bread riots. As industrialization progressed, food supplies became more adequate. Protest shifted increasingly to the workplace and to politics. Bread riots declined and with them the involvement of women in lower-class protest. Bread riots did however occasionally recur in industrial societies, as in France around 1912.

See also Moral Economy; Strikes.

Bretton Woods Agreement

After the 1930s the international system of banking and trade was in crisis. The failing British Empire could not support the gold standard, which collapsed as many nations devalued their currencies and imposed protectionist tariffs. The result was a severe truncation of international commerce. In 1944 over forty countries met at Bretton Woods, New Hampshire, at the United Nations Monetary and Financial Conference to determine the institutional framework for international trade, banking, and economic development for the post–World War II era.

The problems confronting the diplomats and bankers at Bretton Woods were as much political as economic. Would the new institutions that regulated world trade encourage low tariffs and open markets, as favored by the economically and financially stronger nations such as the United States, or would it provide financial assistance to weaker governments that needed aid in rebuilding their economies in order to compete in the global marketplace?

The Bretton Woods agreement established a goal of more liberalized global trade with lower tariffs while providing some assistance to economically weaker, debtor nations. The International Monetary Fund (IMF) was created in order to stabilize national currencies and to encourage the expansion and liberalization of world trade. The IMF established the United States' dollar as the de facto currency of world trade by pegging the exchange rates of other currencies to the dollar. The Bretton Woods conference also founded the International Bank for Reconstruction and Development (the World Bank) to help rebuild the economies of countries devastated by war. The World Bank would also become an important conduit of credit for countries seeking to industrialize.

Bretton Woods did result in greatly expanded world trade. However, the IMF and the World Bank did not play the role of relatively autonomous institutions capable of counterbalancing the economic and political power of the stronger nations. These banking institutions emerged as enforcers of laissez-faire principles on debtor nations, particularly those in Latin America and sub-Saharan Africa. Although key provisions of Bretton Woods have disappeared, and the agreements relating to fixed currency exchanges were abandoned in 1971 as a result of a greatly deteriorating U.S. economy and currency, Bretton Woods' institutions and compromises continue to greatly influence the course of world trade and economic development.

See also Banking System; Development Theory; Great Depression (1930s).

References Brett, E. A. *International Money and Capitalist Crisis: The Anatomy of Global Disintegration* (1983); Cline, William R. *International Monetary Reform and the Developing Countries* (1976).

Brewing and Distilling

Making beer from fermented grain involved techniques going back to ancient Mesopotamia. In the late nineteenth century, industrialization had an impact on brewing by facilitating the construction of larger vats that could increase output and by giving big brewing companies increasing advantages over small, local operations. Improved transportation and the possibility of bottling also favored bigger operations in brewing, while again increasing the availability of commercial beers. In some countries large commercial breweries were among the first new enterprises intruding on largely traditional economies, in the nineteenth century. The great Guiness brewery was one of the first modern factories in Ireland, developing rapidly from 1855 onward after a more modest start. The Cervecería Cauahtemoc of Mexico, which was named after the last Aztec ruler but set up in the 1880s by a businessman of German descent, José Schneider, became so successful that it had to set up a bottle factory as well. Breweries also played a role in late nineteenth-century Japanese industrialization.

Industrial procedures had a bigger impact on the distilling of alcoholic drinks (distilling involves separating alcoholic liquors from fermented materials). Early in the 1800s several inventors—J. B. Cellier-Blumenthal and L. C. Deroux in France, Aeneas Coffey in Britain—introduced continuous stills for recovery. In 1850 new distilling towers were devised that increased output. These developments expanded the production of alcoholic drinks and also tended to increase their potency. Supply factors played a role in the increased drinking that accompanied the industrial revolution.

Britain

The British industrial revolution has drawn more attention than any other because the process was first chronologically, and long set a standard for the world. What caused British primacy? The nation shared many features with other Western societies, but it had dropped serfdom and a strict guild system by the late Middle Ages, giving it a flexible labor force and encouraging the kind of artisan-inventor responsible for the amazing array of British innovations during the eighteenth century. Britain was an especially successful maritime and colonial power, and its export markets motivated industrialization. The British government, though mercantilist until the late eighteenth century, was small and flexible, in contrast to the more heavy-handed French state. Britain's aristocracy tolerated commerce, even allowing aristocratic younger sons to go into business outright without losing status; again this contrasted with the more conservative Continent. British culture, Protestant at base, may have encouraged a special entrepreneurial spirit that was eager to use business success to prove God's favor. Distinctive resource patterns—good location of coal and iron, good riverways, but also an exhaustion of forests that encouraged use of coal to replace charcoal in metallurgy—favored the British development.

Britain's early success spurred high earnings, which meant additional capital for further expansion. Britain—"the workshop of the world"—maintained a world industrial lead well past 1850. British confidence allowed repeal (1841) of regulations that had tried to limit exports of new technology and skilled workers (the regulations had not worked well anyway). British industrial expansion even began to push out agriculture, and the British decided to import foods in exchange for the industrial exports in which they excelled. Early industrialization had costs, however: Compared to the United States and many other parts of Europe, British labor suffered particularly bad urban conditions, unusual exploitation of child labor, and other problems as manufacturers sought to economize.

The next issue of particular interest in British industrialization, after causation and initial success, involves Britain's relative industrial decline from the late nineteenth century onward. Eclipsed by the faster growth of the United States and Germany, Britain began to lag badly in the twentieth century, despite continued innovations such as the development of a television industry in the 1930s. After World War II, particularly, Britain became a decidedly lesser industrial power, still in the top rank but only barely. Why did Britain fade? British cultural values may have been more appropriate for the entrepreneurial phase of industrialization, when individual ingenuity was at a premium, but they were less suited for corporate organization and structured research. British education lagged in technical areas. Resources were less appropriate for late nineteenth century metallurgical techniques than for earlier processes, given the chemical composition of British iron ore. Labor gains, thanks to powerful unions, may have cut British flexibility. Exhaustion after colonial and the world wars played a role as well. The precise combination and concentration of reasons for the decline are debated, as is the relevance of the British example to other still-great but nervous industrial leaders like the United States.

See also Causes of the Industrial Revolution; Standard of Living.

References Deane, Phyllis. *The First Industrial Revolution* (1969); Musson, A. E. *Growth of British Industry* (1979); Wiener, Martin. *English Culture and the Decline of the Industrial Spirit, 1850–1980* (1981).

Bülow Tariff

Passed in 1902, this German tariff established high rates on manufactured but also agricultural goods. It represented a deal between heavy industrialists, who wanted to protect finished products but ideally preferred low food prices, and big landowners, particularly the East Prussian Junkers, who sought to protect all foodstuffs, most particularly grain. This tariff was the famous "marriage between rye and iron," as a combined upper class agreed to compromise at the expense of lower prices for working-class consumers. The tariff was also a response to the rising tariff rates in France and the United States. The government hoped to use the new tariff, named for the chancellor, to bargain with other nations, and in fact the highest industrial rates were not actually imposed. Nevertheless, the tariff fed the growing sense of national exclusiveness and economic competition before World War I.

See also Protectionism.

Reference Gerschenkron, Alexander. *Bread and Democracy in Germany* (1943).

Bureaucracy

Bureaucracy refers to a hierarchy of administrative officials. Bureaucracies are known for set rules of operation and careful record keeping, defined responsibilities, and expert knowledge. Until the industrial revolution bureaucracies grew up primarily in relation to the state and the military, though the Catholic church also maintained an important bureaucracy. The first major bureaucratic tradition arose in China, where officials received explicit training and specialized functions. European bureaucracies began to emerge in the Middle Ages. Training and specialization increased notably in the seventeenth century; grades of military officers and division of functions—combat, supply, and so on—were particularly impressive innovations.

The efficiency of European bureaucracies contributed to some of the functions governments performed in promoting industrialization. Ministries of commerce sponsored technical expositions; artillery officers provided one spur to further training in engineering. Industrialization, in turn, demanded new bureaucratic functions, such as the administration of school systems, welfare operations, and factory inspectorates. Bureaucracies began to expand rapidly in the later nineteenth century as these government activities grew. European bureaucracies by this point were providing models for administration in other societies. Civil service principles, supporting hiring and promotion by merit rather than birth or influence, were adopted in most European countries and the United States in the 1870s, while specialized training opportunities in fields like economics and public health increased as well.

Bureaucratic principles had spread to the private sector by the 1870s, with the growth of large corporations with extensive management operations and specializations according to production, research, procurement, sales, advertising, and so on. In the development of management hierarchies, with detailed promotion procedures and expert functions and training, big business rivaled the state in bureaucratization as industrial societies matured.

See also Managers.

References Chandler, Alfred. *Managerial Hierarchies* (1980); Torstendahl, Rolf. *Bureaucratisation in Northwestern Europe, 1880–1985* (1991).

Business Cycles

During the industrial revolution, years of relative prosperity alternated with slumps. During slumps, levels of employment went down and wages fell, causing immense hardship, including (in the early industrial revolution) higher death rates among workers. Workers pawned furniture, reduced diets, and sometimes returned to the countryside. When prosperity returned, employment went up and wages usually followed, though sometimes after a lag. The year after a slump ended was particularly ripe for strikes or riots; this phenomenon was an important element in the revolutions of 1848, which followed the crisis of 1846–1847. Workers needed to wait for better times to afford the risks of protest and to express the grievances that had built up during a slump. Moreover, they grew impatient for more rapid improvements when the cycle finally turned upward. The frequent oscillations caused by business cycles discouraged workers, reducing their sense that any coherent planning made sense or that they had control over their fate.

Before 1850 slumps were usually caused by bad harvests; prosperity returned when harvests improved. During bad harvests food prices rose, reducing demand for manufactured goods; unemployment could hit one-third of the urban labor force. After 1850 better transportation and agricultural improvements eliminated major food crises in western Europe (though not yet in Russia). A brief slump in 1857 prefigured the more common sort of industrial recession. These modern recessions occurred when production pushed past available sales, for productive capacity had overexpanded in economies where low wages often limited consumer demand. Investments became overextended. Bankruptcies caused investment banks to fail, particularly ones that had offered speculative loans. Bank failures frightened potential investors, so purchases of capital goods (mainly from heavy industry) declined. (Depressions in the United States were termed "panics" for this reason.) This decline led to lower consumption in other industries, and the familiar downward spiral of declining wages and unemployment began. Recovery occurred only when prices fell and interest rates dropped enough to encourage new purchases and new investment. Business orders gradually went up and employment began to recover. Modern business cycles are international in scope. Many slumps have been triggered by bank failures in the United States, and the effects then spread to Europe. Industrial slumps bring lower prices and hit workers less heavily than agricultural failures once did, but they tend to last for several years, causing great insecurity.

The first major recession of this sort was the prolonged crisis of the mid-1870s, which gripped most of the industrial nations. Another recession occurred in the 1890s, and a few shorter ones after 1900 and again after World War I; the Great Depression that began in 1929, a massive global crisis, extended this series of business cycles.

Business slumps had a positive economic function in one important sense. They drove out the less efficient producers—business failures went up rapidly—while employers introduced new methods and more advanced technology to permit them to cut prices and stimulate sales. The result was a more productive economy when the next phase of the business cycle kicked in. Slumps also promoted new business forms, like the trusts and cartels that responded to the 1870s depression by attempting to avoid "over competition."

See also Cartels; Inflation and Deflation; Trusts.

Calico Act

This English law of 1721 was designed to protect English woolen and silk manufacturing against the importation of cotton cloth made in India. It forbade the sale of calico and levied stiff fines against anyone wearing calico material. The Calico Act is an example of the mercantilist interest in using taxes and tariffs to protect national industry. It had a severe impact on traditional cotton manufacturing in India by reducing the available export market. As Indian imports declined, a new English cotton industry took hold, for cotton clothing had become popular. English cottons, in turn, provided the setting for much of the mechanization associated with the early industrial revolution.

See also Deindustrialization; Protectionism.

Canada

Canadian industrialization relied heavily on foreign investments and railway development. Major railway building began in the 1870s. Canadian agriculture, wood pulp, and mineral production grew rapidly, and the nation became a major exporter to western Europe and the United States. Canada has the world's largest holdings of nickel and asbestos, and modern mining equipment allowed the nation to expand output amid a rising standard of living. Extensive immigration around 1900 (2.7 million between the years 1903 and 1914) provided needed labor. After World War I, U.S. investment increased, and U.S. firms located manufacturing subsidiaries in Canada; Canadian automobile production, for example, was one such subsidiary. Canada's industrial economy was unusually heavily tied to other countries and to exports. By the 1950s Canada exported a full third of its total output and imported a third of the manufactured goods consumed. Because of its dependence on import-export trade, Canada suffered greatly from international setbacks like the 1930s depression, but it boomed when war needs or prosperity elsewhere stimulated international demand.

Canadian Pacific Railway

Railroad building began extensively in Canada in the 1870s. The Canadian Pacific was completed in 1905, linking the country from Atlantic to Pacific and connecting the rich western prairie provinces to the international economy. Immigration from Europe to western Canada greatly increased, as did both wheat and mineral output for world trade. The rail line, built mainly with British capital, greatly advanced the Canadian economy, including the significant industrial development in Ontario.

See also Railroads.

Canals

The early industrial revolution created huge new transportation needs, both to ship finished products and, especially, to move raw materials, such as ores, grains, and construction items. Roads were inefficient and costly for heavy goods, and internal rivers were not always well located. An enthusiasm for canals developed in the context of dealing with industrial requirements and encouraging industrial development. Canals also allowed governments, the sponsors of most projects, to take a major role in spurring economic growth. Canal systems spread widely in later eighteenth-century Britain and then, in the early nineteenth century, in western Europe and the United States. The Erie Canal, linking the Hudson River with the Great Lakes, was a striking project, one example of how canal networks flourished throughout the new industrial world.

Construction of canals depended on massive crews of unskilled laborers, or navvies, aided by draft animals but otherwise using manual equipment. Irish immigrants provided much of the labor for canals in the United States. Available cheap labor was vital, and working conditions were harsh and arbitrary.

The importance of canals began to decline with the railroad, which provided faster hauling and more flexible routes. Barge operators frequently tried to delay railway projects, without ultimate success. Canals nonetheless continued to serve industrial needs, and in France, among other places, active canal building continued alongside railway development into the 1880s. A few massive oceangoing canal systems, such as the Panama Canal and the St. Lawrence Seaway, were completed in the twentieth century.

See also State, Role of the.

Reference Way, Peter. *Common Labour: Workers and the Digging of North American Canals, 1780–1860* (1993).

Canning

Canning was a result of the Napoleonic Wars (1799–1815), as the French leader sought alternatives to the high death rate of soldiers from spoiled food and poor nutrition. He set up a Society for the Encouragement of New Inventions, with a prize for a method of preserving food. Pursuing the prize, a candy maker, Nicolas Appert, discovered that air caused food to spoil. In ten years of experiments he found that cooked foods, sealed in tightly corked bottles and cooked again, would remain edible for a long time. He won his prize in 1810. But glass bottles often broke, and an English method that used metal containers or canisters (soon, simply cans) was more fruitful. Canning spread widely, but it was Louis Pasteur's discovery of bacteria's role in food spoilage, in the 1850s and 1860s, that first explained why the method worked. This discovery led to more effective procedures for sterilizing closed containers. Further inventions, like the threaded mason jar (1858) and the rubber sealing ring (1902), advanced the process. Canning served as the basis for a growing food processing industry, more reliable food supplies, and new forms of retailing featuring more elaborate grocery stores.

Capitalism

Capitalism is a system of production in which capital in a variety of forms (money, credit, machinery, and goods) is owned by a relatively small class of capitalists who employ a class of wage laborers to produce the goods, with the owners then expropriating the profits. As a term for economic system, capitalism only came into usage in the mid-nineteenth century; however, historians agree that by the fifteenth century, capitalism had begun to emerge in Europe.

The reason for the evolution of capitalism in Europe is a point of great controversy. Some scholars believe that capitalism first emerged from a crisis in feudalism or manorialism that resulted in capitalistic forms of agriculture in England and to some extent in France and Germany. Other scholars hold that new systems of global trade encouraged the spread of capitalism. In either case, capitalism preceded the industrial revolution, and the changes that capitalism wrought upon European and especially English society enabled the development of industrialization there.

Between the fifteenth and eighteenth centuries, even English society was not yet fully dominated by capitalistic values, for many poor and rich people had not internalized the values of the market. At this stage of capitalism, merchants, big farmers, and planters were the chief capitalists. "Commercial capitalism" helped to lay the groundwork for the industrial revolution by rewarding entrepreneurialism, transforming the role and political form of the state, and building up the necessary financial surplus that would later be invested in industry. By instituting harsher labor systems and more market-oriented patterns of trade, commercial capitalism also began to transform a number of societies throughout the world system—a process that would accelerate in the next two centuries.

Between the late eighteenth and late nineteenth centuries, capitalism and the industrial revolution fundamentally remade European society and, indeed, much of the world. Although capitalism had begun to create an industrial working class, the number of factory workers was relatively small—even by the mid-nineteenth century. However, the process of industrialization quickly began to transform work habits, patterns of trade, and the daily lives of people throughout the world.

This stage of capitalism was relatively competitive, and many inventors and entrepreneurs became rich. Later in the nineteenth century, large corporations and cartels began to monopolize manufacturing in order to maximize their profits. During this phase, the industrial corporations began systematically to exploit the scientific process for new products and processes. Mass production techniques produced more goods than ever before, but, according to the logic of production for profit, the result was increasingly desperate competition among industrialized countries over markets, resulting in a scramble for colonies and captive markets. The rapid expansion of new goods and technologies contrasted with the growing international instability that led to the disaster of World War I.

In order to maximize production for the war, the states of industrialized countries began to take a much stronger role in order to regulate domestic production (and to a limited extent, international trade). During World War I, and particularly during the Great Depression of the 1930s, the laissez-faire ideology of the competitive era of industrial capitalism was abandoned in favor of various forms of corporatism throughout the industrialized world. Britain laid the foundations for its welfare state, and in the United States the New Deal initiated a tentative form of Keynesianism. Italy, Germany, and Eastern Europe experimented with fascism, and the Soviet Union developed an economy in which the state assumed all control over the market. However, the capitalist competition among industrialized countries for markets continued and contributed to World War II.

After World War II the industrialized nations developed much stronger institutions to regulate international trade and finance. From the 1940s until the early 1970s, an unprecedented period of economic expansion occurred that spread capitalist institutions through the world and dramatically improved the standards of living of many workers in industrialized countries. Many observers spoke of mixed systems, in which private capital and capitalist competition continued to motivate business, but state regulation and welfare systems moderated the process. After the late 1970s laissez-faire capitalism gained ground in China and Latin America—reducing the role of the state. Some scholars argue that since the 1970s capitalism has entered a new "postindustrial" phase in which industrial production has become far more globalized than ever before. As a result the position of workers and many local communities have become more destabilized—threatening to undo many of the gains of modernization.

See also Bretton Woods Agreement; Finance Capital; Fordism; Imperialism; Merchant Capital; Moral Economy; Plantations; Research and Development; Science; "Second" Industrial Revolution; Slavery; Stalinism; World Systems Theory.

References Tucker, Robert C. *The Marx-Engels Reader* (1978); Wolf, Eric. *Europe and the People without History* (1982).

Carnegie, Andrew (1835–1919)

Andrew Carnegie exemplified the ruthless industrial entrepreneur of the late nineteenth century, though his rags to riches mobility was unusual. A poor immigrant from Scotland, Carnegie rose rapidly within the Pennsylvania Railroad but left in 1865 and eventually formed his own steel-making company. Much of Carnegie's genius lay in his reorganization of the workplace. Previously, iron and steel were produced in a variety of stages by different firms in scattered locations. Carnegie centralized and reorganized production for maximum speed and efficiency; he quickly became the low-cost producer of steel rails, with a guaranteed market in his former employer, the Pennsylvania Railroad. Carnegie bought additional mills and turned them into low-cost, state-of-the-art production facilities. He also vertically integrated his company, setting up operations in all stages of production, from coal mining to finished steel products. One such venture included a merger with Henry Clay Frick, who controlled vast supplies of cooking fuel, the energy needed to make steel.

During depressions Carnegie slashed prices, forcing other producers out of business; as the market recovered, he raised prices. Carnegie sought to retain his cost advantage by breaking the power of skilled craftsmen, such as the iron puddlers who were essential to the iron-making process. After a series of confrontations with the union in the 1880s, Carnegie threatened skilled workers at his Homestead Works with a pay cut. The workers refused to accept, and Carnegie locked them out. Pinkerton guards who had been sent to escort strikebreakers were driven out of town by strikers. Eventually, the facility was reopened on a non-union basis by the Pennsylvania militia.

Carnegie sold his company in 1901 to J. P. Morgan's United States Steel Company. One of the richest men in the world, Carnegie devoted his subsequent years to philanthropy. Carnegie also served as a spokesmen for the virtues of capitalist competition, espousing Social Darwinist ideals.

See also Homestead Lockout.

Reference Wall, Joseph Frazier. *Andrew Carnegie* (1970).

Cartels

Cartels were voluntary agreements between large corporations to exercise monopolistic control over the market. In the late nineteenth century, national cartels began to form in western Europe that established sales prices, allocated market share among companies, cooperated to block the entry of foreign corporations or cartels into domestic markets, limited production, and sometimes pooled patents or shared technologies. In contrast to the United States, where the formation of monopolies caused widespread alarm (but formed anyway), European governments did not seek to ban cartels but sought to protect the public from flagrant abuses. By the 1930s Germany, Japan, Italy, and much of Scandinavia and Eastern Europe not only enforced cartels' agreements but had begun to encourage the formation of domestic cartels. Critics of the New Deal charged that the U.S. government had adopted a similar policy.

The chemical industry led the way in the formation of cartels. Cartels had proved crucial to the development of the German chemical industry, because collective agreements between companies helped to raise prices, thereby subsidizing the research and development of new products. By the 1880s German chemical companies were hiring university-trained chemists (many had been unable to find academic jobs) and later establishing corporate research and development laboratories. The German cartel maintained its lead over foreign producers by taking out patents abroad—in the early twentieth century, German firms held over 40 percent of U.S. patents relating to the chemical industry and were several times larger than their British, French, or U.S. counterparts. The German cartel's hold over patents blocked foreign chemical companies from beginning production of many different product lines. During World War I the U.S. government effectively subsidized its own chemical industry by distributing patents to its own domestic corporations. In the case of telephone and radio corporations, technologies and patents overlapped and a patent pool was established to facilitate a division of markets; subsequently, some companies concentrated on telephones, others on radios.

German cartels took the lead in establishing international cartels. In 1925 I. G. Farben, which accounted for half of all German production was formed, and soon the German-led dye cartel accounted for almost two-thirds of the international market. Although powerful, the German-led cartel's impact was affected by governmental policies in different countries. In cases where the governments failed to protect small firms, the international cartel bought out or closed down chemical producers; in larger countries where governments were strongly protectionist, local firms were invited to join the cartel. In general, separate agreements were made with U.S. and Japanese firms or cartels. International cartels were often able to use their technological superiority and profitability to force domestic manufacturers into sharing markets. Cartels proved an important factor (or barrier) for countries seeking to build domestic industries with a significant scientific or high-technology base.

See also Capitalism; Finance Capital; Monopoly

Reference Kudo, Akira, and Terushi Hara. *International Cartels in Business History* (1992).

Catalonia

See Spain.

Causes of the Industrial Revolution

The analysis of historical causation involves identifying what combination of pre-existing conditions and new elements brought about significant change. The industrial revolution was a massive change launched by an unusual mix of factors. Basic conditions for industrialization in western Europe included changes in culture emanating from the scientific revolution and the rationalist movement of the eighteenth century known as the Enlightenment. These movements improved scientific knowledge, and some specific scientific advances, as in the study of gasses, directly fed initial inventions like the steam engine. More generally, the Enlightenment promoted beliefs in material progress and in the value of hard work and innovation, forming the outlook of many pioneering entrepreneurs.

The second basic condition for industrialization rested in western Europe's dominant role in the world economy. Since the sixteenth century, England, Holland, and France had dominated world trade. This position brought huge profits, some of which could be converted into capital for further investment. Greater prosperity also encouraged new consumer interests that became quite evident by the eighteenth century, as large numbers of people sought new clothing and other items, providing a clear internal market for manufactured goods. Their dominance of world trade also encouraged Europeans to concentrate increasingly on manufacturing, for manufactured products commanded better prices when they could be exchanged for raw materials or foods in places like eastern Europe or the Americas. Europe's manufacturing gains brought gradual technical improvements in metallurgy and textiles, and by 1700 Europe had the most advanced technology in the world in virtually every manufacturing branch. Finally, increased manufacturing created a work force increasingly familiar with a market economy and ever more skillful. From skilled workers came many of the inventions crucial to industrialization. To an extent, the industrial revolution simply continued these trends in a dramatically new format.

Specific factors triggered the industrial revolution. Under mercantilism, governments became more interested in promoting national industry. Some measures were heavy-handed and counterproductive, like the French government's attempts to regulate craft methods, but other moves, like British tariff protection for the new cotton industry, helped spur change. Britain faced the depletion of its forests, which encouraged businessmen to experiment with coal, rather than wood-derived charcoal, for smelting metals. The most important specific trigger for industrialization was the huge population growth that erupted in the eighteenth century. The populations of

England and Prussia increased by 100 percent between 1730 and 1800, while France gained 50 percent. Supported by new food supplies from the Americas—for instance, the potato—and a lull in epidemic disease, population growth forced many people to seek jobs off the land, making formation of a new labor force easier. Middle-class families produced growing numbers of surviving children, which spurred them to seek innovation simply to sustain their growing families.

Every industrial revolution outside Britain was also caused by knowledge of the power and wealth industrialization could create. Britain's success in the Napoleonic Wars convinced many European governments that they had to imitate simply for military reasons. Businessmen in Europe and the United States saw the prosperity of leading British manufacturers and again vowed to imitate. Russian and Japanese industrializations, later, were prompted by firsthand knowledge of the military power generated by Western industrialization. By providing motivation and example, the imitation factor could supplement other causation—for example, many later industrializers did not have huge capital or a favorable position in world trade, but they could copy strides made elsewhere in textiles and heavy industry.

Other factors need to be considered in explaining industrialization. Resources are obviously crucial. Most industrial revolutions took place in societies with access to coal and iron, though Japan proves that a poor resource position can be overcome. Education may play a role. Most European industrializations began before the existence of a mass school system, but a large minority of the population was already literate. In later industrializations education may be essential to provide a sufficiently skilled labor force plus the basis for necessary technicians.

See also Demographic Transition; Entrepreneurial Spirit; State, Role of the.

References Hartwell, R. M., ed. *The Causes of the Industrial Revolution in England* (1967); Stearns, Peter N. *The Industrial Revolution in World History* (1994).

Central Union of German Industrialists

This group was formed in 1876 during the severe depression of the mid-decade. It grouped leading industrialists, particularly from heavy industry, in an early display of their growing political muscle. The union clamored for tariff protection as the only way to save German industry. Bismarck, Germany's effective ruler, was eager to conciliate this bloc, and he did raise rates in his 1879 tariff, one step toward the growing protectionist climate of the later nineteenth century.

See also Protectionism.

Charity

The tradition of giving money and goods to the poor goes far back in human history. Religious traditions such as Islam and Christianity have long supported charity. Charity connects with industrialization in several ways. First, extensive charity may sometimes have delayed more systematic attempts to deal with working-class poverty. This argument has been made for Russia, where Orthodox commitment to personal charity was extensive and may have impeded more systematic reforms. Second, in Western industrialization many business people and liberal economists argued against charity, claiming that charity simply made workers idle and perhaps encouraged more childbirth, thus making conditions ultimately worse. Instead of charity, workers should be encouraged to help themselves, gain education, and save. Arguments of this sort motivated the Poor Law reform in England. Third, the criticism notwithstanding, charity during the industrial revolution was extensive. Often, middle-class women sponsored charities while their husbands concentrated on business. Some business families sought status and respectability by highlighting their charitable endeavors. Reports on the poverty of urban areas and fear of popular disorder motivated ongoing charity. Thus charity remained a vital resource even as conflicting attitudes and other reform measures took shape.

See also Social Insurance; Underclass.

Chartism

Chartism was a mass movement for democratic rights that flourished throughout England, Wales, and Scotland from 1838 to 1848. While calling on older ideas of the rights of free Englishmen, the Chartist movement was also a major stage in the evolution of protest in an industrial society. Factory workers, particularly in northern England, participated strongly in the Chartist movement, and artisans attempted to use the movement to compensate for their increasingly precarious position in an industrial economy.

Chartism protested the exclusion of the working classes from the extension of the vote in the 1832 Reform Act and also the harsher requirements for poor relief enacted in 1834. The movement took its name from the People's Charter, drawn up by the cabinetmaker William Lovett and published in 1838 by the London Working Men's Association. Chartists demanded universal male adult suffrage and the opening of Parliament to working-class representatives. Women took a subordinate role in the movement, signaling their decline in working-class protest activities. Chartists also urged government-sponsored education and other measures that could facilitate working-class social mobility. The Chartists presented massive petitions to Parliament at several points that were also backed by large gatherings and some riots; factory workers tended to be more prone to violence than artisans. The failure of the final petition, in 1848, effectively ended the movement, but Chartism nevertheless advanced the political consciousness of the working class. At the same time, the Chartist period and the movement's collapse highlighted ongoing tensions between skilled artisans—those, for example, who dominated the London Working Men's Association—and factory operatives. The artisans put more faith in the political system and in respectable if vigorous petitioning. They were suspicious of the newer, less skilled segments of the working class. After the Chartist movement, many artisans turned to separate, largely peaceful craft unionism; a full working-class movement did not resume in Britain for some decades, even as industrialization continued to advance.

Chemical Industry

Until the industrial revolution, chemical production, mostly fairly local, focused on dyes and paints. Only explosives were made on a somewhat larger scale, usually in government-owned or -licensed plants. The rise of a modern chemical industry began with new scientific discoveries in the 1820s. New products were isolated (benzene in 1825) or analyzed (coal tar in 1849). The first aniline dye was synthesized by accident in 1856, and other artificial dyes followed. An organic chemicals industry was poised to take off, and growing demand for fabrics created an obvious new market. New explosives were also invented, beginning with nitrocellulose in 1846; TNT was later developed by the Swedish inventor Alfred Nobel. Work on organic fertilizers advanced in Germany from the 1830s onward. Plastics were introduced, and paper made from wood pulp spread widely from the 1840s onward. The use of chemicals in making metals and other products expanded, though a bit later; this movement included the Hall-Héroult electrolytic process for deriving aluminum from bauxite (1886), which made the mass production of aluminum possible for the first time. Meanwhile, growing uses were found for compounds like sulfuric acid. Finally, demand for soaps exploded after 1860, as bathing became more common. British production of alkalis for soaps tripled between 1852 and 1878.

Amid this explosion, new procedures were introduced to make chemicals with less labor, including larger vats, revolving furnaces, and mechanical roasters. Companies subsidized extensive research to find new ways to make soaps. The Belgian chemist, Ernest Solvay (1836–1922), introduced a new process to make soda, using towers to mix carbon dioxide with ammoniacal brine, recovering the ammonia in a still; the Solvay process gained ground rapidly in making alkali, though Britain lagged, as it did in advanced chemicals generally after 1870. Led by Germany and the United States (which innovated less but copied rapidly), chemical output soared, doubling or tripling in each decade by the late nineteenth century. German sulfuric acid production, for example, more than tripled between 1900 and 1913. The growth of the largely semi-skilled labor force was also considerable, though unionization came slowly in this new industry. In Germany and most other companies, a few big firms cornered an increasing percentage of chemical production, with a diverse array of products from fertilizers to medical compounds. The military and environmental implications of the rapidly growing industrial sector were also important.

See also Cartel; Du Pont de Nemours; Environment; Science.

Reference Landes, David. *The Unbound Prometheus: Technological Change and Industrial Development in Western Europe from 1750 to the Present* (1969).

Child Labor

Child labor has been an essential part of most early industrial revolutions. The long-range impact of industrialization, however, was to reduce child labor. Most industrial societies moved fairly quickly toward a separation of work and childhood and later to a considerable separation of work and early adolescence, defining these stages as necessary for education.

Use of child labor in the early industrial revolution followed from the fact that children from the age of about five had always been used to work. Both employers and worker families found child labor fairly normal. Children received low wages. They could be used on jobs where agility and small size were at a premium. Bobbin boys, for example, tied thread when it broke on looms in the cotton industry while the looms were running, suffering frequent accidents in the process. In early industrial Britain, children were also used to haul coal from the mines or to pick slate from coal before it was shipped to market. British need for cheap child labor drove many cotton factory owners in Lancashire to recruit gangs of children from urban poorhouses. The children were housed in miserable dormitories and often beaten, working alternate day and night shifts. British exploitation of children seems to have been particularly severe, because of the need for low wages and docile labor in this first industrialization process. But child labor sprang up in the factories, particularly in the textile industry, in France, Belgium, the United States, and elsewhere.

Although child labor, even for the very young, was not novel, factory conditions were. Many children worked under the direction of strangers, rather than family members. More frequent accidents and the driving pace of work also posed problems. Middle-class reformers were soon appalled at child-labor practices, particularly because middle-class standards were changing to emphasize growing affection, care, and education for children. Many working-class families depended on children's income, but workers too began to worry about the treatment of children, particularly as factories became more impersonal. There was a growing realization that children were not being trained well, as apprenticeship standards declined. Many child workers were doomed to a life as unskilled factory hands. This situation prompted growing appeals for education to replace work, at least for children under twelve.

Britain, the first industrial society, pioneered child labor legislation, limiting the hours of young workers and then abolishing factory labor for children altogether. Other European countries and several American states followed this lead in the late 1830s

U.S. textile mills, such as this one in the early twentieth century, often hired young girls to work as "spinners," whose job involved mending the breaks in the cotton. Work shifts in such mills often lasted 10–12 hours.

and 1840s. More complex and automatic machinery made child labor less useful in many factory settings, while educational opportunities gradually expanded. Child labor was more common in jobs outside the factories than within by the later nineteenth century in western Europe and the United States, partly because child labor laws became more effectively enforced.

By 1900 a period of schooling was virtually universal in the western industrial countries and also in Japan, which installed a mass education system even before industrialization was fully under way. As childhood became separated from work, families began calculating the expense of having children differently, a major factor in the falling birth rates associated with the demographic transition. In most industrial societies, factory work for young adolescents began to be regulated as well, as the age of first employment crept up past twelve. Population pressures still existed, however, generating families with many mouths to feed, and the need to seek earnings encouraged continued reliance on child labor in most nonindustrial countries well into the later twentieth century.

See also Accidents; Child Labor Laws; Demographic Transition; Education.

Reference Nardinelli, Clark. *Child Labor and the Industrial Revolution* (1990).

Child Labor Laws

Use of child labor in factories and mines prompted concern quite early in the industrial revolution. Though children had always worked, their employment in more dangerous settings, outside the home and sometimes apart from other family members, obviously posed new problems. At the same time middle-class ideas about children increasingly emphasized better care and more education—another source of reform ideas. Meanwhile, however, workers frequently depended on children's earnings to supplement adult wages and employers (though middle class) eagerly sought child labor because it was cheap and docile and trained children for factory life. Employers also had a fierce sense of private property and resented any outside intrusion into their management of their firms.

Child labor reform nevertheless began early. Britain enacted restrictions on the employment of pauper children placed in factories in 1802, and in 1819 Parliament passed a child labor law applicable to all children working in textile mills. The Factory Act of 1819 made nine the minimum age for employment and prohibited a workday of more than twelve hours for children under age sixteen. A new law in 1833 cut the workday to nine hours for textile workers under age thirteen (there were then about 56,000 such workers) and introduced factory inspection for the first time. British laws were revised and extended several times during the nineteenth century, most notably in 1878 when the minimum age for employment was raised to ten and hours for children under fourteen were limited to six. The Factory Act of 1833 also required some schooling for factory children.

British laws helped stimulate legislation elsewhere, so that most industrializing countries began to act on child labor earlier in their industrial revolutions than the British had. Prussia passed a law in 1839. Several industrial states in the United States passed measures and also began to require primary education, though national laws only withstood constitutional challenge in 1938. France passed its first law in 1841, after extensive debate in which many employers claimed that child labor was benign and in which liberal principles were widely invoked to claim that fathers' rights to determine their children's activities and owners' rights to do what they wished in their factories must take priority.

Most early laws were badly enforced. They applied only to larger factories, leaving small shops free to use children as they wished. France began to develop a system of paid inspectors free from employer intimidation only in the 1870s. Also in the 1870s most industrial countries had begun to require primary education, and although this requirement was sometimes evaded, it did cut the use of younger children considerably. By this time, too (earlier in England, beginning in the 1830s), many workers turned against child labor because their children were now being bossed by strangers and because children's low wages could hold down those of adults. In the twentieth century limits on labor were extended to children in their teens in many industrial countries. By the 1920s child labor was quite rare in industrial Europe and North America, and school attendance became virtually universal. Japan, by installing compulsory primary education even before full industrialization, also limited the use of children.

Child labor continued to loom large in most less industrial countries, however. India, for example, passed laws against children in factories, but extensive use of children continued in other branches of the economy, particularly because there was no compulsory education. In the town of Sivakasi, for example, 45,000 children under the age of 15 worked in the local match industry by the 1980s.

See also Child Labor; Liberalism; State, Role of the.

References Heywood, Colin. *Childhood in Nineteenth-Century France* (1988); Trattner, Walter. *Crusade for the Children: A History of the National Child Labor Committee and Child Labor Reform in America* (1970); Weissbach, Lee. *Child Labor Reform in Nineteenth Century France* (1989).

China

China's history of industrialization has been influenced by political factors such as the terms of trade, the basis of state power, and revolution as well as by new technology. The Chinese government in the early nineteenth century attempted to resist incorporation into world trade but was too weak to resist. In the Opium Wars

(1839–1842 and 1858–1860), Britain and France forced the Chinese government not only to allow the sale of opium throughout the country but to make a series of humiliating trade concessions. Other European powers, the United States, and especially the Japanese also won trade concessions, such as allowing foreign-owned banks to issue their own currency. The foreign domination of China prevented the Chinese government from erecting protective tariffs for local industry, although by World War I some industry had developed around Shanghai and Manchuria. The Japanese government's annexation of Manchuria in 1931 and the subsequent war for the conquest of all of China discouraged further industrialization.

The Chinese Communist Party (CCP) came to power in 1949 after a long and bloody war with the Japanese and nationalist forces. The CCP, led by Mao Zedong, had relied on the peasantry (not the urban working class), and Mao charted a uniquely Chinese path to socialism. Heavy industry was initially encouraged, in part to follow the Soviet model of industrialization and to ensure that China would no longer be dominated by foreign powers, but later light industry and agriculture were emphasized. Agriculture was collectivized, but slowly, and there were no purges of party officials or kulaks as in the Soviet Union. After the economically disastrous Great Leap Forward in the late 1950s, industry was tied to the needs of the countryside, producing fertilizer, agricultural machinery, and material for irrigation systems. From the early 1950s until the early 1980s, steel production increased by a factor of thirty and electrical production by a factor of fifty.

After Mao's death in 1976, the CCP under Deng Xiaoping opted for a less ideological and more pragmatic course of action. As Deng often remarked, "It doesn't matter whether the cat is white or black as long as it catches mice." Investment and trade with foreign companies were encouraged and agriculture was decollectivized. Peasants could not own land, but they could buy and sell lengthy leases and they were eligible for compensation for their productive investments. Socialism continued to shape China's economy; for instance, part of the profits from semi-privatized communes in the countryside were allocated to their villages' social spending, such as pensions. However, the government attempted to break the "iron rice bowl" of permanent employment in state firms. Throughout most of the 1980s, industry grew at a 10 percent annual rate (one of the world's highest), and China is today a leading producer of steel, machine tools, and textiles (although its per-capita production is relatively low). Income inequality is growing, and by the early 1990s illegal strikes and demonstrations by workers had increased. Whether China will make the transition from socialism to capitalism, or to something else entirely, remains to be seen—but further industrial advance seems assured.

Reference Riskin, Carl. *China's Political Economy: The Quest for Development since 1949* (1987).

CIO

See Congress of Industrial Organizations.

Chung, Jo Yung

See Hyundai.

Classical Economics

Following the example of Adam Smith, a number of British economists from the early to mid-nineteenth century worked out a system of economic laws that, they argued, described optimal economic behavior and policy. These laws are the foundation of classical economics. Some of the economists have been dubbed the "Manchester School," as they worked in this city. The term "liberal economist" is sometimes also used, though not all liberals agreed fully with classical economics. Although the principal economists were British—T. R. Malthus, David Ricardo, Nassau Senior, and John Stuart Mill—others, including J. B. Say in France, shared similar views.

The classical economists argued that free competition was the desired economic state. They spoke of profits as the reward for risk and saving in a competitive economy. Entrepreneurs would move to operations where profits were promising, and the resultant competition would drive profits down; this was an example of classical "laws" designed to prove how free competition would ultimately work to the general good. Many classical economists argued that wages could not improve much above subsistence, for every increase in wages would draw new workers (or cause workers to increase their birth rate), thus driving the level down again. This view was called the "iron law of wages" and helped label economics "the dismal science." Classical economics also tried to describe rent income and often criticized it as unproductive since it could less fully be brought into the competitive system.

Classical economics helped justify the policies of laissez-faire, including a good bit of indifference to working-class poverty, as well as attacks on tariffs and other restrictions of trade. Proponents of pure classical economists dwindled somewhat after the 1860s—John Stuart Mill even changed his views to allow for more state-sponsored social reform—but classical assumptions have remained an important ingredient in economic theory in the West even to the present day.

See also Keynesianism; Liberalism.

Clothing

The manufacture of clothing traditionally occurred at home, except that the upper classes employed skilled artisanal tailors. The industrial revolution vastly increased the production of thread and cloth, requiring new systems for assembling of clothes. Simultaneously, demand for clothing rose during the eighteenth century. The result was a rapid expansion of hand work. The invention of the sewing machine, in the middle of the nineteenth century, increased the output of workers in the industry and diluted traditional skills, though a great deal of manual manipulation was still required. The result, however, was not a factory system, but a growth of sweatshops that employed primarily women workers. Some sewing was also done by domestic workers. Sweatshops expanded rapidly in cities like New York, Paris, and London in the late nineteenth century. Skills were limited on the new machines, and women workers were abundant. Immigrant workers were often used, as in the New York garment district. The result was long hours and low pay in an industry that, though mechanized to a degree, continued to have high labor costs in relation to the total product. To add to the difficulty, many sweatshops were badly lit and ventilated. Several European governments, and also U.S. states like Massachusetts, introduced some regulation of nonfactory industries around 1900, precisely because of sweatshop conditions in the clothing trade. Unionization also developed, and the International Ladies Garment Workers in the United States became a significant force in the twentieth century. At the same time, the continued search for low-cost labor drove much clothing manufacture to less industrial areas, like parts of the Pacific Rim.

See also Light Industry; Women Industrial Workers.

Coal

See Coal Miners.

Coal Miners

Coal miners were essential players in the industrialization process. Britain's rise as an industrial power was clearly linked to its huge supplies of coal as fuel for iron making, steel mills, locomotives, and steam power in general. Coal was often located in proximity to iron ore fields, and thus coal mining was closely associated with the iron and steel industry. The rapid expansion of mining, without major new technologies, required a great increase in the labor force.

The hazards of coal mining led miners to form unions relatively early, and mine workers' unions were a strategic part of the union movement in Britain, Germany, and the United States. Coal was increasingly important throughout the nineteenth century, but oil began to displace it as a fuel for ships, homes, and factories. By the late 1940s the use of coal was clearly declining; in the United States, many miners lost their jobs to automation. Coal miners have been unable to reassert their once formidable political and economic power, symbolized by the defeat of a major strike at the hands of a conservative government in Britain in the mid-1980s.

See also Congress of Industrial Organizations.

Reference Feldman, Gerald D., and Klaus Tenfelde, eds. *Workers, Owners, and Politics in Coal Mining: An International Comparison of Industrial Relations* (1990).

Cockerill, William (1759–1832)

The Cockerill family played a vital role in the spread of the industrial revolution beyond Britain. William Cockerill brought modern textile machinery to France in the 1790s; Napoleon made him a citizen in 1810. Cockerill operations spread to Belgium, where a machine-building plant in Liège employed two thousand workers by 1812. Cockerill boasted of his ability to import new technology from England just days after it was introduced. By the 1830s the Cockerill operation included the largest integrated metallurgical and machine factory in the world, and it had expanded into mining, shipbuilding, and railroad development. Cockerill realized the quick profits to be made from using British inventions in regions where older methods still predominated; there were risks but less competition. Although Cockerill's role in Belgium was particularly great, the family also spread factories in Germany and by the later nineteenth century (from the parent Belgian company) set up establishments in Russia.

See also Causes of the Industrial Revolution.

Cold War

Because of its length (over forty years) and intensity, the Cold War between the capitalist and the communist world had a large impact on world industrialization between 1948 and 1989. Cold War rivalry between the United States and the Soviet Union, and their respective allies, prompted massive military buildups and weapons research. Many technologies such as nuclear power, satellite communications, and computers were developed first for military use and later applied to the civilian world.

The impact of the Cold War on the Soviet Union and Eastern Europe was enormous. The Soviet Union, which had struggled to industrialize in the 1920s and 1930s, was first devastated by its war with Nazi Germany and then locked in an economic struggle with the United States, the wealthiest, most advanced industrial power in the world. Stalin and his successors favored the development of steel mills and other forms of heavy industry over civilian industries. The military received preferential treatment in labor and materials, which further hampered production for civilian uses (such as housing). The military did have short-term utility and was used to control Eastern Europe and to protect revolutionary governments in China, Vietnam, and Cuba. By the late 1970s, however, an escalating arms race with the United States consumed an increasing portion of the Soviet Union's resources and was a contributing factor to the eventual collapse of its economy.

The military-industrial complex was proportionally smaller in the United States, directly involving about 20 percent rather than nearly 40 percent of the economy by the 1980s, but it nonetheless had a profound effect on that country's industrial development. The relocation and expansion of military industries to the southern and western portions of the United States was crucial in the spectacular growth of cities such as Los Angeles, San Diego, San Antonio, and Seattle. Industries such as aircraft, electronics, and computers became highly dependent upon military support for research and development and then on the government to buy their finished products. A large proportion of the nation's scientists and engineers worked on military-related projects, and the expansion of the university system after World War II was based in part on the need to mobilize a skilled and educated work force in the global struggle. New academic fields, such as computer science, emerged from the military, and established fields, notably physics and electrical engineering, became quite dependent upon military financing.

The Cold War greatly influenced the shape of industrial development in Europe and Asia. In the early phases of the Cold War, the United States greatly desired to stimulate the reindustrialization of West Germany and Japan, but it took steps to prevent either country from remilitarizing. As a consequence, both countries were largely freed from the financial burden of defending their own borders, a decision that by the 1980s the United States was beginning to regret. In fact, some economists view the foreign military expenditures of the United States as an informal way to balance its trade surpluses from 1948 to 1968—and as a contributing factor in its subsequent trade deficits.

The Cold War was a major factor in the rise of Japan, South Korea, and Taiwan as industrial powers. Because these were all "front-line" states (bordering communist countries), the United States helped to underwrite their early efforts at industrialization, offering technical assistance, grants, and eventually access to markets. For instance, the Japanese car industry was given a boost during the Korean War when the United States bought its military trucks.

Although the Cold War technically ended in 1989 with the collapse of the Soviet system, the military continues to play a large role in the United States and Europe. As politicians have discovered, the "peace dividend" that many taxpayers looked forward to in the early 1990s went unrealized as many cities and industries mobilized to save what had become essential to their survival. Some analysts observe that the opportunity costs of continuing to subsidize military industries over civilian ones is a major factor in the economic decline of the United States.

See also Military Industrial Complex; State, Role of the.

Reference Markusen, Ann R., and Joel Yudken. *Dismantling the Cold War Economy* (1992).

Collectivization of Agriculture (Soviet Union)

See Five-Year Plans.

Colonization

See Imperialism.

Combination Acts

In 1799 and 1800, inspired by fear of revolutionary agitation spreading from France, Britain passed acts forbidding combinations (what today are called unions) among workers—effectively making unions and strikes illegal. During the next two decades, the difficult early period of British industrialization, the acts were frequently invoked to justify arrest of working-class protest leaders. They were one factor (similar to laws in most other early industrializing societies) in keeping agitation down. Liberals often supported the acts, arguing that workers should negotiate freely but individually, for any group activity distorted free market competition. As Britain passed through its most repressive phase, opinion shifted, as various leaders (including many liberals) saw that workers needed new rights to balance the power of employers. The Combination Acts were repealed in 1824, though various legal restrictions affected trade unions.

Communism

Communism is the belief that economic production should be socially (or communally) controlled, directed, and owned. Although industrialization caused social upheaval for workers, many observers recognized that the new economic order could not only meet people's material needs but eventually liberate humanity from the scourge of poverty. Although each regional or national movement has its own influences, traditions, and history, the Paris Commune (1871) and the 1917 Russian Revolution are crucial moments in the history of world communism.

The Paris Commune was a complex and contradictory event, and many Communards were influenced by Karl Marx as well as by the anarchism of Michael Bakunin and Pierre-Joseph Proudhon. By operating factories, arming workers (to defend the city from the advancing Prussian army), and establishing free schools, Communards were attempting, and in many ways succeeding, to establish the first worker-run society. The implications of the Commune inflamed the passions of revolutionaries and reactionaries alike. Lenin would later term it a "festival of the oppressed," and many socialists and anarchists looked to the event as a precursor of a society struggling to be born. The upper and middle classes were also obsessed with the Commune, though for obviously different reasons, and they generally tolerated the French government's brutal suppression of Communards: twice as many people were killed as died in the French Revolution (1789–1793).

Many communists believed that self-regulating communities of producers would form the basis of a new society and the communal ideal would play an important role in the Russian Revolution. The Bolsheviks came to power in large part by promising to allow workers and peasants to run the factories and farms. However, whether by necessity (to defeat counter-revolutionaries) or by design, power quickly became concentrated in the Bolshevik, or Communist, Party. In 1921 revolutionary sailors near St. Petersburg (Krondstadt) rebelled against the Bolsheviks' suppression of the self-governing councils (soviets) of workers and soldiers. Many socialists and anarchists viewed the suppression of this commune as the final betrayal of the revolution. Subsequently, "large C" Communism became identified with Stalinist tactics, although "small c" non-communist leftists tried to differentiate the ideal of communism from the flawed but "actually existing" socialism to be found in the Soviet Union.

By the late 1950s the Soviet Union's method of economic development and intolerance of dissent had alienated even Mao Zedong, who advocated a more egalitarian strain of society for China. Under Stalin's heirs, Soviet society had developed an informal social contract that many workers joked was "we pretend to work, you pretend to pay us." By the 1980s the Soviet Union had entered into an economic and political crisis from which it failed to recover, and Chinese leaders had begun to embrace capitalism more fully.

See also Great Leap Forward; Internationals; Stalinism; Syndicalism.

References Avrich, Paul. *Anarchist Portraits* (1988); Claudin, Fernando. *The Communist Movement: From Comintern to Cominform* (1975); Haupt, Georges. *Aspects of International Socialism, 1871–1914: Essays* (1986).

Company Union

The term "company union" is most commonly used to describe a union sponsored by a particular company in order to avoid negotiations with an independent union. Many Western firms intimidated or cajoled their workers into company unions around 1900, sometimes offering paternalistic benefits to its members. The effort won some success but did not deflect the growth of independent unions in Europe and the United States. The related "enterprise" unions represent the workers at a particular firm. Though not "company unions" in the pejorative sense, enterprise unions generally have less leverage with companies than independent labor organizations. Enterprise unions are common in Japan. In the 1950s conservative enterprise unions, aided by most employers, triumphed over left-wing industrial unions that made political and economic demands. Japanese enterprise unions typically maintained that they must help improve their company's productivity, whereas industrial unions saw their role as extending benefits to the entire working class rather than to one set of workers. Although enterprise unions do cooperate with each other in "spring offensives" to win better wages and working conditions, the temptation and pressures to strike an independent deal with one's own employer generally undermine unions' solidarity.

Comprador

In 1842 China was forced by European countries to open several of its ports (e.g., Hong Kong) as conduits for international trade. Compradors were Chinese middlemen (the term is Portuguese in origin) who put their knowledge of China's languages, culture, laws, and economy to use for Western companies—and often amassed their own fortunes. The term comprador has generally been used to describe a class of merchants or ruling class that relies on extensive foreign support to maintain its position.

In nineteenth-century China, merchants had lower status than artisans, farmers, or scholar-bureaucrats (the most prestigious social group). However, compradors' knowledge of Western languages, business practices, and technology made them invaluable to the Chinese government and to Chinese merchants. Compradors often headed Chinese industrial firms, such as the first steamship line, which was formed in 1873. Unlike traditional merchants, compradors generally did not seek to become scholars but preferred to stay in business.

Compradors were able to use networks of Chinese traders to help European merchants expand their trade throughout East Asia. By the early twentieth century, the comprador system began to decline as both Chinese and foreign merchants gained greater knowledge of each other's languages and markets; compradors disappeared entirely in the 1940s.

References Bandarage, Asoka. *Colonialism in Sri Lanka: The Political Economy of the Kandyan Highlands, 1833–1886* (1983); Hao, Yen-p'ing. *The Commercial Revolution in Nineteenth Century China: The Rise of the Sino-Western Mercantile Capitalism* (1986).

Computers

Since the seventeenth century, mathematicians have recognized the desirability of a machine that could automatically process information. In the mid-seventeenth century, Blaise Pascal developed "thinking machines." In the 1830s Charles Babbage and his female programmer, Augusta Ada, used punch cards in their "difference engine." Punch cards were later used in the partial automation of the U.S. Census in the 1890s. During World War II the U.S. military turned to universities and corporate research laboratories, such as Bell Labs, to make important advances in both mechanical and electronic computers, automatic machines capable of rapid, complex calculations. Until the late 1950s computers were expensive, used only by large governmental and corporate bureaucracies. Beginning in the 1960s, however, the size and cost of computers decreased, largely through the use of microchips; computers' speed increased; and their use expanded throughout society. Computers have helped to automate many different kinds of job and, combined with advances in communications technology, have made it easier for companies to decentralize production and distribution.

See also Universities.

Reference Cortada, James W. *Before the Computer: IBM, NCR, Burroughs, and Remington Rand and the Industry They Created, 1865–1956* (1993).

Confédération Générale du Travail (CGT)

Founded in 1894, this French national federation of unions long attempted to bypass the socialist political movement and its various disputing factions. Strongly influenced by the *bourses du travail* movement—local, largely artisanal labor exchanges—the CGT reflected France's strong craft traditions and revolutionary heritage. The movement did embrace industrial federations as well, and combined frequently strident rhetoric with practical efforts to promote union growth. A general strike for an eight-hour day in 1906 brought government repression, and the federation became more moderate. After World War I it was caught in splits between socialists and communists, but remained the largest national union organization.

See also Internationals; Syndicalism.

Reference Moss, Bernard. *Origins of the French Labor Movement* (1976).

Congress of Industrial Organizations (CIO)

The Congress of Industrial Organizations was the largest federation of industrial unions in the United States. It was formed in 1935 as the Committee for Industrial Organization by a number of unionists within the American Federation of Labor who wished to organize unskilled workers in mass production industries. (The CIO changed its name to the Congress of Industrial Organizations in 1938.) After a brief period in the 1920s of "welfare capitalism", in which corporations sponsored new benefit programs, industrialists had responded to the Great Depression in the 1930s by slashing the wages and benefits of their workers. In sharp contrast to previously antiunion administrations, President Franklin Roosevelt signaled his tentative support for unions when he helped to pass legislation that aided unions, such as the National Industrial Recovery Act in 1933 and the Wagner Act in 1935. In the desperate conditions of the depression, workers followed radical leaders who organized mass strikes of truck drivers in Minneapolis and dockworkers in San Francisco. Clearly, many unskilled workers, considered "unorganizable" by the AFL, were ready for unionization. At this juncture, it was the AFL that was not ready to change; it expelled the CIO in 1936.

The CIO used new tactics to organize mass production industries. In 1936 autoworkers in Toledo seized upon a new tactic: the sitdown strike. Because of the continuous nature of production within automobile plants, even a small number of workers who shut down one part of the production process idled hundreds or even thousands of other workers. Workers learned that employers were far less likely to resort to violence inside their plants, because valuable machinery could be damaged. Thus, sitdown strikes forced employers to negotiate with workers, which increased workers' sense of their power: employers had previously refused to even meet with unions. In order to organize workers throughout the industry, however, CIO organizers had to distribute leaflets to workers on the streets, leaving themselves vulnerable to attack. Before the industry was organized, unionists and company guards battled on many city streets around the entrances to factories. The turmoil of the auto industry probably convinced U.S. Steel in 1937 to recognize the CIO union simply to avoid that kind of upheaval in its mill towns.

In a clear break with the AFL, the CIO organized both white and black workers. To this end, the CIO hired many communists, who were staunch antiracists, as organizers. The head of the CIO, John L. Lewis of the United Mine Workers, was an anticommunist, but rationalized his use of communists by observing: "Who gets the bird, the hunter or the dog?" Although many communists remained as officials or employees of CIO unions in auto, meatpacking, and other unions, Lewis fired most of them from unions he controlled, such as steel. In the late 1940s the CIO expelled the communist-dominated unions, leaving the labor movement divided and weak. In the postwar years, the CIO continued to expand its membership but slowly grew more conservative, and in 1955 it merged with the AFL. Though less radical then their predecessors, CIO unions proved instrumental in extending social welfare benefits such as raising the minimum wage, increasing the federal government support for education, and providing care for the aged. The CIO was also instrumental in promoting the passage of civil rights laws in the 1960s.

References Bernstein, Irving. *Turbulent Years: A History of the American Worker, 1933–1941* (1970); Lichtenstein, Nelson. *Labor's War at Home: The CIO in World War II* (1982).

Construction Industry

Throughout the nineteenth century, most home construction was done by small-scale employers using highly skilled workers. Most contractors were former workers themselves. The growth of cities from the early nineteenth century onward necessitated a rapid growth in the construction industry. This growth, plus well-defined skills for carpenters, masons, and others, encouraged the spread of craft unionism throughout the industry. Although most employees retained their skills, there was some innovation in housing construction. Beginning in the 1830s, working-class homes in the United States were made with "balloon" frames of inexpensive wood studs held together with machine-made nails (instead of complex joints); by the 1870s pre-cut studs were widely available. By 1900 new equipment, including mechanized saws and preformed concrete, was altering work patterns. In the 1940s homes for the lower middle class were mass produced throughout suburban "Levittowns." Levitt relied not only on what mechanization was available (power saws, bulldozers) but on a simple, repetitive design in which the work was subdivided, allowing gangs of workers to increase their productivity. Large-scale construction projects, such as skyscrapers, dams, or airports have been dominated by large companies because they require vast amounts of technical expertise and capital—as well as political connections to obtain the contracts.

See also Infrastructure; Kaiser, Henry.

Consumerism and Mass Consumption

Consumerism is the term used to describe "a culture of consumption," which analyzes not only the influence of mass consumption on economic development but also the cultural and social dimensions of what Marxists call "commodity fetishism," a preoccupation with turning human qualities—like beauty—as well as goods into consumption items. Since the mid-nineteenth century, mass consumption of manufactured goods and services has become more important to developed industrial societies.

Some of the most exciting recent work on consumerism has uncovered the origins and rapid gains of the phenomenon in the eighteenth century, particularly in Britain but also to an extent in western Europe and North America. Large numbers of people acquired a new passion for imported goods like sugar, tea, and coffee. New home furnishings and table settings became more sought after. The eagerness for stylish clothing led to a rise in secondhand shops and in clothing thefts. Store owners began to set up more attractive displays and to advertise. Faddism—always a facet of consumerism—supported fluctuations in clothing styles. Early consumerism responded to new opportunities based on Europe's favorable position in world trade. Cheaper clothing allowed ordinary people to mimic and subtly challenge the lifestyles of the upper classes. Above all, consumerism helped set the market for greater output, thus motivating new industry and production methods. Although the pressures of early industrialization reduced the interest of poor urban workers (or work-oriented manufacturers) in consumerism, the pattern was launched; the next round of consumerism, later in the nineteenth century, clearly built upon earlier trends.

While a large portion of manufactured goods (railroads, iron and steel, machine tools, and chemicals) produced by industrial corporations in the mid-nineteenth century were directed toward factories or infrastructure projects, an increasing number of goods, such as sewing machines and processed foods, began to be mass marketed to middle-class consumers. Furthermore, by the late nineteenth century, more middle-class people worked as clerical workers or professionals than as farmers and small businessmen, and consequently their cultural values began to change. The dominant virtues of hard physical work, savings, and self-reliance began to be replaced by new mores that valued leisure and the goods and services available for purchase in the market.

The transformation in middle-class lifestyle (and, equally important, the changed expectations of what daily life should be) was painful and resulted in heightened levels of anxiety. While ministers and the new professions of doctors and psychologists attempted to put the collective mind of the middle class at ease, advertisers began to suggest that consumption of goods could also alleviate troubles. By the late nineteenth and early twentieth centuries, advertisers began to shift from offering technical information about their products to suggesting that their products could fulfill their customers' emotional needs and desires. Interestingly, in order to invoke a higher modern authority, by the 1910s and 1920s many advertisers relied on white-coated "doctors" and "scientists" who promoted their products by promising they would cure real or imagined problems.

Because members of the working class had less money to spend (or saved what little they had to get them through bouts of unemployment), workers were slower to join the culture of consumption. However, many poor families could go to the movies or amusement parks, buy processed foods, or purchase a radio. The lack of workers' purchasing power was seen by some industrialists in the early twentieth century, such as Henry Ford, as a problem. Because industrial workers in mass production industries (such as automobiles or electrical equipment) produced more and more goods, some employers felt they could pay their workers higher wages (which also prevented the unionization of their factories). Nonetheless, it was uncommon before 1920 for working-class families to purchase "consumer durables" such as radios, washing machines, refrigerators, or automobiles.

Many of the Keynesian policies after World War II were directed at expanding the purchasing power of workers and the middle class in developed countries such as North America, Western Europe, and Japan. Consumerism was an important feature that offset the crisis of "under consumption" and prevented the global industrial system from slipping back into depression after 1945. The ability of workers to participate in consumerism (albeit interrupted by the Great Depression in the 1930s) was seen by many workers and most middle-class observers as proof of the genius of the capitalist economic and political system. In 1959 Vice-President Richard Nixon told Nikita Khrushchev in the famous "kitchen debate" that the United States was more of a "workers' state" than the Soviet Union because "44 million families own 56 million cars, 50 million television sets, 143 million radios . . . and 31 million own their homes."

By offering workers the opportunity to improve their standard of living, particularly after World War II in the West, consumerism has long been assumed to have depoliticized workers. Rank-and-file communists recall that during the 1950s it was hard to interest workers in socialism when workers had "never had it so good." Even in Japan, which lagged in consumerism because of low wages and devotion to savings, consumer interests increased by the 1950s, a process encouraged by large department stores and advertising. Before the 1980s many observers argued that Eastern European and Soviet workers chafed under their regimes because they were denied consumer products such as cars. Some scholars have observed that even in the United States the influence of consumerism on politics has more often been assumed than proven; they point to examples of boycotts led by unions or civil rights groups. Current studies of consumerism explore how different groups establish personal meanings by acquiring goods and how consumerist values spread to other areas, as in the "selling" of political candidates.

References Brewer, John, and Roy Porter, eds. *Consumption and the World of Goods* (1993); Cohen, Lizabeth. *Making a New Deal: Industrial Workers in Chicago, 1919–1939* (1990); Fox, Richard Wightman, and T. J. Jackson Lears, eds. *The Culture of Consumption: Critical Essays in American History, 1880–1980* (1983).

Wheeler & Wilson's No. 9 sewing machine was mass marketed to middle- and upper-class consumers through this 1870 poster. In the 1830s and 1840s sewing machines proved too expensive for the middle class, but lower prices in the mid-1870s made them affordable.

Cooperatives

Early industrialization was launched on a firmly capitalist basis, with major firms regarded as the private property of the owner. Not surprisingly, many people who objected to industrialization, at least as currently organized, began to think of alternatives to this arrangement. Ideas of cooperative organization were part of almost all utopian socialist schemes, such as those of Robert Owen in Britain, and Charles Fourier and Pierre Proudhon in France. Utopians argued that private property allowed some people to profit from the labor of others—hence Proudhon's dramatic phrase, "property is theft." A cooperative alternative, or cooperative, in which ownership would be shared by those involved, would distribute rewards equitably and would allow all participants to make decisions about how work was to be organized. Utopian communities in Europe and the United States always used cooperative principles.

The first large-scale cooperative effort originated with the British Rochdale Equitable Pioneers in 1844. The founders, twenty-eight weavers in a town near Manchester, focused on buying groceries, selling them at standard market prices (to avoid annoying other shopkeepers) but then distributing profits to members of the cooperative, in proportion to purchases, at the end of the year. Members also voted on all policy issues, and a small part of the profits were reserved for mutual education efforts. The cooperative flourished, numbering 8,000 branches by the 1870s; by the 1860s the movement branched out into wholesaling and began to manufacture some of the commodities sold. Well before this point, cooperative stores modeled on the Rochdale example began to spread to other countries. In Germany a large cooperative movement sprang up in the 1850s, organized by Franz Schulze-Delitzsch and emphasizing banks and credit societies as well as cooperative stores. Consumer cooperatives never displaced other forms of retailing, though they caused concern to private storeowners, but they definitely added a new option for consumers.

The cooperative movement also spread strongly among peasants in western Europe and farmers in the United Sates from the 1860s onward. Cooperatives could help small agricultural producers acquire seeds, fertilizers, and equipment at lower cost through buying in bulk; they could provide credit; and they could help market and process produce. Cooperatives helped Danish peasants obtain the capital needed to convert to more market dairy farming, and cooperatives in many countries helped sell dairy products at favorable prices. The movement allowed rural producers to bargain more effectively with large wholesalers, shippers, and equipment manufacturers.

Cooperatives were sometimes attempted in factory production, but they rarely succeeded. Because factories seemed to need a management hierarchy, cooperative insistence on lots of participation and joint decision making could prove inefficient. Other cooperatives, trying to be efficient, disappointed their worker-members by failing to change working conditions appreciably.

Corn Laws

Britain began levying tariffs on grain imports to protect its farmers, as early as the sixteenth century; more modern regulations, called corn laws for the generic British term for grain, began in 1660. Rates rose and fell as a result of eighteenth-century legislation. Grain growing increased during the Napoleonic Wars, but when peace returned, farmers (including aristocratic estate owners) faced falling prices. A new Corn Law in 1815 established higher tariffs (though in fact prices continued to fall).

For years thereafter, manufacturing interests battled to reduce grain tariffs; their interest was in cheap food, whether imported or not, so that workers might be given lower wages. The issue was also ideological—liberal theory argued for free trade as the best way to stimulate production and maximize prosperity; and it was symbolic—the growing industrial middle class battled the aristocracy for political power. Several partial reductions did not end the dispute. An Anti-Corn Law League emerged in 1836, headed by the liberal Richard Cobden and backed by many factory owners. The league benefited from the larger middle-class vote allowed in the Reform Bill of 1832. After much agitation, the Corn Law was repealed in 1846, establishing Britain as a leader in free trade.

See also Agriculture; Enclosure Movement; Protectionism.

Corporations

Corporations are companies that can accumulate investment funds from many individual investors. They emerged only after industrialization was well under way. The need to amass extensive capital to form and expand large industrial firms emerged quickly with the industrial revolution. The initial response in Western countries was to apply the joint-stock form, already well established in overseas commerce. Joint-stock operations allowed several wealthy investors to pool their capital to set up such enterprises as new metallurgical factories or railroads. But the conventional joint-stock operation had one obvious constraint: any investor could be held liable for the debts of an entire firm, should it go bankrupt or be sued. This constraint limited the number of joint-stock companies and confined most investors to the ranks of the very wealthy, who could know the industrial operation intimately as well as gain some assurance about the solidity of their co-investors.

One way out of this constraint on pooling capital was through government involvement through government-backed bonds. This method was used for many railroads (in the United States, large land grants to railroads had somewhat the same effect, making investment less risky) and also for big industrial investment banks like the Crédit Mobilier, formed by the French government in 1852 to promote business financing.

The common solution after 1850 was to pass legislation permitting joint-stock companies, or corporations, to form with limited liability—that is, the investor was liable only for the amount of his or her investment. Many countries hesitated to embrace this innovation, worried that it would encourage irresponsible corporate behavior; but the lure of amassing more capital from more diverse investors, including relatively small ones, was too great to resist. Limited liability laws passed in most European countries. France, for example, passed a law in 1863 and further liberalized it four years later. The corporate form spread very rapidly thereafter; it was used in most branches of industry, particularly in heavy industry. Mergers were often arranged in the corporate form, for example, the United States Steel corporation, which carried on the firms of Andrew Carnegie and many mineowners. Joint-stock financing was widely used in investment banking, helping banks assume a growing role in setting up and rearranging industrial operations, particularly toward mergers and vertical and horizontal integrations. Hundreds of corporations formed each decade after 1870 in the major industrial countries, allowing massive industrial expansion and greatly increasing the size of the average firm. Thus, corporations promoted further industrial growth and innovation and also served as the financial basis for the age of big business—an age that still describes most capitalist countries.

Nations seeking to industrialize usually imitated this feature of Western business law. Russia gained its first joint-stock bank in 1864. During the reform era of the 1860s and 1870s, limited liability law was extended, and the number of corporations rose rapidly.

The rise of the limited liability corporation also promoted the growth of business investment on the part of the middle as well as the upper class. It served as the basis for the rapid growth of stock markets, where limited liability shares could be bought and sold. In the twentieth century it became an increasingly international phenomenon, as investment in foreign as well as domestic corporations surged—an obvious way to direct capital from wealthy countries to settings where capital was in short supply but industrial opportunity growing. Also in the twentieth century—quite visibly by the 1920s and again after World War II—the corporate form could support nonproductive investment behavior, as stocks were bought and sold not because of industrial potential but as means of manipulating stock prices and earning windfall investment profits.

See also Joint-Stock Companies; Mergers.

Reference Chandler, Alfred D., Jr. *Visible Hand; The Managerial Revolution in American Business* (1977).

Corporatism

This economic policy was designed to organize an industrial economy in a way that offered an alternative to capitalism and class-conscious socialism. It harks back somewhat to preindustrial traditions in which artisans or merchants organized into guilds or corporations to assure quality of production, harmony within the group over any divisive competitive advantage, and good relations among various segments of the labor force. Corporatism of the twentieth-century variety was touted as a means of checking the exploitation possible under capitalism while also reducing class conflict.

Corporatism was widely discussed in many countries, by certain British socialists as well as by conservative leaders in Europe and Latin America. Fascist leaders, however, actually came closest to implementing corporatism as a policy. Mussolini's Italy moved first. During the 1920s the Italian government abolished strikes and required government approval of all worker associations. Corporatist rhetoric urged collaboration between employers and workers. The government regulated work by adopting an annual vacation with pay and some improvements in social insurance (Labor Charter, 1927). Employer and worker associations were required to cooperate with government agencies. The idea was that each major industry would form an overarching corporation to further labor-management cooperation, topped by a National Council of Corporations. In fact, most of the corporations were little more than paper constructions, though fascist leaders tried to use some councils to coordinate economic policies. Private enterprise still prevailed, along with fairly rapid industrial growth, and the main result of the corporate economy was to undermine independent trade unions. A similar pattern took shape in Nazi Germany.

Corporatist policies also spread to Franco Spain and to parts of Latin America. In Brazil between 1930 and 1945, under the regime of Getulio Varga, corporatist rhetoric flourished, and the government intervened regularly in labor disputes in the interest of preventing strikes. Here too, industrial growth occurred, but labor was held down.

See also Perónism.

Cotton

Cotton, one of the principal fibers to be utilized in mechanized textile production, had been grown and used in manufacture in India but was a new product in Europe in the eighteenth century. Increasing British production (resulting partly from bans on Indian imports) thus fed a new consumer interest, one of the first cases of the connection between industrial production and changing taste. Cotton worked well with machines because it did not break easily. Carding, spinning, and weaving devices were applied from the mid-eighteenth century onward, and because there was little traditional production and so little stake in preindustrial procedures, machines gained ground very rapidly. The utility of cotton was boosted by the invention of the cotton gin, which separated the seed from the fiber of the cotton plant.

Cotton cloth could be dyed and printed in many colors and designs. This, plus its low cost, attracted popular taste, changing clothing habits very quickly. Cotton was

Egypt exported cotton as early as the 1830s, and by the time this picture was taken in 1916, land dedicated to growing cotton had more than doubled. This shipment's final destination was likely to be Egypt's largest customer, Great Britain.

also easily laundered, which improved hygiene. Conversion to cotton clothing was a significant improvement in the standard of living of the lower-class and in the variety and fashionability of apparel widely evident by the 1820s and 1830s. The rapidly expanding production of cotton, a major industrial export, called for increasing supply. Not only the southern United States and India but also Egypt and, later, parts of Africa turned to cotton growing for commercial export. Some of these regions benefited from export earnings, but others relied on poorly paid labor. Some land was put to cotton production at the expense of basic foodstuffs, worsening economic conditions for the local peasantry, as in parts of sub-Saharan Africa such as Mozambique in the first half of the twentieth century. In short, cotton reflected a variety of features, both advantageous and disadvantageous, of industrialization as a global process.

Cotton Gin

The cotton gin was invented by Eli Whitney in 1793 to separate cotton fiber from the seed. Before the existence of this machine, a person had to spend a full day handpicking the seeds from a pound of fiber. With cotton fabric gaining popularity, and machines increasing the output of thread, the need for a better method of initial processing was pressing. The gin feeds harvested cotton through a row of rapidly revolving saws, the teeth of which pull the cotton from the seeds; ribs between the saws prevent the seeds from passing through. The cotton gin not only supported the industrialization of cotton production, it also increased the importance of slavery in the southern United States, where cotton cultivation spread to new areas such as Alabama and Mississippi.

Cranes

Loading cranes, based on cranks (winches) and pulleys, are an ancient device long used by merchants and shipowners. With industrialization, especially by the late nineteenth century, new materials and machines could be applied to cranes, making them bigger, more mobile, and capable of carrying much heavier loads. Metal cranes, using metal cables instead of rope and powered by internal combustion engines, spread in metallurgical plants and on docks and construction sites. Cranes could also be placed on rails, for lateral mobility, or on truck beds. Many unskilled workers, previously employed for crude hauling, were displaced by the new kinds of cranes, though the increasing volume of goods to be moved or loaded preserved some employment. Mechanical cranes and derricks allowed construction of new structures like the skyscraper, introduced in the United States soon after 1900, for which materials had to be lifted to great heights. Mechanical cranes, a logical, fairly simple technical outgrowth of industrialization, thus transformed a number of aspects of labor, transportation, and urban life.

See also Dockers.

Crompton, Samuel (1753–1827)

The inventor of the spinning mule (1779) was one of a long line of eighteenth-century English inventors who established the technological basis for the industrialization of textiles. The mule, like the spinning jenny, contained a movable carriage with spindles, but rollers were used automatically to feed the fibers to the spindles; when the yarn was partly spun, the feed rollers stopped and the spinning was completed at high tension. This made possible the spinning of finer cotton threads for muslins (in contrast to Arkwright's cruder water frame). Thread could be spun not only far faster but also much finer than by the human hand. It was estimated that by 1812 one-half to two-thirds of the English cotton industry depended on mule-spun thread. Both processes, the frame and the mules, are still used in modern textiles. Crompton had to sell his patent for next to nothing because of poverty.

See also Lawrence, Abbott; Textiles.

Crystal Palace Exhibition

Sponsored by Britain in 1851, this great international exhibition, held in an iron and glass pavilion itself a mark of industrialization, celebrated the British industrial lead. Huge crowds of people from all social classes pressed to see the latest industrial wonders in a display designed to convince that industrialization meant progress. Foreign observers were stimulated to greater efforts at imitation, seeing the triumph of British machines, though individual displays, like Krupp's in metallurgy, surprised the British hosts by their sophistication. Many industrial exhibitions followed in the nineteenth and twentieth centuries as a means of competitive display; they spread industrial knowledge, and they certainly showed the increasingly international scope of economic change.

Cunard Steamship Company

This British company, founded by Samuel Cunard (1787–1865) in 1840, was the first great transatlantic steamship line. Steamship development had concentrated in the United States, where it was vital on riverways. But British coastal steamships began to increase after 1827. Seagoing steamships were not developed until 1838, when four steam vessels crossed the Atlantic. The results pleased the owners, though tremendous amounts of coal had to be used. On the basis of these results, the Cunard company launched its service with a fleet of four ships, which had to use about 40 percent of their carrying capacity for coal. Until the 1860s, the Cunard operation focused on shipments of mail. But

The Crystal Palace Exhibition was held in an enormous greenhouse-like building, which covered nearly 2,000 acres and required almost a million square feet of glass.

then improved engine construction, using higher pressures, reduced the coal needs, and the steamship began to come into its own for passenger as well as transport use. Cunard himself introduced iron steamers (1855) and screws instead of paddle wheels (1862). The Cunard line remained a major player in Atlantic and other oceanic operations into the later twentieth century.

See also Steamboat.

Daewoo

Daewoo is a South Korean "chaebol" or holding company. Its strategy in the world market has been to compete fiercely at the bottom rungs of a number of different markets rather than concentrating on a single product. This strategy was remarkably successful. In the early 1970s, for instance, Daewoo produced no ships, but by the mid-1980s it had become the second-largest shipbuilder in South Korea, which had become the world's premier shipbuilding nation. Daewoo's rise depended not only on the assistance of the Korean government but also on the collective technical, financial, and organizational assets of the different companies within the chaebol.

Decolonization

Decolonization is the process by which former colonies rid themselves of direct political and economic control from metropolitan countries. World War II greatly weakened the industrialized European countries with colonies in Asia and Africa (England, France, Holland, and Belgium) and destroyed outright the empires of Italy and Japan. By the mid-1960s, most of the Asian and African nationalist movements had won their independence from colonial powers either through wars (Algeria, Kenya) or mass movements (India, Ghana). However, more difficult than winning political freedom was the struggle for economic independence.

As a matter of policy, most metropolitan countries had shaped their colonies into suppliers of cheap raw materials. Decolonized countries often attempted to industrialize and thereby gain more control over their economic lives and to increase the standards of living of their populations. However, the legacy of colonialization was difficult to overcome. All of the physical infrastructure (railroads, roads) in the decolonized countries had been developed to move raw materials efficiently from the interior to the coast, and the social infrastructure (education, social services) was generally quite underdeveloped. The former Belgian Congo provides an extreme example: upon independence it had less than twenty college graduates. After decolonization, the state played an important role in the industrialization process (or attempt) because former colonies lacked a vigorous class of capitalists and in part because many nationalist leaders were influenced by socialist theories of development. After 1947 the Indian state expanded the educational system, nationalized certain industries, and offered financial incentives for others. In South Korea the state encouraged the formation of large business conglomerates very similar to the zaibatsus of their former colonizers, the Japanese.

Many of these new nations have experienced severe political instability (such as ethnic wars, border conflicts, and political repression) as well as economic turmoil (and by the 1980s the economies of many countries in sub-Saharan Africa were in outright decline). The historical experience of Latin America in the nineteenth century (which also underwent a process of decolonization) suggests that it often takes decades to develop the institutions necessary for a stable nation state. Even a stable nation state, however, is no guarantor of successful industrialization, as the case of Argentina makes clear. The difficulty of Latin American countries to industrialize has led many scholars to analyze the neocolonial policies of industrialized countries, which discourage industrialization by refusing to open their markets to industrial goods or by dumping manufactured goods in local markets and thus undercutting fledgling industrial firms.

In the late 1980s, a third wave of decolonization occurred as countries in Eastern Europe and the former Soviet Union gained their political independence. Much of Eastern Europe was industrialized, but most countries have found it extremely difficult to make the transition from a centralized economy to the capitalist marketplace. In most cases political independence was swiftly followed by severe deindustrialization, which even in the case of the former East Germany (whose citizens received subsidies from its much richer partner, the former West Germany) has been a painful process. A few countries, such as Hungary and the Czech Republic, seem likely to benefit from their decolonization, but most countries (particularly those in the former Soviet Union) appear headed for a prolonged period of political and economic turmoil.

See also Finance Capital; Maquiladora; World Bank; World Systems Theory.

References Grimal, Henri. *Decolonization: The British, French and Belgian Empires, 1919–1963* (1978); Smith, Tony, ed. *The End of the European Empires: Decolonization after World War II* (1975).

Deflation

See Inflation and Deflation.

Deindustrialization

Deindustrialization is the dismantling or destruction of manufacturing or industry. Over the last two hundred years, the dynamic nature of capitalism has generally involved the spectacular rise and fall of specific industries in regions or countries. The history of deindustrialization suggests that market forces, new technology, governmental policies, and industrialists' decisions and investment patterns are possible causes of deindustrialization.

The rise of the British textile industry in the late eighteenth century destroyed the hand-loom trade in Great Britain and textile producers in India. Although the replacement of mechanized looms for hand-powered ones was inevitable in economic terms, the fate of Indian textiles was sealed by the mercantilist policies of the British Imperial government, which actively sought to create a reserve market for British products. The government maintained policies that largely kept India as a captive market for British textile mills; deindustrialization here meant the displacement of hundreds of thousands of workers. Throughout the nineteenth century, the technological supremacy of British industry meant that if national governments could not protect local manufacturers through tariffs, as in the case of France and the United States, the cheaper British imports rapidly displaced local producers. Thus, throughout much of Latin America, many women lost their textile manufacturing jobs in the 1830s and 1840s. As industrialization proceeded throughout the world, even well-established industries could fall. By 1919 jute-weaving mills in Scotland (at least the ones that produced twine and coarse bagging for raw cotton) were successfully displaced by mills in Calcutta, which had cheaper labor and were located closer to raw materials. In some cases, Scottish mills were dismantled and moved to India.

Even within national boundaries, established crafts or industries can be deindustrialized by new technology, market forces, or corporate policies. Advances in mechanized rolling of sheet metal in the 1920s, a response to the rising demands of the automobile industry, displaced many hand-rolling mills in the Pittsburgh region. The petroleum industry replaced whale oil with its own products as a source of light and eventually robbed coal of much of its market for heating homes and powering industry. Large coal regions in Europe and the United States began to experience deindustrialization in the 1920s, which resulted in a massive loss of jobs. Deindustrialization can also result from corporate policies to avoid unions or move to be closer to cheaper labor. After a bitter textile strike in the 1920s, for instance, many New England–based companies shifted their mills to the non-union South.

After World War II, corporations' ties to

specific countries weakened as multinational corporations took advantage of the global lowering tariffs that resulted from the Bretton Woods Agreement. The experience of coordinating production and distribution of goods throughout the world further weakened the ties between corporations and their "home" country. From the 1970s onwards, many U.S. firms shifted their factories to northern Mexico after the U.S. and Mexican governments had reduced tariffs and other trade barriers. As a result of the efforts of the World Bank/IMF, many countries throughout the world have reduced their barriers to foreign investment by limiting taxation and easing restrictions on the export of profits. Not surprisingly, there has been enormous growth in free-trade zones in places as diverse as the Caribbean, Chile, and the Philippines. In this scenario, companies shift production plants from one country to another in search of the most favorable business climate. Sheer international growth has produced new levels of production in important industries such as steel and textiles, resulting in deindustrialization in parts of the United States, Europe, and Japan. Since the 1970s in the United States, deindustrialization has dramatically reduced the size of the manufacturing labor force.

Perhaps the most dramatic case of deindustrialization is occurring throughout the former Soviet Union and Eastern Europe. In the last several years industrial production has fallen by more than 50 percent, partly in response to the shutdown of inefficient facilities. Even relatively modern factories, however—in Poland, for example—have lost their former markets in the Soviet Union and have been unable to find new markets; Western Europe, coping with its own problems of deindustrialization and unemployment, has refused to allow Eastern European producers access to their markets. Another factor resulting from the collapse of the Soviet state is sheer larceny. The proceeds from the sale of valuable machines, raw materials, or products such as petroleum have often simply been stolen by unscrupulous managers. Moscow has become the largest consumer of German luxury automobiles even as many former industrial workers are desperately seeking day-labor jobs throughout Western Europe.

The systematic loss of industry not only results in direct unemployment and massive disruption in many working-class families but also causes a negative ripple effect as service sector workers are displaced. In the United States during the 1970s and 1980s, small feeder companies, such as tool and die shops that relied on contracts with automobile companies, also went out of business. Perhaps the most pernicious effect of deindustrialization is that it reduces tax revenues and weakens the ability of government to respond to economic and social crisis. In the early 1980s some local governments in U.S. "rust belt" towns unscrewed the light bulbs in streetlights because they simply could not afford to pay their electric bills. Numerous corporations have used the threat of relocation to lower their tax bill or to request easing of environmental or safety regulations.

Different countries have responded variously to the current deindustrialization crisis. In the case of the United States, the federal government under both Democratic and Republican regimes has refused to intervene to directly subsidize heavy industry. Aid to hard-hit areas has been minimal; many steel-mill towns in Pennsylvania and Ohio that were deindustrialized in the 1970s and 1980s are still largely devastated. Japanese steel towns benefited from their companies' paternalism, for the companies have subsidized new industries. Because of their strong trade unions and Social Democratic traditions, Western European governments generally expanded unemployment benefits, added jobs in government industries, or increased their emphasis on education. Until recently, French unions have forced their government simply to increase state subsidies to the steel industry there. In the late 1970s Margaret Thatcher in England pioneered the path of radical reduction of government services to workers in order to reduce public deficits.

See also Dual Labor Markets; World Systems Theory.

Reference Bluestone, Barry, and Bennett Harrison, *The Deindustrialization of America: Plant Closings, Community Abandonment, and the Dismantling of Basic Industry* (1982).

Demographic Transition

This term describes the process by which a society's population system changes from the traditional one of high death and birth rates to one with much lower birth and death rates. Usually death rates drop first, then, as people realize the problems associated with the resultant population increase, the birth rates begin to decline as well, gradually restoring greater population stability. The new system, however, is much different from the old, for the percentage of children in society goes down (the lower birth rates) and that of older people rises (due to effect of declining mortality rates and higher life expectancy).

This demographic transition first occurred in western Europe and the United States and was closely associated with industrialization. Rising population in the eighteenth and early nineteenth centuries resulted from declining death rates, thanks to better food supplies and some new sanitation measures. Increasingly, industrial economies helped people realize that a new level of birth control was essential. Middle-class people usually led the way, seeking fewer children so that they could be sure to have the capital necessary to educate the children they did have and to provide them with a start in business or the professions (or for women, marriage) at an appropriate middle-class level. They sought to upgrade human capital while cutting human numbers. Industrialization increased the requirements for education and capital and thus motivated more rigorous birth control. Working-class conversion to new levels of birth control occurred a bit later—1870 is the standard date for western Europe. Workers found that children could not work until they entered their teens and that they also needed some education; their own low wages prompted concern for birth control simply as a matter of family survival, particularly given recurrent economic slumps like the one that hit Europe in the mid-1870s. By 1900 the average family size was dropping rapidly. Ironically, fewer children per family also promoted better care for children, so Europe and the United States also experienced a massive reduction of infant mortality between 1880 and 1920, motivating still further levels of birth control.

Birth control during the demographic transition in the Western world was first accomplished primarily by sexual abstinence or coitus interruptus. Artificial methods were used but were suspect for moral reasons and were not fully reliable in any event. Gradually, however, greater reliance on factory-produced items like condoms and diaphragms (called pessaries in the nineteenth century) increased, which reduced the sexual tension occasioned by the demographic transition.

Other societies that industrialized went through a roughly similar demographic transition as the relationship between fewer children and family and national prosperity was recognized. Birth rates declined in the Soviet Union from the 1920s. Japan's demographic transition, backed by the government and involving considerable use of abortion, occurred after World War II.

Many nonindustrial societies have experienced unprecedented population growth in the twentieth century. Many experts argue that (as the death rate has fallen due to better medical technology and food supplies) these countries must introduce a demographic transition simply to be able to industrialize fully; otherwise the increasing population drains too many resources. In keeping with these beliefs, China, India, and most other countries have tried with varying success to introduce greater population control in the later twentieth century. World population growth rates are beginning to fall. Some societies with expanding industrial sectors have experienced a demographic transition even though the legacy of fast growth will continue to spur population expansion for some decades; these societies include Brazil (1950s), Mexico (1960s), and probably China (1980s). The exact patterns of demographic control necessary or desirable for industrialization are matters of dispute.

See also Child Labor; Green Revolution; Population Growth; Retirement.

References Caldwell, John. *Theory of Fertility Decline* (1983); Coale, Ansley, and Susan Watkins, eds. *The Decline of Fertility in Europe* (1986).

Demography
See Population Growth.

Department Stores

Department stores, which offered a large variety of items for mass consumption, were a clear product of industrialization. They served the need to find new ways to display and sell increasing quantities of manufactured goods. They thus followed the growth of urban shops in the eighteenth century. The stores carried all sorts of products, from kitchen ware to clothes, and geared themselves to wide sales rather than to neighborhood shopping. Department stores were also industrial in their organization: the labor force (sales people) was specialized, largely unskilled, supervised, and trained to be efficient. Discipline imposed on sales clerks, though distinctive in emphasizing the need to be polite and mimic middle-class dress and manners, was as severe as in the factories. Goods were arrayed precisely, in machine-like fashion. Unlike many traditional shops, department stores did not allow bargaining over price and limited chatting and socializing.

The first department store, an expansion of a clothing shop, opened in Paris in the

A late 1880s woodblock depicts the Mitsui Dry Goods Store, a predecessor of the Mitsukoshi Department Store in Tokyo, Japan.

1830s. The idea quickly spread. After the 1850s most Western cities offered several major department stores. Great stores opened in the United States, like Macy's in New York and Marshall Fields in Chicago. Their owners resembled industrialists in seeking to innovate in quest of profit. Department stores were launched outside the West, though most often by Western businessmen. Most of the stores in St. Petersburg and Moscow around 1850 were foreign-owned, the first started by a French businessman. The rise of department stores (called *depato*) in Japan in the twentieth century, some of them unprecedentedly large, was an integral part of the nation's industrial growth; by the mid-twentieth century these stores featured huge arrays of standardized industrial goods including cameras, audio equipment, and other delights of high-tech consumerism.

The spread of department stores provoked massive debate in the late nineteenth century and beyond. Many observers criticized the stores for luring women into excessive consumption and moral decline. Others worried about the impact on the lower classes. Although most department stores shoppers were middle- or upper-class, the stores did seek mass sales, and many poor urban people at least wandered through, developing what one historian has called "dream worlds" of material luxury. New kinds of theft developed amid the opportunities department stores offered; both in Europe and the United States, kleptomania, a new disease, emerged in the 1870s. Its victims were mainly women, often from wealthy families, who stole out of compulsion. Some Russian intellectuals also attacked department stores for their foreignness: "With the colossal houses . . . the former good nature, the conviviality . . . [of shopping] is disappearing. The tenor of life is becoming disciplined, is being chained to the pace of the machine."

See also Consumerism.

References Miller, Michael. *The Bon Marché: Bourgeois Culture and the Department Store, 1869–1920* (1981); Pasdermaijan, Hrant. *The Department Store: Its Origins, Evolution, and Economics* (1954); Williams, Rosalind. *Dream Worlds: Mass Consumption in Late Nineteenth Century France* (1982).

Dependency

See World Systems Theory.

Development Theory

Development theory arose in the late 1940s, elaborated by economists and other social scientists in the United States and in international economic organizations like the World Bank. The theory attempted to identify the changes that could move impoverished, largely agricultural, "third world" economies into the industrial age. Sweeping changes were seen as necessary, but the primary attention of development theory was directed at increasing levels of science and education, introducing new technology, and accumulating capital, on the assumption that these ingredients, similar to those available in the Western industrial countries, would cause governments, labor forces, and entrepreneurs to adjust appropriately. Specific government forms, or prior traditions of work, did not matter much in this scenario. Development theorists paid some attention to agricultural productivity, though they were sometimes accused of neglecting the agricultural majority in favor of showcase industrial projects. With time, they devoted increasing attention to demography, as rapid population increase threatened to prevent significant industrial gains no matter what the inputs of foreign advisors, technicians, or investment capital.

Development theory sought to sum up what was understood about the causes of successful industrialization, though many historians have argued that the summary oversimplified and downplayed human and cultural factors. The theory was spurred by sincere if somewhat patronizing concern about massive world poverty, as colonial regions achieved political independence without corresponding economic gains, and by a desire to improve economic levels to bar the spread of communism in the context of the intensifying Cold War.

Development theory formed the basis of serious policy. In 1949 the International Bank for Reconstruction and Development (World Bank) sent a mission to Colombia that called for sweeping reforms in the name of industrial development. Science, technology, planning, and the guidance of international organizations constituted the launching pads. Special attention was paid, in this and other cases in Latin America, Africa, and Asia, to the problem of capital formation, for albeit some foreign aid was provided, the internal savings rate had somehow to rise by as much as 300 percent.

During the 1970s development theory had to adjust to the stubborn fact that industrialization had not gained ground as rapidly around the world as initial planning had anticipated. New attention went to agriculture, with the "Green revolution" one result of technology applied to farming in the tropics.

Development theory has been criticized for more than overoptimism and vagueness about sources of new capital. It has been seen, like modernization theory, as an unexamined Western judgment on very different world societies. It has been attacked for putting industrial advance ahead of any real attention to poverty, which often has remained untouched by apparent change at the industrial level. The strong planning emphasis has also been questioned, particularly as free-market theories gained ground in the 1980s.

Naive expressions of development theory have declined. Nevertheless, many of the goals and some of the premises of development theory persist in efforts to stimulate industrial growth by cutting rates of population increase, expanding education, or enhancing investment.

See also Causes of the Industrial Revolution; Modernization Theory.

References Escobar, Arturo. *Encountering Development: The Making and Unmaking of the Third World* (1995); Nurkse, Ragnald. *Problems of Capital Formation in Underdeveloped Countries* (1953).

Diesel, Rudolf (1858–1913)

A German mechanical engineer, Diesel developed an internal combustion engine in 1897 that used oil as a fuel. It was more efficient than gasoline engines and simpler in design, making it especially appropriate for large equipment such as steamships and locomotives. Diesel was an example of the later-industrial kind of inventor, because he was formally trained (in Munich). He based his work on other engineers' designs and on the theory of heat engines. He set up a factory to make his engines. In 1913 he mysteriously disappeared from a German ship bound for London.

Diesel engines work on compression ignition, rather than spark plugs. Air, compressed by a piston in each cylinder, ignites the fuel. Diesel oils are cheaper than refined gasoline, and their energy is easily converted to rods that can turn crankshafts, providing rotary power for heavy engines.

Discipline

New forms of discipline were essential for the work processes of early industrialization for three reasons. First, workers operated in relatively large groups. Even though most early factories were small, the owner could not keep his eye on the whole crew, which was composed of strangers unaccustomed to working with each other. Second, powered machinery required unprecedented speed and coordination. If one member of a team operating a machine strayed, the whole machine might have to be shut down, resulting in a great loss of production. Third, factory owners generally shared a rigorous work ethic (for others, and often for themselves as well) that held that good, disciplined work was life's highest goal and the clearest demonstration of good character. Since many workers brought from their rural or artisanal past different work values that emphasized a slower pace with more interruptions, new forms of discipline seemed essential to whip them into shape.

The goals of factory discipline were diligence and regularity. Workers must arrive on time. They must not dirty the material they were working on. They must not sing or chat or wander around. They must obey orders and display loyalty, and of course they must not steal materials. Several mechanisms were used to enforce this unfamiliar discipline. Shop rules stipulated the major regulations and were prominently posted. Fines were administered. A worker who arrived late to work was locked out of the factory for a half-day, receiving no pay and owing an additional half-day's pay as penalty. Watchmen frequently controlled exits and even searched workers suspected of stealing material. Increasingly, foremen were employed to make sure that workers toed the line. They replaced more informal methods of supervision, such as hiring a skilled worker and making him responsible for the behavior of his assistants.

Eventually, the rigor of discipline tended to increase. Workers were told not to try to fix a machine but to leave it to a specialist. The advent of efficiency experts—industrial engineers—in the 1890s signaled an effort to regulate workers' motions ever more strictly, to avoid loss of time. Factory workers were to be made as machinelike as possible. New electrical devices like time clocks systematically checked arrivals and departures.

Although the most rigorous work discipline applied to the factories, new systems spread to other branches of work. Sales personnel and clerks were required to adhere to dress codes and were taught politeness and other forms of emotional control in order to please their bosses and customers. This trend gained momentum in the twentieth century. Some scholars argue that the subtle regulations, particularly over emotional expression, enforced on white-collar workers have now become particularly severe, distorting emotional life even off the job. Airline flight attendants carefully taught to smile no matter what the provocation from a passenger—a major component of company training—are a recent example of workers disciplined to make their public personalities fit the job.

At no stage in the industrialization process did workers accept all the new discipline with docility. Individual efforts to evade rules were legion, and thefts from the workplace expressed defiance as well as desire for material gain. Mocking the supervisors was a favored pasttime—when it could be enjoyed safely. Specific conflicts with foremen were the source of many small but bitter strikes. Larger efforts, in strikes and the union movement, to modify employers' rights unilaterally to determine discipline was a major stimulus to the labor movement from the late nineteenth century onward. On the whole, however, workers increasingly accepted many aspects of industrial discipline, one of the major changes in the human experience of work brought by industrialization.

See also Scientific Management.

References Joyce, Patrick. *Work Society and Politics: The Culture of the Factory* (1980); Pollard, Sidney. *The Genesis of Modern Management* (1965); Stearns, Peter N. *Paths to Authority* (1978); Voss, Kim. *The Making of American Exceptionalism* (1993).

Distilling

See Brewing and Distilling.

Division of Labor

The process of subdividing the role of each worker in the manufacturing process has been a central feature of industrialization since its origin in late eighteenth-century England. In one of the classic examples of the advantages of the division of labor, Adam Smith observed in the 1770s that an artisan working alone could only produce a handful of pins, whereas once the labor process has been subdivided a few dozen workers repeating different tasks in a pin factory can produce thousands of pins. The division of labor has continued because each industrialist or employer has an interest in producing goods more cheaply in order to gain a greater market share or simply to remain competitive.

In contrast to artisans who produced an entire product from beginning to end, factory owners separated workers into skilled,

Service technicians prepare a Boeing 727 turbofan engine for testing at an aircraft plant in Connecticut in 1961.

semi-skilled, and unskilled laborers. In the late eighteenth century, for example, the New England shoe industry relied on the "putting out" system in which rural artisans produced entire shoes in their workshops. In the early nineteenth century, merchants centralized production of shoes in factories; some workers became foremen or skilled workers (such as those who made the patterns that other workers followed), but most employees became factory "hands" who repeated one or two steps in the production process. Shoe factories relied on steam-powered machinery, but the "deskilling" of workers was also a significant factor in allowing shoemakers to raise production of shoes and lower prices. Many of the deskilled workers were women. Given sexual division of labor, women's jobs were always categorized as low-skill, even when (as in garment making) their jobs actually required a number of skills.

Even as industrialization destroyed many workers' pre-existing skills, it also created entirely new skill requirements, as exemplified in the work of puddlers or machinists. By the late nineteenth century, however, most machinists did not create whole machines but were employed in large workshops completing one stage of machine making. Many young workers were still enrolled in apprentice systems around 1900, but only a small proportion of them (less than 25 percent) learned all the different features of the craft. Battles between an increasingly craft-conscious machinists' union and employers set the ground for the counteroffensive led by Frederick Winslow Taylor and the scientific management movement. In the Cold War, military contractors relied on machinists to build aircraft and ships, but both employers and the military eagerly attempted to use automation to create workerless factories.

Because of the increasingly hierarchical division of labor in manufacturing, the number of people engaged in supervisory tasks rose rapidly in late nineteenth-century corporations. These people included both foremen and managers, as well as white-collar employees who staffed the new bureaucracies as accountants, engineers, and low-level clerical workers. These occupations could also become deskilled when new technology was implemented or when new opportunities opened up for men and the old jobs were staffed with women. Secretarial work, for example, once a slot for educated, responsible men, was increasingly divided into filing, receptionist, and typing tasks as women took over the field and new equipment downgraded skills like handwriting.

There is also an international dimension to the division of labor. The pressure on industrialists to shift production to regions or countries where wages are lower has existed since the beginning of the industrialization process. The English textile industry displaced Indian manufacturing (which was often of higher quality) in the eighteenth century, but by the mid-nineteenth century, Indian manufacturers began to displace English mills from low-quality markets such as bagging. However, low wages are only one aspect of industrialists' costs, and the extreme division of labor and the more capital-intensive nature of many industries in developed countries allowed them to capture high-end markets or to dominate mass markets by using high-volume production.

Since the early 1970s, however, the ongoing industrial investment in developing countries has accompanied increasing unemployment in developed countries. For instance, automobile companies have increased investment and production in relatively poor countries such as Brazil and Mexico. Many scholars have argued that the international division of labor has resulted in the shift of low-skill, low-wage industrial jobs to industrializing countries while highly skilled, high-tech, high-wage jobs remain in the advanced industrialized countries. Because multinational corporations are headquartered in industrialized countries, this tendency persisted until the late 1980s, when middle-class jobs began to lose ground. For instance, U.S. corporations are subcontracting the designing of cars to Japanese companies; South Korea has emerged as a site for engineering; and Bangalore, India, has become a site for writing computer software.

See also Assembly Line; Deindustrialization; Fordism; Maquiladoras; Pink-Collar Workers; Postindustrial Economies; Protoindustrialization.

References Braverman, Harry. *Labor and Monopoly Capital: The Degradation of Work in the Twentieth Century* (1974); Montgomery, David. *Workers' Control in America: Studies in the History of Work, Technology, and Labor Struggles* (1979).

Dockers

Dock work was a traditional, largely unskilled operation. Many dockworkers—dockers—in ports like Hamburg, Germany, alternated dock work with agricultural labor, though a more skilled core of ship loaders provided a stable element. Some European ports had traditional organizations of dockers that helped regulate work habits and distribute jobs. Demands for dockers grew with industrialization, as ocean commerce expanded, but supply grew even more quickly than demand, thanks to population increase. By the late nineteenth century irregular employment was widespread. New technology, especially loading cranes, altered the nature of dock work. Around 1900 employers (themselves organized increasingly in large shipping companies) tried to speed the pace of work, using foremen for closer supervision; the tonnage handled per worker rose, even aside from new technology.

In this increasingly industrial atmosphere, a number of big dock strikes erupted: the great 1889 movement in Britain, the 1896 strike in Hamburg, and the 1899 and 1904 protests in Marseilles. The strikes, though usually defeated, helped unionize dockers and other unskilled workers, providing a new and often radical membership for the union movement as a whole for the next several decades. Dock workers, still distinctive in many ways, became part of mass unionism and the industrial working class.

Domestic Manufacturing

This traditional, but capitalist, system of production developed in Europe starting in the Middle Ages. Also called the putting-out system, domestic manufacturing involves work in the home, usually by several family members cooperating in various tasks. Many domestic manufacturers also engage in agriculture, though some are full time. Equipment is simple, usually purchased by the family—a spinning wheel or a hand loom. Domestic workers receive material from an urban merchant, who usually sends out agents to provide the material and give instructions on what product is desired. The workers complete the manufacturing, and the agent then returns to get the thread, cloth, or small metal goods, paying workers by the piece. Workers occasionally go directly to cities to negotiate their own purchases and sales. Occasionally, also, merchants provide the tools.

Domestic manufacturing requires little capital; merchants only have to invest in the raw material. It requires few adjustments by workers, who can pursue a traditional rural family life. (Some domestic manufacturing also occurs within cities.) This is why the system spread so rapidly when demand for manufactured goods went up in the eighteenth century, drawing hundreds of thousands of new workers into the process. The system does not encourage high productivity, however, unless workers are very needy. And there is little supervision of quality. Thus some merchants in domestic manufacturing saw the desirability of shifting to a factory system when it became possible.

In the long run, domestic producers could not compete with factories and equipment. But domestic manufacturing regions survived in western Europe throughout the nineteenth century, and it has been argued that this tenacity often made it easier to set up factories in new areas, rather than trying to get traditional workers to change jobs and locations. By accepting lower pay, getting other family members (particularly women and children) to work harder, and by concentrating either on high quality or very cheap products, domestic weavers could eke out a living for decades, as they did, for example, in parts of France or Ireland.

Domestic manufacturing was not exclusively a European system. It spread in the United States right before industrialization began. It spread also in Turkey, for the production of rugs for Western markets, and in other areas. Domestic manufacturing could actually grow in response to new demand even after industrialization began.

See also Protoindustrialization.

Reference Liu, Tessie. *The Weaver's Knot: The Contradictions of Class Struggle and Family Solidarity in Western France* (1994).

Drinking

Drinking habits were greatly transformed by industrialization. Before the industrial revolution, many British peasants or farm laborers began the day with a mug of beer, and drinking throughout the working day was common (for instance, sailors received a daily ration of rum). In fact, in the United States until the 1820s, it was considered impossible to build a house without liquor on the job site. However, drinking in the preindustrial workplace was closely supervised by the master artisan or owner who determined the timing and amount of drink.

Factory owners desired a sober work force and fired or fined workers who drank on the job. Although many craft workers continued to hold to older traditions, industrialists generally succeeded in changing attitudes towards drinking and work. Indeed, during the nineteenth century, there was a rise in coffee and tea consumption among the urban working classes throughout Europe and North America. Still, industrialists, the middle classes, and some labor leaders were troubled by the fact that many workers spent much of their leisure time in saloons. A saloon offered more than simply a place to drink—it was a site for workers to socialize, find jobs, read the paper (often in immigrant workers' native languages), and enjoy a nickel lunch. After the repeal of prohibition, drinking patterns changed. Saloons were replaced by taverns, which were more accepting of women although most taverns catered to specific audiences that were often segregated by race and class.

See also Temperance.

Reference Rosenzweig, Roy. *Eight Hours for What We Will: Workers and Leisure in an Industrializing City, 1870–1920* (1983).

Dual Labor Markets

Almost all observers would agree that some jobs, such as for large automotive companies, generally pay well and lead to better jobs, while other jobs, such as french-fry cook at a fast-food restaurant, are poorly paid dead ends. Dual labor market theory seeks to explain this situation by showing how jobs are divided into primary and secondary labor markets. Primary job markets consist of jobs that pay decent wages and benefits, offer year-round, full-time employment, and, just as important, provide on-the-job training or opportunities for advancement. The secondary labor market consists of unstable jobs that pay poorly with little or no opportunity for upward mobility. All jobs in the the secondary labor market are entry level; a subsequent job in the secondary labor market is likely to have the same pay, no matter how much time was spent on the first job.

The preindustrial job markets for workers were highly stratified, for the gap in skill and living standard between artisans and the unskilled was quite extreme. When they could, artisans and skilled workers restricted the entry of new workers into their labor markets in order to keep wages high. The barriers to entering these labor markets could be legal, but they were more often a combination of social and technical factors. In the nineteenth century, an aspiring artisan or skilled worker generally had to learn his trade from a knowledgable older man. In the case of puddlers, sons frequently learned how to manipulate molten iron from their fathers. Sometimes, a father would have to retire before his son could become a full-fledged practitioner, which could lead to a certain degree of friction within families. Recruiting new workers from family or friendship networks, however, facilitated the solidarity that ensured the survival of craft unions. It also had the effect of barring women, racial, and ethnic minorities from skilled jobs.

Industrialization undermined or eliminated the skill of many trades, and some historians have argued that this effect created a great deal of homogeneity among workers. Employers' increasing reliance on mechanization and the minute division of labor did effectively deskill many trades, greatly decreasing the time it took to learn to make shoes or weave cloth. However, much evidence suggests that even in factories skilled workers maintained relatively privileged positions. (Their high pay and partial autonomy in the workplace led them to be called "labor aristocrats" in the nineteenth century.) Even after shoemaking and textile factories had emerged, many former artisans became skilled workers or foremen, overseeing the work of unskilled workers, who were sometimes women or recent immigrants. The turnover rate was frequently highest for unskilled workers who occupied jobs in the secondary labor market, while skilled workers were much more likely to stay at their jobs.

In the 1900s large corporations began to develop internal labor markets in an attempt to convince unskilled workers not to change employers. Employees were offered opportunities to improve their pay when they switched jobs within the corporation. Although the difference in skill was often negligible between jobs, many workers welcomed the chance to earn more money and perhaps one day become a skilled worker. Employers generally continued to encourage divisions between skilled, unskilled, and semi-skilled workers in order to discourage the formation of unions. In the U.S. steel industry during the early twentieth century, most of the laborers in the steel mills were Catholic immigrants from eastern and southern Europe. Through internal labor markets, many immigrants had become semi-skilled workers, although employers carefully extended numerous privileges to its skilled work force, most of whom were native-born Protestants. Skilled workers refused to identify with immigrants, contemptuously referring to them as "hunkies" and "dagos." In 1919 unskilled workers in steel sought to build an industrial union movement open to all workers, but skilled workers crossed the picket lines of the immigrants and helped to break the strike.

There has been a strong correlation between race, gender, or ethnicity, and position in industrial job markets. At the turn of the century in the northeastern industrial cities of the United States, the daughters of skilled workers frequently became clerical workers, saleswomen, or telephone switchboard operators. Employers generally reserved these jobs for "American" women, and the daughters of eastern and southern European immigrants had to settle for factory jobs. Although black women were certainly bona fide Americans, they occupied the bottom of the female job market. Employers generally refused to hire black women for either factory or clerical work, and most were relegated to jobs as domestics or clothes washers.

Although unionization of heavy industry raised the standards of living of many black workers (and to some degree of women), the disparity between working-class labor markets increased after World War II. Particularly as manufacturers abandoned inner cities, a process well underway by the 1950s, black workers and recent Chicano and Puerto Rican immigrants were forced increasingly to take low-wage jobs in the service sector. By the 1970s deindustrialization was eliminating the sources of livelihood for many blue-collar workers; black workers were especially hard-hit because they were largely barred from suburban and white-collar job markets. Even when manufacturing jobs have returned, unions have been too weak to force employers to pay high wages; in Los Angeles and New York, many immigrant workers are employed in low-wage "sweatshops" in the garment, woodworking, and electronics industries.

Labor market patterns in Western Europe have followed roughly the same chronology as in the United States. Advancing industrialization reduced skill disparities and separate labor markets in the late nineteenth and early twentieth centuries. But advancing technology after World War II, along with labor shortages in a rapidly growing economy, prompted many native-born workers to move into skilled ranks or out of the blue-collar labor force altogether. Immigrants from other parts of the world filled the unskilled jobs, particularly in service industries like restaurants or transportation. These workers lacked the training to compete for the better-paying positions and were often targets of racial discrimination. Low pay and frequent unemployment characterized this labor sector.

Racial factors often created somewhat separate labor markets, even apart from skill requirements. Employers and workers sometimes sought to exclude or restrict new immigrants from their labor markets altogether. In Australia white workers successfully agitated for legislation to exclude Asian workers, and in California white unionists barred Asians from all but the most menial jobs. Under the apartheid regime, black workers from the South African countryside had to apply for work permits to work in urban centers or even in the gold mines. Polish immigrants to the coal mines of northern France were often deported when unemployment threatened French workers. In response, Polish immigrants formed their own unions to advocate their interests. Today, France and Germany allow "guest workers" to work for a short period before being sent back to Algeria, Turkey, or Poland.

See also Underclass; Work.

References Gordon, David M., Michael Reich, and Richard Edwards. *Segmented Work, Divided Workers: The Historical Transformations of Labor in the United States* (1982); Harrison, Bennett, and Barry Bluestone. *The Great U-Turn: Corporate Restructuring and the Polarizing of America* (1988).

Du Pont de Nemours

This famous Delaware family established a great chemical company, one of the leading business dynasties in the United States. The first Du Pont in the United States was a French-born economist who fled the revolution. His son, a student of the French chemist Lavoisier, set up a plant near Wilmington, Delaware, to provide gunpowder to the U.S. army in 1802. This enterprise was the basis for the Dupont company. Subsequent descendants served in the United States military and government. Thomas Du Pont (1863–1930) made a fortune in coal and iron. Under his presidency (1902–1915), the Dupont company consolidated. The company had branched out from gunpowder to high explosives in the 1880s. It became interested in cellulose products in the 1890s, producing plastics and paints. Under Thomas Du Pont, the product list expanded to several hundred items. In imitation of German chemical companies, a formal research division was established, one of the first in the United States. Dupont took the lead in developing nylon, and after World War II the company became active in nuclear power and developed Teflon and new fibers such as Orlon and Dacron.

See also Research and Development; Synthetic Fabrics.

Reference Hounshell, David, and J. K. Smith. *Science and Corporate Strategy: Dupont R&D, 1902–1980* (1988).

Eastern Europe

Eastern Europe generally refers to the former members of the Warsaw Pact: Poland, East Germany, Czechoslovakia, Hungary, Romania, and Bulgaria. Prior to their occupation by the Soviet Union at the end of World War II, these countries had experienced quite diverse histories of industrialization. By World War I, East Germany, much of Poland, and the western regions of Czechoslovakia were rapidly industrializing, although this effort was interrupted by the politically and economically chaotic interwar period. By contrast, Bulgaria and Romania in the 1940s were still dominated by a peasant economy. Subsequently, the Stalinist model of industrialization, which favored heavy industry, was carried out throughout the region, although even after 1948 important differences distinguished these countries. For instance, the Polish Communist Party allowed peasants to own most of the country's farmland, whereas in Czechoslovakia farms were collectivized into efficient communes whose members received a share of profits, as well as state-run farms, whose employees were paid wages.

See also State, Role of the.

Reference Tampke, J. *The People's Republics of Eastern Europe* (1983).

Edison, Thomas A. (1847–1931)

The "wizard of Menlo Park" was an prolific inventor and industrialist. Edison developed several products that transformed the twentieth century: incandescent lights and electrical street light systems, the phonograph, and the motion picture camera. Edison was more of a tinkerer than a scientist; he distrusted theoretically minded academics, but he did develop one of the first industrial laboratories to bring together scientific minds in his "invention factory." Edison pursued applied research—he wanted his inventions to be commercially viable—and he or his associates patented over a thousand different products or processes. Although Edison believed direct current would provide the basis for electrical systems, he was bested by George Westinghouse and Nikola Tesla, who advocated alternating current. Edison helped form one of the world's largest electrical conglomerates: General Electric.

See also Research and Development; Research Laboratories.

Reference Millard, Andre J. *Edison and the Business of Innovation* (1990).

Education and Literacy

Education has been associated with industrialization in many ways. Regions that have industrialized have usually had relatively high educational levels already. Western Europe had expanded literacy to a growing minority from the sixteenth century onward, and the United States had the most literate population in the world by the late eighteenth century. Japan's preindustrial literacy rate was quite high, and the nation improved it by imposing a universal primary school requirement in the 1870s.

Literacy and numeracy are important to an industrial labor force by providing workers who can do simple calculations, read instructions, and shop rules. Advancing consumerism also depended on people who could read advertisements and product labels. Historians have cautioned, however, against positing too close a link between basic education and industrialization. Uneducated workers often did just as well, in terms of productivity, wages, and mobility, as workers with some schooling; this was true among immigrants to Canada, for example. Even some factory owners have been uneducated, even illiterate. How much education is needed to launch an industrial revolution is thus not entirely clear.

Despite this complexity there is no question that in all cases to date, education continued to expand after the industrial revolution began. Although extensive use of child labor sometimes inhibited schooling, the issue was addressed in child labor laws. Primary education spread because of belief in the economic utility of basic education and because child labor became less useful: children had to be given something else to do and some other controls. Many paternalist employers set up schools for their workers' children. By the 1870s most Western countries required primary education. Schools not only taught literacy and arithmetic skills but discipline, including time discipline, which helped to form habits useful in factories. Schools often tried to teach loyalty to the nation and the existing economic system, with some effect (particularly in societies like Japan, where nationalistic education in the 1920s built on older Confucian loyalty). By the 1890s perhaps as many as 95 percent of all adults in most industrial countries were literate. By then, also, most families, even in the peasantry, had accepted the necessity of education for later work life. Interestingly, education for women made particularly good sense by 1900, for it prepared them for clerical jobs.

Technical education was absolutely vital to advancing industrialization, for a certain number of people simply had to have access to specialized technical knowledge. In very early stages of industrialization, training could be provided on the job. By the mid-nineteenth century, however, schools and night courses increasingly took over part of the task of providing technical knowledge of chemistry, accounting, design, and other skill areas essential to industrial technicians and low-level engineers. Big companies, like Le Creusot in France or Tata in India, set up technical high schools for the most talented graduates of their primary programs and recruited their top skilled workers and foremen from this group. Technical courses spread in most industrial cities, widely attended by artisans. Germany set up technical high schools; U.S. high schools offered technical tracks. Britain, which lagged in providing a technical education system, clearly suffered from the lack of well-trained technicians and managers by the late nineteenth century. Japan and, after 1917, the Soviet Union, used effective technical education to improve the quality of its industrial labor force.

Most countries trying to industrialize in the late nineteenth and early twentieth centuries worked on expanding both primary and technical education, though the strain on resources sometimes limited results. Specific patterns varied. India featured superb technical training for a minority but introduced mass education less rapidly. Latin America moved forward in mass education, with 75 percent literacy by the 1990s, while technical facilities, though expanding, gained more slowly. The cause-effect-cause relationships of industrialization and education remain complex.

See also Child Labor Laws; Universities.

References Graff, Harvey. *The Legacies of Literacy* (1987); Kaestle, Carl, et al. *Literacy in the United States* (1991).

Edwards, Persis

Persis Edwards came to the new textile factories of New Hampshire in 1839 from a farm background. She expected to work only a few years, like most of the new factory hands, intending to save her wages to send back to her rural family or to accumulate as a nest egg for her marriage. Indeed, at one point she wanted to come home but accepted uncomplainingly her mother's decision that the family still needed her wages. Edwards seems fairly representative of this unusual first generation of American factory women, save that her letters have been preserved. In 1839 she wrote a cousin that she liked her job "very well—enjoy myself much better than I expected." But she also felt confined by factory conditions—"could wish to have my liberty a bit more." Some of Edwards's colleagues were a bit bleaker in their assessments, noting their low status and claiming to be "sick" of factory conditions. Fairly well paid and housed in good barracks, most New England factory women stuck it out until they had saved what they wanted; conditions did not begin to deteriorate until the 1840s, when new immigrant workers and increasing employer efforts to lower wages reduced workers' satisfaction. Persis Edwards did finally return home, and she later married.

See also Textiles; Women Industrial Workers.

Reference Dublin, Thomas, ed. *Farm to Factory: Women's Letters, 1830–1860* (1981).

Electricity

Applications of electricity provided new flexibility to the industrial revolution, particularly from the later nineteenth century onward. Electrical energy could be transmitted over long distances, allowing power use well away from the original energy source. It could be applied to large motors or very small ones, permitting power equipment in nonfactory sites and in homes. Thus industrial technology spread to many artisans, housewives, and others using small electrical motors. Applications of electrical energy also created a massive new industry, providing electrical appliances and equipment for a variety of uses. Finally, electrical power could be used not only for motion but also for light and heat.

Industrial uses of electricity depended on prior scientific discoveries: Volta's chemical battery in 1800; Oersted's discovery of electromagnetism; the statement of the law of the electric circuit in 1826; and work by several scientists including Faraday on electromagnetic induction in 1831. Subsequent significant inventions included the electromagnetic generator, in 1866–1867; the ring

Coal-fired plants, such as this U.S. plant pictured in the 1940s, began supplying the industrial world with electricity in the late nineteenth century.

dynamo, producing the first commercially practical direct current, in 1870; and later development of high-voltage alternating current. Advances in the manufacture of cables and insulation and in generator construction were also vital.

Early uses of electricity, like the telegraph, required little power and could be run on batteries, but electrical motors and lighting depended on larger power stations. The first station in Europe was set up at Godalming, in England, by the Siemens brothers in 1881. Coal- and water-powered stations soon sprang up throughout the industrial world. Early stations were small, but it was soon discovered that big stations, close to the power source, were more efficient, even with some power loss in transmission; quickly, additional discoveries reduced the transmission loss, particularly through the use of alternating current. Power stations generating 225 kilowatts over 200 kilometers at 30,000 volts were introduced in Germany in 1891, and advances were rapid thereafter.

Power stations of this sort could run a variety of large motors, city lighting and tram systems, and home outlets. Electricity was applied to trains, with a Siemens model in 1879; to city lighting, in several U.S. cities in 1882; to metallurgy and chemistry in the 1880s (electrical manufacture of sodium, aluminum, and other products); and also to the mechanical kneading of bread, the sewing of clothes, and other shop and sweatshop production branches. Huge electrical equipment companies arose in Germany and the United States; two firms, AEG and Siemens, dominated the German market. Rates of power production multiplied. New industrializers adopted electricity quickly. In Japan, however, use of electricity began slowly, though the Tokyo Electric Light Company formed in 1882. Japanese power-generating capacity rose over sevenfold between 1905 and 1920, then tripled again before 1930. Japanese conversion to electricity was the most rapid in the world by this point, and Soviet expansion of electrical networks was not far behind. Here were clear cases in which latecomer industrializers, with less established commitment to older methods like steam engines, could forge ahead rapidly.

See also Electronics; Hydroelectric Power; Westinghouse, George.

Electronics

Electronics, a branch of the science of electricity, deals with the flow of electrons, or current, passing through vacuum tubes, transistors, or other devices—instead of merely running along a wire. Vacuum tubes, the first electronic device, removed air molecules that interfered with electron flow, amplifying currents and producing signals by oscillation. The simplest tube, the diode, changes electromagnetic waves sent out by radio broadcasting stations into signals that can be heard. Electronics generally uses tubes to control small electrical signals, capable of bringing not only sounds (radio) but also pictures (television). The first practical use of electronics came in the 1890s with the X-ray, which was produced by electronic tubes. Then came electronic tubes in radio, spawning a massive consumer goods industry by the 1920s, as well as a significant shift in home recreation patterns. By the 1950s electronics had become the fifth largest manufacturing industry in the United States, employing over a million and a half workers. Electronics manufacture, featuring fairly simple wiring boards, could also easily be taken up by new industrializers, like Taiwan, giving them a competitive export product early in the industrialization process. Electronics advances in recent decades include computers, microwaves, and other devices widely used both by industry and by consumers.

See also Electricity.

Emancipation of the Serfs

Czar Alexander II emancipated the serfs, or Russian peasants tied to estates owned by nobles or the government, in 1861 in an attempt to modernize Russia, which had been humiliated in the recent Crimean War by industrialized countries; the czar was also seeking to avoid peasant unrest. After emancipation, serfs were no longer owned by their landowner and could buy property, marry, and use the courts. Access to the land remained a crucial question—as it did with freed slaves in the post–Civil War South in the United States, where emancipation had been settled on terms decidedly favorable to landowners. The Russian government eventually loaned money to former serfs to buy parcels of inferior land at inflated prices. The situation drove many peasants further into poverty; as a result of the revolution of 1905, the government canceled these debts. Peasants' dissatisfaction with the issue of land ownership was a major cause of the 1917 Russian Revolution. Nevertheless, emancipation did promote a more mobile labor force and provided some fuel to early Russian industrialization.

See also Feudalism and Manorialism; Serfs.

Reference Zaionchkovsky, Petr Andreevich. *The Abolition of Serfdom in Russia* (1978).

Emancipation and Reconstruction

The emancipation of several million slaves was a major turning point in the economic and social history of the United States and was one of the most significant results of the American Civil War. Because the war destroyed slavery, furthered the growth of industry in the North, and strengthened the ability of the federal government to promote industrialization (by reducing the political power of planters), many historians have labeled the Civil War the "second American revolution." Once the war was over, however, there remained the enormous task of reconstructing Southern society. Freedmen (ex-slaves) were free, but free to do what? Who would control the land, the government, and the direction Southern society would take? Reconstruction is the period between 1863 and 1877 in which many different groups (freed slaves, former slave masters, Northern politicians) resolved these questions.

President Abraham Lincoln had sought to win the war with the South without abolishing slavery but was gradually convinced (by abolitionists and by the difficulties of winning the war) that attracting slaves to the North would deprive the South of its labor supply and provide much-needed troops. Although the date of Lincoln's Emancipation Proclamation (January 1, 1863) is popularly believed to be "the" date of emancipation, historians argue that emancipation is best viewed as a process rather than as an event. For one thing, Lincoln's proclamation applied only to those parts of the South outside of the military control of the United States; within the several slave states loyal to the Union, emancipation of slaves was problematic, for slaveowners loyal to the United States tried to retain their "property." In the Confederacy, the effective end of slavery was tied to the advances of the Union army. However, word of the remarkable document quickly spread throughout the South and resulted in what W. E. B. DuBois termed a "general strike" that mortally wounded the slave regime. Numerous slaves found their way to the Union lines and these "contrabands" proved themselves to be capable and effective soldiers.

Presidential Reconstruction (1863–1866) allowed the vast majority of former confederates to easily reenter political life. Radical Reconstruction (named after the Republican Congressional faction) imposed far harsher restrictions on the political rights of former confederates who had made it clear they would refuse freedmen any significant political, social, or economic rights. During Radical Reconstruction, blacks participated in Republican governments that attempted to broaden educational opportunities and protect the rights of laborers. However, ex-slaves' demands for land redistribution went unanswered and most freedmen ended up as sharecroppers. The political aspects of Reconstruction were bitterly contested in the South, and white Democrats used a combination of terror and appeals to white supremacy against white and black Republicans. By the mid-1870s, Northern Republicans were tiring of the South's constant political turmoil. In 1877, in order to help resolve a bitterly contested presidential election, the last of the federal troops were withdrawn from the South, leaving black voters at the mercy of white Democrats. Within twenty years, most Southern blacks had been disenfranchised. Many historians have argued that the failure of the South to continue the political and social reforms of Reconstruction and the continued reliance on cotton production (and other raw materials) hampered industrialization of the region. The demise of Reconstruction also ended the experiment of federal intervention in order to solve social problems for another sixty years.

See also Black Workers; U.S. South.

References Foner, Eric. *Reconstruction: America's Unfinished Revolution, 1863–1877* (1988); Litwack, Leon. *Been in the Storm So Long: The Aftermath of Slavery* (1979).

Enclosure Movement

The English enclosure movement occurred between the sixteenth and early nineteenth centuries as entrepreneurial farmers gained control over what had previously been "common lands." By requiring owners to fence their lands, an expensive process, enclosure forced many small owners to sell to large estates. During the period of manorialism, the legal status of land was different from its status under capitalism. Land was not unencumbered private property: it often came with certain rights and obligations—peasants could owe dues (payable in cash, agricultural goods, or labor) to their manorial lords and the church. Peasants could also claim "traditional" rights to gather fuel, graze their cattle, and hunt on what was technically private property but had come to be viewed as common lands. In the sixteenth century, market-oriented farmers realized they could increase profits by fencing in or enclosing their land, expelling their tenants (or keeping them from "poaching") and growing cash crops—often raising sheep or growing grain. The enclosure movement helped to create the entrepreneurial ethos and legal system necessary to allow the emergence of capitalism throughout the economy—which in turn facilitated the rise of the industrial revolution. Although estates employed laborers, they did not provide work for the growing rural population. Hence, the enclosure also created a class of landless workers who gradually became employed in protoindustrial manufacturing.

Many societies that became tied to the world system of trade also experienced somewhat similar enclosure movements. In Meiji-era Japan, peasants were denied access to common lands, and the government forced them to pay their taxes in cash, not grain. In nineteenth century Sri Lanka (Ceylon), the British colonial government sold what it considered "waste" lands to English planters who began to raise tea, rubber, and coffee on these mountain plantations. Although Kandyan Sinhalese peasants had used these lands to supplement their incomes, they did not generate products for the market (and thereby were unable pay the taxes in cash) as the planters did. Throughout the world, market-oriented farms or plantation systems were created through similar enclosure movements that caused the decline of peasant producers. Government was crucial in this process of enclosure, for it changed both the legal status of land and the tax requirements.

Although enclosure movements allowed the spread of market-oriented production, the social effects seldom replicated the results in England (creation of capitalism, entrepreneurs, and landless free-wage workers). Occurring at roughly the same time as in western Europe, enclosures in eastern Europe also caused a growth of market-oriented production but caused a tightening of manorial relations—peasants retained some rights to land but had far less freedom of movement than western European workers. The harsh serfdom in Russia and eastern Europe later inhibited industrialization. The spread of the plantation system throughout colonial Asia and Africa in the nineteenth century created economic relationships and social classes that would complicate industrialization efforts in the twentieth century.

See also Decolonization.

References Bandarage, Asoka. *Colonialism in Sri Lanka: The Political Economy of the Kandyan Highlands, 1833–1886* (1983). Neeson, J. M. *Commoners, Common Right, and Social Change in England, 1700–1820* (1993).

Engineering

Engineering is essentially a modern profession devoted to organizing materials and power for human use. Prior to the eighteenth century, design of tools, roads, and mines was a function of artisans, who often operated by trial and error. There was no formal training and little by way of theoretical principles. Growing technical knowledge in Europe and a rising demand for a more organized approach to nature stimulated the emergence of specialized training and a growing body of manuals and textbooks aimed at teaching design. France and other countries began to set up schools of mining engineering and what is now called civil engineering—the design of roads and bridges—in the late eighteenth century. Artillery services in the military also demanded engineering training. Several prestigious technical schools were set up under the Revolution and Napoleon that turned out mechanical and chemical engineers as well. The term "civil engineering" entered the English language about 1750, introduced by John Smeaton, an English engineer. The first formal engineering training in the United States was offered at the military academy, West Point, in 1802. Rensselaer Polytechnic Institute, in Troy, New York, taught engineering from its foundation in 1824 and offered the first engineering degrees in the nation in 1835.

Engineering became increasingly vital to the industrial revolution, educating people not only to plan infrastructure but also to design and adapt equipment, testing materials, and so on. Trained engineers played a growing role in invention, particularly from about 1850 onward, as amateur inventors gave way to organized programs of technical development. By the late nineteenth century, engineers also began to design work systems, plotting efficient routines with their time-and-motion studies. This development led to an increasing association of engineers with management, as well as a new level of intensification of work. Engineers in the United States spearheaded this development, which was capped by the work flow systems devised by Frederick Taylor soon after 1900. New industrializers, like Japan, rapidly developed a training system for engineers. By the late twentieth century, Russian and Japanese production of engineers exceeded that of the West.

The emergence of engineering as a formal profession was complicated. Engineers, particularly in industry, long preserved a trace of manual, artisanal labor; the distinction between skilled workers, capable of installing machinery, and formal engineers was not always clear-cut. Even the development of formal training at technical schools did not eliminate the ambiguity. Technical schools operated at various levels, turning out technicians as well as genuine engineers. It was hard to get engineers to agree that they belonged to the same group, and rival associations often formed. By the late nineteenth century, however, the professionalization of engineering was clearly under way in most industrial countries. Associations were formed, licenses established, and standards of training were raised, with increasing amounts of pure science supplementing the applied work. Engineering training also involved the inculcation of a rigorous work ethic. French technical schools in the late nineteenth century, for example, imposed strict schedules on students that were designed to serve as a model for work life.

See also Technocrats; Universities.

References Layton, E. T., Jr. *The Revolt of the Engineers* (1971); Noble, David. *America by Design* (1977).

England
See Britain.

Enterprise Union
See Company Union.

Entrepreneurial Spirit
The role of businessmen in the industrial revolution is obvious. Particularly in early industrializations, like those of Britain or the United States, where the government role was modest, ambitious, risk-taking entrepreneurs—businessmen who undertake new ventures—played a crucial role in introducing new equipment, factories, and organizational innovations such as corporations. Many of these industrialists seemed to possess distinctive values and energy—an entrepreneurial spirit—that historians have sought to describe and explain as part of understanding what industrialization was all about. Some historians, following the lead of the great sociologist Max Weber, author of *The Protestant Ethic and the Spirit of Capitalism*, have attributed a kind of religious zeal to industrialists, particularly those of Protestant origin, as they sought to demonstrate God's favor by pressing for ever greater industrial success. Other cultural values, including the general Enlightenment faith in progress and hard work and later social Darwinist beliefs in struggle and competition, both caused and reflected the entrepreneurial spirit of nineteenth-century industrialists.

The beliefs of industrialists varied, of course. A few were ardent reformers, like Robert Owen, eager to expand but also anxious to produce better conditions for their workers. Many early industrialists, not surprisingly, sought business success only in order to ape the lifestyle of aristocrats or established merchants. In every European industrialization, a number of factory owners pulled out of industry when they had made some money, buying land and imitating the gentry, or encouraging their sons to enter respectable professions instead of business. At the same time, most industrialists shared with the wider middle class a set of beliefs about the importance of respectability, hard work, education, the weakness but moral virtue of women, and so on. They were quick to criticize workers for excessive drinking or sexuality, and in their shop rules sought to discipline labor according to middle-class standards.

Many leading industrialists, however, went beyond middle-class conventions; they did seem to display a distinctive spirit. These people might introduce new equipment in a given region not once but many times. They schooled their sons to succeed them, establishing family industrial dynasties like the Krupps or the Wendels. France, for example, had many industrialists who pioneered in setting up cotton factories, then branched out into machine building, and soon spearheaded regional railway development as well. Lesser industrialists often recognized (and sometimes criticized) the drive of these leaders. In the north of France, for example, the parents of industrialist Motte Bossut ran a small textile operation; they thought in terms of a family business, keeping an eye on all branches of production and sales themselves. Their son, however, wanted to imitate British success; he thought big and set up one of the first big spinning and weaving factories in the area. His parents lent him some money but refused to set foot in his giant factory because they felt its scale and risk were immoral.

Industrialist leaders had immense self-confidence. They worried about failure but usually felt that God was on their side. "The rich are in effect destined by Providence to be the leaders of work," as one French business paper put it. They took pride in their boldness: "You have everyone against you, and you find no resources other than your own courage." They loved hard work, often refusing to take vacations and feeling extremely uncomfortable when illness kept them from the job. They saw themselves as authors of their own fortune but also, in providing jobs, the source of general prosperity as well—"the soul of the whole industrial development of a country." They pushed for steady growth, confident in the power of their own will to overcome obstacles: "We had then only one goal, only one thought: always to expand."

Religion spurred this spirit. So did new political principles, like those of the French and American revolutions, which seemed to open new opportunities for men of talent and allowed businessmen to claim that they had replaced aristocrats and other traditional leaders as the source of dynamism in their societies. Accidents of personality undoubtedly helps explain why some entrepreneurs had this driving spirit and others were content with more modest success or shunned risk altogether.

Entrepreneurial spirit cannot be measured; its role in industrialization is impossible to quantify. But it was relevant. It also helps explain some of the conflict that industrialization engenders. The same spirit that prompted industrialists to grow also made them peremptory with their workers and intolerant of demands to share power. It was hard to get most of these entrepreneurs, so confident of their own worth, to think in terms of bargaining. It was easy for them to consider workers a breed apart, almost a different species, and therefore manipulable according to the interests of the firm. Several historians have noted the particularly severe discipline imposed by U.S. industrialists in the later nineteenth century. They attacked unions and sought new ways to regulate work in the interests of efficiency, in a context in which many workers were also immigrants and so viewed as foreign as well as socially inferior. Entrepreneurial spirit helps explain why a singularly undemocratic work organization prevailed in one of the oldest Western democracies.

See also Causes of the Industrial Revolution; Entrepreneurs; Liberalism; Religion.

References Pollard, Sidney. *The Genesis of Modern Management* (1965); Stearns, Peter N. *Paths to Authority: The Middle Class and the Industrial Labor Force in France* (1978).

Entrepreneurs, Origins of

New kinds of businessmen played a vital role in the industrial revolution everywhere. Their role was particularly obvious in early industrializations, as in Britain, where the government was not particularly active. But entrepreneurs loom large in early Russian industrialization, in Japan (particularly in textiles), and more recently in places like South Korea. Because early industrial entrepreneurs were by definition willing to take considerable risks, investing in untested new machinery and organizing new kinds of business operations (over 50 percent of all businesses failed in the early industrial period), historians have long been interested in explaining where they came from and why some societies seem to produce more of them than others. By the late nineteenth century the most successful industrial entrepreneurs were becoming part of a new upper class in industrial societies, influencing politics and military activity as well as business; again, the question of origins becomes significant.

Individual industrialists came from all sorts of backgrounds. Different industries obviously had different kinds of access; textiles, with relatively low capital requirements, recruited a wider variety of people than did heavy industry. Some aristocrats became entrepreneurs. A few, often very visible, industrialists came from working-class backgrounds, beginning as factory hands and working their way up through sheer talent and energy. Many cultures liked to celebrate these rags-to-riches stories. This kind of mobility was very rare, however, far rarer than historical myths like to acknowledge. By 1848, for example, only one industrial entrepreneur in Alsace came from a worker background. At the other end, most entrepreneurs were not from established merchant or aristocratic families, which tended to look on these new forms of business as dirty and chancy.

Most entrepreneurs came from families in the middle ranks of society, eager to move up or at least find new ways to defend family position in a changing environment. Some industrialists were former artisans who expanded their operations. Some simply gradually converted shop production into a small factory operation.

Many had initially participated in a domestic manufacturing system as foremen; over several generations the family acquired a bit of capital and set up a small factory. Commercial farmers were another source of industrialists, particularly in the United States and Japan. Most industrialists, in other words, came from families with some commercial or manufacturing experience.

Some entrepreneurs also came from minority religious groups, eager to seize new opportunities for business success to establish themselves precisely because standard educational and political opportunities were closed to them. A disproportionate number of early English businessmen were Dissenters (minority Protestants in an Anglican society). Old Believers in Russia and Protestants in France provided important sources of entrepreneurship. An important theory—the Weber thesis, devised by sociologist Max Weber—argues further that Protestantism provided a culture of self-denial and a need to demonstrate success as a sign of God's favor that was ideal for capitalism. In fact, the religious origins of industrialists, including many Catholics in places like Belgium and northern France, are too diverse to sustain the Weber thesis fully, but some elements may be applicable.

See also Entrepreneurial Spirit; Middle Class; Ruling Class.

References Crouzet, François. *The First Industrialists: The Problem of Origins* (1985); Jaher, Frederic. *The Urban Establishment* (1982); Rubinstein, W. D. *Men of Property: The Very Wealthy in Britain since the Industrial Revolution* (1981).

Environment

From its early stages, the industrial revolution has damaged the natural environment, though the industrialization process can also remedy some of the damage it creates. Early industrialization in western Europe and the United States created massive, smoke-belching factories, whose unsightly intrusion was often noted and deplored. Early railroads cut through farmland, often injuring livestock. Clearer environmental impact came from expanding uses of water power. Dams to facilitate water power created lakes covering former farmland and often disrupting more modest uses of power like mill wheels. Diversion of water for power use affected other users of rivers. A number of environmental court cases focused on these issues. Growing cities also polluted, thanks in part to unprocessed handling of human and animal wastes; this was a major environmental problem, for river and water quality began to decline

By the mid-nineteenth century, environmental problems had widened. The expansion of metallurgy and the development of the chemical industry added to the amount of industrial wastes and by-products, most of which were dumped into waterways. At the same time, concentration of heavy industry radically worsened air quality, because of the intensity of smoke. Slag heaps intruded on farmland, creating eyesores. In this context, countermeasures began to develop. Sewage treatment was advocated, along with underground sewers to reduce urban health hazards. By the 1880s, spurred by several epidemics, regulations about dumping wastes into waterways began to be actively discussed. A strong environmental movement developed in the United States, combining public health officials with wider elements of the middle class, some of whom were hostile to all-out industrialization. Regulations were opposed by most factory owners, and many workers placed the security of their jobs over environmental niceties. Aside from sewage treatment, effective regulation developed only slowly. Nevertheless, from the early twentieth century the quality of waterways in the Western world began to improve. Other measures set aside park lands, like the national parks in the United States, to limit industrial exploitation of nature. Not only regulation, but also new technologies—use of petroleum instead of coal, for example—facilitated some environmental gains. Even smoke abatement occurred. Pittsburgh, a metallurgical center often so blackened by smoke in the 1920s that street lights had to be turned on at noon, reduced smoke pollution notably by

Pittsburgh smokestacks darken the sky in the 1890s. The city's air pollution was so severe that during the 1920s street lights were required during the day.

the 1950s by requiring home owners to use oil and gas for cooking and heating instead of coal.

Water and local smoke problems were tackled with some effect, but air pollution as a whole tended to worsen in the twentieth century, as the geographical range of emissions widened, the internal combustion engine created dangerous exhausts, and the chemical composition of air pollution became more complex. Adoption of tall smokestacks aided smoke abatement locally, but spread pollution to other areas. Thus midwestern smoke harmed forests in Canada through acid rain, while emissions from the Ruhr killed trees and lakes in Scandinavia. There was general agreement that air pollution had replaced water pollution as the leading industrial environmental issue. Beginning in the 1960s environmental concerns became increasingly important in Western society; "Green" parties developed considerable strength in Germany and Holland. The debate about tradeoffs between environmental damage and economic growth continues.

The industrial revolution also had important impact on environments in other parts of the world from the late nineteenth century onward. Expansion of rubber plantations, clearance of land for more commercial agriculture and sheep grazing (for wool), and the spread of mining and quarrying also damage environments in Asia, Africa, and Latin America. Massive deforestation occurred in the nineteenth century, both near industrial centers and around mining and grazing operations outside the West. Brazil cut down tropical forests to make way for coffee plantations, in order to export products to the industrial, caffeine-hungry West. Brazil's later exploitation of its massive rainforest for agriculture and cattle farming, after the mid-twentieth century, has had a deep impact on the chemical balance of the atmosphere.

Industrial revolutions outside the West have typically been at least as heedless of environmental consequences as the West had been, and have added to the overall global effect; indeed, sometimes the pressure to compete with the West has encouraged even more recklessness. Western firms established in other parts of the world often exploited lax regulation to economize on environmental procedures; this was a major issue with U.S. firms with branches on the Mexican border, where chemical runoffs coursed freely over the ground and into waterways. Japanese pollution increased notably during the twentieth century until several serious cases of pollution-induced illness, and the sheer intensity of air pollution, forced more active regulation and the development of a substantial environmental industry by the 1970s. The Soviet Union and its satellites were particularly careless as their industry expanded after World War II amid Cold War competition. Chemical wastes burned out large stretches of land and many waterways. By the 1980s it was estimated that at least a quarter of Russian territory had been seriously damaged by pollution, and the health of many Russians was adversely affected as well, contributing to a rising mortality rate. Projected clean-up costs were mind-boggling, and some sites simply had to be abandoned. China's industrial push after 1978 frankly put growth ahead of environmental quality. Water and air pollution increased; the Chinese referred to airborne emissions in the cities as the "Yellow Dragon," and the nation became one of the leading industrial contributors (after the United States) to the emissions that seem to cause global warming. Countries like China often charge that established industrial powers, with enough wealth to cope with some of their own environmental problems, are trying to impose unduly rigorous standards on the rest of the world.

Environmental history is just beginning to open up as a field of inquiry. We will learn more about industrialization's impacts on the environment and peoples' reactions to them, especially before recent times, in the future. Of course, not all modern environmental issues are directly a result of industrialization itself; sheer population and urban growth also plays a role, even in nonindustrial areas.

See also Minimata Disease; Population Growth.

References Brimblecombe, Peter. *The Big Smoke: A History of Air Pollution in London* (1987); Hays, Samuel. *Conservation and the Gospel of Efficiency* (1959); Hays, Samuel. *Beauty, Health, and Permanence: Environmental Politics in the United States* (1987); Steinberg, Theodore. *Nature Incorporated: Industrialization and the Waters of New England* (1951); Tucker, R. P., and J. F. Richards, eds. *Global Deforestation and the Nineteenth-Century World Economy* (1983).

Erie Canal

Prior to canals, rural areas that were not near rivers or the seacoast were at a severe economic disadvantage due to the extremely high cost of shipping goods by horse or oxcart over dirt roads. The Erie Canal was built between 1817 and 1825 and connected Buffalo with Albany, a distance of 363 miles; goods were then shipped down the Hudson River to New York City and from there to international markets. This infrastructure project was paid for by New York State and was a stunning success—transportation rates from western New York to New York City fell by 90 percent. The Erie Canal made it economically feasible for farmers to export their grain and other products to Europe; river towns in upstate New York, such as Rochester, boomed. Many other states, notably Pennsylvania, also financed the construction of canals in order to facilitate trade with their hinterlands. By the 1840s railroads, which did not have to close in the winter, began to replace canals as a means of connecting markets.

Reference George Rogers Taylor. *The Transportation Revolution, 1815–1860* (1962).

Ethnicity

Ethnicity is an identity based on national heritage and is thus akin to nationalism, although it is generally subsumed under another national identity (e.g., Italian Americans are Americans first and Italian second). Much of the work done by historians of ethnicity has examined how ethnic communities and identities were shaped by the processes of immigration and industrialization, particularly in the United States.

Immigrants to industrial cities of the late nineteenth century United States encountered a situation ideally suited to the creation of ethnic identities. Industrialists hired and placed workers on the basis of their supposed "national character." Slovaks were considered strong and docile, and this stereotype and the process of chain migration (whereby established immigrants helped their family and friends acquire similar jobs) resulted in large numbers of Slovak immigrants working in the coal mines and steel mills of Pennsylvania. From the late nineteenth century through the first decades of the twentieth century, relatively stable employment allowed immigrants to buy homes near their workplace and to establish a network of churches, newspapers, ethnic clubs, and self-help societies that reinforced ethnicity.

Most of the established urban ethnic neighborhoods dwindled or disappeared after World War II with the decentralization of housing and employment. Immigrants arriving from Asia, the Caribbean, and Latin America after World War II encountered volatile job markets that afforded fewer opportunities for upward mobility. As a result, their ethnic neighborhoods have not been as stable as earlier ones.

Like national identities, ethnic identities are not "natural" but have to be created. Before the 1930s, for example, "Italian" migrants to the United States often identified more strongly with their specific village or region of origin than with Italy. Once in the United States, however, Italians were assumed by others to have a common language, cuisine, and culture. The ethnic identity of Italians was shaped by mass media stereotypes, Italian nationalists, and the Italian government, which was itself in the process of creating an Italian national identity in an effort to unite a deeply divided country. Italian ethnicity in the United States began to acquire cohesion in the 1920s, although disputes between fascist and communist Italian Americans deeply divided the community.

The relationship between ethnicity and racial identity is complex and problematic. Though, at least in the United States, there are many similarities between ethnicity and race, many scholars are beginning to investigate the ways in which some migrants (such as Italians) become "white" and others (such as Mexicans or Puerto Ricans) become "black" or "brown."

See also Postindustrial Economies; Racism; Suburbanization.

References Bodnar, John. *The Transplanted: A History of Immigrants in Urban America* (1985); Takaki, Ronald. *Strangers from a Different Shore: A History of Asian Americans* (1989).

Exploitation

The concept of exploitation owes much to the theories of Karl Marx. Marx did not believe that exploitation was created by oppressive working conditions per se; he argued that through a variety of means capitalists were able to "appropriate the unpaid labor" of workers. In part they achieved this end by imposing new forms of work discipline, by lengthening the work day, or by instituting new technology (which Marx believed was also derived from workers' labor). Higher production resulted, but wages did not rise. Marx wrote that the "appropriation of unpaid labor is the basis of the capitalist mode of production . . . even if the capitalist buys the labor power of his laborer at its full value as a commodity on the market, he yet extracts more value from it than he paid for," and this surplus becomes the basis for the increasing wealth of industrialists. Workers' belief in exploitation, whether Marxist or not, motivated many

Workers prepare sugar cane for processing in the Dominican Republic. The majority of this crop will be exported to the United States.

labor struggles, particularly between the 1870s and the 1950s.

See also Capitalism; Marx, Karl; Surplus Value.

Reference Marx, Karl. *Capital: A Critical Analysis of Capitalist Production* (1976).

Exports

Exports are the sale of goods or services from one country or region to another. Countries can rely on high levels of exports without industrialization. For instance, throughout the nineteenth century, actual or de facto colonies (such as India, Argentina, or the U.S. South) were dependent upon exporting raw materials or agricultural products in order to purchase manufactured goods. However, exports are a vital means by which industrializing countries finance the purchase of machinery, technical assistance, or necessary raw materials. Exports do not need to be finished products: in the 1930s, the Soviet Union exported food products to help pay for its industrialization effort, while Argentina in the 1940s relied on its exports of meat and hides to help offset the initial cost of industrialization. Exporting goods is vital to certain latecomer industrializers such as South Korea, whose internal markets cannot absorb their production.

See also Import Substitution; World Systems Theory.

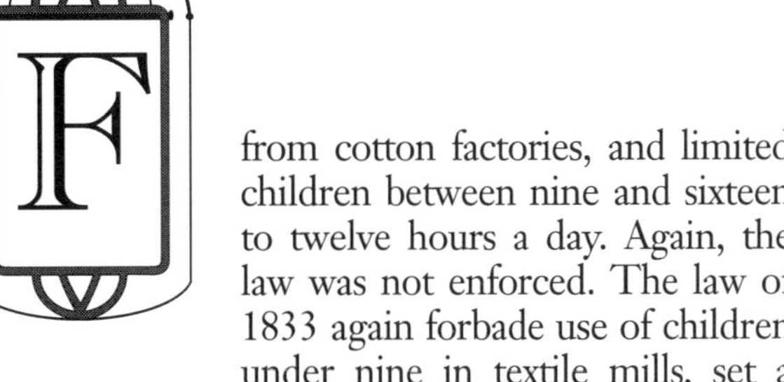

Factories in the Field

The book *Factories in the Field* was written by Carey McWilliams to describe the history of migrant farm workers who toiled in California's enormous commercial farms — what McWilliams termed California's first factories. Unlike farmers in the rest of the country, these rural proletarians would never become independent landowners because the vast majority of available farmland was controlled by a handful of corporations and families (who received subsidized water to irrigate their fields). The phrase "factories in the field" has been applied to other large-scale commercial farming operations, such as eighteenth-century Caribbean sugar plantations that relied on slave labor. Although planters relied on slaves and not free workers for their labor supply, these enterprises were "modern" because planters viewed land and labor simply as inputs that could produce wealth.

See also Slavery; World Systems Theory.

References McWilliams, Carey. *Factories in the Field: The Story of Migratory Farm Labor in California* (1939); Wolf, Eric. *Europe and the People without History* (1982).

Factory Acts

Factory acts were early laws regulating working conditions. Soon after 1800 the British government gradually began to introduce new laws about work, after having removed older restrictions as part of the growing adoption of laissez-faire policies. Knowledge of deplorable factory conditions became widespread, however, forcing a new if still rather limited approach. Various Parliamentary inquiries produced ample evidence of abuse of children in unsafe conditions. The first Factory Act (1802) provided twice-yearly washings for the dormitories of pauper apprentices and forbade more than twelve hours of work. It was not enforced. An 1819 law banned children under nine from cotton factories, and limited children between nine and sixteen to twelve hours a day. Again, the law was not enforced. The law of 1833 again forbade use of children under nine in textile mills, set a nine-hour day for older children, and provided for paid inspectors and some enforcement. The 1842 law regulated women's work in the mines; an 1844 law reduced children's hours of work. The 1847 Ten Hours Act applied to women and children. Men were excluded out of deference to laissez-faire, since they presumably could bargain for themselves. Other regulations dealt with fencing in dangerous machinery, educating child workers, and sanitation.

See also Child Labor.

Fascism

Fascism is a totalitarian ideology and movement that opposes communism while still granting the state a large role in organizing society and the economy. In the 1920s and 1930s fascists came to power in industrializing societies that were in economic crisis, where living standards were low or declining, and where traditions of political democracy were weak—Italy, Germany, Japan, Spain, and Eastern Europe.

In the early 1920s, the first fascist state arose in Italy, led by Benito Mussolini. Although Italy was a "victor" of World War I, the war had caused numerous deaths, economic chaos, and political destabilization. In 1919 communists sought to emulate the 1917 Russian Revolution. They launched a series of strikes and attempted to establish political control through councils (soviets) of workers. Though the strikes failed, they provoked widespread fear among the wealthy. Mussolini, a former socialist, borrowed much of the rhetoric of the left while receiving financial

Thousands of German troops listen as Hitler speaks at the Nuremberg Rally of 1936.

backing from wealthy landowners and industrialists. He used this money to pay and uniform street thugs. Once in power, Mussolini arrested leftists and greatly expanded the state's role in the economy, underwriting the formation of large cartels. The fascist state was unable to raise standards of living or stimulate the Italian economy. Largely to compensate for these failures, Mussolini launched a series of ill-fated imperialist adventures in Lybia, Ethiopia, and Albania.

Fascists (called National Socialists, or Nazis) seized power via the ballot box in Germany in 1933. World War I had devastated the German economy, and the resulting severe inflation ruined many white-collar workers and other members of the middle classes. German fascism, too, was financed by industrialists who feared that workers would turn from Social Democratic parties to communism. Industrialized countries with well-established parliamentary systems tolerated fascist regimes because they seemed preferable to communism. Once in power, Nazis relied upon repression of leftists and other opponents as well as propoganda through the mass media of radio and film to legitimize their rule. Germany quickly launched a military buildup (a kind of military Keynesianism) that stimulated the industrial economy and concentrated production in cartels. Employment increased, though wages were low. Tolerance of big business and profiteering created economic inefficiency. Nazi Germany's attempt to conquer other countries arose from its need for raw materials and markets that had already been seized by advanced industrialized countries, as well as from its theories of racial superiority.

World War II destroyed the fascist regimes in Germany, Italy, Eastern Europe, and Japan—but it did not destroy fascism itself. Francisco Franco, Spain's fascist leader, came to power with the backing of Mussolini and Hitler and survived until the mid-1970s. Quasi-fascist regimes have come to power in Latin America, and fascist movements have gained strength since the 1970s as living standards for many workers and white-collar workers have declined. In countries as diverse as France, the United States, and India, fascists (or those influenced by fascism) have offered racist explanations for their countries' economic (and allegedly moral) decline.

See also Imperialism; Japan; Racism.

References Kershaw, Ian. *The Nazi Dictatorship: Problem and Perspectives in Interpretation* (1989); Laqueur, Walter, ed. *Fascism, A Reader's Guide: Analysis, Interpretations, Bibliography* (1976).

Feminism

Feminism, the movement that works to promote women's rights, has two relationships to the industrial revolution. First, although industrialization did not cause Western feminism, it certainly influenced it; second, feminism in recent decades has greatly affected interpretations of the industrial revolution.

Western feminism resulted from new ideas associated with Protestantism and the Enlightenment, and changes in family structure and limits on women's work developed well before the industrial revolution. In fact, many industrial societies, like Japan, have never developed feminism similar to that of the West in range or intensity. Nevertheless, industrialization encouraged feminism by reducing women's economic role, creating new grievances, while simultaneously promoting an ideology of purity. Middle-class beliefs in the nineteenth century in Western Europe, Canada, Australia, and the United States emphasized women's freedom from commerce and their greater virtue. Many feminists urged new political and economic rights for women on the basis of their presumed virtue; since women were purer, they should have at least equal rights. This element was especially strong in late nineteenth-century feminism. After achieving the vote, and particularly after World War II, feminist concerns shifted more directly to the economic front. Betty Friedan's influential *Feminine Mystique* (1963) argued against women's confinement to the home and helped justify and motivate new work roles. Since industrial society continued to emphasize work as the basis of worth, women demanded their share, particularly as birth rates dropped and educational levels rose (two other results of industrial society).

Contemporary feminist theory has altered the study of the industrial revolution in several ways. It has emphasized gender as a factor in industrialization. The male-centeredness not only of manufacturers but of most male workers, now a commonplace in historical research, is a valuable contribution of the feminist emphasis. The omission of women from most labor movements and the assumptions even of many apparently sympathetic socialist leaders that women's real place was in the home have been more fully grasped, thanks to feminist research. Feminist work has also encouraged historians to consider women generally, not just the minority of women in the factories; hence the new attention to women as domestic servants and the realization of the economic losses suffered by many women as industrialization spread. It has prompted reinterpretation of several standard landmarks in industrial history. Movements to limit women's hours of work, like the British law of 1847, were once seen as belated triumphs of humanitarianism, as reformers finally realized how difficult factory life was for women. Now these same measures are judged to be products of male assumptions about women's frailty and as efforts to limit women's economic competitiveness. Historians of industrialization continue to try to understand the relationship of gender factors to work.

See also Women Industrial Workers.

References Rendell, Jane. *The Origins of Modern Feminism* (1984); Scott, Joan W. *Gender and the Politics of History* (1988).

Feudalism and Manorialism

Feudalism was the dominant legal, political, and economic system in Europe between the eleventh and seventeenth centuries. In legal terms, feudalism was a series of reciprocal obligations between vassal and lord, in which both had obligations to each other. A vassal held land under a lord, in exchange for which the vassal had to provide his lord fees or services (often military). Feudalism was a decentralized system of political authority based on the amount of military force, particularly cavalry, that elites could lead into battle. Both in Europe and Japan, feudalism was associated with frequent warfare. Economically, feudalism was based on manorialism, in which nominally landowning lords exacted fees, taxes, or labor from their tenants. Feudalism ended in western Europe in the seventeenth century and in Japan in the nineteenth century.

Under manorialism, a system of agricultural management in which both serfs and landlords had ownership rights, most people were peasants or tenants on large estates. Population tended to increase beyond the productivity of the land, resulting in famines or plagues. Due to a limited market for goods (mostly luxury goods, such as weapons and textiles) cities were small. Elites could increase their wealth by attempting to extract more financial surplus from their serfs (which peasants resisted) or by expanding their holdings through warfare or colonization. The constant warfare of the period encouraged the formation of stronger states that could resist outside powers or conquer more lands.

By the fourteenth and fifteenth centuries in western Europe, the increased wealth of elites led to more commerce and manufacturing, which adversely affected peasant production (the main source of wealth) by straining food production. In response, elites attempted to increase peasants' dues and taxes. The resulting class conflict fundamentally reshaped the manorial system. Peasants in parts of Germany and France gained clear title to the land, although elites obtained wealth through the state. English elites maintained title to their land and gained higher rents, though they were forced to give their tenants greater day-to-day freedom. Once freed from premarket reciprocal obligations of the manorial system, many producers in western Europe were able to reorient themselves to the rising tide of international commerce. The emerging capitalist system of agriculture and commerce helped to promote the entrepreneurial ethos and to provide the surplus food and population necessary for the industrial revolution.

Manorial systems also developed in eastern Europe, Japan, Latin America, and elsewhere. The conditions of serfs were worst when landlords tried to increase agricultural exports to industrial areas in the eighteenth and nineteenth centuries. Manorial labor proved to be too inflexibly tied to the land for industrialization, which is the reason the system was progressively abolished.

See also Agriculture; Emancipation of the Serfs; Serfs.

References Ashton, T. H., ed. *The Brenner Debate: Agrarian Class Structure and Economic Development in Preindustrial Europe* (1954); Sweezy, Paul M. *The Transition from Feudalism to Capitalism* (1978).

Finance Capital

Finance capital is a concept developed by Marxists around the beginning of the twentieth century to explain the increasing power that banks exercised over industry in capitalist societies. By the late nineteenth century, industrial corporations came to rely on bankers to supply them with capital, either through loans (as in Germany, Japan, and to some extent the United States) or through floating stocks (as in England and the United States). Marxist economists believed that finance capitalists constituted one segment of the capitalist class that exerted a specific political and economic force. Finance capital was believed to be economically and territorially aggressive, resulting in various forms of imperialism including World War I. By encouraging patterns of international industrialization that favored keeping some regions as cheap producers of raw materials, finance capital helped to prevent regions such as Latin America from acquiring enough capital for industrial development.

See also Mellon, Andrew; Morgan, J. P.; Neocolonialism; Zaibatsus.

Reference Hilferding, Rudolf. *Finance Capital: A Study of the Latest Phase of Capitalist Development* (1981).

Five-Year Plans

Five year plans were developed in the Soviet Union in the late 1920s in order to implement Stalin's economic goals of industrialization and collectivization. The Soviet economy was still recovering from the economic devastation of World War I, the revolution, and the civil war, but the first five-year plan in 1928 nonetheless set ambitious targets in heavy industry and agriculture. Unlike the preceding period (the New Economic Policy), where entrepreneurs were tolerated and even encouraged, the first five-year plan made economic decision making the province of the state. Central economic planners attempted to anticipate and coordinate the nation's existing or planned production facilities toward a single goal.

The five-year plan effectively marked the beginning of the Stalinist period of economic development and attempted a bold departure from the dominant logic of capitalism, which advocated (if it did not always follow) laissez-faire principles. Western governments predicted disaster, though in fact their own economies soon succumbed to the worldwide crisis of the Great Depression. Stalin's gambit stimulated an enormous economic boom, a point that communists throughout the world (with strong encouragement from Moscow) were happy to point out. The state poured massive amounts of capital into schemes that established blast furnaces, rolling mills, and various factories throughout the country. One visitor to the Soviet Union in the 1930s remarked that "I have seen the future and it works," an observation that appealed to many unemployed workers.

The five-year plans, which instituted centralized planning, production quotas, and the replacement of markets with a command economy, also created problems for the Soviet Union. Firms were not free to reject poor quality goods but continued to circulate them throughout the economy; machinery made with defective steel had to be made bulkier to compensate. Left-wing critics termed the system a "planless plan" because even central planners abandoned parts of the plan in order to exceed quotas in one sector or factory—thereby creating shortages elsewhere. Despite its limitations, many capitalist countries, including India, South Korea, and Japan have adopted informal five-year plans as a means of galvanizing their economies. In these countries, the government helps to establish national production goals and allocates its resources, tax burdens, and incentives accordingly.

See also Stakhanovites; Stalinism; State, Role of the.

References Nove, Alec. *An Economic History of the USSR, 1917–1991* (1992); Preobrazhenskii, Evgenii Akekseevich. *The Crisis of Soviet Industrialization: Selected Essays* (1979).

Flying Shuttle

This device, invented by the Englishman John Kay in 1733, was intended to increase output in domestic manufacturing. Previously, two weavers were needed to operate a loom, one to move thread vertically and the other to guide it horizontally. The flying shuttle operated in a grooved runway on each side of the loom, propelled by a handle or treadle; it carried the horizontal thread, or weft, automatically. Thus one worker instead of two could operate even a broad loom, and the whole process was speeded by the more rapid movement of the shuttle. Later improvements allowed different shuttles carrying various colors for making patterns. The shuttle responded to the increasing demand for cloth, but it increased demand in turn, necessitating greater production of thread—a key incentive for subsequent innovations in spinning. This was part of the accelerating pattern of technological change. The flying shuttle could be combined later with powered equipment in mechanical looms.

See also Crompton, Samuel; Hargreaves, James; Jacquard Loom; Textiles.

Ford, Henry (1863–1947)

Henry Ford was the "inventor" of the moving assembly line. He created an industrial empire by mass manufacturing automobiles. Ford began making cars in the 1890s and established the Ford Motor Company in 1903. Production of the Model T began in 1908, and by 1913, Ford had utilized the assembly line technique to radically increase the number of cars he produced; prices also dropped steadily, and by the early 1920s the Model T was the most popular car in the world. The River Rouge factory became the world's largest industrial facility, employing 60,000 workers, making its own steel and forging parts, and assembling the finished product. In 1914 Ford shocked the world by announcing a policy of paying five dollars a day for unskilled labor, an extremely high wage. Workers had to live up to Ford's rural Protestant standards of morality and adapt to the monotonous and brutal work regime. The pace of work was so grueling, that Ford workers frequently fell asleep on Detroit's streetcars and "Ford widows" were a staple of workers' humor. Ford's empire began to fray in the 1920s when General Motors began to attract customers by offering a wide selection of styles and models.

See also Fordism; Sloan, Alfred P.

Reference Meyer, Stephen. *The Five Dollar Day: Labor, Management, and Social Control in the Ford Motor Company, 1900–1921* (1981).

Fordism

Fordism, an approach developed by Henry Ford and adopted and modified by many other industrialists, strictly controlled the production process in order to maximize output, sales, and profitability. In the early 1900s automobiles were a luxury item, produced in small batches by groups of highly skilled workers. Ford believed that

A 1924 advertisement

an enormous potential market existed in the United States for a cheap, durable automobile. He sought to meet that demand by mass producing the Model T on continuously moving assembly lines manned by large numbers of semi-skilled workers. Time and motion specialists analyzed the variety of tasks performed by craftsmen in order to meticulously subdivide their skills into actions that could be performed by numerous unskilled laborers. If they could conform to the regime of the assembly line as well as to the strict standards of Ford's Sociological Department, which frowned upon drinking, political radicalism, and other bad habits, workers were promised generous wages. Ford's strategy was an enormous success. In the early 1910s the Model T became the most popular car in

Assembly line auto production at a Highland Park, Michigan, plant in 1914. Between 1908 and 1913, Ford installed assembly lines in all of his factories, an innovation that his competitors quickly adopted.

the world, purchased by professionals, farmers, and even prosperous workers. The company's increased sales, and hence profits, enabled it to continue the welfare programs for its work force.

Ford's labor innovations provoked other industrialists to label him a radical. Leftists sharply criticized Ford for his paternalist attitude toward his work force and called the pace of his assembly line inhuman. However, industrialists who adopted Ford's mass production ultimately undermined the first phase of Fordism. By the late 1920s General Motors, led by Alfred P. Sloan, captured much of Ford's market share by extending credit to consumers and offering them a wide variety of models at a time when the Model T had to be paid for in cash and was available only in basic black. Sloan's strategy undermined both Ford's profits and his paternalism. Although Ford was able to regain much of his market share with the Model A, his self-interested benevolence toward his workers disappeared. The social workers once employed by Ford to investigate workers' living habits were replaced by armed goons who intimidated workers and sought to keep the workplace free of unions.

Between the 1910s and the 1970s, many American corporations applied Ford's approach in a modified form both to their work forces and to the market. The essentials of the system remained the use of assembly line techniques and primarily semiskilled labor, who were rewarded for repetitious work with relatively good pay. Although Fordist companies bitterly fought unions in the 1930s, Fordism eventually managed to survive the unionization of the industrial work force. A major turning point came in the lengthy, bitter strike of 1946. The United Auto Workers argued that GM should "open its books" in order to reveal that it could provide workers a substantial raise without raising the price of its cars. In the end, workers got their raise only after the union acquiesced to GM's price hike. Throughout the postwar period, GM and other Fordist employers retained strict control over the marketing of their products and continued to insist on "management's right to manage" the workplace. The union won a privatized welfare system for its members, with substantial health and pension benefits, but these gains came at the expense of workers who worked for companies in more competitive sectors of the economy through rising car prices. Although Fordist companies continued to automate the workplace, which eliminated jobs and degraded the work environment, their workers' standard of living continued to rise until the early 1970s as mass consumption became an accepted fact of life.

Elements of Fordism had become dominant in most advanced industrialized countries, but the system began to unravel in the 1970s. Companies in the United States began to lose their monopoly position in the market when competition from abroad undercut their prices. High wages were only one factor in the demise of Fordism; more importantly, management had become accustomed to passing along their poor investment decisions to consumers. Global industrialization undermined the ability of Fordist firms to force others to subsidize their social contract. Fordist employers eventually abandoned their unofficial social contract with their work forces by laying off workers and cutting wages and benefits. Fordism was so entrenched, however, that it is still in the process of being unmade in some parts of the economy.

Post-Fordist corporate strategy seeks to adapt to a far more competitive international market by adopting "flexible production," using a variety of plants and firms throughout the word to manufacture products rather than centralizing production in the home country. As a social system, post-Fordism is still being implemented, and its consequences will be global. It will clearly foster the spread of industrialization throughout the world and has already contributed to the stagnation or decline in living standards among many workers in advanced industrialized countries.

See also Long Waves of Capitalism.

References Gramsci, Antonio. *Selections from the Prison Notebooks* (1971); Lichtenstein, Nelson, and Stephen Meyer, eds. *On the Line: Essays in the History of Auto Work* (1989 [1971]).

Foreign Trade

Foreign trade has been a crucial aspect of all countries' efforts to industrialize. Mercantilist theories had been discredited by the nineteenth century, but most countries sought to promote exports in order to promote employment and to protect their currencies. Throughout most of the nineteenth century, when English manufacturing was the most advanced in the world, England advocated free trade, arguing that countries should pursue industries in which they held a "comparative advantage." However, most industrializing countries (such as the United States, Germany, and Japan) sought varying degrees of protectionism for domestic industries—as did English manufacturers in the twentieth century when their industries became increasingly uncompetitive.

The difficulties that industrialized countries faced in regulating trade among themselves led to the colonization of Africa and Asia in a search for markets. Another attempt to regulate international trade was the creation of cartels that allocated market share between countries. In the 1920s and 1930s, the informal institutions that could have countered "trade wars," such as the gold standard, broke down, and increasingly protectionist measures, such as the Smoot-Hawley Tariff in the United States, resulted in a sharp curtailment of global trade. While the Soviet Union and fascist regimes in Germany and Italy attempted to create a measure of "autarky," or independence from foreign trade, all regimes relied on technology or raw materials from abroad, which had to be paid for by exports.

After World War II, the United States (now the world's largest creditor and exporter) created new institutions to regulate foreign trade. Free trade would be the goal of international agreements, although that trend was balanced by institutions such as the World Bank that provided loans to weaker economies. Between the 1950s and the 1990s, these institutions helped to increase the size of international trade by over ten times; in the 1950s imports and exports accounted for 10 percent of the U.S. economy, and in the 1980s that figure had grown to 25 percent. Although the United States ran a significant trade surplus until the early 1960s, it was balanced by the Marshall Plan and by assuming the responsibility for the defense of Germany and Japan. Direct military spending in Asia and Europe was another way the United States countered its trade surpluses. By the 1960s high levels of military spending contributed to the erosion of the balance of trade for the United States. By the 1970s Germany and especially Japan emerged as the world's strongest export economies. Unrestrained trade remains the goal of international agencies (such as GATT), although regional free trade zones such as the European Union and NAFTA may signal a turn to regional trade "cartels."

See also Bretton Woods Agreement; Division of Labor; Imperialism; Import Substitution; Smith, Adam.

Reference Itoh, Makoto. *The World Economic Crisis and Japanese Capitalism* (1990).

Foremen

Early in the industrial revolution, factory owners realized that they could not supervise all their workers directly. They employed intermediaries, called foremen, to oversee and often also to hire and fire. (These agents were sometimes called overseers, as in New England textiles.) Foremen had also worked in the old putting-out system, bringing orders to workers in the countryside and picking up products; so the idea of a subordinate director of labor was not new. In factories, foremen often acquired considerable personal power. The quality of work life often depended on the foreman's personality, for although most foremen began their lives as workers themselves, many became harsh and arbitrary. Many small strikes occurred over brutal treatment by foremen, and physical blows and sexual intimidation of women were not uncommon. By the early twentieth century, the power of foremen was being diluted; employers no longer trusted them to run the work process at maximum efficiency. Engineers now studied factory arrangements and set basic work rules, which foremen were supposed to carry out. By the 1920s, beginning in the United States, foremen were also expected to quench potential labor protest, becoming grievance experts who knew how to control their own emotions in the interests of calming workers down. The position remained an important one, and foremen still formed an important bridge between labor and management, but the heyday of the foreman was over.

See also Engineering.

France

French industrialization began in the 1820s with the establishment of several large metallurgical firms, the expansion of coal mining, and the rapid spread of factory production in textiles. This stage involved active imitation of Britain and imports of British equipment (generally illegal, by British law), as well as employment of British workers when skilled French operatives were lacking. Heavy industry concentrated in the north, in Lorraine, and in a few scattered factory towns like Le Creusot; the most modern textile center emerged under the auspices of Protestant manufacturers in Alsace. Industrial growth accelerated with concerted government backing during the Second Empire (1852–1870), when the main railroad network was completed, and government-sponsored banks stimulated industrial capital. France was hurt by the loss of

Alsace and much of Lorraine in the Franco-Prussian War (1871), but industry grew in 1900 and again in the 1920s. The Great Depression hit France late but fairly hard. Very rapid industrial growth characterized the post–World War II period, when French became one of Europe's industrial leaders.

France's lack of extensive coal holdings (the nation had to import coal from England) in combination with possibly undue government protection and relatively slow population growth held industrialization back in the nineteenth century, though growth rates approximated those of Britain. France emphasized light industry and luxury goods production (furniture and silk), pressing craftsmen into more rapid, uniform manufacturing operations. This characteristic accounted for a large artisanal voice in French trade unionism. Silk workers in Lyons, for example, pressed to work faster and with less artistry, recalled earlier rhetoric from the Revolution of 1789, in arguing for new political rights to provide greater voice and status. From the 1880s until 1914, French unionism included more radical goals and heavier emphasis on producer control than was common to union movements in other countries. By 1900 France also employed more women workers than Britain or Germany, though the rate of urban growth still lagged slightly. Historians used to charge France with a lack of dynamic entrepreneurial spirit, but their claims have faded as France's rapid productivity gain has been better understood. It is nevertheless true that French industry, particularly during the nineteenth century, was overshadowed by the more impressive growth of Germany.

See also Confédération Générale du Travail; Germany; Syndicalism.

Reference Cameron, Rondo. *France and the Economic Development of Europe, 1800–1914* (1961).

Franchise

The history of the franchise, or voting rights, is more a part of political development than of industrialization, but there is an important connection between franchise and industrialization. As industrial working classes became better organized, they typically pressed for voting rights, believing that if they had a voice in government they could win important legislation to improve their lot. Chartism in England was an early expression of this impulse in the 1830s and 1840s. German workers sought political rights in their early socialist movements. Where voting rights were slow to come to the urban working class, as in Belgium, Austria, and Italy, important agitation, including general strikes, ensued between 1900 and 1914. The desire for franchise was a vital ingredient in the revolutionary agitation among Russian workers in 1905 and 1917, as well. Where voting rights came early, however, they could provide workers enough voice in the political process to actually limit the development of political radicalism. For example, free male workers gained the vote in the 1820s in most U.S. states, before industrialization had really begun. As a result, the labor movements they formed did not reflect a sense of exclusion from the political process. This aspect of the U.S. labor movement has often been used to explain why socialism gained far less ground in the United States than in Europe or even Japan.

Most commonly, voting rights were granted to male workers after several decades of industrial developments—1867 in Britain, the 1860s in Germany. When the vote came, governments fairly quickly began to develop programs that would appeal to the working class, in order to prevent the growth and radicalism of socialism. The German leader Otto von Bismarck's social legislation of the 1880s exemplifies this reaction, though it actually failed to blunt the socialist movement. From the late nineteenth century, use of the vote helped European and U.S. workers, socialist or not, to gain new laws regulating conditions of work and developing welfare programs. A similar pattern developed in Japan in the 1920s, when the government began to encourage more protective policies in the major companies, including greater employment security, as well as heightened nationalism as means of improving relations with new working-class voters.

See also State, Role of the.

Free Economic Society

This organization, based in St. Petersburg in 1765, was one of several in Russia that preached technical improvements similar to those being introduced in British farming. The society maintained contact between Russian leaders and the economic practices of the West. Only a few estate owners actually introduced new measures, however. For the most part, greater grain output for export was achieved by requiring more labor from the serfs.

Free Trade

See Protectionism.

French Revolution

The French Revolution (1789–1793) has generally been interpreted by Marxists as one of the great "bourgeois" revolutions—a political corollary or preparation for the industrial revolution. Many historians have revised the view that the French Revolution was based primarily on a class conflict between a rising capitalist bourgeoisie and a feudalistic aristocracy, noting, for instance, that most revolutionaries were themselves aristocrats (albeit ones that criticized royalist practice and ideology). However, France's revolution did transform the political and legal framework of the French state and spurred the development of a capitalist and industrial society.

The French Revolution arose out of the enormous social and fiscal crises of the feudalistic and manorial "ancien régime," or "old order." The constant warfare of the French king had bankrupted the state, and its escalating demands for taxation led aristocrats to call a parliament to limit the king's expenditures. The aspirations of other social classes for political representation and economic relief, however, resulted in a far more radical and democratic regime than that envisioned by the king's aristocratic critics. A fierce struggle ensued between political factions from different social classes over how to democratize society and reform the ancien regime. Artisans' guilds were abolished, which allowed workers more flexibility in adjusting to the new forms of production and technology that were emerging. Internal tariffs on commerce were dropped. Peasants managed to eradicate their manorial payments, although the dissolution of the manorial system allowed the introduction of more efficient forms of agricultural production—which ultimately harmed the peasantry.

The French popular struggle to reform the old order led to a counterattack by conservative monarchies that plunged Europe into a long series of wars, concluded only when Napoleon Bonaparte (the usurper of the revolution) was defeated in 1815 by allies led by a smaller but far more industrialized Britain. Although artisans, peasants, and the urban poor had ceased to control political power relatively early in the revolutionary process, the principles of political democracy and new economic legislation spread far beyond France's borders. The French Revolution established new legal codes to regulate trade, property, and labor that aided the spread of the industrial revolution throughout Europe.

See also Le Chapelier Law; Revolutions of 1848.

References Goodwin, Albert, ed. *The American and French Revolutions* (1965); Lefebvre, Georges. *The French Revolution* (1964).

Frontier Settlement

The development of white settler colonies throughout the Americas, Africa, and Australia beginning in the sixteenth century helped to spread the industrial system throughout the world. These settler societies frequently expanded the amount of farmland in production for the global marketplace by further colonizing the country. Frontier settlement offered

European societies an outlet for excess population, expanded the amount of raw materials available for the urbanizing population, and provided important markets for manufacturers.

The social cost to the indigenous peoples was profound. Throughout the Americas, most indigenous inhabitants died from disease, although war and outright theft of land also occurred when Europeans expanded into already settled areas or grew impatient with the sometimes slow rate of the Indians' decline. In parts of Latin America where the pre-contact population had been large and in Africa, indigenous people became a significant source of labor for farms and later industries, although whites reserved the best jobs for "civilized" workers.

In most cases, white settler societies exported agricultural products and minerals to centers in Europe. Throughout the nineteenth century in Australia, Argentina, and New Zealand, exports enabled the upper classes in the white populations to enjoy relatively high standards of living. Strong personal, cultural, and financial ties to Europe facilitated the transfer of technology and capital necessary for industrial production and efficient agriculture and mining. By the mid-twentieth century, settler countries that had not successfully industrialized, notably Argentina and New Zealand, began to suffer economically, both because the prices of raw materials declined and because European countries ended their preferential trading relationships.

See also Dual Labor Markets; Primitive Accumulation; Racism; South Africa; United States.

Reference Denoun, Donald. *Settler Capitalism: The Dynamics of Dependent Development in the Southern Hemisphere* (1983).

Fulton, Robert (1769–1815)

Robert Fulton is best known for designing the first commercially successful steamboat, the *Clermont.* Born in rural Pennsylvania, Fulton early showed a talent for design, making skyrockets for a town celebration and household utensils for his mother. Apprenticed to a jeweler, he went to Europe to become an artist. He traveled widely in Europe, studying science and mathematics. Fascinated by technology, he designed various canal boats and locks, plus a dredging machine for cutting canal channels. In 1797 he began to work on a submarine, creating several prototypes but failing to gain full backing either from Napoleon or from the British. In 1802 a U.S. ambassador urged him to concentrate on the steamboat. His first effort, launched on the Seine River, sank because its engine was too heavy, but a second model worked. Fulton ordered a new engine from England and returned to the United States, building the *Clermont* in 1807. It became a regular passenger vessel on the Hudson. Part of the boat's success owed to Fulton's concern with passenger comfort. Fulton built a small fleet for use on various rivers, and he continued work on military warships and underwater guns.

General Commission of Free Trade Unions (Germany)

The major German labor federation was formed in 1890 under the auspices of the Social Democratic Party. The "free" union movement was distinct from important though smaller Protestant, Catholic, and Polish organizations. The German federation formed at roughly the same time as major national union federations in other countries, when working-class leaders felt the need for greater coordination and more political influence in the face of the growing power of employer federations and giant corporations. The German federation was distinctive in its close and sometimes subordinate relationship to the Socialist Party; French unions stayed more separate from politics, and in Britain unions were actually more powerful than the Labour Party itself. The German federation did press socialists for greater pragmatism, for members wanted to see concrete gains, and it deviated somewhat from socialism in the attempt to recruit union members. Initially composed primarily of craft unions, the federation grew to encompass the growing industrial movement. Although local movements often insisted on great autonomy, the influence of the federation grew fairly steadily; in 1896 it was even able to expel a printers' union for bargaining too closely with employers. The federation was disbanded by Hitler, then revived after World War II.

See also Internationals.

German General Workingmen's Association

Formed in 1863 under the leadership of the socialist Ferdinand Lassalle, this group was instrumental in launching the German labor movement. Lassalle believed that workers must first acquire the vote and then use it to transform private enterprise and wage labor into a full cooperative system that would treat workers fairly. A number of German cooperative societies and artisans were attracted by this notion, which appealed to older ideas of guild structure while meeting modern industrial and political conditions. The new association did well for a time, but suffered from poor leadership after Lassalle's death in a duel in 1864. It was increasingly outstripped by the more strictly political Marxist Social Democratic Party, and it merged with the party in 1875. The united group made a bow to the idea of producers' associations (a compromise that infuriated the purist Marx), but in fact its program was Marxist. Nevertheless, the Lassallean movement had helped launch the most important trade unions in Germany.

See also Franchise; Utopian Socialists.

Reference Geary, Dick. *European Labour Protest, 1848–1939* (1981).

Germany

German industrialization began a bit late by West European standards. Most parts of Germany retained the guild system into the 1840s; this helps explain the absence of German inventions in the early period. Separate states retarded commerce until the formation of an internal customs union (the Zollverein) in the 1830s. States even introduced different rail gauges, hampering transportation. German textiles suffered badly from British competition.

But German coal mining and metallurgy expanded rapidly in the 1830s. Iron production grew at the rate of 14 percent per year in the 1840s to supply the new rail network. German iron and coal resources were excellent and benefited further by the acquisition of Lorraine in 1871 after the Franco-Prussian War. National unification in the 1860s removed local impediments to trade, and a booming population provided labor and markets.

German industrialization had several special features. Once launched, growth was very rapid. The special concentration on heavy industry focused the economy and linked it to military goals. Government involvement was extensive. Germany was also a center of business combination; mergers and trade associations allowed businessmen to inensify their political and economic power. Capital-intensive heavy industry, the role of big investment banks, and government backing furthered the growth of cartels. Two or three firms predominated in industries like chemicals and electrical equipment. By the late nineteenth century there were three hundred cartels in Germany, with extensive market control and political influence. Steel and coal cartels set production limits for each member, to keep prices up.

The speed of German growth antagonized many traditional social elements, like artisans and small shopkeepers. Conflicts with labor and socialism—the German Socialist Party was the largest in the world by 1914—pushed big business to back repressive measures. These traits have been seen as part of Germany's "special path" *(Sonderweg)* in modern history and suggest how such a modern society could also generate Nazism amid the dislocations following World War I and the Great Depression. Historians have also noted, however, how many aspects of Germany's industrial history resemble those of other societies; the comparative judgment is complicated. Germany's special economic zeal resumed after World War II, with the rapid growth of the Federal Republic of Germany, as the nation regained a decisive share of world economic leadership.

See also Krupp; Siemens.

References Henderson, W. O. *The State and the Industrial Revolution in Prussia* (1958); Landes, David. *The Unbound Prometheus: Technical Change and Industrial Development in Western Europe* (1969); Lidtke, Vernon. *The Alternative Culture: Socialist Labor in Imperial Germany* (1985).

Gilchrist-Thomas

This process allowed fuller use of the important iron ore deposits in Lorraine (held mostly by Germany in the 1870s) and Sweden, which were excessively high in phosphorous. A variety of engineers worked on this chemical problem, but the answer was found by two British amateurs, Sidney Thomas, a police court clerk, and Sidney Gilchrist, a chemist in a Welsh iron works. By mixing limestone with molten iron and relining blast furnaces, they were able to draw the phosphorous out. Major steel companies like Wendel and the Rheinische Stahlwerke paid small sums to lease the patent fights on the process and began a huge expansion of production in 1879. The process was fundamental to the spectacular rise of German heavy industry. Gilchrist and Thomas were the last examples of the great early industrial tradition of artisan-tinkerers as sources of invention; from this point almost all gains came from research divisions in big companies.

See also Invention; Iron and Steel Industry; Open Hearth; Research and Development.

Glassmaking

The art of glassmaking extends back to ancient times—about 3000 BCE. Until late in the industrial revolution, it was a highly skilled operation, with glass containers individually blown and window and mirror glass hand pressed. Volume was limited, and considerable artistry was involved. Demand for glass rose in the nineteenth century. Window glass was particularly sought after. With discoveries in electricity, light bulbs had to be blown; the first bulb was produced in 1879 in the Corning Glass Works. By the 1880s glass companies in Europe and the United States expanded the processing of glass, using larger melting pots to stir the substance as it was made from sand and soda. A semiautomatic machine for making bottles was also introduced in France in 1859. Less skilled workers were used, and several labor conflicts suggested that skilled workers were beginning to feel threatened. Still, major technological developments lagged simply because the product was so fragile. In 1897 a continuous process for annealing plate glass was developed by a Pennsylvania company, cutting three days from the production time required for a sheet of plate glass. In 1902 a Belgian, Emile Fourcault, invented a machine to draw a continuous sheet of glass. The following year a machine to make bottles automatically was introduced in Ohio, while a French inventor devised laminated glass. Developments in glass composition and manufacturing were fairly steady thereafter, with a window-glass drawing machine introduced after 1908 and an automatic machine to blow electric lightbulbs invented in 1926. Glassmaking became a major factory industry, and the skill component involved was dramatically reduced.

Reference Scott, Joan. *The Glassworkers of Carmaux* (1974).

Gold Standard

The gold standard, by which the value of money is pegged to the supply of gold, was an integral part of the international banking system under which national currencies were converted upon demand into gold. It arose in the late eighteenth century with the rise of British economic power and lasted until the 1930s when Britain could no longer enforce it. Allowing merchants to trust the currencies of foreign merchants through the gold standard helped to facilitate international trade. The gold standard broke down, however, during periods of political turmoil and war, such as in the late eighteenth and early nineteenth centuries during the French Revolution and Napoleonic Wars and World War I.

The gold standard was a central feature of laissez-faire economic policy, and it was an important mechanism in regulating the international economy throughout the nineteenth century. Countries had strong incentives to keep trade surpluses in order to maintain gold reserves (and hence the strength of their currency). Although from the 1790s to the 1890s the United States was a net importer of capital, consistently running a trade deficit, it remained on the gold standard and retained the confidence of bankers. When a country experienced a depression, people often converted their money into gold, and the government (or central bank) defended the value of the currency by buying gold from other banks, thus attracting capital to the country. Other central banks (particularly the Bank of England) cooperated by lending the affected government capital to maintain the gold standard.

Although new discoveries of gold in nineteenth-century South Africa and the United States expanded the de facto money supply, the gold standard also placed a check upon inflation because the amount of gold was relatively inflexible. With the financial demands of the American Civil War on the federal government, the gold standard was partially abandoned (from 1862 until 1879) in favor of nonredeemable paper currency or "Greenbacks." The issuance of paper money resulted in substantial inflation that favored debtors, such as farmers, who could repay loans with "cheaper" money. Bankers successfully argued that the government should return to the gold standard, which as a result contracted the money supply throughout the 1880s and 1890s. Prices of agricultural and manufactured goods fell relative to the price of gold and farmers and other debtors had to repay their loans with more expensive money. Farmers in particular complained that they were being "crucified upon a cross of gold."

By World War I the gold standard had begun to break down as an international system. The decline of the British economy prevented the Bank of England from maintaining the system's inviolability by intervening to aid troubled currencies and economies. The unwillingness of the United States or other creditor countries to assume Britain's role in maintaining the standard was a contributing factor to the breakdown of international trade in the 1920s and 1930s, and countries went off the gold standard and devalued their currencies to cheapen their exports. By 1936 all the major industrialized countries had abandoned the gold standard. The Bretton Woods Agreement of 1944 established new mechanisms (under the guidance of the United States) to regulate international trade and banking. The dollar (backed by gold reserves) became the standard international currency, although by 1971 the failing economy of the United States had forced its government to abandon the convertibility of dollars into gold.

See also Banking System; Finance Capital; Populism.

Reference Eichengreen, Barry. *Golden Fetters: The Gold Standard and the Great Depression, 1919–1939* (1992).

Gompers, Samuel (1850–1924)

Samuel Gompers was an English-born cigar worker who became the first head of the American Federation of Labor. With the exception of one year, he led the organization from its formation in 1886 until his death in 1924. Cigar workers were a skilled, literate, and radical group of workers who frequently hired a person to read to them newspapers, books, and articles on labor issues and socialism while they worked. Thus, early in his life, Gompers was influenced by socialism, although he is best known for laying the conservative foundations upon which the U.S. house of labor was built. Gompers believed that workers would not benefit from "utopian" goals of cooperatives, independent political parties, or unions of unskilled workers who could not easily force employers to recognize their unions. Gompers instead advocated "pure and simple unionism," eschewing political affiliations, radical tactics, or socialist goals in favor of wages, benefits, and moderate political reforms.

See also Congress of Industrial Organizations; Industrial Unions; Industrial Workers of the World.

Reference Kaufman, Stuart Brace. *Samuel Gompers and the Origins of the American Federation of Labor, 1848–1896* (1973).

Goodyear, Charles (1800–1860)

Charles Goodyear invented the vulcanization of rubber, which allowed crude rubber to retain its elastic and waterproof qualities at high and low temperatures. He was investigating how rubber was affected by mixing it with sulfur when he spilled or left some of the mixture on a hot stove—the result set him on the road to uncovering the process. However, Goodyear was unable to retain patent rights in Europe or effective control of the process in the United States. He died penniless in 1860; the company that bears his name was formed in 1898 by Benjamin Franklin Goodrich.

See also Invention.

Gould, Jay (1836–1892)

Jay Gould was a speculator and railroad tycoon who built a great fortune during the building of a national network of railroads in the nineteenth century. After making a small fortune on Wall Street, Gould entered the railroad business in 1867 by joining the board of directors of the Erie Railroad. In the 1860s and 1870s railroads were rapidly expanding, and great fortunes were made and lost by issuing stock, frequently in a watered-down form, and manipulating the setting of freight rates in a rough-and-tumble struggle for access to capital and control of markets. The Erie eventually went bankrupt, but not before Gould bested Cornelius Vanderbilt, who remarked after his experience with Gould that "it never pays to kick a skunk." In 1885 Gould was forced by the Knights of Labor to sign a union contract on one of his western railroads; within a short time, however, Gould had crushed the union.

See also Great Strike of 1877; Railroads.

Reference Klein, Maury. *The Life and Legend of Jay Gould* (1986).

Great Depression (1930s)

The Great Depression was a lengthy, severe global economic crisis that had far-

A victim of the plunging New York stock market attempts to raise money in 1929.

reaching social and political consequences. The depression affected every country in the world economy, which meant the only major exception to the depression was the Soviet Union. The crisis was severe not only in industrialized countries such as Britain, Germany, and the United States but also in countries or colonies that primarily exported agricultural goods or raw materials, such as Argentina, Ceylon (Sri Lanka), and South Africa.

The root causes of the crisis were not only the tendency of the capitalist system to overproduce goods but also the political and economic resolution of World War I. That war required Germany in particular to pay large reparations to France, England, and other allies; Germany's ability to export goods and services to foreign markets was limited because of high tariffs. The economies of the major European allies, England, France, and Italy, were weakened by the economic costs of the war. Even in the United States, the "roaring 20s" had many "sick" or troubled industries, including steel, coal, and textiles. The U.S. government's demands that their World War I allies repay their war loans regardless of their ability to pay spurred demands by the European Allies that a devastated Germany honor its reparations. The result was a severe inflationary spiral in Germany that undermined the faith of many of its citizens in parliamentary democratic government. The financial crisis soon extended to world trade as many countries raised their tariffs in an attempt to protect domestic industries and raise the revenue for financial obligations. At the same time, overproduction in agricultural and raw materials areas such as Latin America caused lower earnings and reduced the markets for industrial exports from Europe and the United States. Between 1929 and 1933 world trade diminished by about 70 percent.

Although there were important differences among the ways that industrialized countries attempted to resolve the crisis, varying from the New Deal in the United States to fascism in Germany and Italy, there were some common themes. Even among many businessmen, faith in the market's ability to resolve the crisis was severely eroded. The gold standard, which had been currency's previous mark of stability, was abandoned. Beginning with fascist Italy, many countries adopted some form of corporatism, which meant that the government attempted to mediate the interests of different social groups or classes. Governments everywhere took a larger role in the economy: the United States preferred to subsidize and coordinate private industry, while the Italian government had a larger direct involvement in its own economy than any other country except the Soviet Union.

The failure of industrial countries to resolve the depression was a major contributing factor not only to the rise of fascism in Japan, Spain, Italy, and Germany, but also to World War II. In the wake of that war, there was a widespread effort on the part of industrial countries to coordinate tariffs, stabilize currencies, and attempt to resolve diplomatic and trade disputes peaceably.

See also Bretton Woods Agreement.

Reference Garside, W. R., ed. *Capitalism in Crisis: International Responses to the Great Depression* (1993); Nash, Gerald D. *The Great Depression and World War II: Organizing America, 1933–1945* (1979).

Great Leap Forward

The Great Leap Forward began in 1958 and was an attempt, led by Mao Zedong, to catapult China into the industrial era by harnessing the Chinese people's revolutionary zeal. In the first (and only) five-year plan, China borrowed heavily from the Stalinist model of development and emphasized heavy industry. Mao felt that the Soviet model of development left agriculture relatively underdeveloped; Mao sought to utilize the reservoir of potential labor and energy in the countryside so that China could "walk on two legs." The status of technicians and economic planners declined in favor of rural communes that sought not only to increase output of grains but to help the Chinese steel industry grow by 15 percent a year by building small pig-iron furnaces. Mao's plan failed and resulted in widespread economic and political chaos. The Great Leap Forward also helped to precipitate the split with the Soviet Union in 1960.

Reference Lippit, Victor D. *The Economic Development of China* (1987).

Great Migration

The Great Migration is the term for the mass movement of black workers from the southern United States to urban industrial centers in the North, West, and South in the early twentieth century. Until World War I, industrialists blocked black Americans from factory employment, arguing that they were inherently unfit for industrial labor. When the war caused industrial production to explode and interrupted established patterns of immigration, industrialists responded by actively recruiting southern blacks. Although hundreds of thousands of black men, women, and children became industrial workers and urban dwellers in the South, the northern dimension of the Great Migration was most influential in transforming the culture, politics, and economics of the black community.

Although blacks were denied equal access to jobs, housing, and public facilities, northern blacks earned more money and had greater freedom to form their own organizations and institutions than their counterparts in the South. Furthermore, northern blacks were able to vote, a fact which eventually undermined the political support for segregation within the Democratic Party. Blacks' experiences with unions was particularly problematic. During World War I unions affiliated with the American Federation of Labor attempted to organize the mass-production industries of meatpacking and steel. Most unionists found it difficult to accept blacks as full-fledged union members; consequently, most black industrial workers remained skeptical of "the white man's union." Strikes to establish unions failed, and many blacks crossed picket lines; the competition for jobs helped to contribute to the violent race riots that shook many northern cities in 1919. Most blacks had realized that the North was no paradise, though the mass migration back to the South, which many southern whites had predicted, failed to materialize.

Although urban dwellers (both black and white) frequently viewed migrants as fresh from the fields, most black migrants had had some experience with industrial employment. Traveling to Chicago, New York, or Los Angeles was frequently the culmination of a process in which southern blacks took jobs in local sawmills, regional industrial centers, and southern cities. Even after black men and women found urban jobs, they retained social ties with friends and family by periodically returning to the South, often to work for a period before returning to industrial employment. Interrupted by the Great Depression, the Great Migration began again in the 1940s and continued until the 1970s, when deindustrialization decimated the urban black community.

See also Dual Labor Markets; Urbanization.

Reference Trotter, Joe William, ed. *The Great Migration in Historical Perspective: New Dimensions of Race, Class, and Gender* (1991).

Great Strike of 1877

By 1877 railroads were the largest single employer of U.S. workers. In the midst of a severe economic depression, railroad owners slashed wages, and workers responded by refusing to operate equipment in what became known as the Great Strike of 1877. Attempts by companies to run the trains with managers or strikebreakers led to bloody confrontations among militia, workers, and sympathizers from working-class neighborhoods. After militia members killed several demonstrators in Pittsburgh, workers destroyed a great deal of railroad equipment and temporarily drove the militia out of the city. Although the strike eventually failed, it raised the specter of working-class insurrection established by the Paris Commune of 1871. The strike's failure and the subsequent blacklisting of militants convinced many union leaders that only conservative tactics could preserve workers' organizations. Among the most lasting results of the strike were the professionalization of the National Guard and the establishment of armories in working-class neighborhoods to prevent similar riots.

See also Knights of Labor.

Reference Foner, Philip S. *The Great Labor Uprising of 1877* (1977).

Gosplan

See Five-Year Plan.

Green Revolution

The "Green revolution" (1960s) involved new agricultural technology, chemical fertilizers, and more productive seeds, developed mainly by U.S. agricultural experts, to increase output in many Third World countries. The Green revolution had particularly great impact on India and Southeast Asia. Indian food production had not kept pace with population growth, forcing food imports in the 1960s and threatening famine; the results severely reduced industrial growth. The Green revolution restored India's self-sufficiency in food, allowing resumption of overall economic growth in the 1970s. The revolution also benefited those farmers with enough money to invest in new materials, widening rural divisions and leaving the rural majority still desperately poor; it did not assure a general improvement in economic conditions, though it may have prevented deterioration.

Hammer, Armand (1898–1990)
Armand Hammer was a U.S. businessman (and art collector), best known for his role as a trader and entrepreneur in the Soviet Union. Hammer grew up in poverty, the child of Russian immigrants. His father became a doctor and was also a fervent communist activist. Armand Hammer took over his father's failing drug business and made a fortune selling tincture of ginger (a concoction that contained alcohol) during the early phases of prohibition. In the early 1920s Hammer traveled to the Soviet Union and used his father's reputation as a good communist to establish business deals. Hammer prospered during the New Economic Policy period, by importing grain and Ford tractors and exporting furs, leather, and lumber for a 5 percent commission on each end of the deal. He also established a pencil factory, which enabled the fledgling regime to forego imports from Germany; when his production costs dropped, Hammer exported the product. By the late 1920s he had lost favor with the Soviet regime, and for the next thirty years he concentrated on building a fortune in the United States, largely in the oil industry. After 1961 Hammer again helped arrange deals between the Soviet Union and the United States.

Hargreaves, James (d. 1778)
Hargreaves, a weaver by trade, was the inventor of the spinning jenny (c. 1764, patented in 1770). He utilized earlier British inventions that had tried unsuccessfully to automate part of the manufacturing of thread and yarn. Growing demand for the product had prompted the Society for the Encouragement of Arts, Manufactures, and Commerce to offer a prize for a spinning machine, which Hargreaves won. His jenny used a wheel to rotate the spindles that wound fiber into thread, but the drawing out and twisting of the fiber were mechanized, whereas on the traditional spinning wheel these processes were performed by hand. Early jennies contained only eight spindles, but the number was rapidly increased. Although it was operated by hand power and was used in the home, the principles of mechanizing the twisting process could later be applied to powered equipment. The jenny thus advanced protoindustrial manufacturing while paving the way, technically, for outright industrialization in cotton spinning.

See also Arkwright, Richard.

Heavy Industry
See Iron and Steel Industry.

Holding Company
A holding company seeks to control other companies by holding strategic amounts of their stock. This allows the holding company to amass technical expertise, patents, and capital and to exert a monopolistic influence on a market. In many cases, a holding company (such as American Telephone and Telegraph or U.S. Steel) holds the stock in order to own or manage its subsidiaries. In Japan, holding companies such as Mitsubishi were called zaibatsus (or financial cliques) and exercised enormous influence after the Meiji era. The Japanese government provided zaibatsus with informal subsidies; in the case of Mitsubishi, the subsidies supported the company's shipping monopoly. The zaibatsu controlled a network of other companies through an internal bank, intermarriage, and appeals to loyalty. Although formally disbanded during the U.S. occupation of Japan, zaibatsus still function in all but name.

See also Cartels; Corporations; Finance Capital.

Holy Monday

The idea of taking Monday off was an old custom among European artisans in many countries. Many craftsmen argued that, if Sunday must be devoted to the family, they also needed the next day free from work in which they could pursue their own leisure interests—often including a good bit of drinking. This day became known as Holy Monday. Some factory workers, when their wages were high enough to permit the indulgence, maintained the Holy Monday tradition as well. Employers, including craft employers eager to regularize their workers' habits as their share in the industrialization process, fought Holy Monday vigorously, fining workers for absences and threatening dismissal. Here was a quiet battleground between older customs of more leisurely work and the new demands for regular timing and pace brought by the industrial revolution. Gradually, the Holy Monday tradition declined, though lower worker productivity on Mondays (thanks to recuperation from the weekend) leaves a trace of the tradition even in advanced industrial societies in the late twentieth century.

See also Discipline; Work.

Homestead Lockout (1892)

A lockout is essentially a strike by the owner, and in the case of the Homestead Lockout, the owners were Andrew Carnegie and his partner Henry Frick, who refused to allow their employees into the steel mill until workers repudiated their union. The showdown between Carnegie's skilled work force, who criticized the growing economic power of monopolists as incompatible with the democratic political ideals of the United States, was widely covered in the press of the time. The local government was sympathetic to the workers, and the entire community rushed to repulse armed Pinkerton guards whom owners had hired to suppress the strike. Several workers and Pinkertons were killed. Workers won the battle but lost the war. At the urging of Frick, Pennsylvania's governor called in the state militia, who helped to crush the union. The lockout revealed the limitations of craft unionism and workers' political rights in the face of the growing power of large industrialists.

Reference Krause, Paul. *The Battle for Homestead, 1880–1892: Politics, Culture, and Steel* (1992).

Honda Motor Company

This company was founded in 1948 to produce motorcycles. It did not produce automobiles until 1962, but by the mid-1980s Honda was the third-largest car company in Japan. By the 1980s Honda produced 60 percent of the world's motorcycles by producing high-quality, fuel-efficient engines and aggressively appealing to the middle class, claiming that "you meet the nicest people on a Honda." A relative maverick within the Japanese system, Honda is not part of a zaibatsu or "group." In 1974 the Japanese government encouraged its carmakers to curb their exports to the United States, but Honda refused. That year Honda introduced its innovative CVCC engine, which drastically reduced auto emissions without the use of a catalytic converter. In 1979 Honda built a factory in Marysville, Ohio, and by 1985 it was the fourth-largest carmaker in the United States.

Hours of Work

Industrialization lengthened the working day and required more disciplined forms of labor. Struggles between workers and industrialists over the length of the working day became an enduring tension of industrial society. In the early nineteenth century, most industrial workers labored six days a week, twelve or more hours a day. Trade unionists struggled for a shorter workday, often arguing that this would protect women and children. Employers resisted shortening the workday, arguing that it would make their factories unprofitable and allow workers more time for drinking. Working-class advocates of the shorter workday maintained that increased leisure would not only alleviate unemployment but allow workers sufficient time for rest, a decent family life, and opportunities to improve their minds. Although many strikes fought for shorter working hours, the most significant gains came as a result of political agitation, for example, that of the Chartists in England. Hours for children and women were often regulated by law before those of adult men.

As a result of strikes and political agitation, the working day for most U.S. and West European workers had fallen to ten hours a day, six days a week, by 1900. The trend was far from universal, however. Although the eight- or ten-hour day had been common in the United States' iron and steel industry of the 1880s, the destruction of unions in the 1890s allowed industries to institute a twelve-hour day and a seven-day week. Workers knew furnaces needed to be run continuously or else they become damaged, but they maintained that employers could afford to hire more workers and shorten the work week. Until the 1920s, when workers' protests and the muckraking accounts of journalists resulted in an eight-hour day, steelworkers had to endure the "long turn" every other Sunday when they would work two back-to-back turns. One steelworker recalled that by three in the morning of the long turn, you could die and not even notice.

Until the 1920s workers' calls for a shorter working day had often been linked to their demands for greater control over the workplace. Employers refused to cede their control of the workplace but did reduce their workday, so that by the 1940s a forty-hour week had become the norm. Despite periodic demands for a thirty-hour week, most unions dropped the quest for shorter hours. By the 1970s the working day of most workers in the United States began to lengthen as people worked longer (or took additional jobs) to compensate for falling wages. By the late 1980s the average U.S. worker was working the equivalent of an extra month a year, and the trend is accelerating as real wages continue to fall. Due to their strong unions, workers in Western Europe came to enjoy far more leisure; though daily hours of work might slightly exceed U.S. workloads, most European workers enjoy at least six weeks of vacation a year. In South Korea, Japan, and other Pacific Rim industrial countries, unions are weaker, and a six-day work week is common for factory workers. Among white-collar employees in Japan, mandatory (and unpaid) overtime is compulsory and *karoshi* (death from overwork) remains a serious problem.

See also Dual Labor Market; State, Role of the; Workers' Control.

References Cross, Gary. *Time and Money: The Making of Consumer Culture* (1993); Roediger, David R., and Philip S. Foner. *Our Own Time: A History of American Labor and the Working Day* (1989); Schor, Juliet B. *The Overworked American: The Unexpected Decline of Leisure* (1992).

Housework

Industrialization has radically transformed the nature of housework. In the nineteenth century, the growing separation of the family from economic production meant that the unpaid labor necessary for social reproduction and preparing workers for the labor market (that is, housework) increasingly fell on women alone. Prior to industrialization (and for much of the nineteenth century), before a woman could cook, clean, or wash, she had to spend an hour or two hauling water into the house and then manipulating the stove to heat it. Chopping and hauling wood to heat the home and water also required a substantial amount of time and effort. Although entrepreneurs created numerous labor-saving devices, most were of limited utility and the favorite "labor-saving device" for those who could afford it was a maid or servant. Most servants in the United States were Irish, German, or Slavic women immigrants and, increasingly in the twentieth century, black women. Advances in technology did ultimately influence housework, however, and by the mid-nineteenth century, most women in cities used coal instead of wood, which burned hotter and required less work. Feeding the stove or furnace (and periodically cleaning the stove and house of soot) was still a burden nonetheless. Sewing machines made making clothing at home easier, though it could still be a time-consuming chore. The most significant advances came later in the nineteenth century, with indoor water, gas, and then electric lights (which did not leave soot); still, many working-class families in the United States did not receive these amenities until well into the twentieth century. Also in the twentieth century, electrically powered machines such as mechanized washing machines or electric vacuum cleaners began to ease the burden of middle- and then working-class women's housework. Most scholars of housework have observed that industrialization did not free women from housework, because standards of cleanliness rose in tandem with the advances of new technology. Furthermore, many jobs once done by men (such as delivering produce) were shifted onto women. These observations notwithstanding, the demands of housework had declined sufficiently in the twentieth century to allow middle-class women to dispense with their servants and begin a career, as well as to take on the demands of housework—or the "second shift." (Many white working-class women and most black women had always worked.)

In most of Europe and the United States, the demands of housework have been addressed by new technologies adopted by individual families. Nineteenth-century socialists advocated that many of the demands of housework be solved by using new technology to collectivize the tasks. The Soviet Union attempted to free women from housework by establishing state-run (and subsidized) daycare centers, laundries, and restaurants. This experiment was successfully implemented by many Eastern European societies after World War II but has been abandoned with the return to market-driven policies. Housework continues to be a significant burden for women in all societies.

See also Women Industrial Workers.

Reference Cowan, Ruth Schwarz. *More Work for Mother: The Ironies of Household Technology from the Open Hearth to the Microwave* (1983).

Hydroelectric Power

As demand for electricity went up in the 1870s, with the invention of the electric motor, street lighting, and other developments, the need to expand generation became obvious. One quick recourse involved use of hydroelectric power—water power—to generate electricity. By the 1880s hydroelectric lighting systems were being installed in mountainous sections of central Europe and Scandinavia. Tramways were powered by hydroelectric generation. Large factories, already using water power, found it more convenient to produce electricity and apply it to motors for the machines in the plant.

Hydroelectric power did not require any new inventions outside the electrical field. The hydraulic turbine had been invented in 1832, and by the 1880s it was possible to design a turbine to meet the requirements of any power site, from a small mountain stream to Niagara Falls. The first electric plant at Niagara, opened in 1881, had two turbines. A new powerhouse was begun in 1891, with ten turbines connected with generators rated at 5,000 horsepower each. Europeans tended to emphasize smaller installation, but in large numbers. Switzerland had 561 20–99 horsepower plants by 1914, but only 6 of 10,000 horsepower or more. Like all electrical power generation, hydroelectric power focused increasing attention on long-distance transmission. Research on this subject began in the 1880s, with experiments steadily improving efficiency from initial levels of 39 percent energy loss. Work in Italy on alternating current, begun in 1886 by Circhi and then carried on by others, including Nicola Tesla in the United States, allowed transmission over more than 100 miles with less than 10 percent loss by the early 1900s.

Hyundai

Created by entrepreneur Chung Ju Yung, this company was one of the mainstays of South Korean industrialization after World War II. Chung Ju Yung was a villager who walked 150 miles to Seoul to take a job as a day laborer in the 1940s. He soon opened a modest business of his own, which expanded steadily as the South Korean economy began to take off after the Korean War. By the 1980s Hyundai had 135,000 employees and offices in 42 countries around the world. Visually, it governed Korea's southeast coast, building ships and automobiles. The highly paternalistic company built thousands of housing units for its low-wage labor force and sponsored technical schools to supply technicians. It used traditional rituals to tie workers to each other and to the company, building an arena for *tae kwon do,* the Korean martial art, and beginning work days with group exercises. Hyundai workers seemed to respond favorably, putting in six-day weeks with three vacation days per year and participating in reverential ceremonies when a fleet of cars was shipped abroad or a new tanker launched.

See also Japan.

I

Immigration and Migration

Migration occurs when people move (either permanently or temporarily) from one country or region to another—generally from farms to cities or rural industrial centers (such as coal mining camps). Immigration is the movement of migrants to a new country; emigration occurs when people leave a place. Although famines, wars, and ethnic or religious conflict have affected migration flows, the most common reason for the mass movement of people is economic. The common image that pre-industrial life was a settled and stable one is simply wrong. Many poor peasants migrated to other regions to find seasonal work and artisans in the journeyman stage traveled in order to find work and build up their skills.

Industrialization built upon these earlier migration patterns and transformed them. By creating new centers of employment (often in cities) industrialization facilitated the permanent shift of millions of people from "field to factory." Many migrants were initially "sojourners," that is, temporary migrants who frequently traveled short distances, but most became urban workers. Industrialization also made migration easier through improvements in transportation technology (canals, railroads, and steamships). The ongoing process of industrialization, migration, and immigration resulted in transforming the composition of most countries involved in the world economy.

In the sixteenth and seventeenth centuries, the dramatic decline of indigenous population of the Americas (over 80 percent died after contact) and the rise of silver mines and plantations for sugar, rice, and tobacco created an enormous demand for labor that colonial powers generally filled through the enslavement of several million Africans as well as with European laborers. This pattern continued in the nineteenth and twentieth centuries because the rapid industrialization of the United States created a large demand for workers. Apart from African slaves, most immigrants prior to the 1830s came from Britain and Germany. During the early phases of industrialization, the Irish were slotted into the unskilled labor market. Many of the servants in industrial cities were Irish women. Many, though not all, migrants from England, Wales, Scotland, and Germany became artisans and skilled workers. In addition to their labor, many of these workers contributed to the development of the trade union and socialist movements.

In the past, historians assumed that migrants were "the uprooted"—overwhelmed by the difficulties of finding work and creating identities for themselves in a new country. Although historians still document the frequently harsh experiences of migrants, most historians today view migrants as "transplanted" and emphasize migrants' creative/adaptive strategies. Migrants used their family or personal contacts to find out information about local working or housing conditions; after they migrated, these contacts were helpful in finding jobs (chain migration). To the enduring frustration of trade union organizers, many migrants judged their difficult working and living conditions abroad against even worse conditions at home—a factor that inhibited protest. However, once workers believed they had been wronged, their immigrant cultures were often a formidable base for solidarity. For instance, one of the largest (and generally unacknowledged) strikes in the United States was conducted by the Chinese immigrants in 1867 working on railroads in California.

During the "second" industrial revolution (late nineteenth to early twentieth

Early twentieth-century immigrants arrive in the New World. Advertisements placed in European newspapers by American factories and railroad companies lured millions of people across the Atlantic during the nineteenth century.

centuries) Eastern and Southern Europe became the United States' primary source for industrial laborers. There were important differences between migrants: the vast majority of (largely impoverished) Slovak villagers ended up as laborers in Pennsylvania's coal mines and steel mills while better-off Czech migrants settled in midwestern cities as artisans or farmers. Many Italians were "birds of passage" and frequently returned to Europe (or migrated again to Argentina). In the Western part of the country, Asian and Mexican migrants were important sources of labor to build railroads and to work in the mines or on the plantations. By 1924, nativist sentiment and the demands of the American Federation of Labor succeeded in passing laws that drastically reduced immigration. Changes in the law meant that during the Great Depression of the 1930s, immigrant radicals (or simply unemployed immigrants) were deported. Migrants were also an important factor in colonial regimes. In the nineteenth and twentieth centuries, plantations in Asian and African colonies created large scale movement of workers. During the nineteenth century, the British Imperial government encouraged the settlement of several million Indian laborers to work the rubber, tea, coffee, and coconut plantations of South and East Africa, Sri Lanka, and Malaysia. By 1948, there were more than a million Tamil laborers in Sri Lanka (then Ceylon). The newly independent Ceylonese government sought to repatriate several hundred thousand of the now unwanted workers. The Indian government refused to accept the return of these laborers, fearing that it would set a precedent that might result in the influx of several million impoverished workers. While a substantial number of these "Indian Tamils" (many of whose families had lived two or three generations in Ceylon) were expatriated, many others were rendered stateless—a status that many still hold nearly 50 years later.

After World War II, most immigrants to the United States came from Latin America or Asia. Many Mexican, Haitian, and Puerto Rican migrants came because their economies were faltering or collapsing; many Cubans, Salvadorans, Vietnamese, and Filipinos, because their countries were experiencing substantial political upheaval or revolutions. Many of these immigrants did not find factory jobs, but obtained work in the service sector as cooks, waitresses, and janitors. The political concerns of the Cold War were an important factor in influencing immigrants' experiences. In the 1980s, Nicaraguans were assumed by the U.S. government to be political refugees from Nicaragua's leftist Sandinista government (and because they could find work legally, they faced less abuse from employers), while Salvadorans, whose right-wing government was supported by the United States, were assumed to be "economic refugees" and had difficulty obtaining legal work.

Even before World War II, other industrial areas besides the United States were magnets for immigrants seeking factory jobs from poorer, agricultural societies pressed by population growth. British industry in the nineteenth century used many Irish workers. Poles in the early twentieth century migrated to the industrial regions of Britain, Germany, and France. After World War II, immigration to industrial Europe came from Africa, Turkey, the Indian subcontinent, and the Caribbean. As in the United States, many immigrants found work in the unskilled sector, with better factory jobs reserved for the native born. Though less dependant on immigrant labor (having a substantial pool of underemployed people in its own hinterland) postwar Japan also imported workers from Korea and Southeast Asia, another example of how the labor needs of industrialization, together with global population growth, continued to create dramatic patterns of population movement.

See also Argentina; Dual Labor Market; Great Migration; Urbanization; World Systems Theory.

References Bodnar, John. *The Transplanted: A History of Immigrants in Urban America* (1985); Moch, Leslie. *Moving Europeans: Migration in Western Europe Since 1650* (1992).

Imperialism

Although empires have existed for thousands of years, the industrial revolution was influenced by, even as it significantly changed, the meaning of imperialism. As one historian has pointed out, "Empires and emperors were old, but imperialism was new" to the late nineteenth century—the term "imperialism" only came into popular usage in the 1880s. It referred to the rapid spread of European conquests in Africa, Asia, and the Pacific. Beginning in the seventeenth century, global commercial empires provided Britain and France with surplus capital to finance their industrialization efforts—in Portugal and Spain, however, colonial possessions did not significantly aid industrialization. Throughout much of the nineteenth century, Britain's colonies (notably India, South Africa, and some Caribbean islands) provided it with a reliable supply of raw materials and a captive market for industrial goods. Particularly in the late nineteenth century, many industrial or industrializing countries sought relief from a prolonged depression (caused in part by overproduction) in imperialism. Between 1875 and 1914 countries as diverse as Britain, Germany, Japan, and the United States quickly conquered and colonized Africa and most of Asia—a total of one-quarter of the world's surface.

Imperialism provided "metropolitan" countries not only with cheap raw materials and captive markets but with an opportunity to build common political ground for capitalists, the middle class, and workers. Although relatively few Europeans, Americans, or Japanese actually migrated to a colonized country as workers, supervisors, or administrators, all members of the metropolitan country were made aware (through the mass media) of their nation's superiority over technologically (and allegedly morally) inferior peoples. As such, imperialism provided much-needed social and political stability to metropolitan countries experiencing tremendous class polarization.

Besides outright conquest, industrialization offered technologically and economically advanced countries new ways to control other regions. Throughout the nineteenth century, England's superior industrial production provided it with de facto economic control over nominally independent nations in Latin America. Countries like Argentina were dependent upon Britain to buy its exports of raw materials (in this case meat, hides, and grain). When Britain suffered a depression or when world war closed shipping lanes, Argentina's economy was hit hard, and it could not afford to purchase manufactured products. The attempt by Latin American nations to modernize their economies drew them further into Britain's economic orbit as they sought technical expertise and capital. Until 1914, Britain was the world's foremost lender, and this position gave its bankers a powerful amount of control in structuring the economies of Latin American nations.

In the twentieth century, the attempts of other industrialized countries—notably Japan, Germany, and Italy—to replicate Britain's economic success through outright imperialism resulted in the devastation of World War II. Global conflict so weakened the metropolitan centers that most of the countries colonized during the previous four centuries were able to gain their independence. The present ability of industrialized countries to use loans and other means to control the terms of trade (and, by extension, the economies) of decolonized nations has caused many to term the new relationship neocolonialism.

See also Decolonization; Finance Capital; Neocolonialism; World Bank; World Systems Theory.

Reference Hobsbawm, Eric. *The Age of Empire: 1875–1914* (1987).

Import Substitution

Import substitution is the practice whereby governments encourage domestic production of goods previously imported. In the 1930s the weakening demand in Europe for meat and hides from Argentina meant that the country could not afford to import manufactured goods; in response, the government supported the rise of domestic industries. Iran adopted similar policies in the 1920s and 1930s to reduce its economic dependence on Europe. In South Korea and Taiwan in the 1950s, textiles were among the first industries encouraged by their government. Import substitution is typically (or hopefully) a prelude to an economic "takeoff" that will lead to the production of goods that can be exported. In the case of Taiwan, an export-oriented garment industry developed in the wake of the successful industrialization of the textile industry. Even when a full industrial revolution does not develop, import substitution spreads mechanization and forces the world's industrial leaders to concentrate on more advanced production sectors.

See also Foreign Trade.

India

By the middle of the twentieth century, India was one of the ten largest participants in world trade, yet Indian society as a whole was only partially industrialized. By the time of its independence in 1947, industrial production was concentrated near Bombay, along the country's western coast, and in the east, in the region surrounding Calcutta. However, the level of mechanization in India was low, and its output of manufactured goods per person was increasing at a slower rate than industrializing countries such as Mexico. Even today, though India has a large industrial sector, its rural population engaged in agriculture is even larger and growing fast. The successes and limitations of industrialization in India were strongly influenced by its economic development as a British colony from the mid-eighteenth century until 1947.

British imperial policy favored British-manufactured goods and displaced Indian textile makers, who were forced to produce for the lower ends of local markets where low profit margins retarded investment in industrial production. From the early nineteenth century until the 1940s, India was an important market for Lancashire's textiles, and as British manufacturers lost other markets they sought to adjust the tariff to protect the Indian market. Nevertheless, industrial textile production did begin to develop in India in the 1850s, although it did not really blossom until the 1870s. By 1914 India was the world's foremost supplier of jute (twine and bagging for cotton) and its textile mills were significant on the world market. After the 1920s Indian entrepreneurs began to displace expatriate British managers of industrial facilities, a process aided by a strong Indian entrepreneurial tradition and the ideological demands of the growing nationalist movement. However, large industrial companies, such as that of Jashmed Tata (by the 1940s, the world's twelfth-largest steel company) were rare.

Although commodity production of tea, cotton, and jute transformed much of the Indian countryside into plantations that produced raw materials for the world market, most Indians remained peasants, and land holdings remained small. Unlike Argentina, where the entire population became dependent upon the cash economy, India was still dominated by (to some degree) self-sufficient peasants. Literacy rates under the British remained low until the twentieth century, when they slowly began to rise. The poverty and relatively low productivity of the countryside acted as a drag on the expansion of the industrial sector. For instance, although the Indian railroad system is one of the world's largest, it is chronically short of rolling stock to transport its passengers, and the situation is exacerbated by the many Indians who cannot afford to pay but manage to ride anyway.

After independence, the Indian government sought to accelerate industrialization by providing credits to crucial sectors such as steel and electrical power and by expanding the country's school system. Major urban centers grew rapidly, often beyond the ability of the government to provide basic services. The parliamentary form of government, frequently jettisoned by newly independent revolutionary or nationalist governments elsewhere, proved remarkably resilient in India, although preindustrial loyalties of caste and religion provided the basis for divisive conflicts. Industrial production has continued to expand, helping to produce sizable working and middle classes, but most Indians are hard-pressed peasants. By the 1990s the country was able to produce sophisticated military equipment, but much of its population remained mired in poverty.

Reference Tomlinson, B. R. *The Economy of Modern India, 1860–1970* (1993).

Industrial Workers of the World

The Industrial Workers of the World (IWW) were formed in 1905 as a revolutionary syndicalist union. The founding convention in Chicago brought together socialists, anarchists, and veteran hard-rock miners (copper, lead, etc.), radicalized by bitter struggles with mining companies in the western United States. The goals of the fledgling union were high; one participant called the formation of the union the "constitutional convention of the working class." The IWW bitterly criticized the conservatism of the American Federation of Labor (AFL) and sought to organize all workers, regardless of skill, race, or nationality, into unions. They believed industrial unions would allow workers to "bring to birth the new world from the ashes of the old." The IWW led numerous militant strikes, and about three million people passed through the organization until it was destroyed by the U.S. federal government after World War I. Although the IWW still exists, its influence radically declined in the 1920s and most militant Wobblies (as IWW activists were called) joined the Communist Party.

Unlike most unions that grew out of the social solidarity of skilled workers in relatively stable neighborhoods, the Wobblies built a union movement among transient workers, particularly in the great plains and in the West. In the early 1900s, farming was partially mechanized, but farmers still relied on large numbers of migrant laborers to harvest their crops. Living conditions for workers were crude, and workers put in long hours. However, if the crops were not harvested in a timely fashion they would spoil, and Wobblies frequently exploited this situation by urging workers to strike, or more commonly to simply work slower or to sabotage equipment. The union was represented by traveling delegates who collected dues from workers in the fields. The most common form of traveling for these hobo-workers was by hopping freight trains, and Wobblies would sometimes enforce solidarity by only allowing union men to ride in "their" boxcars. A similar tradition arose among timber workers, particularly along the West Coast, but also in the pine woods of the South. The IWW organized white and black workers into the union, an act which cost numerous union men their lives. Violence at the hands of vigilantes was a common form of retaliation on the IWW and part of the reason that Wobblies advocated "striking on the job," which was their term for sabotage, was that traditional strike methods were not only futile but could be lethal. Union activists did try to defend their civil liberties, and when small-town police prevented Wobblies from speaking, the union frequently flooded the town with union men until the city fathers tired of paying to put up union men in their jail. The IWW opposed World War I, and Wobblies' advocacy of sabotaging the war effort brought them into conflict with the newly formed FBI. Fear of the Bolshevik revolution led the United States into a full-blown "red scare" after the war ended, and many Wobblies were lynched or murdered and their organization destroyed.

See also Workers' Control.

Reference Dubinsky, Melvyn. *We Shall Be All: A History of the Industrial Workers of the World* (1969).

Industrial Unions

Industrial unions are organizations that represent all the workers at a particular firm or in an entire industry. Rather than consisting only of skilled workers, industrial unions also include the unskilled and the semi-skilled machine operators. After a work process has been sufficiently subdivided or automated, employers can easily replace workers, thus making solidarity between skilled and unskilled workers during strikes an absolute necessity if unions are to survive or succeed. Because of the long history of racism, sexism, and nativism in the craft unions of the United States, industrial unions in that country often developed a philosophy of representing all workers regardless of race, gender, religion, or national origin. In Europe as well industrial unions had a social agenda because they frequently developed in tandem with labor or Social Democratic parties. Revolutionary anarchosyndicalist unions were also influential in France, Spain, and Latin America.

The significance of industrial unions becomes clear only in the context of the history of their predecessors, craft unions. In the early phases of industrialization, unions were generally made up of highly skilled craft workers. Unskilled workers were frequently not able to join the unions, sometimes because skilled workers felt that the unskilled did not have the requisite technical skills, social status, or personal self-control to regulate the organization of their workplace. In the nineteenth century, a few British trade unions opposed extending the franchise to all workers. Furthermore, there was often a fair amount of day-to-day tension between the skilled and the unskilled. One of the legacies of the artisanal mode of production was that skilled workers often continued to direct unskilled workers on the job site.

By the late nineteenth century, employees, particularly in mass production industries, were increasingly organized on a national basis, either through industrial firms or cartels, which allowed them to bypass the local and regional organizations of most craft unions. Many workers saw the need for industrial and national organization, but the actual dynamics of union organizing made industrial unionism an elusive goal. In 1880, for instance, unskilled dockworkers in London established a union, but the organization was destroyed by an employer counteroffensive in 1893. In the United States, a massive influx of immigrants from eastern and southern Europe accompanied the cartelization of mass production industries. Many native-born residents or more recent immigrants from northern Europe viewed the new immigrants as undesirable, and furthermore as a cause of the decline of workers' organizations and standards of living. In the 1870s and 1880s the Knights of Labor attempted to organize all workers regardless of skill, race, or gender. After some stunning initial successes, the union unraveled, in part because many workers refused to accept black members, although the primary reason was that unskilled workers had little leverage on their employers. The national federation of craft unions, the American Federation of Labor, largely retreated from social and political concerns, as did the mass production industries, choosing largely to concentrate on the economic or "bread-and-butter" concerns of its skilled members. By the turn of the century, however, national confederations of unions were established in Germany, England, and France, and they all had at least one million members. Industrial unions that united workers across skill levels gained ground, particularly in heavy industry, the chemical industry, and among dockworkers.

Industrial unions were not established in the United States until the formation of the CIO in 1935. Led by the United Mine Workers, the CIO organized important mass production industries such as steel, auto, electrical equipment, rubber, and aircraft. In many unions, radicals, communists, and former IWW members were organizers and often gained local office; several CIO unions had close ties with the Communist Party. Blacks, women, and immigrants gained a wider, though far from full, voice in the workplace and in the unions. Many workers used the CIO as a political vehicle, although not a revolutionary one; the CIO helped to make industrial workers a crucial component of the Democratic Party and Franklin Roosevelt's New Deal. The power of the CIO was perhaps strongest between 1946, when several million workers struck to regain or improve their standard of living, and 1948, when the CIO helped reelect Democratic president Harry Truman in a stunning political upset.

At the height of its power, the CIO was undermined by changes in government policies. In 1947 Truman confronted a Republican Congress, which overturned his veto to pass the Taft-Hartley Act, a law that greatly restricted the actions of the CIO. Unions were prohibited from making political contributions, the closed shop (in which new workers were automatically enrolled in the union) was banned, and all union officials had to guarantee that they were not communists. In order to abide by the last provision, the CIO drove eleven unions with communist ties out of their federation, and most were destroyed by both the government and other unions "raiding" their members. Although the CIO unions continued to grow in numbers and influence until the 1960s, the growing conservatism of labor law has made it more difficult to organize new workers, and today most industial unions are declining with their industries.

In Europe, industrial unions had a different history. The fascist regimes in Germany and Italy both restricted the independence of unions, although in the postwar period industrial unions affiliated with social democratic parties regained much of their previous strength. In many cases, unions won not only better wages and social benefits, but a direct role in shaping industrial policy. Often, union leaders are also members of corporate boards of directors.

Although Soviet workers were also organized in industrial unions, in practice these were almost completely dominated by the communist governments. In the early 1980s, however, Solidarity, an independent industrial federation of Polish workers, emerged and forced the government to make important political and economic concessions before it was temporarily suppressed. Unions also played an important role in the transformation of the Soviet Union in the 1980s and 1990s.

The concentration of workers in industry has given them common experiences and employers and has made it possible for workers to organize to overcome common problems. Throughout the history of industrial unions, their formation and health have frequently been influenced by political as well as economic trends. Repressive regimes often suppress trade unions and even murder trade unionists. There are also cases of industrial unions weakening or toppling repressive governments, as in Poland in the 1980s or the actions of Nigerian oil workers in the 1990s. The most serious challenge to industrial unionism probably lies in the increasing power of multinational corporations to shift production from one country to another. Although there are cases of industrial unions cooperating across national borders, that chapter of history largely remains yet to be written.

See also Confédération Générale du Travail; Division of Labor; Socialism.

Reference Lichtenstein, Nelson, and John Harris Howell. *Industrial Democracy in America: The Ambiguous Promise* (1993).

Industrial Workers

Industrial workers have often been at the forefront of work organization and labor discipline. In the late eighteenth century, merchants organized decentralized "putting out" systems of production that employed rural workers working in their homes. In the nineteenth century, work was centralized in factories and industrial workers experienced tighter supervision, longer hours of work, and a faster work pace, a regime that quickly extended to other workers. Thus, industrial workers differed from craft workers who had different traditions and work sites. By the end of the nineteenth century, industrial workers were increasingly concentrated in large factories where industrialists could achieve greater levels of efficiency from new forms of work organization, such as the moving assembly line. In the 1920s there were over 60,000 workers in Henry Ford's River Rouge automobile factory—an extreme case, but one that exemplified the tendency toward the rapid growth and centralization of industrial workers.

Many Marxists in the nineteenth century believed that the expansion of the industrial revolution and of industrial workers would create a unified, disciplined, and politically conscious class that would fight for socialism. Industrial workers were certainly at the forefront of most social democratic parties and movements, but the substantial differences between workers' skills, wage levels, and political expectations (often influenced by race, gender, or ethnicity) made class solidarity problematic. Industrial workers were not the whole working class, though they were the most rapidly growing segment. Early in the twentieth century, Lenin observed that whereas many people called industrial workers "proletarians," this was a political identity, not a demographic one. More workers aspired to be the foreman in the factory than the militant who wanted to overthrow capitalism.

Because of the importance of industrial firms to the economy, organizations of industrial workers have often wielded great political and economic strength. Russian factory workers were essential in toppling the czar in the communist revolution of 1917. However, most industrial workers eschewed revolution for reform. In the United States, the formation of the Congress of Industrial Organization in the 1930s created durable unions of industrial workers and strengthened the New Deal. Although "globalization" of industrial production had always been a reality, this trend began to accelerate in the 1960s and 1970s, undermining the importance of industrial workers in industrialized countries. Industrial workers began to decline numerically in the most advanced industrial economies. As late as the 1970s, strikes by British coal miners toppled national governments; in the mid-1980s, the crushing of a coal miners' strike by Margaret Thatcher's government had enormous political symbolism.

See also Black Workers; Dual Labor Markets; Industrial Unions; Postindustrial Economies; Protoindustrialization; Welfare State; Women Industrial Workers.

Reference Montgomery, David. *The Fall of the House of Labor: The Workplace, the State, and American Labor Activism, 1865–1925* (1987).

Inflation and Deflation

Inflation describes a condition of rising prices. Prices can rise because the supply of money increases (when the stock of precious metals grows or governments print more money), driving up the price of goods, or inflation can occur when demand exceeds the amount of goods available. Deflation is the reverse: either because supply exceeds demand or because the amount of money in circulation diminishes, prices fall. Economic historians debate the relative importance of money supply versus supply and demand for goods. When money supply drops in relation to business activity, the value of the unit of money goes up; in inflation the reverse prevails. But efficiency (tending to cut costs and prices) or growing consumer demand (tending to raise them) plays a role as well.

During the early industrial period in most Western countries, an inflationary situation did not prevail. Prices went up during the Napoleonic Wars, when military demand and supply shortages created bottlenecks; this encouraged further industrialization in Britain. But during much of the nineteenth century prices were stationary or falling; money supply declined in relation to the growth of economic activity, while increased output kept pace with or outstripped demand. Temporary inflation occurred when harvests were bad, driving food prices up, but there was no systematic trend. Deflation was the more normal pattern. Limits on money supply, tending to reduce prices, helped motivate businessmen to seek ways to cut costs in order to continue making profits. New gold supply from California, in the early 1850s, created some inflation, but this ended in 1857 and deflation resumed.

Inflation began to loom as a greater problem around 1900, when consumer demand sometimes exceeded supply. New discoveries of gold in Australia (1851), South Africa (1887), and the Klondike (1896) began to increase the money supply, also pushing prices up. Several protests against rising prices occurred after 1900. Rampant inflation occurred during and after World War I, when governments spent massive amounts of money without raising taxes, thus increasing overall demand. French prices stood at an index of 356 in 1919 (1913=100), 509 in 1920. Austrian inflation reached a multiplier of 14,000, and German and Russian levels were far worse. These inflationary conditions could temporarily spur industry, because businessmen were eager to borrow for expansion knowing that, as prices continued to go up, their debt would be less costly when it came time to repay simply because the unit of money would be worth less. But post–World War I inflation was ultimately destabilizing, hurting people on fixed incomes, encouraging speculation rather than solid investment, and reducing overall confidence. Thus inflation was a major factor in Europe's interwar economic woes. Britain, running against the tide, deflated its prices by returning to the gold standard in the 1920s, but this made British exports more expensive and hurt the economy. The British abandoned this policy during the Great Depression of the 1930s, when prices fell everywhere.

Inflationary tendencies continued, though at a lower rate, in the industrial world after World War II, and governments tried hard to keep the problem in check. Rapid inflation in many developing countries, like Brazil, was a major economic problem after World War II; demand, including government expenditures, went up rapidly, raising prices and reducing the value of money. This trend could discourage foreign investment and certainly pressed living standards for most wage earners, though industrial growth often continued.

The history of inflation during the period of industrialization suggests that rampant price increases are socially and economically damaging. The relationship between milder inflations and economic growth is less clear; at some points, by making credit cheaper, it stimulates borrowing, which can in turn increase industrial capacity. At the same time many late twentieth-century governments, stung by the post–World War I experience, sedulously attempt to keep price increases at moderate levels even at the expense of short-term economic growth.

See also Business Cycles.

Reference Feldman, Gerald. *The Great Disorder: Politics, Economics, and Society in the German Inflation* (1993).

Infrastructure

Successful industrialization efforts have relied not only on new technology or entrepreneurialism but on the creation of a physical and social infrastructure in which economic change could take place. Infrastructure refers to facilities like roads, sewers, or schools that are essential to economic life but not directly productive.

Physical infrastructure projects have generally been the responsibility of the state. European governments helped support industrialization by building canals and railroads. The Japanese government also sponsored expansion of port facilities and shipyards, a vital part of industrialization in a country dependent upon ocean trade. In the United States, federal, state, and even local government helped to finance the building of nineteenth-century transportation networks such as roads, canals, and railroads and, in the twentieth century, highways and airports. The Erie Canal greatly expanded exports of grain and manufactured products from New York, and several other states attempted to duplicate New York's success. The federal government offered lucrative land grants to railroads in the West; the economic costs to a city or region that were bypassed by a railroad were severe, and therefore localities frequently underwrote bond issues so that they could be linked to a main line. The decline of the U.S. railroad system in the twentieth century was caused in large part by the shift of federal subsidies to the automobile.

Although automobiles rapidly became the center of the U.S. economy, carmakers relied on the government to provide the street and highway network required for "mass automobility." Partly through a tax on gasoline, federal and state governments spent billions on highway construction—even more in the 1930s than in the more prosperous 1920s. The location of highways proved crucial to suburban land developers. Ironically, the government could build roads that made land more valuable, but it was prohibited (unlike many European governments) from purchasing land that would accrue in value after the construction of roads. European governments generally used gasoline taxes to subsidize public transportation, while most streetcar systems in U.S. cities were dismantled by a consortium of automobile and automobile-related companies. After World War II, the federal government launched a massive program to build "superhighways." Ostensibly a defense measure (an imitation of fascist Germany's Autobahn), the superhighway program, along with subsidies for suburban home ownership, helped to solidify the development of auto, home, and highway construction industries.

Industrialization has also relied on systems of mass education and universities. An educated work force has provided the technical skills, flexibility, and discipline for latecomer industrializers to develop a modern system of manufacturing. The university system in the United States rapidly expanded after the 1862 "land grant" system to schools that offered technical and agricultural education. Engineering and scientific researchers quickly developed strong links with corporations and have provided much of their research and development. During the Cold War, government-sponsored military-related research provided an additional subsidy, both to the university system and to defense companies. The Japanese state built on the already strong pre-Meiji education system by emphasizing technical skills and nationalism. After their independence from Japan in 1945, South Korea and Taiwan expanded their education systems, particularly technical instruction, and their highly skilled work force was a major contributing factor to the success of their industrialization drive. From the nineteenth century onward, public health facilities such as sewer and water systems have been vital features of industrial infrastructure, making industrialized cities more livable for workers and helping to improve their productivity.

Since the mid-1970s, most industrialized countries have developed a serious financial crisis. As a result, support for education has been limited or cut. In Europe, university students must pay an increasing amount of tuition, whereas once the state paid the entire amount; stipends to students have been reduced or fail to keep up with inflation. In the United States, direct and indirect subsidies to universities, and education in general, have been cut. Tuition rates for universities and colleges have risen at twice or more the rate of inflation. Technically trained workers are still readily available, but an increasing number of skilled workers are unemployed.

Faced with large deficits, states often choose to delay maintenance of physical infrastructure. In the Soviet Union, where everything was owned by the state, roads, oil pipelines, and even nuclear power plants were allowed to deteriorate to the point of collapse. Stalin's five-year plans neglected infrastructure in favor of production and the road and rail system suffered. Ultimately, this policy created production bottlenecks and environmental damage, contributing to the Soviet Union's industrial decline in the 1980s. In the United States, the infrastructure of roads, bridges, and waterways, particularly in urban areas, has reached a critical stage. In the late 1980s, delays in repairing an underground tunnel (which would have cost several hundred dollars) eventually flooded much of downtown Chicago, resulting in the loss of several hundred million dollars worth of business.

The financial crisis for industrialized states is undeniably critical, but among industrializing or nonindustrialized countries it is far more acute. In Africa, the university system is failing, and many development agencies refuse to provide aid, arguing that Africans will only need low-level skills anyway. Hundreds die because hospitals lack such necessities as rubber gloves. The global nature of the infrastructure crisis has led some scholars to wonder whether the industrial system has begun a process of "modernization in reverse."

See also Postindustrial Economies; Professionalization; "Second" Industrial Revolution; State, Role of the; World Bank.

Reference Noble, David F. *America by Design: Science, Technology and the Rise of Corporate Capitalism* (1977).

Instrumentalism

This term is used to describe a fundamental new attitude toward work that partially replaced the older belief that jobs should provide identity or be defined in terms of unchanging effort (what British unskilled workers called the lump o' labor). Instrumentalist workers accepted the idea that work could change and even intensify, if it was viewed as an instrumemt to a better life (higher earnings, shorter hours) off the job. Instrumentalist workers thus could bargain for gains in exchange for some loss of skills or diminished control or interest on the job. Instrumentalist goals began to surface in the mid-nineteenth century among British skilled workers. They later spread even more widely among semi-skilled factory workers in most Western industrial countries, and they influenced the goals of many labor movements.

See also Discipline; Standard of Living; Work.

Interchangeable Parts

As complex machines became more important in manufacturing, issues in their own manufacture loomed larger. Before the eighteenth century most machinery and weaponry was assembed by hand, with metal pieces individually cut out for each item. The one exception was in boring cylinders for cannon, where some equipment beyond hand tools was used. Industrial parts manufacture was expensive. It was clear that production of parts separately, in large quantities, would be more efficient as soon as enough accuracy could be achieved that they were interchangeable in assembling the whole item.

As early as 1700 the Swedish engineer Christopher Polhem tried to manufacture accurate separate parts. He applied water power to all possible stages of production, assembling the individual parts later on. But the equipment available was too crude to have much effect. In 1785 a French manufacturer, Honoré Le Blanc, began to produce muskets with interchangeable parts, using standardized jigs to guide workmen cutting out the different segments. The results of his work were limited because hand crafting was essential, but they were being publicized by 1791.

A further breakthrough toward interchangeable parts was accomplished by Eli Whitney and Simeon North in making firearms under contract with the U.S. government, though Whitney claimed more uniformity than he really achieved. North's work, between 1798 and 1816, was more vital because he worked on uniform parts *and* the specialized machinery to make them, in what became known as the "American System." By the early nineteenth century guns could be produced in quantity by assembling standardized, accurately molded parts chosen at random in each necessary category. British manufacturers, some of whom worked for a time in the United States, began to produce pulleys and other equipment for the navy on the basis of interchangeable parts. Again the security of a military contract was essential for the innovation required: Marc Brunel and Samuel Bentham designed 44 separate machines capable of producing most of the parts needed for a finished pulley block. The machines variously cut pieces, bored and shaped them, turned and riveted them, and polished the most exacting parts. Although some work still had to be accomplished by hand, machines enabled 10 semi-skilled workers to do work otherwise requiring 110 skilled operatives. The principles of interchangeable parts were progressively carried into the manufacture of all sorts of machinery and equipment, including engines. Fully automatic machine building was not completed until the late nineteenth century, but interchangeable parts provided an essential basis for the mass production of crucial technology in growing volume and with decreasing costs.

See also Boring Machines; Machine Building; Springfield Armory.

Internal Combustion Engine

This engine operates by means of a channeled explosion: as gasses expand in a confined space, such as a cylinder, a piston is driven in the direction desired. The possibility of such a device, driven by regularly repeated explosions, was discussed as early as 1678 by Abbé Hautefeuille. The first practical version was developed only in 1859, however, when Etienne Lenoir brought forth a motor fired by a mixture of gas and air. The motor consumed too much gas to be practical, but the principle was established, and from then on a variety of tinkerers and engineers worked on further development. N. A. Otto produced and patented the first practical gas engine in 1876, and within a few years more than 35,000 of them were at work all over the world. This engine had many advantages over steam: it was more efficient, particularly in small industry, cleaner, and the feed could be automated, saving the labor of shoveling coal. Early motors were fixed in location, using gasses emitted as byproducts from metallurgical factories. When liquid petroleum fuels were developed, the motor could also be mobile, and its greatest uses turned out to be in transportation, in engines for ships, and, ultimately, in automobiles. The motor's invention stimulated the search for new sources of petroleum, which was initially very expensive. Oil engines were in use in Russia in the 1870s, based on the great Baku oil fields. Western-owned fields first emerged in southeast Asia (1898) and Texas (1901); at this point European navies began to convert to petroleum. By the 1920s this fuel was rapidly displacing coal for many uses, creating a major rebalancing in labor forces and older industrial economies alike. Many coal-producing regions began to decline, and the scramble for control over oil fields became one of the major themes of the twentieth century.

International Monetary Fund

See World Bank.

Internationals

The internationals were organizations that attempted to articulate and coordinate the interests and movements of the growing working class throughout the industrializing world. The fate of the three successive internationals has reflected larger transformations of socialist ideology and organization. The First International (1864–1876) was formed by a collection of radicals, utopian socialists, anarchists, and unionists. The organization helped to spread radical ideas but fell victim to the conflict between the communist Karl Marx, who argued that workers' organizations needed to carefully study social and economic conditions before formulating their goals and actions, and the anarchist Michael Bakunin, a believer in spontaneous revolt. The Second International (1899–1920) was dominated by the socialist parties of Germany, France, and Austria, among others. Despite a long tradition of advocating the solidarity of the working classes, and therefore noncooperation with wars between industrial countries, all major socialist parties endorsed World War I. The Third or Communist International (1919–1943) arose out of the failures of the socialist parties and the dramatic success of the Russian Bolshevik Party. Although the Communist International initially asserted that workers' revolutions in countries such as Germany, Italy, or France would take precedence over conditions in Russia, the failure of revolutions in these countries led the Third International to demand allegiance to the Russian revolution. Until Stalin dissolved this international in 1943 (out of solidarity with his allies in the fight against fascism), loyalty to the Bolshevik Party was ruthlessly and often brutally enforced. Although a failure in Western Europe, the Third International did promote revolutions in China and Eastern Europe.

See also Russian Revolution of 1917.

Reference Haupt, Georges. *Aspects of International Socialism, 1871–1914* (1986).

Interstate Commerce Commission

The Interstate Commerce Commission (ICC) was established by an act of Congress in 1887 to regulate railroad rates after great political pressure from U.S. farmers who depended on railroads to get their goods to market. The enormous power railroads exercised over interstate commerce and the frequent use of rebates to favored customers (subsidized by higher rates paid by other consumers) helped to legitimize the creation of the ICC, which was authorized to prevent "unjust or unreasonable" charges. What "unreasonable" meant in practice was unclear, and because railroad companies exercised great influence on the regulatory board, the ICC's interpretation of that term frequently favored cartels. Railroad companies themselves had requested government regulation because fierce competition between companies was resulting in the ruin of many railroad lines. The ICC is an example of the important role government frequently plays in regulating markets, often by limiting competition among firms. In the early years, however, informal rate agreements came undone as firms undercut their competition. The regulatory power of the ICC has extended to all surface transportation: rails, trucks, water traffic, pipelines. Many regulators today leave the ICC for careers with rail or trucking firms.

See also Populism; State, Role of the.

Reference Kolko, Gabriel. *Railroads and Regulation, 1877–1916* (1965).

Interventionist Government

Interventionist governments adopt explicit policies to affect economic and social patterns. Pinpointing the role of government —the degree and impact of government intervention—in the industrial revolution is difficult. All industrial revolutions have involved government action. All have also required government to stop enforcing certain traditional policies—like supporting guild restrictions on technological innovation. Government roles have varied, however, and they have been debated; liberal economists have attacked government in the name of open competition, a particularly important theme in the industrialization of Europe and the United States.

Some of the common policies governments have adopted to encourage industrialization include promoting technological knowledge by sponsoring commercial fairs and technical schools; expanding educational systems; using government funds and rights of eminent domain to sponsor big improvements in infrastructure, such as railway development or the modernization of ports; and using police and laws to help limit worker protest, particularly during early industrialization. Even within this category variety exists. Most governments backed educational growth (in the United States, this was up to state governments), but Britain lagged a bit, in part because of uncertainty that this was an appropriate government activity. Although all governments helped railroad construction, the British government did relatively little, whereas the United States gave huge public lands to private companies; the French government planned and built the tracks but let private companies run the lines under state license; and the German government built and operated most lines directly.

In general, later industrializers relied on governments for more intervention to spur economic growth than had been the case in Western Europe and the United States. Governments could help a society like Russia catch up technologically and also compensate for lack of capital and entrepreneurial tradition. The Japanese government, with its powerful Ministry of Industry, was even more active than its Russian counterpart, building most of Japan's initial heavy industry directly. Pacific Rim industrializations in the 1950s and 1960s involved extensive government planning, for example, in encouraging exports; thus the Taiwanese government during the 1960s installed elaborate planning mechanisms designed to make the most of limited capital and resources, while rapidly expanding schools and technical learning. Many industrializing areas, including India and Latin America, also relied heavily on government intervention to further their process of change. Latin American governments, reacting to the 1930s depression, took a quite activist economic role. Brazil, for example, built a new steel industry and then launched a successful computer sector under government sponsorship. Only in the Soviet Union and Eastern Europe, however, did a government try to run the industrialization process entirely, doing away with virtually all private initiative. Government intervention in the economy has been somewhat cyclical. In the early industrialization of the West, liberals focused strongly on getting government out of the business of protecting older methods; some also fought high tariffs, though with varying degrees of success. After 1850 government intervention tended to increase. Governments helped organize investment capital, as in the big banks sponsored by the Second Empire regime in France. Armaments expenditures rose, in part to provide markets for heavy industry. Governments began to intervene in labor conditions by regulating children's and women's labor, supervising safety, and, beginning in the 1880s, providing some social insurance programs. The general idea here was to use government inspection and some tax monies to limit the worst abuses of industrial operations. In most industrial countries of the twentieth century, this approach blossomed into the welfare state, in which governments offer a wide range of social programs to protect its citizens economically against the worst problems of aging, unemployment, and illness. Increasing concern with environmental regulation after World War II added yet another regulatory area.

In the 1970s world opinion shifted again to oppose too much government regulation. A number of governments have sold off selected state enterprises—thus Mexico "privatized" over half of its government companies in the early 1990s. Free market competition was encouraged in China after 1978 and then in Vietnam. In the 1990s India, too, began to reduce government regulations and encourage foreign business. The idea was that too much government activity, even if helpful at first, proved stifling. The prosperity of the West and Japan, with extensive private sectors, and the failure of the Soviet command economy system in Russia, helped spur this move. Government policies still vary—the United States is unusual in having no government planning office. Almost everywhere, however, intervention is much more extensive than it was in the nineteenth century, and the proper mix continues to be debated.

See also Child Labor Laws; Laissez-faire; Social Insurance.

References Gordon, Linda, ed. *Women, the State, and Welfare* (1990); Haggard, Stephan, and Chung-in Moon. *Pacific Dynamics: The International Politics of Industrial Change* (1989); Skowronek, Stephen. *Building a New American State: The Expansion of National Administrative Capacity, 1877–1920* (1982); Smith, Thomas. *Political Change and Industrial Development in Japan: Governmental Enterprise, 1868–1880* (1955).

Inventions

Inventions were crucial in setting off and sustaining the industrial revolution. Early inventions, occurring mainly in eighteenth-century Britain, were designed to improve productivity within the existing economic system; thus they focused on domestic manufacturing. With the steam engine, inventions began to apply directly to the need for factories and novel sources of power. Many countries contributed to the list of important industrial inventors. Britain headed the pack, but France and the United States contributed strongly; by the late nineteenth century, Germany and Sweden joined in, particularly in electronics and chemicals.

Inventions had occurred before, of course, though often anonymously. Until the fifteenth century, Asia, particularly China, had provided world technological leadership; China, for example, had introduced printing, paper, and explosive powder. The focus shifted to Western Europe several centuries before the industrial revolution. During the eighteenth and nineteenth centuries, the pace of invention greatly surpassed all historical precedent. Several millennia previously, around 4000 BCE (that is, several millennia after the introduction of agriculture), a number of vital discoveries converged: the invention of writing, the wheel, the use of metals. These inventions spread over many centuries, however, and thereafter the rate of major invention actually was fairly slow. The rate and scope of inventions in the industrial revolution were thus unprecedented.

What caused the surge of invention around the onset of industrialization? Analyses must take account of individual genius, but this factor does not explain timing. New opportunity, in the form of growing markets for goods, was clearly involved. Most inventors were quite conscious of working to fill a need. Once the wave of inventions began, each one triggered the next. That is, new devices for weaving created greater need for thread, which provided a target for inventors to think about the spinning process. Early machines created needs for making machines more efficiently—hence another target, devising interchangeable parts that could be turned out more easily. Along with opportunity came new scientific discoveries that guided many inventors. New knowledge about the behavior of gasses contributed directly to improvements in the steam engine; study of electricity led to the telegraph and the electric motor. Science also provided inventors with a belief that nature could and should be understood and controlled and that technical progress was both possible and desirable.

Most early inventors came from artisanal backgrounds, though there was diversity. British artisans, especially, with no strict guild tradition and with incentives provided by patent protection, seemed to have a genius for devising new methods. This early kind of inventor is often dubbed "artisan-tinkerer." Some early inventors, with or without artisanal background, received scientific training and not a few had artistic experience clearly relevant to design. Some inventors proved to be very bad businessmen and ended in poverty, their devices exploited by other entrepreneurs. Others were quite successful, either on their own or in partnership with men who could provide capital. Many inventors gained great prestige, in a society that was coming to value economic growth.

The style of invention began to change by the 1830s, and the artisan-tinkerer tradition faded by the 1870s; Gilchrist and Thomas, in metallurgy, are sometimes called the last of the breed. Increasingly, trained engineers and scientists, often working in teams in university or industrial laboratories, produced the significant inventions. Big businesses and governments realized that invention was too important to be left to chance, and the need for more training and laboratory funding became essential. More formal research and development work underlay many nineteenth-century inventions in industrial chemistry and electronics.

See also Engineers; Interchangeable Parts; Patents; Technology.

References Habbakuk, H. J. *American and British Technology in the Nineteenth Century: The Search for Labor Saving Inventions* (1962); Kranzberg, M., and C. W. Pursell, Jr., eds. *Technology in Western Civilization* Vol. 2. (1977); Hounshell, David. *From the American System to Mass Production, 1800–1932: The Development of Manufacturing Technology in the United States* (1985).

Invisible Hand

See Smith, Adam.

Iron and Steel Industry

The iron and steel industry was a crucial component of the industrialization process, particularly in the "second" industrial revolution. Cheap and abundant iron and steel eased the development of railroads, machine building, and armaments in Britain and undergirded the country's economic and military strength. Because iron and steel were necessary for the development of other manufacturing as well as for a modern military, many governments (German, Japanese, Russian, and Soviet) stimulated the rise of heavy industry for its military as well as economic importance. Jashmed Tata, a late nineteenth-century industrial leader in India, believed that the country's future strength (after it ceased being a colony of the British Empire) would require a strong iron and steel industry. In fact, until the 1980s, the overall economic and military strength of a country was generally measured by its steel production.

Iron had been produced by ancient Indians, Chinese, and Africans, and in the seventeenth century the process began a slow but significant technical change in England and then throughout Europe. Beginning in 1619, English iron makers, confronting diminishing supplies of wood, began to replace charcoal with coal as the fuel for the smelting process (by which iron ore is heated and transformed into iron). Horse and, later, steam power was used to blow air over the baths of molten iron, and the air intensified the heat in the blast furnaces. In the seventeenth century iron puddling was developed in England, which allowed higher quality iron to be produced.

The demand for iron began to explode in the 1830s as the railroad industry demanded huge amounts of iron for its locomotives, rails, and rolling stock. The rapid expansion of railroad networks spurred the expansion and technological development of the iron and steel industry. The world's premier steel industrialist, Andrew Carnegie, named his first steel mill after the head of the Pennsylvania Railroad, J. Edgar Thomson. By using Bessemer converters, Carnegie was the first to produce steel rails, which were cheaper and far

Open-hearth steel production at an early twentieth-century mill in the United States. Until the 1940s, America was the world's largest steel producer.

more durable than those made of iron. The Thomson Works was the first mill to rationally integrate all of the steps in making steel, and it achieved new economies of scale. Carnegie brought together the facilities to create iron (blast furnaces), convert iron into steel (Bessemer converters, later open hearth furnaces), and rolling mills to give the metal the proper temper. (By the 1960s the dramatic decline of the railroads nearly caused the Thomson Works to close.)

Steel mills required vast numbers of unskilled laborers, although about one-quarter of all steel workers were highly skilled; they operated furnaces, cranes, and railroads, or repaired the machinery. Employers made distinctions between skilled and unskilled workers in terms of pay and status. In the United States, most skilled workers until the 1930s were native-born white Protestants. Conflict among workers hampered the creation of an industrial union in steel until the 1930s. The union enabled some Catholic workers, but almost no black workers, to rise into the ranks of the skilled. Work in steel mills was notoriously dangerous. Around the beginning of the twentieth century in Pittsburgh, over a hundred men were killed in an average year. Even after the work had become much safer, employers blocked women from the mills and steel workers developed a distinctive masculine ethos around their strength and ability to withstand the extremes of heat and danger of the furnaces.

The availability of increasingly cheap steel helped to revolutionize many aspects of daily life. Mass-produced nails allowed U.S. builders to eschew complicated joints in favor of frame houses. Steel wire enabled telegraph companies to connect national communication networks. In the late nineteenth century, steel wire permitted the construction of such engineering marvels as the Brooklyn Bridge and, by 1919, the paper clip. By the 1910s steel beams made possible the construction of skyscrapers; steel plate had already transformed shipping and naval warfare. Steel pipe allowed oil companies to drill and transport oil along lengthy pipelines.

Steel was essential for industry and warfare. In order to build a modern navy and to industrialize, the Japanese government subsidized the construction of a steel industry in the late nineteenth century—even though the country had no iron ore and meager coal deposits. Stalin recognized the importance of steel and made it a top priority of his first five-year plan. In the 1920s and 1930s, illiterate peasants, revolutionary workers, and foreign technicians struggled in the Ural mountains, under incredibly harsh weather conditions, to construct the blast furnaces and rolling mills required for an industrial economy.

From the 1890s until the 1940s, the United States was the world's largest and most advanced steel maker. After World War II, however, there was an explosion of iron and steel production throughout the world. German, British, Russian, and Japanese mills were not only rebuilt, but their capacity was greatly expanded. Many new producers emerged in countries as diverse as South Korea, Brazil, Poland, and China. The result was an enormous worldwide surplus of production. A good deal of it was exported to the United States as steel or as automobiles or appliances. Large U.S. companies failed to reinvest enough capital to remain competitive, and many of the country's mills had closed by the 1980s. Parts of U.S. mills were sold to firms in China, Brazil, and South Korea.

See also Accidents; Deindustrialization.

References Brody, David. *Steelworkers in America: The Nonunion Era* (1960); Carr, J. C., and W. Taplin. *History of the British Steel Industry* (1962); Warren, Kenneth. *The American Steel Industry, 1850–1970: A Geographical Interpretation* (1973).

Israel

This new state, established in 1948, quickly built an industrial base. Earlier Jewish settlers had extended commercial agriculture by setting up new irrigation systems and producing goods like fruits and eggs that could be sold abroad. New Israeli settlers from Europe had many craft and commercial skills, and extensive foreign aid, particularly from the United States, supported the industrialization effort. Israeli industrialization focused on the production of consumer goods, including construction materials, for use within Israel and potential export. Development of an armaments industry was also a high priority. Israel gained extensive export sales in the West, Turkey, and parts of Africa. Imports were essential to provide necessary raw metals and advanced machinery. By the 1960s a quarter of the population worked in manufacturing, as Israel was the clear industrial leader in the Middle East.

Jacquard, Joseph (1752–1834)

One of the leading French inventors of the early industrial revolution, Jacquard devised a machine for weaving nets. His main contribution, the Jacquard loom, wove complicated figured patterns, advancing the industrial manufacture of high-quality cloth by allowing the application of power machinery to designs that were not geometrically repetitious. It used punched holes to guide the machine in producing any particular pattern, facilitating alterations of a design; this innovation much later was picked up in the early computers.

Japan

Many of Japan's institutional arrangements that made its industrialization possible (a highly skilled, low-wage work force and coordination between industrialists and the government) were established in the late nineteenth century as the country struggled to develop an economically viable empire. Although Japan was a latecomer to industrialization, world trade, and power politics (being self-isolated until the 1850s), the Japanese government quickly made up for lost time. As other Asian countries became outright colonies of industrialized European powers or found their independence severely compromised, Japan quickly mastered industrial production and became a colonial power in its own right. In 1895 Japan won from the Chinese government commercial concessions in Korea and annexed Taiwan; in 1910 it formally annexed Korea. In 1905 Japan achieved great-power status when it decisively defeated the Russian navy. Not all foreign adventures were successful. Japan's intervention in the Soviet Union in the 1920s was financially costly and provided no lasting benefits. However, Japan's colonies provided Japanese companies with access to raw materials (coal in Korea, food in Taiwan) and markets for industrial goods.

Beginning in the Meiji Restoration, the Japanese government subsidized certain zaibatsus or "financial cliques" and allowed them to monopolize key areas of the economy. In return, the zaibatsus helped the government to achieve its national economic goals. A key component of Japan industrial development strategy was to keep its wages low as a competitive advantage. This approach meant, however, that the domestic market was always underdeveloped and zaibatsus were forced to go abroad in a search for markets as well as to find natural resources. The Japanese government also encouraged the manual production of silk cloth by women (who had been sold into labor by their families). Here was a vital source of foreign currency to help support industrial purchases and supplies. By the 1930s Japan's strategy was paying off with factory production expanding rapidly, and Japan made large inroads into the markets of other imperial powers. Japanese textiles had captured half of the Indian market (previously an exclusive preserve of British manufacturers). Japan was the second-largest exporter to Morocco (after France), and when tariffs were raised on colonial markets, it aggressively exported to Latin America. Other industrialized countries retaliated by raising tariff barriers—a major factor contributing to Japan's attempt to grab what it needed by force.

Japan's war for annexation of Manchuria in 1931 and its subsequent attempt to militarily construct an "Asian Co-Prosperity Sphere" throughout the Pacific was a desperate gamble to gain access to raw materials and markets. Military production was also the rationale for creating an automobile market, for the Japanese government wanted to have an independent supply of

Workers at a semiautomated auto plant in Zama, Japan, in 1980.

trucks and jeeps. The result, World War II, was disastrous, for at the war's end, Japanese industry was decimated; millions of demobilized soldiers and unemployed colonial officials and expatriates competed for what few jobs remained.

In 1945, the United States intended to limit Japan's industrialization, but by the late 1940s, confronted with a communist government in China (and then a war in Korea), the U.S. government favored the reindustrialization of Japan and limited punishment of its fascist leaders. Partly at the insistence of its allies, the United States required that Japan remain demilitarized, which shifted the focus of Japanese business and government to its domestic market. Japan expanded its domestic economy through Fordist strategies of raising the purchasing power of its working class (although weak unions meant that wages always fell well short of advances in productivity). The lack of military spending did not end the close cooperation between government and businesses and eventually turned into a strategic advantage as Japanese companies (unlike many of their U.S. counterparts) specialized in civilian products. Japan's export drive accelerated in the late 1960s and 1970s to offset the rising prices of raw materials, particularly oil. By the 1980s Japan was running a substantial trade surplus with many of its trading partners, particularly the United States.

See also Imperialism.

References Itoh, Makoto. *The World Economic Crisis and Japanese Capitalism* (1990); Sumiya, Mikio, and Koji Taira. *An Outline of Japanese Economic History, 1603–1940: Major Works and Research Findings* (1979).

Japanese System of Employment

In the Japanese system of employment, large companies offer their permanent employees a lifetime of job security in return for extreme loyalty. Under this system, workers are paid on the basis of their seniority, not on the job being performed. The earnings of an employee typically start out low and peak after twenty or so years with the firm; real wages decline rapidly thereafter. The lure of eventually earning higher pay is an important factor in preventing workers from leaving their jobs or protesting such practices as mandatory overtime or relocation to a new part of the country. Not every employee is eligible for the system; large auto factories, for instance, rely on temporary workers who are laid off during slack periods or when the factory is being retooled. Women are far more likely to be temporary workers who work on a piece-rate basis. The system began to take shape in the 1920s, when advancing industry began to require more skilled workers. As the system spread, it promoted company loyalty and weakened independent unions.

Reference Gordon, Andrew. *Labor and Imperial Democracy in Prewar Japan* (1991).

Joint Stock Companies

These capitalist enterprises, which combine funds from several investors, originated in the investment needs of long-distance trading firms in Britain. Partnerships were formed for each voyage, but during the seventeenth century the partnerships evolved into a durable investment in a company. The company would decide on particular ventures without needing to assemble a new partnership each time. Various joint stock companies developed, but the East India Company and its new charter of 1657 is taken as the first common use of this method of organization. Similar companies developed in the Netherlands at about the same time. Unlike partnerships, joint stock companies also issued stocks that could be transferred to other owners.

Although early joint stock companies applied mainly to trade, they were also available for industry. A number of metallurgical and mining ventures, in France and Germany as well as Britain, required so much capital that the joint stock form was essential. Most early railroad companies were also joint stock ventures. Joint stock arrangements were much more novel outside western Europe; the first ones appeared in Russia only in 1864, for commercial banking. The principle of the joint stock company also underlay the later development of the corporation, though the latter required additional legislation to limit the liability of each investor. Under traditional joint stock arrangements, any one investor could be held liable for the entire debts of the enterprise, which obviously discouraged use of the form, particularly by smaller capitalists.

Journeymen

See Artisans.

Kaiping Mines

These mines played an important role in early Chinese industrialization and highlight the difficulties the process encountered in the late nineteenth century. The mines, north of Tianjin, were opened in 1878 to provide coal for steamships newly plying Chinese rivers and canals. The first permanent railroad in China was built in 1881 to carry Kaiping coal to the Chinese-owned steamer fleet. (An earlier rail line had been built by Europeans but was torn up by the Chinese government in protest against imperialist interference.) The mines ran up large debts, and the steamship line—the China Merchants' Company—was badly administered and lost ground to British companies working the Chinese rivers. The mines were taken over in 1900 by a foreign consortium headed by the American Herbert Hoover. The early venture was an exception to China's general policy of neglect, as industrialization was mainly brought in by foreigners in their newly acquired treaty ports, and its rocky start both reflected and furthered the nation's indecisiveness about modern industry at this point.

See also Imperialism; Latecomer Industrialization; State, Role of the.

Kaiser, Henry (1880–1967)

In the 1930s and 1940s, Henry Kaiser helped to develop the U.S. West and built an industrial empire by employing mass production techniques in construction and shipbuilding. Another crucial factor in Kaiser's success was to take advantage of contacts within the New Deal government, which loaned Kaiser capital and purchased many of his products. In the 1930s Kaiser helped to coordinate construction of key infrastructure projects, including the Hoover and Grand Coulee dams, which provided the West Coast with enough power to rapidly expand its industrial production of aircraft and ships during World War II. During the war, Kaiser adapted the assembly-line techniques of the automobile industry to shipbuilding. Practically from scratch, Kaiser trained and housed a massive work force, and by the end of the war Kaiser's shipyards had built one-third of the U.S. merchant fleet.

Reference Foster, Mark. *Henry J. Kaiser: Builder in the American West* (1989).

Kawasaki Shipyard

The Kawasaki shipyard was set up by the Japanese government when it realized that building steamships was a vital national response to Western industrialization. The shipyard also played a crucial role in moving Japan away from wider dependence on imports of European machinery. In 1907 the yard produced the first locomotives and coaches in Japanese history, thus replacing several decades' reliance on Western supply for the nation's burgeoning rail network and foreshadowing the boom in heavy industry after World War I, as Japan moved into its second stage of industrialization.

Kay, John

See Flying Shuttle.

Keynesianism

Keynesianism refers to the economic theories and policies of John Maynard Keynes (1883–1946). Keynes was a British economist who rejected the laissez-faire verities of the nineteenth and early twentieth centuries. In 1923 he wrote a *Tract on Monetary Reform* that attacked the gold standard, previously considered the only way to ensure the stability and strength of national currencies. But Keynes is best known as the "author" of "interventionist" government, arguing in the midst of the Great Depression of the 1930s that governments could play a positive role in managing their national economies, particularly by using deficit spending to stimulate buying power ("priming the pump") and ending the downward economic cycle.

Keynes's theories were adopted by the New Deal state in the United States and were an important theoretical underpinning of the welfare state in Europe. In practice, Keynesianism viewed the state as the manager of industrial capitalism, controlling and directing public and private investment during booms and stimulating demand by aiding the unemployed during its "busts." Although Keynesianism has become viewed as inherently inflationary, Keynes urged the British government to finance wartime expenditures through compulsory savings (saving bonds) in order to avoid inflation during World War II. The British government, however, preferred more traditional methods of financing, and serious inflation did ensue. Keynesian theories (although not those of Keynes himself) were applied to the postwar institutions of international banking, trade, and development through the establishment of the World Bank/IMF. More active government planning and spending helped protect postwar industrial economies from severe depression.

Political conservatives were uncomfortable with the increasing role of government in the economy and society, fearing that instead of managing capitalism it was opening the door to "creeping socialism." In practice, however, conservative politicians (along with their Liberal, Labour, and Social Democratic counterparts) accepted Keynesianism in Britain and the United States. By 1971, arch-conservative Richard Nixon publicly confessed, "I am a Keynesian." However, the economic crisis of the mid-1970s proved immune to Keynesian economic measures; the attempts to stimulate a recovery from the depression that began in 1973 resulted in both sluggish growth and inflation: stagflation. Although Ronald Reagan formally rejected Keynesianism in favor of supply-side economics, the massive deficits that he ran up in the 1980s (and the resulting economic expansion) suggested that Reagan owed more to Keynes than he wished to acknowledge.

See also Bretton Woods Agreement; Fordism; Long Waves of Capitalism; Military Industrial Complex; Socialism.

References Collins, Robert M. *The Business Response to Keynes, 1929–1964* (1981); Heilbroner, Robert L. *The Worldly Philosophers: The Lives, Times, and Ideas of the Great Economic Thinkers* (1986).

Knights of Labor

The Noble and Holy Order of the Knights of Labor was formed in 1869 as a secret association of Philadelphia tailors, but by the early 1880s it had around 100,000 members of all trades throughout the United States. The Knights were an industrial union, which meant they were open to workers regardless of their craft (or lack of one). The idea that all employees of one company should belong to one union instead of separate craft unions made sense to many workers who were aware of the growing national organization and power of industrialists. Unlike the American Federation of Labor, the Knights did not simply define its membership by occupation; it allowed almost anyone to join (except bankers, lawyers, gamblers, and liquor dealers) who wanted to improve the status of laboring people. Farmers, small businessmen, and wage workers were members. Unlike most unions, women were allowed to join, and after 1883 black workers could join segregated locals; however, Asians were rigorously excluded.

In 1884 railroad workers went on strike (against the advice of the Knights' leadership) against an operation owned by Jay Gould. The intercraft solidarity of the strikers was successful and by 1886, 700,000 people had flooded into the Knights, making it the largest union in the country. In 1886, however, Gould provoked the Knights into another strike in which he decisively defeated the union.

In the public mind (or rather that of the mass media) the events of 1886 linked the moderate Knights with radical and socialist union advocates. In 1886 Chicago was wracked by a number of strikes seeking to establish the eight-hour day; Chicago Knights participated in a solidarity rally with socialists and anarchists in Haymarket Square. The rally ended in disaster; someone (whether anarchists or the police is still disputed) threw a bomb that killed several policemen; the police opened fire, killing several demonstrators. Haymarket became a rallying cry among radicals, particularly after several immigrant anarchists were executed on the basis of very flimsy evidence; Haymarket was also the basis of the first red scare in the United States. Most Knights were not socialists, but the association damaged the respectability of Knights in the eyes of many middle-class sympathizers. More damaging, managerial counteroffensives similar to that of Gould decimated the strength of the Knights throughout their former strongholds. By the early 1890s the Knights were in irreversible decline.

In practice, the Knights combined elements of trade unionism with the political ideals and specific reforms of a social movement. The Knights also set up producer cooperatives. Throughout the 1880s the Knights established themselves in many industrial areas as a force in local government, but they failed to establish themselves as a permanent labor party. By defining "labor" broadly, the Knights allowed many people to identify with their movement but also enabled other parties to borrow their rhetoric to win back voters. Particularly in the South, the Knights' real and imagined emphasis on racial equality led many whites to eschew the Knights.

See also American Federation of Labor; Racism.

References Fink, Leon. *Workingmen's Democracy: The Knights of Labor and American Politics* (1983); Rachleff, Peter. *Black Labor in the South: Richmond, Virginia, 1865–1890* (1984).

Krupp

The Krupp family pioneered modern heavy industry in Germany, in the coal-rich Ruhr region, and went on to enter the ranks of the German upper class by the later nineteenth century. Alfred Krupp was born in 1812 into a merchant family in Essen. His father had not done well, twice being swindled by partners when he tried to establish steel factories. Alfred set about to repair the family fortunes. He was sent to work in a factory at the age of 13 and the next year launched his own operation on the basis of a meager inheritance. Adept at using advanced technologies developed by others, he single-mindedly pursued a policy of expansion, branching from the manufacture of scissors and hand tools into metallurgy and mining. The Krupp firm, further developed by Alfred's descendants, became one of the great integrated companies in Germany, creating a vast investment market from raw materials such as coal to finished products such as armaments. Later Krupp leaders played a significant role in national policy, encouraging military expenditure and producing much of the artillery used on the German side in the world wars. The Krupp conglomerate was modified by the victorious allies after World War II but continued under managers outside the family.

See also Corporations; Iron and Steel Industry; Latecomer Industrialization; Military Industrial Complex.

Kulaks

Although kulaks were wealthy Russian peasants who spearheaded commercial agriculture in the villages after 1905, this was primarily a political, not an economic, category developed by the Bolsheviks in the years following the 1917 revolution. Although the Bolsheviks had distributed land to the peasants, their support was weakest in the countryside, and kulaks were often blamed for withholding grain—which allowed the Bolsheviks to escape responsibility for the state's contribution to shortages because of poor planning.

During the Stalinist period of the collectivization of agriculture, kulaks' cattle, horses, and grain were especially subject to seizure. Kulaks themselves could be deported to forced labor camps or prison. Stalin's methods were particularly brutal; in many cases, peasants' seed grain was seized, and the state allowed millions in the countryside to starve. Although wealthy peasants were most vulnerable to deportation, it was quite easy for a vengeful official or a spiteful neighbor to label anyone a kulak. The "dekulakization" of the countryside convinced many peasants to emigrate to industrial centers in order to escape the harsh punishment the Stalinist regime meted out to opponents, real and imagined, of its rural policies.

See also Lenin; New Economic Policy.

Reference Fitzpatrick, Sheila. *Stalin's Peasants: Resistance and Survival in the Russian Village after Collectivization* (1994).

L

Labor Turnover
This term refers to the frequency with which workers leave any given firm or industry—the greater the frequency, the higher the turnover. High labor turnover is normally undesirable for a firm, because it requires recruiting and training a series of new workers, rather than relying on increasing experience and loyalty.

High labor turnover was endemic in the early industrial revolution in most regions. Changing jobs gave workers a sense of control over their lives and some hope for a slightly better future. Some workers, of course, could not leave a firm because they were too poor or insecure, and some were sufficiently skilled that they did not wish to leave. Early New England factories, for example, had a very stable skilled worker core. Many workers, however, even risked considerable poverty for the sake of changing jobs and getting some break from the normal routine. Some (such as black migrants from the U.S. South) returned to the countryside periodically, particularly during harvest periods when rural labor was in demand. Others wandered to different cities, simply hoping for a better break. Geographical mobility was extensive in the nineteenth century, often complicating family life. Artisanal tradition had involved a good bit of wandering for young workers as part of training; this tradition carried over to industry in some cases. Even unskilled workers, like Slavic immigrants to the United States, shifted jobs frequently. Frequent economic recessions encouraged turnover, because workers, who were often fired during slumps, developed no loyalty to particular firms. In boom times, different firms deliberately tried to woo workers away from their rivals, to build their own labor force with more experienced operatives.

High labor turnover translated into striking statistics. The average Japanese worker in 1900 stayed with a firm less than two years. Turnover was often particularly high among women, who as supplementary earners were likely to quit work on marriage and who moved around a lot. Turnover in the Ford automobile factory around 1908, with a large staff of immigrant workers, was up to 1000 percent per year.

Employers made major efforts to reduce turnover, particularly among the harder-to-replace skilled workers. They instituted paternalist programs, like company housing or mutual aid, so that workers would lose more than a job if they left the company. Early industrial firms often offered bonuses for workers who completed a multiyear contract. In 1915 Ford instituted a $5 day for unskilled workers who showed steady work habits and a respectable home life. Japan's massive program of employment security, launched in the 1920s, was aimed at the turnover problem. Not all these measures worked; particularly in Europe and the United States, workers' desire for flexibility and their resentment of industrial conditions generated a long-standing turnover problem. Turnover did tend to decrease with time, however, for older workers with family responsibilities had less flexibility than their younger counterparts. Likewise, workers who bought into consumerist goals, wanting to maximize their earnings, might take fewer risks in changing jobs. The history of turnover in the industrial economy provides important insight into patterns of work and employer-worker relations.

See also Immigration; Scientific Management; Work.

References Meyer, Stephen. *The Five Dollar Day: Labor, Management, and Social Control in the Ford Motor Company* (1981); Stearns, Peter N. *Lives of Labor: Working in a Maturing Industrial Society* (1975).

Labour Party

British working-class politics have been distinctive. Many British workers long backed either the Liberal or the Conservative party, both of which, after workers got the vote in 1867, paid some attention to working-class demands. Despite or perhaps because of a strong union movement, Marxism did not catch on, though some efforts were put forward by Marxist leaders. The Labour Party took shape in the 1890s. The Labour Representation Committee, formed in 1900 as a merger of labor groups, grew slowly, but a House of Lords decision that unions could be sued (Taff Vale Case) gave it new support by 1906. As it gained, the party was heavily influenced by unions and also by the intellectual Fabian Society, an articulate socialist group advocating deep-seated reform rather than revolution.

By 1919 the party replaced the Liberals as one of the two top British political forces. Its rule during 1945–1951 installed the British welfare state, with an extensive national health plan, government-built housing, and nationalization of key industries like coal mining as a means of reducing the power of capitalists over workers.

Laissez-faire

The economic doctrine of laissez-faire, or "let do," emphasizes the importance of allowing individuals to pursue their economic self-interest free from government interference. Acquisitive individualism provides the best motives for people to work hard and innovate, and free competition among individuals is most conducive to economic progress and prosperity.

Laissez-faire doctrines developed in the eighteenth century and served as the basis for the economic writings of Adam Smith, whose *Wealth of Nations* was the most influential treatise during the early industrial revolution. The doctrines were opposed to the principles of mercantilism, which had called for extensive state intervention. Most economists continued to support laissez-faire ideas through the middle of the nineteenth century. The philosopher and economist John Stuart Mill, for example, wrote in 1848 that "every restriction of competition is an evil, and every extension of it, even if for the time injuriously affecting some class of laborers, is always an ultimate good." Laissez-faire advocates opposed old restrictions on innovation like the guilds; they attacked tariffs; and they often argued against combinations of working people that might restrict wage competition. Government, in the laissez-faire view, should be nothing more than a policeman, making sure that competitors played fair and did not conspire to limit individualism.

Laissez-faire ideas were very influential in early industrialization in western Europe and the United States. Old regulations were abolished, allowing freer introduction of new technology and freer expansion of business. British policy, particularly, was affected by laissez-faire, and the size of British government actually shrank somewhat in the mid-nineteenth century. Many businessmen embraced laissez-faire ideas, though they often used them selectively. It was not uncommon for an American industrialist to advocate laissez-faire against some incipient trade union or labor law, while asking for tariff protection or a government land grant to a new railway company.

The importance of laissez-faire ideas continued into the twentieth century, although in practice they seem less important in increasingly interventionist states. The ideas became more complicated as the size of business units grew; should giant corporations be allowed to develop or should the government limit them in the name of really free individual competition? Many laissez-faire advocates also expanded their notion of essential government services, as in arguing that publicly supported school systems were needed. In addition, laissez-faire ideas were attacked as leading to excessive capitalist profits and inadequate attention to the needs of the working class and the poor. Socialist theorists developed alternatives to the laissez-faire vision, and their ideas increasingly affected actual policies.

Finally, most societies that industrialized later, like Russia and Japan, made no pretense of embracing literal laissez-faire, for they used government policies openly and actively. On the whole, then, the impact of this doctrine declined after the early industrial period in the West, but its imagery remained powerful, particularly in the United States.

See also Liberalism; Social Darwinism; State, Role of the; Subsidies.

Reference Heilbroner, Robert. *The Worldly Philosophers: The Lives, Times, and Ideas of the Great Economic Thinkers* (1961).

Latecomer Industrialization

Societies that industrialize well after the initial industrial revolutions of western Europe and the United States have some special advantages and disadvantages. These "latecomers," including Japan, Russia, and more recently the Pacific Rim, have been able to imitate advanced technology and business forms; they did not have to start back at early British industrial levels. They can also copy ingredients of the process that developed more haphazardly in the West—as in setting up formal education systems early on. On the down side, however, late industrializers always face intense competition from established factory centers; it takes decades to rise to the top level, and some industrializers, like Russia, have not yet managed to do so. Interference from more advanced industrial competition is always a problem. Latecomers typically lack the capital or the culture that induced industrialization in the West; they have to change more structures in order to clear the decks for industrialization. Thus Japan's civil strife in the 1860s altered political forms, and then the Meiji reforms began to alter Confucian culture in the interests of introducing more scientific training. Russia tried to industrialize with less prior change and paid the price in revolutions in 1905 and 1917, when structures and cultures altered with a vengeance.

Latecomer industrializers always have to encourage but also manage imitation of foreigners and outright foreign investment. Japan was cautious in this regard; Russia was less so, until the 1917 revolution when foreign contacts were limited. They usually employ the state to help organize capital and form many industrial companies outright; this stratagem compensates for some other deficiencies. Latecomers must find goods to export in order to earn foreign exchange to pay for pilot equipment. Japan emphasized silk production, Russia foods and raw materials. Sometimes latecomer industries, pressed to catch up, may be even more careless about environmental problems than other industrial societies; this was certainly the case in Soviet Russia and Eastern Europe.

Latecomer industrializers, in other words, face some specific issues that differ from those of other societies, even as they engage in what is broadly speaking a common process.

References Gerschenkron, Alexander. *Economic Backwardness in Historical Perspective* (1962); Stearns, Peter N. *The Industrial Revolution in World History* (1994).

Latin America

Most Latin American countries gained their political independence in the 1820s and 1830s, but as exporters of raw materials they remained economically dependent upon industrialized countries throughout the nineteenth and much of the twentieth centuries. Deindustrialization of traditional manufacturing workers occurred under the pressure of British industrial goods. Despite the new nations' economic and social reforms in the mid- and late nineteenth century, most of Latin America's population remained peasants, although an urbanized working and middle class emerged in Argentina, Brazil, and Mexico. In the 1940s, under Juan Perón, Argentina began a policy of import substitution that succeeded in building an industrial economy. By the 1970s Argentina's inability to export manufactured products began to undermine its industrial economy. After World War II the Mexican and Brazilian governments sought to build the infrastructure for successful industrialization (roads, rails, electrical, and educational systems). In the 1980s both countries began to attract export-oriented factories from Europe, Japan, and the United States, although whether this effort will result in economic independence remains to be seen.

See also Maquiladoras; World Bank; World Systems Theory.

Reference Keen, Benjamin, and Mark Wasserman. *A Short History of Latin America* (1984).

Lawrence, Abbott (1792–1855)

One of the early New England industrialists, Abbott Lawrence headed a group of Boston financiers who built a textile center at a site on the Merrimack River—now Lawrence, Massachusetts—in 1845. One of his partners, his brother William, had already set up the first corporation to manufacture woolen goods. The partners built a stone dam to harness waterpower and erected rows of workers' houses to attract a labor force and economize on wages. That drew large numbers of immigrant workers to what was one of the classic one-industry communities in the United States. The new company was a second-generation textile operation, far larger than its predecessors and with greater capital resources. Lawrence and his fellow investors also had unusual political influence, which allowed the company to regulate waterways in the Connecticut basin, to the detriment of many local farmers and artisans. The city of Lawrence also gained fame much later, in 1912, as the center of a huge and bitter strike involving over 20,000 workers that led to some improvements in worker conditions in the textile industry. In the 1920s many Lawrence mills failed or moved south in search of cheaper labor.

Lawrence, Massachusetts

See Lawrence, Abbott.

Le Chapelier Law

Enacted in 1791 during the liberal phase of the French Revolution, this law abolished guilds and forbade other worker associations. It was designed to promote free competition and innovation by holding down labor protest. The law signaled the basically middle-class character of this phase of the French Revolution, and it was similar to anti-labor rules in most early industrial societies. The law was fully repealed only in the 1880s. Up to that point, the French government retained the right to intervene against labor organizations and arrest leaders.

Lee Kuan Yew (1923–)

Lee Kuan Yew was the first prime minister of Singapore when it became self-governing. Lee at first attempted to maintain a commonwealth with Malaysia, but by 1965 he had led the ethnically diverse city-state to full independence. Under British rule, Singapore had always been an important commercial port; Lee sought to supplement that activity with industrialization. Exports were vital, as internal markets were far too small to absorb industrial production, and Lee eventually encouraged a shift from production of labor-intensive goods to more capital-intensive ones. Singapore's strategic location, its skilled work force, pro-trade policies, and efficient government allowed it to make good use of foreign capital. Lee used the government to promote economic policies that promoted industrial growth, full employment, and a rising standard of living; elections and civil liberties, however, were suppressed under one-party role. Lee's experiment succeeded in creating a wealthy, export-oriented industrial society with a well-educated population and remarkably efficient government.

See also Pacific Rim.

Reference Turnbull, C. M. *A History of Singapore, 1819–1988* (1988).

Lenin, Vladimir Il'ich (1870–1924)

Lenin was a founder of the Russian Social Democratic Workers' Party (Bolsheviks) and the leader of the 1917 Russian Revolution. A fervent Marxist who argued that international capitalism created the conditions for proletarian revolution, even in Russia, Lenin believed that his party would be the vanguard of workers' struggles, guiding workers away from reformist goals and toward socialism. The Bolsheviks' highly disciplined cadres helped the fledgling revolution survive the myriad problems it confronted, including counterrevolution and invasion by England, Japan, and the United States. However, in the face of war, the Bolsheviks refused to allow workers' organizations to function independently, and workers' soviets and newspapers were suppressed or strictly controlled; gradually, economic, political, and military planning were taken over by the Bolsheviks.

Although fiercely anticapitalist, Lenin proved remarkably flexible in adjusting to the economic and political chaos provoked by world war, revolution, counterrevolution, and civil war. During the civil war, industrial facilities were nationalized, that is, taken over by the state, and most goods were no longer sold in the market but were instead produced by quota and distributed through rations. After the civil war production was a fraction of what it had been in 1913 and Lenin launched the controversial New Economic Policy, which reintroduced markets for many products, particularly agricultural goods.

Lenin believed that industrialization would spread the conditions for socialism throughout the country. Before he died, Lenin warned the Bolshevik Party to beware of the growing power of Joseph Stalin, but it was too late. Lenin's life, party, and revolution provided a blueprint for many revolutionaries, particularly in underdeveloped countries, who sought to industrialize and build socialism at the same time.

See also Kulaks; Stakhanovites; World War I.

Reference Fisher, Louis. *The Life of Lenin* (1966).

Liberalism

This political movement originated in western Europe during the eighteenth-century Enlightenment under the influence of the political theories of philosopher John Locke. Many liberals supported the industrial revolution, and many industrialists in Europe, the United States, and Latin America were liberals, at least in orientation. Liberalism gained ground in Europe beginning in the 1820s, the same time the industrial revolution was taking shape. Revolutions of 1830 in France and Belgium thus were liberal, at least initially.

Liberal political movements believed in constitutional government and personal rights such as freedom of religion and the press. They backed the spread of education. They were hostile to traditional restrictions on economic freedom, such as guild regulations. Some liberals believed in laissez-faire. In general, however, liberals did not seek systematically to exclude government from economic activity. Many businessmen, though politically liberal, supported tariffs; this was true in the United States. Liberal leaders often urged government involvement in measures to promote economic growth, such as railroads. Some liberals, as they learned more about working-class misery, came to back certain reforms, like child-labor legislation. As the nineteenth century wore on groups like the British Liberal Party supported increasing government intervention in the welfare area. A Liberal government in Britain enacted the National Insurance measure of 1911, which first provided unemployment insurance. Similarly, liberals in the United States backed increasing government intervention during the New Deal.

Liberalism, in sum, was rarely entirely identical with the narrow interests of industrialists, though they were often linked to liberal groups in the nineteenth century. Always eager for individual freedoms, liberals often urged government-backed reforms. Therefore, liberalism necessarily varied greatly from place to place and tended to change over time; as liberals became more interventionist, they usually lost most business support, as in western Europe and the United States by the early twentieth century.

Liberalism never widely caught on in Russia and Japan, and industrial revolutions in these countries had little to do with liberal policies. In Latin America liberalism was an active movement in the nineteenth century. Liberals usually backed government encouragement for industry. Their eagerness for economic growth could lead them to impose harsh measures on groups—for instance, the Indians—linked with more traditional economic practices. As in the United States, liberals often tried to press Indians to support private property and other "modern" concepts and were quite willing to coerce in the name of progress.

Except in the United States and to an extent Britain, nineteenth-century liberalism failed to catch on with working-class groups. This could result in growing identification of liberalism with the cause of business—as in Germany after 1871—and in a growing loss of liberal power thanks to the rise of socialism. Still, liberal beliefs and policies, though variable, related to the growth of industry in the West during crucial decades of the nineteenth century. In the late twentieth century liberal beliefs in relatively free markets and low tariffs revived almost worldwide, as a means of encouraging global industrial development.

See also Classical Economics; Protectionism.

References Love, Joseph, and N. Jacobsen, eds. *Guiding the Invisible Hand: Economic Liberalism and the State in Latin American History* (1988); di Ruggiero, Guido. *A History of European Liberalism* (1927).

Light Industry

This term refers to consumer goods industries, like textiles, leather, processed foods, tools, and (more recently) small appliances. Different industrial revolutions placed different emphases on light as opposed to heavy industry. Russian (and Soviet) industrialization was notorious for underplaying light industry, to the detriment of consumer standards. German industrialization also stressed heavy industry, in part because British factory imports, earlier, had weakened German textiles (1820–1830). By contrast, France and Italy, with poor iron and coal resources, emphasized light industry strongly, developing small, mechanized factories and shops. Within any industrialization process, light industries typically employ more women than heavy industry does, and offers lower wages in part because of more intense price competition among relatively small firms.

See also Electronics; Women Industrial Workers.

Linen

Linen was one of the most commonly used fibers in preindustrial Europe. It was made from flax, a plant that could be widely grown throughout most of Europe. Linen production was hard to mechanize, however, because the fiber broke easily. Factory production began, haltingly, only in the 1840s. Linen products thus declined in the face of factory cottons and wools, and linen goods became a low-paying, largely female craft specialty. Traditional linen-producing areas, like rural Brittany, parts of Belgium, and Ireland, suffered growing unemployment. Ironically, commercial linen production had increased on the eve of industrialization, serving the needs for military uniforms during the Napoleonic Wars; in Northern Ireland, linen weaving was as essential as the potato for the survival of rural Protestant families. This earlier demand made subsequent deindustrialization all the more severe.

See also Textiles.

Literacy

See Education.

Long Waves of Capitalism

Most people are aware of the "boom-bust" cycles of capitalist economies from personal experience or from reading the newspapers. Over the last sixty years, economists have increased their knowledge of the causes of business cycles, and their recommendations have influenced the policies of government, greatly reducing the length and severity of depressions (now termed recessions). However, social scientists have begun to investigate the causes and consequences of much longer economic cycles that take decades to resolve. These "long waves" of capitalist development include short-term business cycles within them but are spread throughout the entire world system of trade. Unlike business cycles, the resolution of long-wave cycles involves the transformation of a wide variety of business, social, and political institutions and relationships.

The generally accepted periodization of cycles of economic expansion are late eighteenth century to 1815, 1850–1873, 1897–1914, and 1945–1973. Periods of global depression are 1815–1850, 1873–1897, 1920–1945, and 1973 to the present. Although economic growth occurs within depressionary cycles (such as the one since 1973), living standards of workers remain stagnant or decline, unemployment grows, and many industries and firms (such as steel in most industrialized countries) become unprofitable. Such periods of depression or crisis destroy the social, political, and business institutions that had developed in the previous expansionist cycle and had enabled capitalism to expand and grow. When new institutional arrangements are constructed, capitalism begins to expand.

During the 1890s, for instance, the rise of monopoly capitalism not only centralized financial and productive power in the hands of cartels and corporations (instead of the relatively competitive period that had preceded it), but labor relations were also transformed. In the United States, craft unions in the iron and steel industry were crushed in the Homestead Lockout, and railroad unions were tamed through a number of bloody confrontations. The weakness of workers relative to industrialists facilitated a faster pace of work, the creation of more intense forms of workplace discipline such as Taylorism, and eventually the moving assembly line. The rapid expansion of production required that industrialists develop new relationships with consumers—encouraging a consumer culture through aggressive advertising and credit. This complex of institutional arrangements proved highly successful through the 1920s, but the Great Depression of the 1930s revealed corporations' inability to manage the entire economy. In the 1930s and 1940s a new set of institutional relationships developed that gave the state a far larger role in managing the industrial economy.

See also Capitalism; Fordism; Keynesianism; Mass Marketing; New Deal; Welfare State.

References Gordon, David M., Richard Edwards, and Michael Reich. *Segmented Work, Divided Workers: The Historical Transformation of Labor in the United States* (1982); Mandel, Ernest. *Long Waves in the History of Capitalism: The Marxist Interpretation* (1978).

Luddites

In the late eighteenth and early nineteenth centuries, laws and customs that had protected the wages and working conditions of British workers were gradually overturned, ignored, or abandoned. In 1809 regulations governing the woolen industry were repealed; in 1813 the apprentice system was suspended, and, the next year, the minimum wage. In addition, as steam-powered looms and shuttles were introduced to the textile industry, previously skilled workers' wages fell and working conditions deteriorated. Luddites were bands of disaffected British workers and artisans who resisted the new order and wrecked machinery during the late eighteenth and early nineteenth century. The rioters came to be called Luddites because factory owners were warned ahead of time of retribution by "Ned Ludd" or "General Ludd" (a probably mythical leader) if they did not agree to changes in wages and working conditions. Luddites raised bread-and-butter issues but also resented and resisted the degradation of political rights and social status of artisans and workers in the early phases of the industrial revolution. Workers turned to Luddism after trade union actions had been banned by the government and workers could find no relief in the courts or parliament. After the Combination Acts, unions continued to operate in secret and ostracized, beat, or sabotaged "blackleg" or non-union workers or artisans. Luddism was an extension of this activity and like many pre-industrial "riots," Luddites relied not only on the social solidarity of a group of protestors but on a wider community as well. The riots sometimes occurred in daylight, and the secrecy of the actions could have been betrayed by other workers who witnessed the riots. One police informer reported that "most every creature of the lower order both in town and country are on their side." Some magistrates also sympathized with workers' hostility to machines.

Luddites sometimes accomplished their immediate aims of a rise in wages, although riots also led to severe repression by the government. By 1812 (in the midst of a war with Napoleon) armed Luddites clashed with both mill owners and the army, and over ten thousand troops were in the field against General Ludd. The protests threatened to become a national movement and change the government that had ignored their plight and denied them their traditional rights. Repression won the day, however, and enough workers were hung to break the movement. The fact that industrialization at this point was a largely rural phenomenon hampered workers' ability to communicate with each other and coordinate activities. Many Luddites became members of the Chartist movement, although there was not another mass insurrection of workers that threatened the government. The sabotage of new machinery and ostracism of strikebreakers remained fixtures among English workers, but the slow legalization of trade unionism and the gradual extension of the right to vote to male propertied workers throughout the nineteenth century made the insurrectionary activity of Luddites appear bizarre to later historians and workers. However, attacks on machines were common in many early industrial periods, such as France in the 1820s. By the twentieth century a Luddite had come to mean anyone who futilely and irrationally seeks to oppose new technology.

See also Arkwright, Richard; Moral Economy.

Reference Thompson, E. P. *The Making of the English Working Class* (1963).

McCormick, Cyrus (1809–1884)

Cyrus McCormick helped to mechanize farm production by inventing and mass producing farm equipment, such as the mechanical reaper he perfected in the 1830s. His invention allowed horse power to be substituted for human power, a significant advantage for large-scale grain farmers on the enormous prairies of the United States. McCormick ensured high-quality products by building his own factory and adopting mass-production techniques. He guarded against competitors by carefully patenting his subsequent inventions. McCormick's acumen as a businessman, utilizing advertising and advancing credit to customers, gave him a near monopoly on agricultural implements for much of the mid-nineteenth century.

See also Mass Marketing.

Reference Pursell, Carroll W., Jr. *Technology in America: A History of Individuals and Ideas* (1981).

McCormick Reaper

See McCormick, Cyrus.

Machine Building

This industry was both result of industrialization and vital to its expansion. The new inventions in textiles and the steam engine obviously had to be manufactured. At first, prototypes were made by industrialists like James Watt, and traditional metal shops were used to provide materials; but ultimately the industry had to emerge on its own. The Boulton-Watt collaboration involved a machine tools shop in which numerous steam engines could be constructed. Real progress in developing procedures for the production of standardized machine parts awaited the very end of the eighteenth century and beyond. Increased knowledge in the manufacture of clocks and other precision instruments played a crucial role. New equipment included accurate lathes, on which machine parts could be cut; various types were available by the late eighteenth century. All-metal lathes, pioneered by Henry Maudslay in England and David Wilkinson in the United States, constituted a significant advance, for they provided minutely accurate screws for machines. New boring engines allowed more accurate construction of metal cylinders, of the sort used in engines. Lathes and boring engines set the basis for the development of interchangeable parts, which a Swedish engineer Christopher Polhem, had worked on as early as 1700. By 1785 a Frenchman named Le Blanc was making muskets on the basis of interchangeable parts, presumably by cutting patterns for each part to guide the workmen. The most influential achievements stemmed from the firearms manufacture organized by Eli Whitney and Simeon North in the United States, as well as from the manufacture of naval pulleys in England. Different machines cut and bore each part identically, so that machines could be assembled by putting them together.

Early machine-building operations depended on skilled workmen. Most shops were small, and, although the skills were new, an essentially artisanal atmosphere prevailed. Much labor was recruited from the ranks of trained metalworkers. Skilled unions, like the Amalgamated Society of Engineers in Britain, brought these workers into the ranks of craft organization. Later in the nineteenth century a new generation of inventions permitted more automatic machine construction. Automatic riveting and boring machines, attached to electrical or gasoline engines, allowed semi-skilled workers to build equipment like ships' engines and locomotives. These developments greatly expanded output—for example, in

World War I, when women workers were widely used. They also produced important labor conflict over the boundaries between skilled and factory operatives.

See also Wilkinson, John.

Reference Derry, Kingston, and T. I. Williams. *A Short History of Technology* (1961).

McKinley Tariff

The McKinley Tariff (1890), named after Senator (later President) William McKinley (1843–1901), aimed to protect industrialists, workers, and farmers from international competition. Typically, the Republican Party, of which McKinley was a member, advocated protective tariffs to shelter U.S. industries, whereas the Democratic Party supported tariffs only as a source of government revenue. McKinley's tariff was notable because it was far higher than most protective tariffs, and it was intended to be permanent and not just to support the rise of infant industries.

Malthus, Reverend Thomas Robert (1766–1834)

Thomas Robert Malthus was a British middle-class economist. He is most famous for his argument that whereas population can expand geometrically (1, 2, 4, 8), food production can expand only arithmetically (1, 2, 3, 4). Hence, Malthus defended wars, plagues, famines, and morality as checks on population. People who were influenced by Malthus's ideas on population defended the refusal of the British government to intervene massively in the Irish famine, since the deaths of Irish peasants were "inevitable." It was after reading Malthus that Thomas Carlyle declared economics to be the "dismal science." Malthus was the first economist to try to figure out the causes and consequences of what he called "gluts," which later economists would term depressions. Malthus's followers (Malthusians) tended to oppose welfare for the poor, which would increase their birth rate; some of Malthus's followers worked hard to encourage birth control in the nineteenth and early twentieth centuries within middle-class reform organizations but also in some labor movements.

See also Population Growth.

Reference Heilbroner, Robert L. *The Worldly Philosophers: The Lives, Times, and Ideas of the Great Economic Thinkers* (1986).

Managers

A manager is someone who directs a business or professional operation without owning it. Whereas people like managers existed before the industrial revolution, the term and the importance of managerial activity result from advancing industrialization. In the early industrial revolution in western Europe and the United States, most factories were managed by their owners, or at least by one member of an owning partnership. Maintaining older values, many factory owners placed great emphasis on the importance of their personal direction of most basic activities. They tried to run the factory, oversee supplies and sales, and keep up with the latest technology. If they needed additional staff help, they often turned to family members.

Fairly quickly, however, it became clear that expanding factories could not operate as a one-man band. Some activities had to be released to managers, who would take basic directions from owners but would have considerable latitude in running day-to-day operations. The expansion of corporations, where ownership was diffuse, also required increasing recruitment of managers. By the late nineteenth century, most industrial operations (and also many department stores, public utilities, and other activities) depended on direction from managers. Most managers were recruited from middle-class ranks. Some regretted the fact that they could not own outright; a number of British managers in the later nineteenth century believed that they had been downwardly mobile. But talented individuals could rise into management as well.

Managers on average had somewhat different interests from owners, and the tone of the industrial economy may have changed as operation was separated from ownership. Many managers were more highly educated than owners, and in a better position to apply new technology and to organize systematic industrial research. During the twentieth century the professional levels of management expanded; in Europe, for example, a "new breed" of manager took over many large enterprises after World War II, with backgrounds in engineering, economics, or law. Managers sometimes applied a longer-term perspective to their operations than owners did, less concerned about short-term profits. They may also have been more willing than owners to share some decision-making power with trade unions, less concerned with defending every owner prerogative and more eager for labor peace. These distinctions cannot be applied in every case, but it is possible that the rise of management over more traditional owner direction contributed to other shifts in industrial operations from the late nineteenth century onward.

See also Bureaucracy; Scientific Management.

References Chandler, Alfred. *The Visible Hand: The Managerial Revolution in American Business* (1977); Nelson, Daniel. *Managers and Workers: Origins of the New Factory System in the United States, 1880–1920* (1975).

Mao Zedong (1893–1976)

Mao Zedong led the Chinese Revolution (1949), which brought the Chinese Communist Party to power. Mao was the first Communist to emphasize the peasantry, rather than the urban working class, as a revolutionary force. As the leader of China, Mao sought to develop industry, but he also focused a great deal of attention on transforming the countryside. Collectivization of agriculture occurred more slowly and with far less brutality than in the Soviet Union. The first five-year plan was carried out from 1953 to 1957. It was somewhat successful but was followed by the overly ambitious Great Leap Forward. Mao's ideology stressed not only the necessary role of the revolutionary party but also egalitarian principles. Egalitarianism was emphasized during the Cultural Revolution (1966–1969), for example, piece rates for industrial workers were abolished and were only reinstalled in 1978 under Deng Xiaoping. Mao's policies, while sometimes inhibiting industrialization, helped to develop China's human and physical capital.

Maquiladoras

Maquiladoras are foreign-owned, export-oriented manufacturing plants located in Mexico. After 1945 Mexican workers could legally migrate to the United States through the *bracero* program, until it was terminated in 1964 by the United States. In 1965 Mexico and the United States began the Border Industrialization Program in order to create jobs in northern Mexico, thereby stemming illegal immigration. Under the maquiladora program, Mexican laws that limited foreign investment and U.S. import tariffs were relaxed. By the late 1980s over 300,000 Mexicans worked in over 1,500 factories throughout Mexico.

In the 1960s and 1970s, most maquiladora factories were in low-wage, labor-intensive industries such as garment making and electronics, and the majority of the employees were women. Although wages were relatively high for Mexico, working conditions were harsh (job-related diseases and injuries were common), and labor turnover was high. Since the 1980s, more capital-intensive industries such as automobiles have entered Mexico, and maquiladoras employ more skilled workers and professionals, an increasing number of them men. Some technologically advanced firms have developed in Mexico to provide services to foreign-owned factories. However, the Mexican government has discouraged workers from forming independent unions. Furthermore, because more people migrate to maquiladora areas than can find jobs, unemployment remains high in industrializing regions. Critics of the program also point out the burden that unrestrained industrialization and urbanization has placed on the delicate desert environment. The benefits of the system to the process of Mexican development are widely disputed.

Initially, the maquiladora program worked to the advantage of corporations in the United States that sought to take advantage of relatively cheap labor in order to win shares of foreign markets. The program became a more important source of foreign revenue to Mexico, however, after the collapse of oil prices in the early 1980s. In the wake of the devaluation of the Mexican peso, labor prices became even cheaper than before, and investment from Japan, Europe, or Canada accounted for half of all new investment in Mexico. Because of their Mexican factories, Japanese and European corporations can circumvent tariffs or quotas set by the United States. After the approval of the North American Free Trade Agreement in 1994, the maquiladora program, with its problems and potential, will continue to expand. Scholars predict that more small and medium-sized companies will also take advantage of the opportunities for investment in Mexico.

See also Deindustrialization; Division of Labor; Foreign Trade; Import Substitution; Postindustrial Economies.

References Faemi, Khosrow, ed. *The Maquiladora Industry: Economic Solution or Problem?* (1990); Fernandez-Kelly, Maria Patricia. *For We Are Sold, I and My People: Women and Industry in Mexico's Frontier* (1984).

Marconi, Guglielmo (1874–1937)

Marconi, an Italian engineer, developed what was first called wireless telegraphy, or radio. He was born into a wealthy Irish-Italian family and was early drawn to the study of electromagnetic waves. On his father's estate, he first set up an apparatus to receive and send signals by electrical waves, reaching longer distances than any had ever done before. The Italian government was uninterested, so Marconi sought funding in England, taking out a patent in 1896.

He formed the first wireless company the following year, installing wireless sets in British lighthouses. He sent the first wireless message across the Channel, a distance of 85 miles, in 1899. Radios were soon used on ships and proved vital in signaling emergencies. Marconi built a station to send signals across the Atlantic in 1901, managing to send a very faint "S" sound. Marconi continued to add to the distance radio messages could be sent, later experimenting with short waves. He commanded an Italian radio division in World War I.

Marconi's radio method involves the beam system, to and from aerials. A cathode-ray tube system was developed at almost the same time, by Ferdinand Braun. The two men shared the Nobel Prize for physics in 1909. Radios soon became vital not only for faster and more flexible communication but also to transmit entertainment, adding to the growing stock of consumer items.

Markets

People have traded commodities in markets for centuries, but the market as a system whereby land, goods, and labor (or services) can all be treated as commodities only arose in Europe in the last 500 years. In addition to the social and economic changes engendered by the rise of capitalism, the expansion of the market system helped to create an entirely new scholarly discipline: economics.

Adam Smith was one of the first economists to investigate the operation of the market system. Smith argued that competition among producers in a free or unregulated market becomes self-regulating—producers that attempt to overcharge customers are displaced by manufacturers with more modestly priced or better quality wares. The self-regulating nature of the free market, or what Smith termed the "invisible hand," became an important fixture of laissez-faire economic theory, which opposed governmental regulation of businesses or intervention to aid the poor. Smith castigated the assumptions of mercantilist governments that assumed that international trade was a zero-sum game; instead, Smith argued, free trade would allow different countries to specialize in products or services in which they developed a comparative advantage. However, Smith acknowledged that the government was not the only limit on free markets and noted that producers frequently attempted to circumvent the market by fixing prices or establishing cartels.

Despite the importance of laissez-faire as an ideology, even in the nineteenth century virtually no markets were free; they were regulated by national or imperial governments. Although the industrial revolution had made it possible for manufacturers to produce vastly increased amounts of goods, the question of who would buy these goods was more problematic, and access to markets, whether domestic, colonial, or foreign, was of crucial importance to industrialists. The success of latecomer industrializers all depended upon government's direct subsidies (notably the railroads) or indirect subsidies via tariffs. The quest for markets for individual goods was a contributing factor to the rise of imperialism.

Labor markets reflected the impact of growing number of workers selling their labor. Employers often tried to undercut pressures that might have raised wages by encouraging an increase in the labor supply. For example, industrialists often attracted immigrant workers to industrializing countries or used growing numbers of women or children.

By the late nineteenth century, the rise of large-scale corporations and cartels changed the dynamics of the market system. By acquiring their own sources of raw materials, transportation, and marketing systems (vertical integration), corporations created "internal markets" for goods, services, and labor. For instance, U.S. Steel had its own "captive" iron and coal mines whose products were transported to steel mills on the corporation's own system of ships and trains. The steel was sold to affiliated companies that produced ships, railroads, and skyscrapers. Competitors faced high costs to enter industries with technically advanced corporations that could also manipulate the market by dumping products at a loss, launching crippling lawsuits, or pressuring other corporations to boycott the newcomers' goods. Thus, though the invisible hand of the market does eliminate inefficient producers in the long run (often by competing corporations or cartels), in the short and medium run, the "visible hand" of the corporation plays a decisive role. Over the last twenty-five years, many corporations have turned to more flexible arrangements with their work forces and suppliers.

See also Capitalism; Mass Marketing; Postindustrial Economies; Profit; Protectionism.

References Heilbroner, Robert L. *The Worldly Philosophers: The Lives, Times, and Ideas of the Great Economic Thinkers* (1986); Chandler, Alfred D., Jr. *The Visible Hand: The Managerial Revolution in American Business* (1977).

Marshall Plan

In 1947 Secretary of State of the United States George C. Marshall (1880–1959) proposed a plan to rebuild the countries devastated by World War II. In the wake of the war, Marshall feared that Europe's economy would continue to decay and eventually fall under the influence of local communists and the Soviet Union. In the words of its namesake, the policy was directed "not against any country or doctrine but against hunger, poverty, desperation and chaos. Its purpose should be the revival of a working economy in the world so as to permit the emergence of political and social conditions in which free institutions can exist." At a point when capitalism was politically vulnerable, the Marshall Plan subsidized the expansion of the system of private enterprise.

The Marshall Plan offered a sharp contrast to the debilitating burdens placed on the defeated powers after World War I. Between 1945 and 1952 the United States offered approximately 20 billion dollars in grants (and several billion more in loans) to former allies and enemies in Europe and Asia. The Marshall Plan prevented economic bottlenecks from developing and encouraged the reindustrialization of Europe in order to expand world trade (and, coincidentally, to provide an immediate market for U.S. capital goods). The Marshall Plan allocated its grants only to countries that structured their economies along procapitalist lines; furthermore, countries were required to coordinate their economic planning in order to stimulate an international division of labor (this ultimately resulted in the Organization of European Economic Cooperation). The Soviet Union refused to accept the conditions of the Marshall Plan and prevented Eastern Europe from accepting grants or loans from the United States.

In both economic and political terms, the Marshall Plan was a remarkable success. Between 1950 and the late 1960s, Western Europe underwent a period of rapid economic growth. By 1963 the European economy was 250 percent larger than it had been in 1940. Furthermore, Western Europe enjoyed a period of social cohesion that allowed the liberal parliamentary system to take hold in Germany, Italy, and other industrial countries. The Marshall Plan undermined the appeal of the communist strategy of industrial development that yielded relatively lower standards of living for the majority of its citizens. The Marshall Plan established one crucial aspect of foreign aid in the post–World War II era, that capital loaned to recipient nations has to be spent in contracts with firms from the lending nation. However, nearly all subsequent aid through the World Bank or the U.S. Agency for International Development was in the form of loans, not grants.

Reference Wexler, Imanuel. *The Marshall Plan Revisited: The European Recovery Program in Economic Perspective* (1983).

Marx, Karl (1818–1883)

Karl Marx was a German philosopher whose all-embracing analysis of capitalism has endured as a basis for studying economics, society, and politics. Marx had an important influence on the nineteenth-century socialist movement through his numerous polemical and analytical writings on economics and contemporary political events. Marx often collaborated with Friedrich Engels, and their work has had a profound influence upon many activists, workers, and scholars.

Marx was born to a middle-class Jewish family, which sent him through the German university system. Marx earned a Ph.D., but the anti-Semitic policies of the Prussian government prevented him from obtaining a faculty position, and Marx plunged into a career as a liberal journalist. Marx's polemics caused the government to suppress the paper. By 1843 Marx had embarked on a journey through France, Belgium, and England. Partly in response to his contact with socialistic workers, Marx began to work out a critique of capitalism, which in his view inherently alienated workers; Marx also elaborated a humanistic vision of communism in which peoples' physical, social, and psychic needs would be realized.

By the late 1840s Marx had started to work out his theory that the driving forces of history have been changes in forms of production. Marx viewed capitalism as a revolutionary force that not only dramatically increased the productive capacity of humanity (through the industrial revolution) but transformed all social and political relationships as well as cultural and intellectual forms. In Marx's view, the revolutionary forces unleashed by capitalist and industrial production would periodically cause crises (more profound than depressions) that could enable the working class to someday come to power. Marx and Engels were commissioned by a group of revolutionary workers to write the *Communist Manifesto*, which appeared in print during the revolutions of 1848. Repression, however, not workers' republics, was the immediate result of these revolutions, and Marx spent the rest of his life in self-imposed exile in England.

Despite the failure of the 1848 revolutions, Marx continued his work in exile, throwing himself into organizing the first workers' International, writing for news-

Philosopher, economist, historian, and revolutionary, Karl Marx believed that capitalism and the industrial revolution would make socialism possible.

papers, commenting on political events of the day (such as the Paris Commune of 1871), and producing his monumental study of capitalism. Marx received some money from his writings, but his chief support came from Engels, whose family owned textile factories—still, Marx and his family lived in poverty. Many of his writings were published posthumously by Engels. Marxism became the leading intellectual support of socialism and communism, though it was subsequently adjusted and modified. Marx's insights about social classes and power inform much research on the industrial revolution to this day.

See also Lenin; Long Waves of Capitalism; Primitive Accumulation; Surplus Value; Utopian Socialists.

References McLellan, David. *Karl Marx: His Life and Thought* (1974); Marx, Karl. *Capital: A Critique of Political Economy* (1967).

Marxism

Marxism is the intellectual tradition that applies the theories and methods of Karl Marx (1818–1883) to history, economics, and society. Although Marx is generally known as an economic theorist, his work attempted to depict the dynamic historical relationships among economics, society, politics, and culture. The social and intellectual history of Marxism has been influenced by the development and reorganization of industrial capitalism and the working class itself.

Marx argued that the economic development of societies and the struggle between social classes have been the forces behind fundamental historical change. Marx saw history as a constant struggle between classes over the means of production. In his day, the crucial struggle pitted workers against capitalists, and Marx foresaw that workers would triumph, and an egalitarian society of abundance with no government would eventually follow. Consequently, Marx himself and many Marxists were involved in what Marx termed the "workers' movement" (trade unions, Internationals, and socialist parties). However, Marxism was not so much a theory of insurrection as a way to guide workers toward socialism through a better understanding of the workings of capitalism. When Marx began his analysis of capitalism, the industrial revolution was still a relatively recent phenomenon and the working class still relatively small. Ironically, it would be the consolidation of industrial capitalism through what Marxists termed monopoly capitalism and imperialism that would throw Marxism and the socialist movement into turmoil. As a few large companies took over most production—monopoly capitalism—and Europe expanded its colonies, working-class conditions became more complex, which generated various disputes about Marxist predictions and prescriptions.

Marxism provided a grand revolutionary theory of history and a scathing critique of capitalism, and it impressed many workers and political leaders. But Marxism was a fractured and argumentative intellectual tradition, claimed and contested by those believed that a classless society could only be won via revolution (such as communists) and those who favored more gradual reforms (such as Social Democrats). Those divisions became more pronounced during World War I, when many reformists supported the war— in violation of their pledges to international solidarity among workers—and revolutionaries opposed the war. The split between reformists and revolutionaries deepened after the war. Revolutionaries helped create the first "workers' state" in relatively backward Russia, not in the more advanced industrial countries with stronger social democratic parties such as Germany, Austria, or Hungary. In 1919–1920 insurgent workers in Germany and Austria attempted their own revolutions and were repressed by social democratic parties.

Since the 1920s Marxism has been strongly influenced by the Leninist tradition, which gave the crucial role of leading the workers' movement to the highly disciplined workers' party, rather than to the trade unions. Because communists were the only major group who resisted fascism in France and Italy, Marxists enjoyed an important political and intellectual role after World War II. Furthermore, Marxism-Leninism became an important ideology for revolutionaries in Latin America and in decolonization struggles in Asia and Africa. Marxist-Leninists began to argue that although industrialization was necessary for a socialist society, revolution itself was more likely in countries on the periphery of the world system.

In Europe, communist and social democratic parties helped to improve the standards of living of workers via the welfare state; ironically, most communist parties became nearly as reformist as social democratic parties. And though communist parties in Eastern Europe, Asia, or Latin America improved living standards for the mass of its citizenry, none was able to create a classless society of abundance. In fact, many dissident Marxists began to argue that the Soviet Union's Communist Party had itself become a new ruling class. The loyalty to the Soviet Union demanded by communist parties stifled the creativity of Marxist intellectuals, whose work was generally of a lower quality than before the 1920s. In fact, after the 1940s an increasing number of Western Marxists refused to affiliate with communist parties, and the center of Marxist thought decisively shifted to the university system. In the postwar world, investigations into philosophy, art, history, and literature rather than economics, organizing, or politics became the norm for Marxists in Western countries.

The growing crisis and subsequent collapse of socialism in the Soviet Union, Eastern Europe, and the rest of the world has caused many Marxists to renounce the possibility, and even desirability, of a socialist society. Marxism nonetheless retains some vitality. As early as the 1920s, a dissident tradition, led by Communists such as Antonio Gramsci and Leon Trotsky, began to criticize the excessively totalitarian nature of the Soviet Union and the Communist parties' inability to effectively resist fascism. The insights and intellectual frameworks of Marxists such as Gramsci and Trotsky have become increasingly important to intellectuals and some branches of the Communist movement.

See also Communism; Russian Revolution of 1917; Stalinism.

Reference Anderson, Perry. *Considerations on Western Marxism* (1976).

Masculinity

The industrial revolution undermined traditional masculinity but permitted important new expressions of masculine power and competence. Industrial workers had little access to property, but because preindustrial masculine maturity had been based on ownership, workers continued to insist on trying to control their wives and children. Industrial work forced men to labor under the supervision of others and reduced the demand for many traditional masculine skills, such as weaving. Even sheer strength could be challenged by machines, as the nineteenth-century U.S. folk song "John Henry" demonstrated. For the growing middle class, industrialization meant office work, where, again, masculine physical prowess could be hard to demonstrate.

Men in both the middle and the working classes reacted to these challenges by vaunting masculinity in new ways from the late eighteenth century onward. Many European and American men sought sexual domination over women: taunts and even violent sexual attacks against women workers increased during the period of early industrialization. Middle-class men, as in Western Europe and the United States in the mid-nineteenth century, promoted the ideology that men were the stronger sex, alone capable of work and political action, whereas women, gentle and moral, were essential to care for the home. Workers and reform-minded businessmen alike supported laws that limited women's hours of work, thus promoting the domestic sphere as proper for women while also making them less competitive in the workplace. Workers often excluded women from trade unions and limited their role in protests, while developing a strongly masculine leisure culture that emphasized drinking, fighting, and sports. This working-class machismo lasted well into the twentieth century. Crucial to all urban classes was the nineteenth-century emphasis on the man as principal breadwinner, whose arduous work and earnings were vital for his family's survival. Men who proved incapable of supporting their families were considered abject failures.

Some of the initial assertions of masculinity were modified as women demanded new rights. Nevertheless, the industrial definition of masculinity, the product of major changes and stresses, continues to exercise some influence even at the end of the twentieth century.

See also Dual Labor Markets; Feminism; Franchise.

References Carnes, Mark, Clyde Griffen, et al. *Meanings of Manhood* (1990); Stearns, Peter N. *Be a Man: Males in Modern Society* (1990).

Mass Marketing

Mass marketing systems designed to sell products to large number of buyers arose in the late nineteenth century as corporations sought to capture or create large-scale demand for a rapidly increasing volume of products. Before the 1850s merchants advertised the availability and prices of their wares in local newspapers; by the 1860s companies had begun to aggressively advertise their products using pictures, stories, and photographs in newspapers and national magazines. Companies sought to differentiate their products from those of their competitors and were able to take advantage of improvements in packaging technologies (canning, paper wrappers, and so on) to build a distinctive "name brand" for household products such as soap, canned foods, and kerosene as well as more expensive items such as sewing machines and farm implements.

The sewing machine was the first major "consumer durable." By the 1870s its manufacturers had developed many of the production, advertising, and distribution techniques that would later be applied to most products. In the 1830s and 1840s, sewing machines were unwieldy, relatively expensive items, and disagreements among companies over who held patents to crucial technologies discouraged improvements. In the late 1850s, companies established a "patent pool"; as a result, the quality of machines improved and prices eventually dropped. In the 1860s, for example, the members of the patent pool sold less than 80,000 units a year, but, by the mid-1870s, sales had risen to over 350,000 a year—with many of the machines exported to England and other foreign markets. Singer emerged as the dominant company, in part because customers could place an order with a traveling sales agent or purchase a sewing machine directly from the company rather than depending on large retail outlets.

After the 1870s mail-order commerce increased as department stores took advantage of the lower postal rates that resulted from the completion of a national railroad network. In 1872 the Montgomery Ward company published its first catalog, and by the 1890s many other companies, notably Sears and Roebuck, had also published massive catalogs. Mail order catalogs, important in their own right for increasing the sales of certain products, also offered residents of isolated rural communities a wider range of products. The catalogs also helped spread the culture of consumerism beyond the middle-class patrons of urban department stores. Mail-order catalogs became such a fixture of U.S. culture that many observers lamented the decision of Sears, Roebuck in the late 1980s to cease publication of its annual catalog.

By the end of the nineteenth century, industrialists had created national and international markets for a wide variety of products. Large corporations or cartels, such as Westinghouse and General Electric, had the resources to take advantage of the emerging advertising industry and were in the best position to exploit national markets. Early on, corporations sold not only their products but their corporate image. In 1908, for instance, AT&T advertised the virtues of a "regulated private monopoly" in the telephone industry. By the 1910s and 1920s, advertising increased in importance for corporations and solidified as an indus-

The cover of the 1896 Sears, Roebuck catalog. The mail order catalogs made millions of people in the countryside familiar with the growing diversity of mass-manufactured goods.

try in its own right. In the heady days of the 1920s, advertisers claimed that by stimulating demand, they could even end the phenomenon of business cycles, in which production and employment fluctuated radically.

One of the most important pioneers of mass marketing was Henry Ford, who mass produced the Model T, a durable, cheap "car for the great multitude." Ford's business became the world's largest industrial company, but by the late 1920s General Motors had begun to produce Chevrolets that offered consumers more options than Ford's Model T. Although a few industrialists, notably Ford, believed advertising was a waste of money, even he found it necessary to advertise in order to compete with General Motors. By the late 1920s carmakers were attempting to lure customers by subtly changing each annual model. Critics charged that companies refused to use all of their new technology in each new model and in fact engineered a short product life—what was called "planned obsolescence."

Certain mass-produced and mass-marketed products have come to symbolize the appeal of industrialized countries' consumerism. Companies such as McDonald's, Coca-Cola, or Levi's have developed world markets by offering consumers a strictly standardized product produced in conditions closely resembling an assembly line. According to these companies' considerable advertising, consumers are purchasing not only food, drink, or clothing but flexibility, freedom, and fun.

See also Cartels; Multinational Corporations; Sloan, Alfred P.

References Marchand, Roland. *Advertising the U.S. Dream: Making Way for Modernity, 1920–1940* (1985); Tedlow, Richard S. *New and Improved: The Story of Mass Marketing in America* (1990).

Mass Media

Mass media, communications outlets designed for mass consumption, emerged first in the form of large-circulation daily newspapers. Middle-class papers like the New York *Tribune* began bidding for larger audiences after the mid-nineteenth century, but the true mass press, selling to one to two million readers, arrived in the 1890s, with offerings like the London *Daily Mail* or the Berlin *Lokal-Anzeiger*. Industrial technology was essential to the mass media. Improvements in printing, which can be dated to the 1830s, included faster, steam-driven presses and methods of translating photographs to the printing press. Cheaper manufacturing of paper came in the 1850s from using wood pulp instead of rag. In the 1890s, automatic composing machines allowed semi-skilled typesetting from keyboards to replace highly skilled manual setting. Advances in photography facilitated illustration.

Industrialization also created large urban audiences—literate, but eager for entertaining, even sensationalized fare. Bold headlines, simple writing, and features such as sports, women's columns, and comics, offered readers escape from the daily routine. Advertisers reached these consumers with eye-catching pitches for cosmetics, clothes, bicycles, and diet products. Advertising revenues helped keep prices low; the mass-circulation papers sold for just pennies in 1900.

The principles of mass newspapers—advanced technology, simple and dramatic messages, and abundant advertisements—extended to later mass media, from radio to television.

See also Advertising.

Meatpacking

Beginning in the seventeenth century, preparation of meat was controlled by small-scale commercial butchers. In the late nineteenth century, large corporations with centralized production facilities (packing houses) displaced local butchers, effectively industrializing this branch of food processing. The new companies relied on a detailed division of labor along "disassembly lines" to produce meat that was canned or shipped fresh via refrigerated railroad cars through national (or, in the case of Argentina or Australia, international) distribution networks. In the United States, corporate meatpacking followed the development of large-scale commercial cattle raising and helped to spur the creation of factorylike feedlots in which hundreds of thousands of animals were prepared for slaughter. In *The Jungle*, Upton Sinclair savagely described the brutal working conditions of immigrant workers in the Chicago meatpacking industry in the early twentieth century. Middle-class readers focused on the images of rotten and spoiled meat and pressed for government inspection—leaving workers to struggle alone to improve working conditions, for durable industrial unions were not established until the 1930s. In the mid-twentieth century, industrialists took advantage of trucking technology by locating smaller packing houses in rural areas, near a ready supply of animals and frequently non-union labor.

See also Armour, Philip Danforth; Industrial Unions.

References Barrett, James R. *Work and Community in the Jungle: Chicago's Packinghouse Workers, 1894–1922* (1987); Sinclair, Upton. *The Jungle* (1988).

Mechanization

Mechanization refers to the replacement of human skill or power by machines. Powerful forces encouraged mechanization: the industrial revolution involved a shift from human, wind, and animal power to steam, electricity, and oil, while the logic of capitalism forced employers to attempt to replace workers with machines whenever possible. The basic principle of mechanization relied on power-driven machinery to produce more than workers could manage with hand tools. Mechanization began first in the eighteenth century in manufacturing processes (such as textiles or shoemaking), but by the early nineteenth century mechanization had proven to exercise a pervasive and powerful influence over the lives of ordinary people. Even when people did not come into direct contact with machines, mechanized products replaced previously homemade goods such as textiles or candles, encouraging a greater dependence upon the market.

By the late nineteenth century, mechanization had completely transformed the homes of ordinary people with domestic production equipment, such as sewing machines, and manufactured consumer items, such as kerosene lamps and factory-produced rugs and wallpaper. By the 1920s the spread of electric power, combined with central heating and indoor plumbing, allowed new levels of comfort for middle-class families—changes that were accompanied by new standards of cleanliness. The spread of air conditioners later in the century allowed many people to control indoor temperature throughout the year. The spread of air conditioning to urban workers and the southern United States has had the effect of slowly undermining older forms of summertime sociability that centered around the porch. As people have gained greater control over their environment, distinctive regional forms of architecture have declined, to be replaced by standardized tract housing.

Mechanized transportation and communication has transformed people's sense of time and space. Railroads and steamships lowered the costs of the postal system, allowing increased business and personal communication. Telegraph networks accelerated this process and enabled newspapers to cover national and international news with greater speed. Prior to the electric streetcar, most people lived within walking distance of their workplace, but by the late nineteenth century the middle and upper classes in the United States could commute from semi-rural suburbs. By the 1910s, the automobile accelerated the process of suburbanization, and the decentralization of business was influenced by "automobility" and telephone networks that facilitated communication between branches of a corporation. The effects of mechanization on the lives of ordinary people continue to accelerate.

See also Automation.

Reference Giedion, Siegfried. *Mechanization Takes Command: A Contribution to Anonymous History* (1969).

Meiji Restoration

Japan was the first non-European country to successfully industrialize. In the mid-nineteenth century, Japan was a feudal society, closed to contact with the world and dominated by a class of warriors or samurai; today it is the world's most advanced producer of automobiles, steel, and electronics. Japan's rapid transformation began in the 1850s, when Russia, the United States, and Britain forced the Tokugawa government to open Japan's ports to commerce. The response of the Japanese government to this external challenge to its authority laid the groundwork for Japan's industrialization. The Meiji restoration was the period between 1868, when the Japanese emperor called Meiji, or "enlightenment," was "restored" to power, and 1912, when the emperor died.

The opening of Japan to foreign traders created a political crisis for the nation's ruling class of samurai warriors. The crisis was eventually resolved by restoring (at least symbolically) the emperor as the nation's leader. The Meiji restoration was less a return to monarchy, however, than a complete transformation of the social and economic basis of the nation from feudalism to capitalism. A small group of bureaucrats (acting in the name of the emperor) enacted far-reaching land reform. Samurai were quickly stripped of their feudal privileges in exchange for stipends; many samurai became bureaucrats in government and industry. Although Japanese farmers had extensive experience with commerce, they could no longer pay their taxes in kind (for instance, with rice) but had to pay cash. Common lands previously used by poorer peasants to gather wood or graze cattle were sold to individuals. The economic surplus gathered by the state provided the basis for industrialization schemes.

The Meiji government also transformed education, stressing nationalism, loyalty to the emperor, and technical fields of study over Confucian ethics. Japan had had high rates of literacy before 1868, and the Meiji regime improved upon this tradition. Universities were established to train the new bureaucratic, business, and technical elites. The Meiji government actively supported industrialization by establishing facilities and then selling them off to favored companies, which generally received monopolies. In the 1870s, the Mitsubishi zaibatsu (business combination) was given a government loan to buy a shipping company previously owned by a European company. Other zaibatsu were also extended remarkably favorable terms to purchase factories, although the government itself ran the railroads, telegraphs, and armories. The government favored policies that kept wages low in order to maintain a competitive advantage in world markets.

Although the government's policies caused widespread hardship for the majority of the population and centralized economic power in a few hands, Japan did avoid becoming reliant upon foreign producers or banks. For instance, the Japanese government relied on foreign technicians to set up a centralized mint and banking system, but unlike the governments of China and India, the Japanese government expelled the foreigners within ten years. In fact, the government's concern with developing itself as a major military power was a dominant theme in its pursuit of industrial development. As one historian observed, "By 1910 Japan had completed the largest battleship in the world, the Satsuma, but had built no textile machinery at all."

See also Enclosure Movement; Imperialism.

Reference Akamatsu, Paul. *Meiji 1868: Revolution and Counter-Revolution in Japan* (1972).

Mellon, Andrew (1855–1937)

Andrew Mellon was the son of a prominent Pittsburgh banker, Thomas "Judge" Mellon. Andrew Mellon joined his father's bank in 1874 and assumed control of it in 1882. Mellon built his fortune by supplying capital to emerging industries and gaining substantial holdings in such companies as oil (Gulf Oil), aluminum (Aluminum Company of America or Alcoa), and coke making (Koppers). Always alert for business opportunities, Mellon helped to establish a construction firm that made locks for the Panama Canal. In 1921 President Warren G. Harding named Mellon secretary of the treasury, a post he held until 1932. Mellon favored lowering taxes on the wealthy and paying off the government's debt, policies that became the subject of much derision during the Great Depression. An indication of his wealth (and taste) can be gauged by the fact that Mellon's personal donation of art and capital constituted the initial collection of the National Gallery of Art.

See also Finance Capital.

Mercantilism

This set of economic beliefs dominated European thinking during the seventeenth and much of the eighteenth centuries. It fit well with the growing military and diplomatic competition among national monarchies. Mercantilists sought economic systems that would maximize national wealth; above all, they wanted to increase the supply of precious metals and the tax base of the national government. Believing that the total wealth of the world was a fixed quantity, mercantilist theories advocated measures that would help one's own nation get a larger slice of the pie, automatically diminishing other nations in the process.

Characteristic mercantilist devices included high tariffs to promote internal manufacturing; promotion of exports; abolition of barriers to internal trade and improved roads; acquisition of colonies to assure cheap imports of raw materials that would not diminish the national treasure; and detailed regulations to encourage consumption of goods produced at home, to promote national industries, and so on. France, under Louis XIV and his finance minister Colbert, became a mercantilist center in the late seventeenth century. A version of mercantilism called cameralism spread in central Europe, helping monarchs like Frederick the Great of Prussia to promote the cultivation of potatoes to increase population (another mercantilist goal), to encourage foreign merchants to settle in Prussia, and to sponsor expositions to promote new technology.

Mercantilism helped prepare the way for industrialization in some respects. Promotion of shipbuilding or tariff protection of new industry could have positive results. For instance, mercantilist encouragement to exports spurred some industry and trade. Detailed regulations of methods of work attempted by Colbert, however, probably dampened innovation. By the middle of the eighteenth century, economists were attacking mercantilist ideas, arguing that wealth was not a fixed entity but could be increased and claiming that unfettered competition, not protection and regulation, would best serve prosperity. Adam Smith was the liberal economist who most decisively unseated mercantilist beliefs. Elements of mercantilism unquestionably survived, particularly in the temptation to use tariff policy as an element in national competitions, even though the theory itself disappeared.

See also Laissez-faire; Protectionism; World Systems Theory.

Reference Hecksher, Eli. *Mercantilism* (1953).

Merchant Capital

Merchants helped to break down feudalism in Western Europe and supplied nascent industrialists with capital, raw materials, and markets; in short, merchants played an important role in the industrial revolution. Merchants actually profited, however, from circulation of commodities, not from production. Therefore, merchants could work with a variety of social forms other than wage labor, such as slavery and sharecropping. "Merchant capital" is how some historians have described the double role that merchants have played not only in the circulation of commodities but in the creation of social systems within the world system. According to the Marxist view, merchant capital is opportunistic and strengthens social systems that rely on unfree labor—even as it helps draw those societies deeper within the nexus of production for the market. Merchants have also sometimes distrusted industrialization and looked down on industrialists as newcomers and exploiters.

See also Profit.

References Fox-Genovese, Elizabeth, and Eugene D. Genovese. *Fruits of Merchant Capital: Slavery and Bourgeois Property in the Rise and Expansion of Capitalism* (1983); Miller, Joseph C. *Way of Death: Merchant Capitalism and the Angolan Slave Trade, 1730–1830* (1988).

Merchants

Merchants are people who trade goods, and their social and economic role long predates industrialization. All urban societies have merchants, and some traditions, such as that of Islam, give merchants a vital social status.

Merchants have been essential to industrialization in many ways, even as industrialization has forced important changes and even hostility among merchant groups. European merchants had been expanding their activities well before the industrial revolution, indeed since the Middle Ages. Trade overseas, from the fifteenth century onward, helped establish new markets for manufactured goods while bringing new capital to European shores. By the eighteenth century various merchants were stimulating a domestic market to express new tastes for products such as textiles and pottery. Merchants also helped organize the expanding domestic manufacturing system to supply goods for their trade. Urban merchants bought quantities of raw material that was distributed to workers in their homes, then returned as finished products to the merchants for wider sale. In all these ways—by stimulating markets, acquiring capital, and promoting manufacturing—merchants helped set the stage for industrialization in Europe and the United States.

Nonetheless, many established merchants suffered from industrialization. They disliked the change. They found factories dirty and despised the upstart industrialists who, however, might well soon be earning more money than their conservative colleagues. Many old merchant firms failed; such failures were a common pattern in Meiji Japan. Other enterprises survived but stagnated, their families sometimes producing intellectuals, like the Brahmins of Boston, critical of industrial life in the name of higher cultural values. Other established merchants partnered with new entrepreneurs, supplying capital but staying out of the factory process itself.

Industrialization quickly generated new needs for merchant activity. Merchants willing to innovate, to devise new methods of disposing of vast quantities of goods, participated directly in the ongoing industrial revolution. Pioneers of department stores or, in the United States, mail-order operations helped fuel industrial sales. Many innovations utilized some of the same principles of standardization, division of labor, and intensive direction of workers that had proved successful in factories. At this level, the industrial revolution stimulated a great change in merchant life, including new opportunities and access to new wealth.

Industrial cities also generated growing numbers of smaller merchants, who also sold a multiplying array of goods to rising urban and village populations. Some shopkeepers expanded, becoming full-blown merchants. Others, however, preserved a family business—the famous mom-and-pop store—and hovered uncertainly on the edges of the industrial world. Many shopkeepers disliked aspects of industrialization, including the expansion of big corporations. Many, drawing their clientele from workers, sympathized with labor protest. By the late nineteenth century, some had turned to rightist movements like the anti-Semitic parties in France and Germany to express their insecurity in a world increasingly dominated by big business. This shift underlay anti-industrial protest through the fascist decades of the twentieth century and again demonstrated the complexities of the relationship between merchants and the industrial economy.

See also Causes of the Industrial Revolution; Department Stores; Domestic Manufacturing; Entrepreneurial Spirit; Merchant Capital.

References Braudel, Fernand. *The Wheels of Com-*

merce (1979); Cipolla, Carlo, ed. *The Fontana Economic History of Europe* (1970).

Mergers

Mergers, the joining of two or more companies together, occurred at all stages of the industrial revolution. They were part of the reason for the growth of average firm size, as bigger firms offered efficiencies and economies of scale over their smaller counterparts. Many early industrial firms merged smaller operations as partnerships. In the late nineteenth century, mergers played a vital role in vertical integration, in which companies developed operations at all stages of the production process, from new materials to finished goods. Steel companies like Carnegie merged with coal mines, creating a chain of reliable supply, from raw materials up to the finished product. Shipping companies like Japan's Mitsubishi merged with shipbuilding operations. Mergers also began to allow companies to gain new international subsidiaries, a pattern that accelerated in the twentieth century. Mergers might be friendly junctures, like the partnerships in the early textiles or pottery industries, or unpleasant takeovers of weaker rivals. In capitalist countries in the twentieth century some mergers had nothing to do with productivity advantages but with stock manipulations and tax breaks, raising questions about the impact of certain mergers on the overall economy.

See also Corporations; Multinational Corporations.

Methodism

See Religion.

Mexico

The present Mexican government was born in a long and bloody revolution (1911–1920) in which peasants and workers sought to gain access to land and decent jobs. The struggle was inconclusive; workers and peasants gained many legal rights, but they were enforced sporadically. Mexico's chief assets in this period were mineral—by 1920 Mexico was the world's second largest oil producer and the industry was nationalized in 1938. Some industrial development had occurred before the revolution—in brewing, for example—but the revolution itself set back the economy. The government encouraged industrial growth after World War II with a strong emphasis on steel, petrochemicals, and infrastructure projects such as improving roads and electrical systems. Over a quarter of the labor force entered the manufacturing sector and began to acquire some consumer goods. Although the economy grew rapidly, it failed to provide decent jobs to many workers and peasants, many of whom migrated to the United States for seasonal or permanent employment. The large role of the state (which accounted for one-fifth of all jobs) was reversed in the early 1980s, when falling oil revenues and a mounting debt crisis pushed Mexico's elite to deregulate large parts of the economy. Although many foreign companies have set up factories in Mexico, it is unclear whether they will raise standards of living and resolve Mexico's long-standing crisis.

See also Maquiladoras.

Middle Class

The middle class is not easy to define. As it emerged in the nineteenth century in Western Europe, it fell beneath the aristocracy; its members did not have titles, and they did not possess as much wealth as the great magnates, but they did rise above the working classes. Middle-class people did not work with their hands: they normally owned property or had a professional skill. On average their educational levels were higher than those of the working classes.

Many members of the middle class had developed a common culture. They believed in science and in the importance of business and economic growth. They had faith in progress and liberal values. They wanted political rights and constitutional government. They adhered, at least in principle, to an ethic of hard work. Many of these values informed the willing participation of the middle class in the industrial revolution, in which they served as factory owners and merchants or as lawyers or doctors assisting other segments of the middle class.

At the same time, however, certain segments of the middle class, even while embracing seemingly common values, responded to the industrial revolution quite differently. An older segment of the middle class, sometimes called the bourgeoisie, was accustomed to preindustrial urban life. They thought in terms of security, not change, and did not willingly invest in new industry. Some of these people opposed industrialization outright, sympathizing, for example, with working-class protest against factory conditions. Some merchants thus backed strikers in factory towns such as Paterson, New Jersey, or supported Luddism in England.

Professional people often resented the gains of factory owners. During the industrial revolution many professionals updated their credentials, claiming access to important new knowledge (like advances in medical science) and imposing new tests and licensing procedures. These new professional standards helped doctors and lawyers participate in industrial society, but tension still arose. Individual professionals sometimes supported labor movements or other activities directed against industrialists. Thus a professor of philosophy, Jean Jaurès, spearheaded French socialism around 1900.

The most successful factory owners pulled away from the middle class into a new upper middle class with special ties with the aristocracy. Even in the United States, where no aristocracy existed, a plutocracy emerged after the Civil War that had little contact with ordinary middle-class folk, though they might advocate some common values.

In the late nineteenth century, a lower middle class developed, composed of people with no property but engaged in nonmanual occupations such as school teaching or clerical work. Again, this group could share middle-class values—it was much less likely to unionize, for example, than blue-collar workers—but its employment conditions resembled those of other workers.

Analyzing the middle class during the industrial revolution means, then, understanding the tension between shared conditions and values and very different specific reactions, including attitudes to industrialization itself. The middle class did, however, define standards of polite behavior, support generally liberal politics, and foster business and technological change that on balance provided a favorable context for industrial growth. It tended to criticize real or imagined working-class habits, like heavy drinking, in the name of respectability. Societies that began to industrialize later, like Russia by the 1890s, also developed a middle class in the process, though the group was smaller and spoke with a weaker political voice. Middle classes, defined in terms of mid-level wealth, business or professional commitment, and some shared values, have also been identified in societies with growing industrial sectors in the twentieth century, such as Latin America and India.

In industrial societies themselves, middle-class definitions have become still more complicated during the twentieth century. In the United States, growing affluence and the dominance of some middle-class values led a vast majority of the population to claim it was middle class by the 1950s. Blue collar workers joined the class, in their own estimation, simply because of a shared standard of living. As more members of the middle class became employed as technicians, managers, and professionals rather than as independent owners, several criteria of the nineteenth-century middle class clearly changed. Middle-class culture also evolved. The kind of respectability defined in the nineteenth century obviously shifted when the middle class embraced consumer values more fully, tolerated more expressive sexuality, and fostered new roles for women. Some core values, however, including faith in science and technical progress, survived. As nonmanual labor expanded, the middle class naturally grew quite rapidly, making it still a vital ingredient of industrial society.

See also Ruling Class; White-Collar Workers.

References Ghosh, Suniti. *The Big Indian Bourgeoisie. Its Genesis, Growth and Character* (1985); Pilbeam, Pamela. *The Middle Classes in Europe, 1789–1914. France, Germany, Italy and Russia* (1990); Stearns, Peter N., and Herrick Chapman. *European Society in Upheaval: A Social History since 1750* (1992).

Middle East

This historic region between the Mediterranean and the Indian Ocean now consists of many nations and varied economies. As a whole the Middle East was slow to respond to Western industrialization. The dominant Ottoman Empire was not an innovator in economic policy, and Muslim tradition discouraged imitation of Christian Europe. The region lagged behind technologically in the seventeenth and eighteenth centuries. The growth of European military power led to takeovers of key areas (particularly in North Africa) by the mid-nineteenth century and to increased political and commercial pressure on the Ottoman empire itself. Several reformers, notably Muhammed Ali in Egypt, attempted to spur industrial growth, without major success. The Ottoman Empire did begin to encourage mining and infrastructure; a postal system was established in 1834, a telegraph system in 1855, and railway construction began in 1866 onward. In the meantime, European commercial influence grew. Oil was discovered in the Middle East early in the twentieth century, and for decades it was exploited mainly by Western companies. In 1912 a European conglomerate formed the Turkish Petroleum Company to exploit reserves in Iraq; Saudi Arabia was dominated by the U.S. Standard Oil Company beginning in the 1930s.

Successful industrial efforts began to take shape, though slowly, after World War I. A new regime in Iran practiced the policy of import substitution; that is, it set up enough factories to supply most national needs and reduce dependence on imports. Iran also managed to retain some control over its oil reserves. Turkey meanwhile developed its own industrial base. In 1961, after individual oil-producing nations gained more control over oil profits by nationalizing or heavily regulating the Western companies, the leading oil producers formed the Organization of Petroleum Exporting Countries (OPEC). This strategy increased oil profits immensely by providing investment funds, and petroleum-based industries, technical training, and some wider industrialization all increased. To be sure, no full industrial revolution occurred; climate, population growth, and heavy military expenditures all hindered rapid development. Nonetheless, substantial industrial sectors existed in most Middle Eastern countries by the late twentieth century.

Military Industrial Complex

When Dwight Eisenhower left the office of the U.S. presidency in 1961, he warned the country of the growing power of a "military industrial complex." Eisenhower was referring to the increasingly symbiotic relationship between the military and the corporations that had become dependent upon military contracts during the Cold War. In fact, the relationship between the military and manufacturing has been important for five hundred years.

The rising European economic dominance over the world system of trade in the sixteenth century was due in large part to Europeans' use of superior cannons and ships. Military competition among emerging European nation states for control over shipping lanes and sugar plantations in the seventeenth and eighteenth centuries fostered the rise of the industrial system. England encouraged its manufacturers, particularly of cannons, guns, and ships, to compensate for the relatively few sailors and soldiers that it could muster.

Throughout the nineteenth century, the perceived military requirements of gov-

U.S.S. Liberty *ships under construction in 1943. Mass manufactured ships, produced with newly trained women and black men, were crucial to the Allied victory in World War II.*

ernments had an enormous impact on industrialization in many countries. Many of the new technologies and organizational innovations used in the development of the U.S. factory system were begun in the Springfield Armory, a weapons center in western Massachusetts. The global arms race among European powers throughout the nineteenth century expanded the industrial base of many countries as each government sought a domestic supply of armaments. Indeed, the Krupp family built an industrial empire by supplying the German government with military equipment. Russian industrialization resulted in no small part from the desire of the czars for military equipment. By the early twentieth century, the Meiji government of Japan had built its first battleship, though it had yet to build its own textile machinery. Although the British navy retained its dominance in the naval arms race prior to World War I, the British steel industry and shipyards did not keep up, and gradually these manufacturers became reliant upon the government to purchase its goods.

Although military spending stimulated the development of many industries, the human cost of this form of development has been staggering. The nineteenth-century arms race of the European "great powers" culminated in the deaths of millions of soldiers and civilians in World War I. The inability of industrialized countries to pay the financial and social costs of the first world war contributed to revolution in Russia, the decline of British military and economic power, economic chaos in Germany, and the rise of fascism in Italy and Germany. Many governments sought to escape from the Great Depression of the 1930s via what some have termed military

Keynesianism. Backed by its powerful industrial cartels, Germany's fascist regime stressed military production. Many of the white-collar and middle-class professionals who had been unemployed found new jobs and status in the military. The only resolution to the threats of fascism and depression was another world war whose social costs were also enormous.

Preparing for World War II allowed the New Deal government of Franklin Roosevelt to reinvigorate the economy of the United States. In industries as diverse as steel and aircraft manufacturing, the government financed the building of new factories, paid to train new personnel, allowed large corporations to manage the facilities, and then purchased the output. In contrast to World War I, profits were limited, although in World War II the contractors were much more likely to be large corporations or cartels than small businesses. After the war the new factories were sold at a substantial discount to their corporate managers. Although many industries reconverted to civilian uses, the Cold War required that the economy remain on a permanent war footing. Resources were directed into the universities and the aerospace and computer industries. With the end of the Cold War in 1989, reconverting these industries to peacetime use has proved difficult, and companies have simply closed facilities rather than operate in more competitive markets. In part, this response is an economic decision, for many companies have simply grown uncompetitive, although some companies calculate that the government will continue to fund projects rather than cause distress to politically mobilized communities.

See also Finance Capital; Imperialism; Iron and Steel Industry.

References Markusen, Ann R., and Joel Yudken. *Dismantling the Cold War Economy* (1992); Schaeffer, Robert K. *War in the World System* (1989).

Miners' Federation

See Miners' National Union.

Miners' National Union

This union, formed in 1863, was one of the first durable industrial unions in Britain. The strong community cohesion of miners' villages plus the rigorous conditions of work provided an excellent basis for unionism, and British miners played a major role in the national labor movement well into the twentieth century. At the same time, varying conditions in different mining areas made national coordination difficult; regional unions often predominated. The miners' union largely supported the Liberal Party, but in 1888 a radical segment split off and formed the Miners' Federation. This division launched a major growth period of industrial unionism more generally. A flurry of bitter strikes erupted as employers tried to increase miners' output. The federation played a significant role in the emerging Labour Party and in some of the great strike movements of British history, including the strikes of 1912–1913 and the General Strike of 1926. At the same time, miners' notorious independence and spontaneity often caused them to race ahead of organized union structure, creating significant tensions between direct action and official federation policies.

See also Coal Miners; United Mine Workers.

Minimata Disease

This disease involved methyl mercury poisoning of residents of Minimata village and other communities who ate fish contaminated by the discharge from a chemical plant. The symptoms were classic mercury poisoning: death or a comatose state, loss of speech, or sensory-motor disturbances. By February 1972, 282 Minimata cases were reported, with 60 deaths. Wide publicity of this and several other chemical poisoning cases in Japan ultimately provoked great concern. A small group of Japanese scientists worked for public awareness in the 1960s, leading to a strong environmental movement and more stringent regulations. The ruling party, concerned about a divisive political issue, adopted environmentalism as its own cause after this episode. Major lawsuits were directed against polluting companies, and heavy damages were assessed.

Ministry of International Trade and Industry (MITI)

The Ministry of International Trade and Industry (MITI) is the post–World War II name of a crucial bureaucracy that has shaped Japan's industrial policies from the 1920s through the present. MITI's roots originate in the Meiji era, with its direct predecessor, the Ministry of Commerce and Industry, which was founded in 1925. The ministry first changed its name in 1943 to the Ministry of Munitions, then to MITI in 1949. During the Meiji era the government itself owned many factories, but MITI functions by establishing national economic policies and encouraging companies to meet its goals through low-interest loans, tax incentives, access to new technology, and foreign currency. MITI's experiences during wartime have shaped its postwar view that Japan is engaged in an economic struggle for survival whose success requires the resources of the entire country. Although critics of MITI fault its elitism and the favoritism it shows to large companies, MITI has engineered impressive economic growth: in 1975 the Japanese economy was more than twelve times larger than it had been in 1950, and it continues to grow.

MITI symbolizes the unique prestige and power of Japanese national bureaucracies, which before World War II had reported directly to the emperor, making bureaucrats relatively autonomous from elected officials. These prewar bureaucrats believed they represented national rather than narrow political interests, although this view became discredited: many Japanese came to blame the bureaucracies for launching World War II, a war whose results were disastrous for Japan. After the war, the U.S. occupation stripped the power of zaibatsus (financial cliques similar to holding companies) and military bureaucracies, but allowed MITI to retain broad controls over the economy. As soon as possible, certainly by the 1960s, MITI restored the zaibatsu system in all but name, using its control over capital for investment and its access to foreign currency to rebuild heavy industry.

Although some Western observers argue that the Japanese "national character" accounts for MITI's power over the national economy, MITI was in fact responding to Japan's weaknesses after the war. Capital and foreign currency were in extremely short supply, and MITI directed what capital was available to projects that it felt would also help rebuild Japan's industrial power. The government's underwriting of loans allowed companies to expand well beyond what more fiscally orthodox bankers would have allowed. The result has been a system of highly concentrated industrial companies directed by cadres of market-oriented bureaucrats. Some observers argue that the system incorporates the flexibility of capitalism while disciplining it through rigorous national industrial policies somewhat akin to the Soviet model of development.

See also South Korea.

Reference Johnson, Chalmers. *MITI and the Japanese Miracle: The Growth of Industrial Policy, 1925–1975* (1982).

Mitsubishi

The Mitsubishi company has been one of the mainstays of Japanese industrialization from the mid-nineteenth century on. The company was formed by a feudal samurai, Iwasaki Yataro (1834–1885), who had managed armaments procurements for a feudal lord, buying foreign weapons and ships. Iwasaki proved efficient in reorganizing older businesses for arms purchases. Under the Meiji regime he set up an independent company while still assisting former feudal nobility and providing jobs for samurai. Iwasaki converted the company into his personal property in 1873, naming it Mitsubishi. He relied heavily on the loyalty of his staff of former samurai. Mitsubishi competed directly with the government shipping line for coastal trade, soon forcing it out of business by using more modern ships with a less cumbersome bureaucracy. In 1875 the government bought eleven new iron steamers, loaning and ultimately giving all of them to the new company with massive subsidies. The goal was to have Mitsubishi compete directly with U.S. and British companies in the trade between Japan and China—and by 1877 Iwasaki had bested the foreigners. Mitsubishi began then to expand beyond shipping, thanks to its massive capital. It bought a maritime insurance company and moved into banking. Despite the widespread dislike of Iwasaki for his huge profits and overbearing personality, Mitsubishi withstood competition from a new shipping company, ultimately taking it over with government help. The conglomerate first borrowed, then bought, a big shipyard from the government and also operated some coal mines. Expansion continued in the twentieth century, as Mitsubishi moved into metallurgy, armaments, and automobiles. Even before World War II, the company had proved adept in making collaborative arrangements with foreign firms like the U.S. company George Westinghouse, which helped to update Mitsubishi's technology. By the 1960s Mitsubishi had emerged as one of the great multinationals, with production facilities and export opportunities around the globe.

See also Military Industrial Complex; Multinational Corporations; State, Role of the.

Reference Patrick, Hugh, ed. *Japanese Industrialization and Its Social Consequences* (1976).

Modernization Theory

This theory was developed by U.S. sociologists during the 1950s and 1960s, although it built on earlier work by the great German sociologist Max Weber. The theory holds that a number of processes were intertwined in the development of modern industrial society. Therefore, one could look at Western history as a model for a whole host of processes that other societies would have to go through in order to industrialize. One could develop various kinds of measurements to determine how "modern" a non-Western society was; perhaps one could even set off a modernization process by introducing some of the factors that had been involved in the process elsewhere.

Industrialization and accompanying technological change were unquestionably part of the modernization process, but the theory focused more attention on other features that could help prepare for industrialization or that would be wrapped up in industrialization itself. Political modernization consisted of developing new functions for the state and more efficient bureaucracy, plus attracting greater popular loyalty. In some renditions of the theory, political modernization should also consist of establishing democracy. Education was clearly part of modernization, and a modernizing state would necessarily develop an educational system. Population control was another widely accepted ingredient of modernization. So, too, new attention to children (including education) and, possibly, more intense affection factored into the process. Modernization for women meant a reduction in patriarchal controls, new legal rights, and greater education. Greater belief in science was a key element of cultural modernization. Some observers also talked of a modernized personality—open to change, eager for progress, individualized. On the basis of these criteria, modernization theorists defined some societies as modernizing, other societies as lagging in modernization.

Modernization theory has become less popular in the final decades of the twentieth century than it was in the 1950s and 1960s. Many historians have criticized its ethnocentrism: at its simplest, modernization theory argues that all societies should be measured on the basis of their resemblance to the West. Even in the case of Western history, modernization has been attacked for lumping too many separate developments together and implying that history moves in a single direction. Critics point out that industrialization did not always bring the same political forms (was Nazi Germany more or less modernized than democratic Britain?). It did not produce the same conditions and outlooks for workers as it did for the middle class, or for women as for men. (Again, at their simplest, modernized personalities sound very much like the standards developed for Western, middle-class males.) The industrial success of Japan further qualified modernization theory, for Japan became a leading industrial power without becoming Western; the idea that individualized personalities were essential to modernization was clearly silly, given the group-oriented style of modernized Japan.

Modernization is, nevertheless, a term in current usage. Its survival partly reflects unexamined assumptions; many U.S. citizens, for example, still judge other societies by their own and use the term modernization to cover this evaluation. The term has also come to have a narrower application. The word "modernization" is often applied to economic change to mean, essentially, industrialization or more intense industrialization; thus a reference to the "modernization" of the Brazilian economy usually means that manufacturing is increasing, more advanced technology is being used—that the economy is, in short, industrializing.

Though modernization is a contested term employed variously and vaguely, it may still be useful. Most societies in the twentieth century have undertaken some common kinds of change, partly in imitation of what the West did earlier: they have expanded education, improved public health, introduced more scientific training, granted new legal rights to women (including voting), adopted new technologies, and tried to improve the training of bureaucrats. Many countries have introduced these changes in hopes that they would foster greater industrialization. These similarities do not mean, however, that all societies have homogenized or that all are about to reach the same industrial level. Modernization clearly does not describe all major social patterns; in some "modernizing" societies, for example, crime goes up, while in others it goes down; in some "modernizing" societies women lose economic functions, while in others they gain new ones. Used carefully to describe some limited but important changes that have been associated with industrialization, modernization may still be a valid historical term. Certainly many policymakers, from the leaders of post-independence India, to Witte, Lenin, or Gorbachev in Russia, have believed that certain kinds of changes might induce greater industrialization, and they have agreed on what a fair number of these changes are.

Modernization theory is an ambitious attempt to explain patterns associated with industrialization by looking at history. The theory can be rejected. If used, it must be defined carefully in the knowledge that it can be rendered poorly and that it definitely does not describe the whole of modern history.

References Black, Cyril E., et al. *The Modernization of Japan and Russia* (1975); Levy, Marion J., Jr. *Modernization and the Structure of Societies* (1966); Rozman, Gilbert, ed. *The Modernization of China* (1980).

Money

Money has played a crucial role in the rise of capitalism, the modern world system of trade, and the industrial revolution. In early industrialization, many people had to adjust to a money-based economy rather than subsistence production and barter. The idea of working for money was distasteful to some, but monetary operations became increasingly accepted. Establishing a common currency was frequently a difficult task for national governments, but once accomplished it greatly facilitated domestic and international trade. By the fifteenth century, gold and silver coins were used as currency. They were gradually replaced by promissory notes (redeemable in specie) that were issued by individuals, banks, or governments. By the late eighteenth century, the gold standard had emerged as a de facto international monetary standard, and most national currencies could be converted into gold. By the 1920s money increasingly meant paper currencies that were not redeemable for gold but were backed by the credibility of national governments and the strength of national economies. After World War II, an increasing amount of money changed hands in the forms of checks and credit cards, continuing the trend away from the gold standard.

Monopoly Capitalism

Monopoly capitalism was the term developed by Marxist economists, who sought to understand the transition from a competitive economic system in the eighteenth and early nineteenth centuries to one dominated by a relatively small number of cartels and corporations, a process that began at the end of the nineteenth century. Spearheaded by financiers, large-scale corporations and cartels began to dominate the increasingly complex industrial production processes in key sectors of the economy, such as steel, oil, and chemicals. The monopoly positions of these companies generally enabled them to maintain their technological superiority, thereby limiting the ability of newcomers to enter the market. At the same time, profits rose and controls over labor increased as a result of limits on competition.

The state played an important role in the formation of monopolistic firms. In Europe and Japan, governments actively encouraged the establishment of cartels that could take advantage of economies of scale. In fact, the developing modern states in Germany and Japan were themselves shaped by the industrialization process led by monopolistic companies. The decline of laissez-faire economic practice caused widespread unease among workers and especially the middle classes in the United States. Although in the early 1900s "trust busters" such as Theodore Roosevelt became a staple of reformist politics, the government did little to prevent the formation of monopolies in the auto, steel, chemical, and electrical equipment industries. Since the 1940s, in fact, all industrialized governments have actively subsidized monopoly firms, particularly those in the military sector.

Monopolistic companies were the first to use scientific management in their workplaces. Companies established dense layers of white-collar bureaucracies to supervise employees and to keep track of the goods and services passing through the corporations' own "internal markets." Some Marxists argued that the concept of monopoly capitalism also applied to Eastern Europe and the Soviet Union, whose governments likewise relied on policies of scientific management, vast bureaucracies, and military spending. New firms have emerged in capitalist societies to compete with established monopolistic companies, but until the 1970s the trend toward centralization appeared to be a global phenomenon. The fall of Stalinist regimes throughout the world and the dramatic decline in the numbers of people employed by powerful corporations such as U.S. Steel and IBM have led some economists to argue that the world has entered a new historical stage—that of the postindustrial economy.

See also Finance Capitalism; Imperialism; Sherman Anti-Trust Act.

References Baran, P. A., and P. M. Sweezy. *Monopoly Capital: An Essay on the U.S. Economic and Social Order* (1966); Braverman, Harry. *Labor and Monopoly Capital: The Degradation of Work in the Twentieth Century* (1974).

Moral Economy

E. P. Thompson used the term "moral economy" to make sense of how and why poor people resisted the extension of capitalism in the eighteenth century. In the preceding centuries, bread and grain were sold for set prices, and the moral economy of the poor (who perceived "fair" prices to be just) contrasted sharply with the emerging values of market economics. During periods of economic hardship, the poor rioted, sometimes merely seizing grain or bread but other times selling it at "fair" prices. These riots were not always disorderly: in many cases, rioters turned over to the miller or baker not only the money the rioters had collected but also the empty sacks! In the workplace, the moral economy tended toward a stable production process with few changes in the pace of work and informal controls and favors between employers and employees.

Rioting was an important part of the preindustrial political culture of European cities. For centuries, elites had used "the mob" to mobilize popular support for their policies, and poor people had rioted when their conditions deteriorated—for instance, when the price of bread increased or other forms of hardship arose. Appealing to the moral economy of paternalistic elites via riots proved to be a relatively effective way for the poor to protest the encroachment of laissez-faire capitalism. By the early nineteenth century, however, the ruling class had become firmly wedded to the emergent values of the market, and without the tolerance of elites, bread riots and similar protests became far less effective.

The preindustrial moral economy of the poor influenced later movements such as Luddism, cooperatives, and socialist utopianism. Building on Thompson's work, historians have examined the alternative values of the poor as they have been expressed in churches, trade unions, and everyday life.

See also Corn Laws; Women.

Reference Thompson, E. P. "The Moral Economy of the English Crowd" (1971).

Morgan, John Pierpont, Sr. (1837–1913)

J. P. Morgan created an enormous financial empire, the "House of Morgan," that dominated U.S. economic life in the late nineteenth and early twentieth centuries. Morgan was the son of a wealthy banker, Junius P. Morgan, and through their connections to English banks, the Morgans became a conduit for capital to U.S. firms and the U.S. and Latin American governments. In 1877 the Morgans loaned the U.S. government enough money to pay the salary of its army until Congress could reconvene and appropriate the money. In 1893 J. P. Morgan helped to stop a panic among railroad companies and as a result acquired a controlling interest in many of the companies. Morgan also helped to create several enormous industrial firms, such as General Electric, International Harvester, and the first billion-dollar corporation—U.S. Steel. Morgan controlled his holdings through a system of interlocking directorates, whereby members of the firms' boards of directors sat on other companies' boards and represented the interests of the Morgan family.

See also Finance Capital.

Reference Carosso, Vince P. *The Morgans: Private International Bankers, 1854–1913* (1987).

Morse, Samuel F. B. (1791–1872)

Morse invented the first successful electric telegraph and the Morse code. Like several other U.S. inventors, including Robert Fulton, Morse was an artist as well as a scientist, with scientific training at Yale and artistic work in England. (After a difficult apprenticeship, he became a well-known portrait painter.) He learned from a shipboard conversation in 1832 that electricity could be sent across wire, and he immediately thought of the telegraph. Making his idea a reality required amassing savings from his art, however, and he was not able to demonstrate a prototype until 1837. A partnership improved the financial picture, though Morse was able to interest neither the U.S. Congress nor foreign backers. A widely publicized display in 1842 failed, but Morse did win some congressional funding in 1843 and strung a telegraph wire from Washington, D.C., to Baltimore. The first message, in 1844, was "What hath God wrought?" Telegraph systems spread widely thereafter, becoming vital to business and military communication. Morse won great fame at home and abroad and amassed considerable wealth.

Multinational Corporations

Multinational corporations (MNCs) are companies that operate simultaneously in

Assembly line automobile production at Ford's plant in Mexico. Built in the 1980s, this facility was designed to be the company's most efficient and modern plant and is one site in a "global assembly line."

several different countries. For instance, Ford Motor Company is one of the largest automakers in the United States, the largest in Europe, and has major facilities in South Africa, Brazil, India, and Japan. Ford's "globalization" started early: in the 1920s Ford had factories in nineteen countries. If Ford were a country, its GNP would be larger than those of Hungary and Israel combined—and oil companies such as Exxon are still larger.

MNCs frequently have diversified portfolios. Philip Morris was originally a maker of tobacco products, but by the 1980s it had become the world's second-largest food producer and the seventh-largest industrial firm in the United States. Beginning in the 1940s, Ford extended credit to its customers so they could buy its cars, but in the 1980s it followed the lead of Japanese carmakers and diversified into all forms of banking. By the early 1990s Ford was the United States' second-largest lender, with $115 billion in loans.

Although MNCs are headquartered in one country, the fact that they operate in numerous countries makes it in their interest to act as good "corporate citizens." MNCs typically staff their overseas branches with foreign nationals and make contributions to local charities and politicians. Before World War II Henry Ford both personally received a medal from Adolph Hitler and became one of the top three suppliers of military goods to the United States. (Ford's German operations also supplied the Nazi army.)

The "home" country of an MNC generally receives the profit from overseas operations. For instance, General Motors' European and Asian companies subsidized the U.S. division throughout the tough times of the 1980s. However, a MNC's first loyalty is to itself and self-interest transcends national allegiances. One U.S.-based watchmaker built a factory in American Samoa that enters the United States tariff-free. The president of the company explained that "we were able to beat the foreign competition because we *are* the foreign competition." In the 1980s Ford cut its payroll by over 100,000 workers, mostly in the United States, and built its most efficient, modern plant in Mexico. Although Ford's close financial connection to Mazda (dating from the 1970s when Ford bought one-quarter of its Japanese rival) allowed Ford to reopen a Michigan factory, much of the design work for the car assembled in Michigan was done by the Japanese, and the engines were produced in Mexico. Ford has been working to produce a "world car" of one design that can avoid tariffs and be manufactured within the national boundaries of any of the several different countries in which Ford operates plants.

Some economists argue that since the mid-1970s the global industrial economy has become more flexible. Large companies such as IBM, General Motors, or U.S. Steel had by this period become "dinosaurs," precipitating a shift of the center of economic activity and entrepreneurialism from huge enterprises to small and medium-sized companies. In many cases, however, MNCs have simply chosen to subcontract manufacturing or design work to smaller companies. In Germany and the United States, large companies generally experience the fastest growth—and have the smallest chance of going out of business. Japanese multinationals such as Mitsubishi continue to diversify product lines and establish operations in every inhabited continent. MNCs retain enormous advantages: for instance, in order to stay competitive in the computer or superconductor industry, companies must be able to invest $1 billion into a new product line—well beyond the capacities of most entrepreneurs.

Most MNCs are based in industrialized countries, and the vast majority of global investment and trade by these corporate giants occurs in Europe, North America, and East Asia. About 20 percent of MNC investment occurs in industrializing countries and only 2 percent in Africa. While the "lean and mean" MNCs survive in the "postindustrial" global economy, their former workers and the communities that once housed factories or offices do not fare particularly well. Whereas unemployment and poverty are highest in nonindustrialized countries, even in the United States 14 percent of the population lives below the official poverty line, and industrial jobs, the traditional avenue of upward mobility, have been disappearing.

Since the 1970s, the power of MNCs has grown, in relative terms, vis-à-vis the power of nation-states. As noted above, many MNCs are larger than small or medium-sized countries. Even large, powerful countries, such as the United States, attempt to regulate MNCs only loosely. Approximately 60 percent of foreign-owned companies operating in the United States do not pay tax to the federal government. Foreign-owned MNCs often "lose" money in their U.S. subsidiaries by overcharging for parts or services, thereby avoiding taxes. Ultimately, however, governments regulate international trade, and even the largest MNCs have responded, albeit reluctantly, to the policies of industrialized countries.

See also Cartels; Deindustrialization; Entrepreneurial Spirit; Foreign Trade; Monopoly Capitalism; Postindustrial Economies.

References Barnet, Richard J., and John Cavanaugh. *Global Dreams: Imperial Corporations and the New World Order* (1994); Harrison, Bennett. *Lean and Mean: The Changing Landscape of Corporate Power in the Age of Flexibility* (1994).

National Aeronautics and Space Administration (NASA)

NASA was created in 1958 by the U.S. government. When the Soviet Union launched the first satellite in space in 1957, many believed the Russians' scientific and technical expertise had triumphed; the U.S. government desperately sought to counter this notion by succeeding in the space race. By 1968 NASA had landed a man on the moon. The space program helped to develop the system of satellite communications and weather prediction as well as military capabilities such as spying and attack warnings. By the 1970s satellite communications were commercially viable, and in the 1990s the amount of data transmitted via space continues to expand rapidly. Although many technologies spun off from NASA have proven commercially viable, military applications still provide the political impetus for such programs as the Space Shuttle, which was launched in 1981.

See also Military Industrial Complex.

Reference McCurdy, Howard E. *Inside NASA: High Technology and Organizational Change in the U.S. Space Program.*

National Miners Union

Formed in 1856, the National Miners Union (NMU), led by Alexander MacDonald, attempted to build a national organization of coal miners in Britain. Because a previous national federation, the National Union of Miners, had been destroyed by a disastrous 1847 strike, the NMU opted for a less confrontational style. It attempted to improve workers' lives through parliamentary action rather than through strikes, and it achieved some success in the 1860s. Miners' wages had largely been stagnant since the 1840s, and in the 1870s, in part due to new levels of unionism and a boom in heavy industry, wages of miners finally improved. In the 1880s employers counterattacked and once again succeeded in lowering wages; the NMU disappeared in that decade, supplanted by the more militant Miners Federation of Great Britain.

See also United Mine Workers.

Nationalism

From the perspective of the 1990s, nationalism and nation-states appear to be permanent and natural if problematic features of world society. Yet nationalism is a relatively recent phenomenon that has been fundamentally shaped by the development of international capitalism and industrialization over the last 250 years.

Some historians argue that a sense of nationalism, an intense emotional bond shared among citizens of a country, is best understood as an "imagined community." Because the vast majority of the members of this national community will never meet each other, the bond between them (even if heartfelt) must remain for the most part abstract and "imagined." Moreover, before people can be French, Brazilian, or Japanese, the national identity must be conceptualized and articulated (or imagined) by nationalist movements, intellectuals, or the state.

By the sixteenth century, most European states were becoming more powerful, a process aided by the emerging world system. The quest for colonies and new markets placed new military and administrative demands on governments, but new sources of taxes and profits allowed central governments to build more powerful armies and bureaucracies—which strengthened their hand vis-à-vis the aristocracy. The emerging form of government could not rely on the old forms of deference and the authority of feudalism. Nationalism became an important way for these new states to legitimize themselves to their populations.

Since the sixteenth century the rapid spread of printing presses facilitated the diffusion of ideas through books, pamphlets, and newspapers, publications that arguably reshaped the mentality of literate and even illiterate people by subtly imposing national identities and boundaries on their mental landscapes. Pamphleteers played an important role in spreading nationalist and democratic ideas during the English revolution of the mid-seventeenth century and during the American and French revolutions of the late eighteenth century. It might be more appropriate, however, to speak of a plurality of nationalisms developing in a country than of the development of a single national identity, for different movements and social classes often vigorously contested the national image promoted by the government. For instance, radical revolutionaries attempted unsuccessfully to address economic inequality as well as questions of political rights and representation in the midst of the English, American, and French revolutions. The process of defining what the nation would mean and who would be a citizen required decades to resolve. Throughout the nineteenth century in Europe, Latin America, and the United States, propertyless workers struggled to obtain the vote. Although poor white workers in the United States obtained the franchise in the 1830s, the question of the rights of blacks contributed to the American Civil War and was not resolved until the 1960s. Some scholars argue that racialized slavery and imperialism have shaped the boundaries of specific national identities and nationalism more generally.

Nationalism contributed to industrialization. Nation-states such as Britain or France that had had "bourgeois revolutions" led the way in creating the legal and physical infrastructure that supported the process of industrialization. At the same time, new urban workers, torn from traditional local loyalties, were often open to the solidarity of nationalism. Even states without strong parliamentary systems found nationalism to be an important aid in the industrialization process. Since the Meiji era, the Japanese government has sought to instill a nationalist sensibility that accepts the necessity of sacrifice of ordinary people in order to industrialize. The government was notably successful in using the education system to promote reverence for the emperor in particular and respect for authority in general. Certainly, "mass" state institutions such as the military or public schools have enabled governments to shape the national identities of its citizens. These institutions, as well as the new forms of propaganda found in radio, film, and television, have been important features of the new nation-states that emerged in Africa and Asia as a result of decolonization in the twentieth century.

Ironically, until the 1980s many scholars believed that in places with "stable" nation states, such as Europe, nationalism was declining in importance. The bloody conflicts that have shaken the former Soviet Union and much of Eastern Europe have demonstrated that nationalism is still a potent force. Although most of the new European states are experiencing severe deindustrialization, most of them were formed on the premise that shared national identities would result in stability, democracy, and prosperity.

Since the mid-1970s the increase of global economic insecurity has contributed to a sharp rise in nationalism even within established nation states. For instance, British nationalism has not simply continued "naturally" from older nationalist traditions but has undergone a transformation, in part economic and in part political. The relative decline of British industry had been a trend since the late nineteenth century, but in the 1970s deindustrialization began to result in the wholesale loss of jobs in coal mining, steel, and other manufacturing districts—causing cuts in the social services formerly provided by the welfare state. At about the same time, the press began to emphasize a "crime wave" that implicitly blamed disorder on South Asian and particularly Afro-Caribbean immigrants. The Conservative Party, led by Margaret Thatcher, successfully articulated a new set of nationalist values that stressed self-reliance (as opposed to reliance on the welfare state), the need for cooperation in industrial relations (as opposed to workers' support for unions), and the return to "traditional" values (in contrast to new immigrants).

See also Chartism; Emancipation; Ethnicity; Imperialism; Racism; Revolutions of 1848; State, Role of the.

References Anderson, Benedict. *Imagined Communities: Reflections on the Origins and Spread of Nationalism* (1983); Balibar, Étienne, and Immanuel Wallerstein. *Race, Nation, Class: Ambiguous Identities* (1991).

Nationalization

Nationalization occurs when a national government assumes ownership of an industry or a sector of the economy. Advocates of nationalization believe that government can provide services more cheaply than private companies, that only governments can treat workers fairly, or that only government can provide the capital necessary for an industry to survive. Whereas mail service in the United States has been a government monopoly since the 1790s, the main movement toward the nationalization of industry began in the late nineteenth century, when unions and socialist parties agitated for government control over monopolistic industries. In 1894 a resolution in the relatively conservative American Federation of Labor called for the nationalization of the rail and utility industries—radicals had wanted all industries nationalized. The most extreme case occurred in the Soviet Union when the state seized control of the entire economy after 1928. However, most scholars view nationalization as occurring within a market economy—resulting in what some have termed "state capitalism."

Many European and Latin American social democratic parties called for the government to assume control of key industries as a prelude to socialism.

Nationalization has often been adopted by weaker industrializing countries. Under Italy's fascist government of the 1920s and 1930s, a large portion of the economy was nationalized. Although the government used socialistic rhetoric to justify government intervention, in practice the regime sought to socialize losses and privatize profits. Beginning in the 1920s, South Africa's government ran important industries, such as railroads and steel, because private firms were unable or unwilling to assume the risk. When the white supremacist National Party came to power in 1948, additional industries were nationalized in order to build a planned capitalist economy that provided decent jobs for whites. The question of compensation for existing companies was often controversial. Foreign companies in Mexico had underestimated the value of their holdings to avoid taxes and were paid a "fair" price. In Eastern Europe and Cuba, assets were often seized—a point that led to problems with foreign governments such as the United States. In the case of Mexico, a leftist nationalist leader seized control of the foreign-dominated oil industry in the 1930s and used the profits to expand the country's industrialization. Although many nationalized companies were sold during the 1980s, PEMEX, the national oil company, remains an important source of revenue, jobs, and national pride for Mexicans.

The best-known case of nationalization occurred in Britain after World War II. In 1945 the British Labour government launched a major wave of nationalization that brought the coal, steel, transportation (rail, canals, and long-distance trucking), and utilities industries under government ownership. Even the Bank of England was nationalized. By 1951 the government owned 20 percent of the economy. Other European countries also turned to nationalization, often to combat the popular appeal of communist parties. For instance, France's conservative postwar government nationalized a higher proportion of the economy than Britain did, because of the popular appeal of communism.

In the postwar period, many governments assumed control of key industries and continued the process of "socializing losses and privatizing profits." In 1944 France's conservative government took over many coal companies, banks, utilities, the Renault auto company, and munitions. (Rail and communications had been nationalized before World War II.) These measures were taken to keep the left from nationalizing even more of the economy.

Britain's Labour Party had argued that nationalization would be the first step toward building socialism, yet many specific plans for nationalization had been formulated by the Conservative Party in the 1930s. Although the Conservatives raised ideological objections to nationalization, they simply continued to manage the nationalized industries when they regained power in the 1950s. Even under a Labour government, managers from private corporations directed nationalized industries, and government-owned corporations were run on the same principles as private companies. One miner complained that "the mine bosses are the same . . . The Coal Board in London is made up of big bosses and ex-admirals . . . Nationalization hasn't changed anything." Although trade union leaders also helped to direct nationalized companies, most workers believed that "they had simply become bosses."

If nationalization did not result in socialism, nationalized industries did provide the basis for an expanded welfare state. Between 1945 and 1951 the nationalized British housing industry built over a million low-cost homes for workers. The nationalized telephone and communication industries provided good, low-cost services to consumers and decent wages for their workers. Because of free health care, pensions, and other forms of social spending, workers' standards of living rose—approaching those of the lower middle class.

These improvements notwithstanding, leftist critics of British nationalization pointed out that the industries that were nationalized had ceased to be profitable and that for every dollar of compensation, which was relatively generous, the government had to spend 80 cents to improve the industries. The only industry that was profitable at the time of its nationalization, steel, was privatized in the 1950s and then renationalized in the 1970s when it had become a liability to its owners. The resultant financial drain upon the state by national industries (combined with high military spending) plunged the British economy into periodic crises that culminated in the reduction of social welfare spending.

In the 1980s the Conservative government of Margaret Thatcher argued that the English economy needed to be weaned from "socialism" and begin the process of privatization. In what was to be the model for many countries with nationalized industries, state-run companies were sold to private companies who generally slashed payrolls, raised prices, and reduced services. The trend toward privatization accelerated in the 1980s, in part because of market forces and in part because the World Bank and the International Monetary Fund often require that countries privatize companies in order to receive emergency loans.

Reference Cochran, Ben. *Welfare Capitalism—And After* (1984).

Nehru, Jawaharlal (1889–1964)

India's first prime minister after independence, Nehru differed from the great nationalist leader Mahatma Gandhi on the subject of industrialization. Gandhi's vision had embraced an India full of traditional crafts; he viewed Western industrialization critically, and he did not want the class divisions and exploitation he saw in the West to mar modern India. Nehru disagreed, seeing poverty as India's most urgent problem. A socialist and intellectual, Nehru advocated centralized economic planning. Under his leadership a system of five-year plans was initiated in 1951 that called for steady growth; heavy emphasis went to agriculture, however, simply because of the burdens of population growth. Funding for industry and mining went up in the second plan, 1956–1961, and production in iron, coal, and power capacity began to rise rapidly (iron ore output almost tripled, while power capacity doubled). Although he emphasized the power of his Planning Commission, Nehru never undermined extensive private enterprise, which in fact became more profitable under his regime.

Neocolonialism

Neocolonialism is a term applied to countries that have achieved political independence but are still economically dependent upon "metropolitan" industrialized countries. For instance, many scholars have sought to understand why most of Latin America, which was freed of Spanish rule by the 1820s, remained an impoverished provider of raw materials to Britain, the United States, and other countries. Even Argentina, which by the early twentieth century had gained one of the highest standards of living in the world through its export of meat, hides, and grain, failed to industrialize, and over the course of the twentieth century, most Argentineans have experienced a dramatic decline in their standard of living.

The history of colonialism is crucial for "underdeveloping" neocolonial countries. In Africa, European governments sought to develop their colonies into producers of raw materials such as copper, coffee, rubber, or food products. Infrastructure projects, such as railroads, connected ports with mines or plantations and were not designed to stimulate industrialization. If peasants were unwilling to work as wage laborers, taxation policies forced people to work in order to earn cash. The British government sometimes imported Indian laborers to work on the African plantations. Education was generally downplayed, because clerical or skilled positions were held by Europeans.

By the time these former colonies achieved independence, their position in the world system of trade had been established. Most postcolonial governments found it difficult to escape the colonial legacy. If they sought to industrialize, they needed to acquire technical skills, raw materials, and machinery from industrialized countries, which necessitated a greater dependence upon the exports of raw materials. During the 1960s and 1970s, newly decolonized countries in Africa and Asia as well as in Latin America found ready sources of capital from private banks or development banks such as the World Bank. However, prices of raw materials plummeted before industrialization efforts could take off, and debtor nations found it difficult to make their loan payments. Short-term loans allowed countries to repay their earlier loans, but banks have increasingly forced governments to impose "structural adjustments" (cuts in the minimum wage, and food and education subsidies) in order to receive additional loans.

See also Colonization; Decolonization; Development Theory; Finance Capital; Immigration and Migration; Imperialism; Péronism; World Systems Theory.

References Frank, André Gunder. *Latin America: Underdevelopment or Revolution* (1970); Rodney, Walter. *How Europe Underdeveloped Africa* (1981).

Neurasthenia

This disease was defined and widely popularized in the United States by such doctors as S. Weir Mitchell in the 1880s and 1890s. Its symptoms ranged from fatigue to various psychosomatic complaints. Doctors attributed the causes of this disease, particularly in middle-class men, to the pace of industrial life: the ambitions and exertions of businessmen were unnatural, though socially useful. (Other groups might develop neurasthenia for other reasons: neurasthenic middle-class women, for example, were blamed for idleness; working-class male sufferers for debauchery.) Neurasthenia was an early term for the symptoms later known as nervous breakdown, stress, or "burn-out." Whether fully real or partly imaginary, it was a disease closely connected to industrialization. Treatment consisted of healthy exercise and recreation, including vacations, and it provided a good formula to justify leisure for groups dominated by the industrial work ethic. Neurasthenia disappeared as a label by 1900, but the basic diagnostic category persisted in defining tensions stemming from industrial life.

See also Work Ethic.

Reference Gosling, F. *Before Freud: Neurasthenia and the American Medical Community* (1988).

New Deal

The New Deal is generally understood to be the period between 1933 and 1938, when President Franklin D. Roosevelt created the institutional foundations of the U.S. welfare state. Roosevelt was elected in the midst of the Great Depression of the 1930s, when millions were unemployed and both agriculture and industry faced crises of overproduction and underconsumption. Many historians agree that Roosevelt saved industrial capitalism from itself by alleviating the protracted social and economic crisis. In order to stimulate an economic recovery, Roosevelt involved the federal government in the economy (and in social concerns) to the largest extent since the Reconstruction after the Civil War. Although many of the particular programs were only partially successful, the New Deal signaled an end to the laissez-faire philosophy that had dominated federal peacetime policy.

During the first phase of the New Deal, Roosevelt undertook cautious economic reforms. The new president inherited an enormous crisis in the banking system. Public confidence in the banking system as a whole was falling because many banks could not allow depositors to withdraw their money due to ill-chosen speculative investments made by bankers during the 1920s. Rather than nationalize the banking system, as some observers demanded, Roosevelt called for a "bank holiday" and then passed a series of laws to put the private banking system on surer footing. New laws regulated banks' financial policies (requiring certain ratios of reserves to loans, for instance). Roosevelt also created the

Franklin D. Roosevelt (left) on the campaign trail in 1932.

Federal Deposit Insurance Corporation (FDIC) to ensure that even if banks did fail, depositors would not lose their savings. The banking system recovered and confidence in the economy slowly grew.

Part of Roosevelt's National Industrial Recovery Act (NIRA) recognized workers' right to organize unions—marking an important change in the relationship between the federal government and the labor movement. Previous administrations had offered unions little support, and the dominant union federation (the American Federation of Labor) had come to oppose any alliance with government. Following NIRA, however, there was an upsurge in union organizing that ultimately resulted in the Congress of Industrial Organizations (CIO). The CIO unions actively lobbied the government to help poor people by intervening to strengthen labor laws, build low-cost housing, and create social security measures for the indigent, unemployed, and elderly.

The New Deal also offered subsidies to industry and agriculture. NIRA encouraged industries that raised wages to set higher prices in order to cause a mild inflationary cycle and stimulate the economy. Farmers were given price supports and paid to reduce acreage—a policy that drove many sharecroppers off the land. (Roosevelt did not want to alienate conservative southern Democrats by supporting black and white sharecroppers.) NIRA was eventually declared unconstitutional, but it formed the basis for subsequent programs. The New Deal stimulated new welfare measures to aid the elderly and unemployed; the Social Security system, initially intended to alleviate poverty among older Americans, ultimately encouraged mass retirements. In other areas, New Deal welfare measures were more limited than similar measures in European welfare states.

Although the New Deal helped stimulate the economy, the depression only truly ended when the government began to prepare for World War II. The government not only placed military orders with business—in many cases, the government actually built the factories and allowed corporations to manage them. As the secretary of war remarked: "If you . . . go to war . . . in a capitalist country, you have to let business make money out of the process or business won't work." (The policy of "military Keynesianism" would continue to dominate economic planning during the Cold War.)

Because many of the government's subsequent social and economic policies originated in the New Deal or were inspired by it, historians generally argue that the New Deal actually extended into the 1970s. During that decade, the political coalition of city dwellers, farmers, and white and black workers began to unravel, and the federal government's commitment to social programs, such as aid to cities or the poor, began to be sacrificed.

See also Industrial Union; Social Insurance.

References Cohen, Lizabeth. *Making a New Deal: Industrial Workers in Chicago, 1919–1939* (1990); Hawley, Ellis W. *The New Deal and the Problem of Monopoly* (1966).

New Economic Policy

The Soviet Union was economically devastated by the political, social, and economic chaos created by World War I, the 1917 Russian Revolution, and the resulting civil war. In 1921 production of agricultural and industrial goods was a fraction of what it had been in 1913—depending on the industry, between 5 percent and 20 percent of 1913 levels. One reasonable estimate is 20 percent of prewar production. (Industrial production across Europe was generally one-third to one-half its prewar levels.) During the civil war (1917–1921), "war communism" had been instituted and market controls had been abandoned; that is, industrial production had been controlled by the government and agricultural goods had frequently been requisitioned by Red Army units. Designed by Lenin to spur recovery, the New Economic Policy (NEP) allowed heavy industry, foreign trade, and banking to remain state monopolies, but private producers (particularly peasants) gained greater freedom to produce and sell agricultural and consumer goods. During the NEP period (1921–1928), the Soviet Union also experienced social and cultural experimentation and a wide range of political debate among communists over how to build an industrialized socialist society.

Under the NEP the state favored agricultural production and light industry (particularly those products directed toward agricultural use). As a result peasants did produce and market more food, although severe drought in the Volga region caused severe famine, and international relief was allowed into the Soviet Union for the first (and only) time. By 1923 the price of agricultural goods had fallen by one-third against industrial goods, and planners (and city dwellers) worried that peasants would withhold grain in protest.

Many party officials were disturbed by the pro-market attitudes of peasants, retailers, and small manufacturers—particularly the ostentatious wealth of the "nepmen" such as Armand Hammer. Although industrial production reached the pre–World War I levels in 1926, unemployment among workers remained high, and some critics of the NEP argued that if industry was to be developed, the manufacturing sector would have to receive greater subsidies. Furthermore, many Bolsheviks remained skeptical of strengthening the peasantry, the social group with the weakest commitment to the revolution, and these Bolsheviks argued that if socialism was to be built, then workers, the chief supporters of the revolution, would have to see improvements in their standard of living. The NEP ended in 1928 when Stalin extended his dictatorial control over the Bolshevik party. Also in 1928 Stalin instituted the first five-year plan, which ended the experiment with a "mixed economy" in favor of a state-run economy.

Reference Fitzpatrick, Sheila, Alexander Rabinowitch, and Richard Stites, eds. *Russia in the Era of NEP* (1991).

Oil

Although petroleum was used in small quantities for lubrication, medicine, and lighting before the nineteenth century, industrialization helped to transform the quantity of oil available and the way oil was used. The first commercial drilling for oil was done in 1859 in Pennsylvania. The oil industry relied heavily on science: even the initial refining of oil into kerosene in the 1860s relied on the research of university-trained chemists. The transportation of oil via pipelines clearly relied on the resources that other industrial fields had made possible. In the form of kerosene, oil quickly displaced other sources of artificial lighting, such as whale oil and coal gas. Cheap kerosene helped to lengthen the amount of time that ordinary people had for reading or working. Oil production quickly became a global phenomenon; the Russian oil fields of Baku quickly emerged, by the 1890s, as a source of oil for Europe, and the oil fields in East Asia and the Middle East were developed by the 1920s. By this point, oil was displacing coal as the staple fuel of industrial societies. Oil was vital to the Allied victory in World War I; one British general observed that they had "floated to victory on a wave of oil." In the twentieth century, oil became a fuel for automobiles and industry, and chemists helped to create many new products, such as plastics, and to transform old ones, such as textiles.

See also Rockefeller, John D.; Synthetic Fabrics.

Reference Yergin, Daniel. *The Prize: The Epic Conquest for Oil, Money and Power* (1991).

Open Hearth

The open hearth is a furnace that converts pig iron into steel. The iron is heated to extremely high temperatures, in large part by using special bricks that reflect heat back into the furnace. The open hearth produced steel more quickly and in larger batches than the Bessemer converter, although, like the Bessemer, the open hearth was also developed to circumvent the labor of puddlers, the highly paid workers who had stirred molten iron to remove impurities. Perfected by Charles and William Siemens in the 1860s and 1870s, the open hearth spread widely in the 1880s when it was adapted to use cheaper grades of iron. Ironically, the open hearth created a new class of highly skilled workers, although because employers controlled the pace of technological change, open hearth workers never developed the kind of workplace autonomy that puddlers had enjoyed. From 1900 until the 1950s, most steel in the world was produced in open hearths. After World War II new processes made steel faster and cheaper, although many U.S. firms operated their open hearths until the 1980s. The open hearth is an example of how industrialists accelerated technological change in order to expand production and to gain greater control over the workplace. The overreliance of American firms on the open hearth in recent decades suggests that eschewing technological innovation is dangerous in a global system of competitive capitalism.

See also Bessemer, Henry.

Reference Krause, Paul. *The Battle for Homestead, 1880–1892: Politics, Culture, and Steel* (1992).

Owen, Robert (1771–1858)

Owen was a prominent cotton manufacturer, who made a great deal of money in the early stages of the British factory system. A paternalist, he also sought to better his workers through factory schools and other measures. Troubled by growing class divisions and worker poverty, Owen turned in the 1820s to a variety of reform movements. He formulated an elaborate plan for social reorganization on a cooperative basis, whereby communities would organize work so that all people could benefit from "the increase of scientific productive power." His cooperative vision inspired a number of people, particularly artisans, to form utopian producer cooperatives. A number of these cooperatives were set up in the United States, such as the community in New Harmony, Indiana. Opposition to his vision led Owen, in Britain, to support direct working-class organization, and he helped form one of the first serious trade union movements during the 1820s. Textile workers formed a Grand Central Union in 1829, and then a wider variety of union movements joined the Grand National Consolidated Trades Union of 1834, backed by Owen. It promoted Owen's cooperative goals but also talked of a general strike to win an eight-hour day. Owen believed that much shorter working time, given the power of modern industry, would easily suffice to "saturate the world with wealth." Employers resisted this new union with lockouts before any strike could be attempted, and it collapsed. Owen stands as a major representative of utopian socialism and early worker organization, but he is also a symbol of the troubled conscience that industrialization could induce in some of its beneficiaries.

See also Cooperatives.

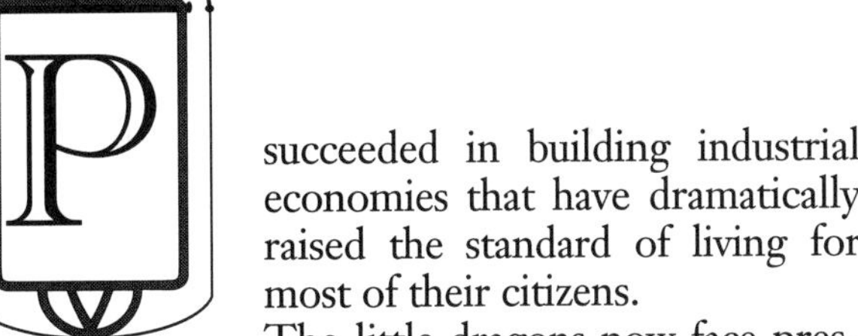

Pacific Rim

In the 1970s and 1980s the rapid industrial growth of East Asian countries inspired some scholars to define the Pacific Rim, or countries that border the Pacific, as having replaced the Atlantic seaboard as the most important area of world trade. In the 1980s the U.S. trade deficit with Japan increased from $14 billion to over $50 billion before declining by about a one-fourth—a fact that affects the increasing amount of U.S. trade with Asia. Furthermore, cross-Pacific investment is an important aspect of corporate restructuring in both Japan and the United States and is particularly significant in Mexican and Latin American industrialization efforts.

Japan had long been an industrial nation, but the industrialization of the four "little dragons" (South Korea, Singapore, Taiwan, and Hong Kong) largely occurred after 1945. In part, the success of the little dragons was due to the Cold War policies of the United States, which extended generous financial and technological aid to these countries and eased tariffs for their exports. Military spending in the region was another boost to their economies; for instance, as late as 1960 about 10 percent of Japan's GNP came from military spending by the United States. These Asian countries all followed policies that encouraged the creation of low-wage, highly skilled work forces, and they used the state to direct resources toward companies that could export products onto the world market. Culturally, they all (like Japan) shared a Confucian heritage that encouraged cooperation and discipline. Until the late 1980s, Pacific Rim countries had authoritarian governments that limited workers' protest, and some maintain an authoritarian cast still. Though the environmental costs have been high, and unions have been crushed, Pacific Rim countries have succeeded in building industrial economies that have dramatically raised the standard of living for most of their citizens.

The little dragons now face pressure from other Asian countries that seek to replicate their success by offering employers access to disciplined, low-wage workers. Beginning in 1978 China began to emphasize the role of the market in aiding its long-standing efforts to industrialize. The government dropped its barriers to foreign investment, and many employers from Europe, the United States, and particularly from Japan and the little dragons have helped turn China, with over 100 million industrial workers, into the world's fastest-growing economy. Many of the abandoned steel mills in the United States have been shipped to China to supply its economy with metal. Although China is currently running a significant trade deficit (except with the United States) its leaders are hoping that its industrialization effort will replicate the success of other Asian countries. Competition also increases from Malaysia, Indonesia, and Thailand, which export to more industrialized parts of the Pacific Rim.

See also Deindustrialization; Maquiladoras.

References Aikman, David. *Pacific Rim: Area of Change, Area of Opportunity* (1986); Thompson, Roger C. *The Pacific Basin since 1945* (1994).

Panama Canal

Construction of a canal to connect the Atlantic and Pacific oceans was begun by a French company in 1881, but the company soon went bankrupt. In 1903 President Theodore Roosevelt, who recognized the advantages of a Panamanian canal to international trade and to the U.S. navy, helped to instigate a revolt in the then Colombian district of Panama. Roosevelt's administration quickly recognized the new regime, which in turn leased the United States a ten-mile wide strip of land for a canal that would be subject to U.S. sovereignty. Construction began in 1906 under the command of the U.S. military and was completed in 1914. The canal itself was a marvel of engineering. Entire mills in Pittsburgh were engaged in constructing components for its series of locks. Mechanized earth-moving equipment, as well as modern medicines (to counteract malaria and yellow fever) were essential to completing the project. The canal symbolized the military and diplomatic power of industrialized nations over less industrialized countries and the increasing importance of oceanic trade; it also indicates the growing role that governments have played in developing crucial infrastructure projects.

See also Erie Canal; State, Role of the.

Park Chung Hee (1917–1979)

Park Chung Hee was the ruler of South Korea from 1961 until his assassination in 1979. Park came to power through a military revolt, and under his authoritarian rule, Korea became an industrial power. Park liked to think of his regime as a Korean version of the Meiji regime, whose reforms helped make Japan into an industrial giant. Under Park, companies that helped the government meet its five-year plans were subsidized. Unlike many military governors, Park took pains to make sure that subsidized companies were economically efficient; companies were encouraged to invest and discouraged from expatriating profits abroad or into nonproductive assets. Park ignored parliamentary forms of government, such as elections, but the U.S. government tolerated him because he was a committed anticommunist.

See also Rhee, Syngman.

Patents

Patents are government-backed grants of exclusive use to inventors of new devices, designed to allow inventors a period of exploitation before others can legally use the devices. Patent owners can of course license to others. The idea is to provide a clear incentive to invent; if others could copy right away, the inventor would gain little advantage from his creative effort.

Modern patent law began in England in 1624, with the Statute of Monopolies. The law was passed at a time when royal power was under attack, as part of a parliamentary effort to limit the king's right to sell special privileges to sell or manufacture. The law made an exception, however, for "the sole working" of "any manner of new manufactures" to the "first inventor and inventors of such manufactures." Various court interpretations progressively refined this meaning of patent law. The patent system was criticized by manufacturers, who wanted the free use of inventions, but the system survived and became the model for patent law in many other countries, including the United States. France, for example, created new Patent Laws in 1791 as part of the revolution. Patent rights have a definite term of years, though they can be renewed; they are not designed to keep an invention from general use forever. Almost certainly, patent law helped spur the huge series of inventions in Britain in the eighteenth century, even though inventors did not always in fact profit from their work. Patent law also supported the capitalist system underlying most industrial revolutions.

Paternalism

Paternalism is an ideology that views employers and employees as being members of the same "family," guided by the fatherly employers. Prior to the industrial revolution, much economic production did occur in the homes of artisans who assumed the role of both father and employer to their apprentices. However, many artisans abused and exploited their charges, and the abandonment of the artisanal guild system throughout the late eighteenth and early nineteenth centuries freed many journeymen from their onerous obligations, allowing them to find jobs earlier in life and thereby control more of their own work and home life. In the southern United States, slaveowners espoused an ideology of paternalism, arguing that slaves were part of their family. Most freed slaves desired to reunite their own families and wanted little to do with their old "family," although some freedmen sought to use the ideology of paternalism to their advantage to obtain access to land or credit.

Paternalistic employers try to show that not all their decisions are based on market forces alone, but that they care for the workers as individuals, take interest in their personal lives, and even provide housing and medical care. In the early nineteenth century, mill owners in Lowell, Massachusetts, found themselves obliged to adopt a paternalistic attitude in order to remain attractive to laborers in their new textile mills, many of whom were women from New England farms. The mills provided housing for the women and strictly regulated their time, requiring them to pray and attend educational courses because it was understood that for them wage labor was a temporary activity before becoming wives to farmers or artisans.

Textile mill owners sought to use paternalism to compensate for low wages—and to keep unions out of the mills. Workers who engaged in strikes could be evicted from company housing and denied access to the company store or doctor, which in rural areas were the only available facilities. Metallurgical companies in France and Germany used paternalistic devices such as company housing to benefit valuable workers, reduce wage levels, and expand employers' control over workers' private lives.

Paternalism has been a halfway house between preindustrial and industrial work relations, at the same time functioning as a coercive and "generous" way to manage a modern work force. Steel companies in the United States engaged in "corporate welfare" in the 1910s and 1920s, offering skilled workers housing subsidies and opportunities to buy stock. Similar policies were followed by Tata, the Indian steel firm. Union movements typically battled paternalism while trying to shift company spending to straightforward benefit programs such as pensions. Even after the U.S. steel industry was unionized, companies continued to hire the family members of "good" employees, offering a powerful incentive to work hard. In one case, eight members of one family worked at the same mill. Japanese companies have also used the ideology and practice of paternalism to encourage employees' loyalty to their corporations. Whereas some employees obtain lifetime employment, those who engage in strikes or refuse to transfer to a new factory can be summarily fired.

Reference Dublin, Thomas. *Women at Work: The Transformation of Work and Community in Lowell, Massachusetts, 1826–1860* (1979).

Peasantry

Peasants are subsistence farmers whose relationship to the cash economy is limited either by choice or by lack of alternatives. The relationship of peasants to industrialization is important, if indirect. Despite a characteristic cautiousness, peasants often innovate, using new methods to increase food production for sale to urban markets or taking advantage of new opportunities such as education. Peasants are often a source of revenue for industrialization projects, certainly the case during the Meiji period in Japan, as well as in the Soviet Union. Governmental policies that demand taxes paid in cash (rather than in kind payments or through labor) often force peasants to move off the land and become members of the working class. Peasant rebellions over inequitable land distribution have been a major factor in precipitating revolutions in Russia and China. The process of modernization unleashed when socialists gained power generally transformed peasants' lives in unforeseen ways. Industrialization has reduced the total number of peasants, although they still may be a majority of the world's population.

See also Populism.

Perónism

Perónism is the term for a populist form of corporatism practiced in Argentina by Juan Domingo Perón (1895–1974) and his followers. Under Perónism, the state intervened in the economy to benefit industry and workers. Perón was part of a June 1943 coup of young military officers; Perón rose to power by successfully appealing to the masses of urban poor, known as the "shirtless ones." Under his rule, trade unions gained impressive wage increases and the state provided generous social welfare benefits such as old-age pensions and unemployment relief. The political cost for this arrangement was that workers' organizations had to cede their independence to the state; Perón's wife, Evita, ran the unions until she died in 1952. Although Perónism favored workers and industrialization over rural landowners, the traditional political elites, Perón did not institute land reform and his overall strategy was not revolutionary. He used the state to control international trade and thereby use Argentina's agricultural surpluses to subsidize industry. The military ousted Perón in 1955. Though Perónistas and unions were periodically able to return to power, they have been unable to make the historic compromise of Perónism pay lasting economic or political dividends.

See also Corporatism; Fascism.

Reference Peralta-Ramos, Monica. *The Political Economy of Argentina: Power and Class since 1930* (1992).

Petroleum

See Oil.

Piece Rate

Piece rate refers to the practice of paying workers not by the hour or day but by the actual amount of work performed. The practice was a favored technique of so-called scientific management, which sought to increase productivity, generally by breaking up group tactics that aim at the restriction of labor. In the early-twentieth-century steel industry in the United States, for example, many hourly wage workers could receive "tonnage" rates if they met their production quotas. Piece rates were often used in the automobile industry and the garment trade, which have a high degree of mechanization and where labor has been minutely subdivided. Many craft workers, in the building trades and elsewhere, used local unions to resist piece rates. Although the practice can operate to some workers' advantage, many workers and unionists criticize the practice as one in which workers are "sweated" for extra production.

See also Stakhanovites; Taylor, Frederick Winslow.

Pink-Collar Workers

The term "pink-collar workers" refers to white-collar occupations that have become thoroughly feminized, such as secretary, typist, and nurse, but in which "respectable" clothing is worn on the job. Pink-collar workers generally achieve less pay and status than their masculine counterparts. This inequity generally has more to do with the ways that work is geared to women than with the actual content of the work, although the two factors are frequently interdependent. In the late nineteenth century, telephone operators in the United States were usually men, and they received good pay and a large degree of latitude at work; when the job became feminized in the early twentieth century, women received lower wages and "required" closer supervision. In the mid-nineteenth century, secretarial work was a province of literate men who were well compensated for taking care of the correspondence (and keeping the secrets) of powerful men; female secretaries perform similar duties for fewer rewards.

See also Women; Women Industrial Workers.

Reference Norwood, Stephen H. *Labor's Flaming Youth: Telephone Operators and Worker Militancy* (1990).

Pinkertons

Pinkertons was a private detective and security firm founded by Allan Pinkerton

(1819–1884) in 1853. Although Pinkerton had himself been an advocate of Chartism in England, in the United States his company earned its reputation by providing armed guards to companies during strikes. Pinkertons were often used to intimidate strikers and escort strikebreakers across picket lines; among unionists, the Pinkertons represented the power of corporations to transcend the power of elected governments by hiring their own private armies. In the Homestead Lockout of 1892, unionists succeeded in driving Pinkertons out of town—only to find themselves confronted by the Pennsylvania National Guard, which helped Andrew Carnegie run his mill with non-union workers. The Pinkertons contributed to the fact that throughout the nineteenth and much of the twentieth centuries, strikes in the United States were violent affairs. As Jay Gould remarked: "I can hire one half of the working class to kill the other half."

Plantations

Plantations were large farms that produced cash crops such as sugar, cotton, rubber, and tea. The owners (planters) of plantations or estates owned the land and frequently the labor force as well. The plantation system arose in the sixteenth century, particularly in the Americas, and produced many of the raw materials for the industrial revolution. Plantations have continued to shape the social and economic relationships of the countries that they dominated.

In the sixteenth century, sugar plantations established in the Caribbean and Brazil imposed harsh labor regimes on both African slaves and indentured servants from Europe. Planters gradually moved toward using African slaves as the main source of labor power—a decision that was based largely on economics—because planters could buy a slave for little more than it cost to hire an indentured servant for several years. The racialization of slavery also allowed planters to use poor whites as their political allies, for slave revolts were a constant fear in plantation societies. Slavery was abolished at different points during the nineteenth century throughout the world, but the plantation system survived and spread, relying on wage labor in some regions, bonded laborers, or peasants who worked part of the year for wages across much of Africa, Asia, and Latin America. Although workers were often paid in cash, working conditions remained harsh, and many peasants in the new colonies resisted becoming laborers for the plantations. British planters in Sri Lanka (Ceylon), Malaysia, and East Africa often used bonded laborers (bound to work for a period of several years) from India and China rather than (or in addition to) the domestic labor supply.

After decolonization, newly independent countries with developed plantation systems initially fared well in the international marketplace. Until the late 1960s, Sri Lanka was able to maintain its trade surpluses with industrialized countries in spite of its growing population. Sri Lanka's favorable balance of trade enabled it to create one of Asia's most developed welfare states, with an extensive university system and generous food, health, and transportation subsidies. The prices for Sri Lanka's main exports, tea and rubber, gradually fell, however. In the case of tea, other Asian and African countries (often at the urging of the World Bank) produced tea—and the resulting oversupply caused prices to fall. Other countries also expanded their coconut plantations, and changing consumption patterns in Europe and the United States exacerbated the price fall. The price of rubber fell because the invention of synthetic rubber during World War II gave buyers an alternate supply. Sri Lanka's worsening balance of payments eventually caused its welfare state to collapse, and as people groped for a reason for the fall in their standards of living, tensions among ethnic groups degenerated into civil war. Although not all countries with plantation systems have plunged into civil war, countries that entered the world system through the plantation system have often had a difficult time industrializing their economies. Plantation systems tend to depend on cheap labor and limited technology, poor workers depress the internal market for manufactured goods, and plantation employers can discourage the development of an industrial sector that would attract workers and raise wages elsewhere.

See also Development Theory; Neocolonialism; World Systems Theory.

Reference Wolf, Eric. *Europe and the People without History* (1982).

Plastics

Plastics is basically a twentieth-century industry. The term derives from the Greek word, "fit for molding." Plastics have various chemical compositions, derived from wood, cotton, and other materials, including ammonia and formaldehyde. Plastic was first discovered by French chemists in 1828. Molding began in the United States about 1850 for novelty items such as combs and jewelry boxes, and plastics began to replace wood, ivory, and ceramics, at least in cheaper goods. Experiments continued in the United States; the greatest step occurred in 1907, when Leo Baekeland discovered phenol-formaldehyde resins, marketed under the trademark Bakelite. Cellulose acetate plastics were introduced in 1927, advancing the possibilities for heat molding. The plastics industry expanded rapidly as new materials and uses were discovered. A light industry, plastics spread widely in several early industrial revolutions of the twentieth century, such as that of Taiwan, providing opportunities in export sales in consumer goods. Workers in plastics are primarily involved with mixing the chemical materials, but there are also skilled jobs in shaping and in designing products.

Poland

The industrialization of Poland began unevenly in the nineteenth century while the country was ruled by the Austrian, German, and Russian empires, though significant industrial centers arose in areas like Ludz. Many Polish workers emigrated to other European countries or to North America. A basic industrialization process was completed only after World War II. In 1945 Poland had great difficulties to overcome: one-fifth of the population had been killed and the country's borders were redrawn—Stalin forcibly relocated millions of ethnic Poles from the Soviet Union into Poland, and large numbers of ethnic Germans were driven into East Germany. Stalin also denied Poland access to Western resources during the period of reconstruction, though Poland nevertheless managed to exploit its massive coal deposits and build an industrial economy. Heavy industry was favored, though Polish communists allowed peasants greater control over the land than Soviet communists allotted their own peasants. Workers' discontent with harsh living conditions and lack of civil liberties periodically erupted in riots. In the 1970s Poland borrowed heavily from the West to finance consumer goods for workers as well as new industrial projects such as shipbuilding, automobile factories, and food processing. Western Europe largely refused to open its markets to these goods, thus accelerating the crisis of the Polish state in the 1980s.

See also Eastern Europe.

Reference Dziewanowski, M. K. *Poland in the Twentieth Century* (1971).

Police Regulation Law

This law was introduced by Japan in 1900, after the first serious labor unrest broke out in the late 1890s. Several unions had emerged, and though they were moderate, they staged a strike in 1898 to protest the firing of "agitators" and to demand better treatment. The Police Regulation Law of 1900 made it virtually a crime to organize and lead workers out on strikes. Several labor groups, including a 1901 Social Democratic Party, were disbanded under this law. The law resembled provisions in other early industrial societies that had outlawed labor organizations, but it was particularly severely enforced. The Japanese union movement was stunted as a result, and workers turned increasingly to political action. A Federation of Labor emerged in 1919, calling for revision of the Regulation Law. A major shipyards strike in 1921 against Kawasaki and Mitsubishi was broken up by army troops; three hundred leaders were arrested, which made the remaining movement more radical. Finally, in 1925, the government began to be more flexible and revised the Regulation Law to eliminate restrictions on labor activities, though violence was still controlled and compulsory arbitration was required in some industries.

Poor Law

The Elizabethan Poor Law of 1601 responded to the growth of propertyless workers as the English economy became more commercial. It authorized localities to provide aid (mainly in kind) to the poor and unemployed. This system seemed incompatible with the principles of an industrial economy, and it was reformed in 1834. Business leaders wanted more consistent policies that were not dependent on local whims, and they sought lower taxes; they were also convinced that many poor people abused the system, getting public aid when they should be working. The views of liberal economists, who were hostile to government assistance programs in the name of free competition, supported this change. The Poor Law reform measure provided central controls over the system. Relief funds were cut and more rigorous tests were to be applied to applicants, so that able-bodied people would be forced to work. Workhouses were established for those who did receive aid, and their conditions were deliberately made unpleasant and discouraging. Workers attacked this change—it was one of the causes of the Chartist movement—but the reformed system continued to be the basis for British relief of poverty until the twentieth century. While the Poor Law reform was intended to foster better administrative practices, it is rightly remembered for the punitive approach to poverty associated with many leaders of the industrial revolution.

See also Enclosure Movement; Underclass.

Population Growth

Population levels are tied to industrialization in complex ways. Too much population, it has been argued, can prevent a full industrial revolution. Some demographic growth, however, is a vital economic stimulant. Finally, industrial revolutions cut population growth rates, with important consequences.

Most societies that industrialized had first experienced population growth. In western Europe, massive population growth began about 1730. Levels doubled between 1750 and 1800 in Britain and Prussia; they increased 50 percent in France. The causes of this growth were the utilization of more efficient foodstuffs, notably the potato, and a coincidental reduction in epidemic disease; major plagues disappeared until a recurrence in the 1830s. Improvements in urban sanitation played a minor role. Better food and less disease meant that more children survived to adulthood, which increased the population and also augmented the number of available parents, increasing the population even more. This cycle continued for several generations. Population growth provided new markets for goods. It also made it more difficult to survive in agriculture; more and more rural children had to look for other work, for the land was insufficient to support them. Countries with lower population growth, like France, felt this pressure less and found it more difficult to recruit a factory labor force. Population growth generally forced workers to accept factory conditions, move to cities, or emigrate. Population growth in middle-class families could spur innovation. Finding that more of one's children survived to adulthood and needed to be supported at a middle-class level could be a direct motivation to business expansion and investment in unfamiliar technology.

Russia, too, experienced population growth before industrialization. Japan's population grew rapidly, thanks to new public health measures and improved agriculture, before and during the early industrial decades.

Too much growth, however, particularly in already crowded conditions, can drain some of the resources and capital needed for industrial investment. This argument has been used to explain why Latin America, India, and China have been slower to industrialize. Certainly, twentieth-century growth rates have been unprecedented in most nonindustrial countries, as China and India come close to a billion people each. Modern medicine and agriculture, fruits of international industrialization, spurred this growth. How great this problem is, in terms of retarding industrialization, is widely debated. South Korea is one of the most densely populated countries in the world, but it has managed to launch an industrial revolution. Many societies, like China since 1978, have actively sought to cut population growth to facilitate industrialization.

All successful industrial revolutions to date have led to rapid drops in birth rates, as families adjust to the fact that children can no longer earn money and devote more attention to improving their standards of living. This demographic transition has affected Japan, Western Europe, Russia, and North America. The transition can be uneven, and some groups reduce their birth rates more rapidly than others; ironically, poorer groups often maintain higher rates (which was not the case before industrialization). The transition also increases the percentage of older people in the population. This new demographic structure presents its own problems to industrialized societies in the twentieth century.

See also Demographic Transition.

Populism

Populism refers to farmers' protest movements. Since the fifteenth century, the rise of capitalism and industrialization has transformed the economic basis of farming throughout the world. Farmers (who are generally considered to be more market-oriented than their relatively self-sufficient peasant counterparts) supplied burgeoning urban markets with agricultural goods but in the process became increasingly dependent on manufactured goods such as plows, bags, fertilizers, and tractors. Once farmers became enmeshed in the "cash nexus," they became vulnerable to variations in prices and demand for agricultural and manufactured goods. Though farmers occasionally enjoyed relatively favorable "terms of trade," as for example during the period just before and during World War I, farms have become increasingly capital-intensive since the late nineteenth century, resulting in the forced eviction of most small-scale farmers from the land. In response to the often negative changes that the industrialization process has wrought on their lives, farmers have instituted a number of protest movements.

Beginning in the 1870s, farmers in the United States began to agitate against the fall of agricultural prices and the increasing cost of credit. What has become known as the Populist movement initially challenged railroad and manufacturing cartels, or "trusts," that charged high rates for transportation and necessary goods (such as bagging for cotton). Populists also targeted the federal government's gold standard policies that favored bankers over creditors. The Populists argued for a more flexible currency that, being based in part on agricultural production, would respond better to the needs of "producers" and not concentrate power in the hands of the banking system. At its height in the 1890s, the Populist movement's People's Party polled over one million votes even in the face of massive and brutal repression in the southern United States. It eventually "fused" with and disappeared into the Democratic Party. The Populists had an important influence on the course of political reforms, including railroad regulations, but they did not succeed in saving large numbers of small-scale farmers from economic ruin.

Not all farmers' movements have been failures, however. In twentieth-century France and Japan, farmers have been able to pressure their governments for generous subsidies, allowing many small farmers to remain economically viable.

Populist movements face a variety of obstacles. The dispersed nature of settlement in the countryside complicates communication, and the often substantial class differences between richer and poorer (or landless) farmers make it difficult to articulate and maintain political unity. For instance, although Populists attempted to address the needs of both sharecroppers and farmers who owned their own land, the movement clearly favored wealthier farmers. Likewise, as a result of resistance by southern Democrats to the Populists' interracial politics, the movement maintained separate organizations for whites and blacks. In the twentieth century United States, rich farmers have been able to form powerful cooperatives (such as Sunkist) and to influence federal policies, whereas sharecroppers have had little luck in influencing policies, and their unions have crumbled in the face of state and vigilante violence.

See also Agriculture; Kulaks; New Deal.

References Goodwyn, Lawrence. *The Populist Moment: A Short History of the Agrarian Revolt in America* (1978); Shanin, Teodor. *Peasants and Peasant Societies* (1987).

Postindustrial Economies

Since the 1970s employment in the manufacturing sectors of industrialized countries have been stagnant or in decline. In Europe, the United States, and Japan, jobs in "smokestack" industries such as steel, textiles, and auto have declined as companies have continued to institute automation or have shifted production to newly industrializing countries such as Mexico, South Korea, or China. The shift of industrial production to new locations has been accompanied by advances in computer and communication technology that has allowed multinational corporations to coordinate the production and distribution of goods on a worldwide basis. Some observers believe that the result has been the emergence of a global "postindustrial" economy.

Many economists have heralded the emergence of a postindustrial economy that is based upon "high-tech" non-industries such as computers, communications, and the service sector. For instance, from the 1950s onwards, New York City has lost many of its blue-collar industries (printing, garments, metal working) as policymakers have encouraged the rise of white-collar employment in media, finance, and real estate. Firms that continue to rely on rigid divisions between managers and workers will fall victim to companies and nations that have more educated and flexible work forces. In the 1980s many old industrial companies, such as IBM or General Motors, lost market share to newer, more nimble companies. Supporters of postindustrial theory point to the fall of the Soviet Union as a result of the failure of the country's communist planners to adapt to a more competitive global market, and many economists worry that firms in the United States may also lag in adapting to new realities.

Critics point out that postindustrialism is not so much a new era in economic development as an acceleration of industrialization on a worldwide scale and note that the changes have neither empowered workers nor improved their standards of living. Whereas flexibility may be a virtue for companies in the global marketplace, "leaner" corporations have resulted in an increasing number of workers who are denied permanent employment. Since the 1980s most of the jobs created in the United States and increasingly in Europe and Japan are low-wage, temporary positions. One historian has observed that "postindustrial" New York City has a wider gap between rich and poor than it did in the 1940s and that, after a brief boom in the 1980s, the numbers of high-wage jobs in finance and media are actually lower in the 1990s than they were in the 1970s. Particularly in the United States and Europe, workers' incomes since the 1970s (if adjusted for inflation) have actually fallen.

Postindustrial technologies may intensify industrial conditions of work. Though some people forecast big changes in work thanks to computer linkages—work may become more decentralized, more self-paced—it is also clear that computers can allow closer monitoring of the pace of work and afford supervisors new ways to keep track of what employees do on the job.

See also Dual Labor Markets.

References Harrison, Bennett. *Lean and Mean: The Changing Landscape of Corporate Power in the Era of Flexibility* (1994); Harvey, David. *The Condition of Postmodernity: An Inquiry into the Origins of Cultural Change* (1990).

Potato

The potato was a New World crop, originally domesticated in the Andes. Its use began to spread to Europe only at the end of the seventeenth century, when prejudices against new foods declined. The potato was an immensely efficient crop, allowing families to survive on smaller plots of land, which in turn fueled Europe's massive population increase in the eighteenth century—up to 100 percent in Britain and Prussia. Population increase stimulated markets for manufactured goods and also expanded the labor supply; both of these developments contributed directly to the industrial revolution. When diseases began to affect the crop, notably the potato blight of 1846–1847, resultant famine generated new patterns of emigration. Large numbers of Irish immigrants swelled available industrial labor in the United States and elsewhere.

See also Agriculture; Population Growth.

Primitive Accumulation

Primitive accumulation is a term developed by Karl Marx to explain the origins of wage labor, or how producers (future proletarians or members of the working class) lost economic alternatives to wage labor. He uses the term primitive not simply because force and robbery play a large role in this process but also because it is part of the prehistory of the capitalist era. He believed that the enclosure movement, by which the English aristocracy drove peasants from common grounds (fields and forests), was a classic example of primitive accumulation. Another example was when England forced Spain to allow English traders to supply African slaves to Spanish colonies. As Marx writes: "If money, according to Augier, 'comes into the world with a congenital blood-stain on one cheek,' capital comes dripping from head to foot, from every pore, with blood and dirt."

Private Property

Private property, a guiding principle of capitalist economies, emphasizes undisputed individual ownership of production goods, such as land, equipment, and business. Most societies that industrialized had fairly well-established laws about private property. Even inventions were protected as property by patent law. Russia, by abolishing serfdom in 1861 and then issuing more standardized legal codes, firmed up its property laws prior to industrialization. A few societies faced groups, such as Native Americans, wedded to more communal property concepts. The U.S. government and Latin American governments have pressed these groups either to isolate themselves or to accept private property arrangements as the basis for a more commercial economy, and significant tensions have resulted.

Though private property was not caused by industrialization, the industrial revolution exacerbated the division between property owners and nonowners. The people who controlled the factories and earned the main profits were owners who thought of their enterprise as their property. Workers were people who had no access to significant property; they were proletarians. Not surprisingly, many workers and many socialist theories attacked private property because it subjected certain people to the control of property owners at very unequal rates of reward. Utopian socialists as well as Marxists argued for more communal arrangements, so that everyone would share in decisions and earnings. A few alternative communities were set up. Only the communist system, however, seriously attempted industrialization without significant private property. Under the Soviet system in Russia, and in later communist societies in Eastern Europe and China, the state owned factories in the name of the people. The system worked well for establishing basic industries, but it seems to have broken down as a structure for keeping industrial growth going. Thus most communist systems between 1978 and 1985 began to tolerate more private property as an incentive for economic innovation.

Private property remains a legal bedrock for capitalist industrial societies. However, the growth of corporations from the 1870s onward progressively diffused ownership. Big industrial corporations are property, but they are not individual property as the early factories were. Industrialization in this sense also complicates property arrangements.

Productivity

Productivity describes the output generated by the average worker in a given factory, industry, or the whole economy, when calculated to include the costs of equipment and resources. The industrial revolution was intended to increase per-worker productivity by using new machines, greater labor specialization, and intensified supervision to improve efficiency. Once an industrial revolution started, productivity tended to continue to expand, though in recurrent bursts rather than a steady progression, as new equipment and greater work discipline were introduced.

Early industrial revolutions could generate massive productivity gains in a given industry, but the simplest figures can be misleading. This is an area where the sophisticated quantitative methods of the "new economic history," or cliometrics, have provided important refinements over a conventional historical understanding. Mechanical spinning allowed a single operative to produce over fifty times as much thread as a hand worker could do, though some assistants were also involved on the machine. However, labor went into the machines, the fuel, and other costs, which makes actual productivity gains hard to calculate. Other equipment was less spectacular: early mechanical looms increased production by 50 percent to 100 percent per worker, which is why handloom weavers, if they concentrated on certain grades of cloth, long continued to compete. Again, overall productivity calculations are complex. When spinning and weaving of cotton (the most industrialized textile fiber) are considered together with the costs of machines and fuel, productivity gains in Britain have been estimated at about 3.4 percent per year by 1812 and at about 2 percent (since the biggest gains had already been achieved) by 1860.

Power-driven printing equipment, mechanical kneading machines for bread dough, larger metallurgical furnaces—these were other developments in the late nineteenth century that heightened productivity. The result was greatly increased output, with a labor force that did not grow correspondingly. In textiles, in fact, productivity gains allowed a smaller number of workers to generate rapidly rising output, and domestic workers were gradually cut back.

Early industrial revolutions did not, however, result in rapid overall productivity gains, which is one reason some historians dispute the term "revolution." The primary reason is that more productive methods were applied only to a small part of the economy, not to the whole. In Britain by 1850 over 80 percent of cotton production was in mechanized factories, but only about 40 percent of wool production had been transformed. British woolens, as a result, had about .9 percent annual productivity improvement during the early industrial period—impressive

Mechanical innovations, such as this early printing press, revolutionized the printing process. Mechanization of the work process was a crucial part of increasing workers' and society's productivity.

over time, but not spectacular in the short run. Construction and other craft sectors, pressed to develop more efficient methods at least to some extent, had expanded, while agriculture remained extensive and operated with only limited new equipment (in Britain there was at most a .4 percent annual productivity gain). Furthermore, early industrialization required massive growth in coal mining where, except in transporting material from the mines, there was little technological innovation; as pits deepened, per-worker productivity might actually decline. Finally, the withdrawal of some workers from the formal labor force, such as most married women, was another constraint on overall productivity.

Productivity gains, then, varied greatly during early industrialization. High in cotton and also transportation, they were more modest in other textiles and in iron and sluggish in nonfactory sectors.

Later industrializations, applying new equipment and methods to more branches of the economy, often generated higher overall productivity improvements. This phenomenon formed the basis for national product growth rates of 9 percent to 10 percent in a number of twentieth-century cases: Japan in the 1950s and 1960s, Spain and Italy in the 1960s, and China in the 1980s.

Productivity improvements in individual industrial sectors, even in nineteenth-century industrial revolutions, remained fundamental, for increased productivity was the source of the greater output of goods that required new sales and export outlets and ultimately a new consumerist mentality. It was also the source of new tensions between employers and workers. Employers, to assure their own profits and pay for new equipment, had to arrange that most productivity gains not return to workers in the form of higher wages. Hence they often tried to cut wages or, more commonly, to switch to hourly scales (rather than piece rates) so that more production would not result in higher earnings. Workers, obviously, recognized this strategy and often felt cheated. Employers also began to press workers to augment their productivity even beyond what new machines assured, when they realized how much productivity meant in terms of competitive costs and satisfactory profits. This realization informed the general efforts to speed the pace of work not only in factories but also in crafts and mines in the late nineteenth century. At the same time, however, higher productivity did ultimately allow higher living standards for many workers, plus shorter hours of actual work and fewer family members involved in work.

Industrialists, for their part, tended to press for higher productivity somewhat sporadically. When sales were good there was little reason to change methods; more workers could be hired. One of the "purposes" of the economic cycle and recurrent slumps was to weed out less productive firms and prompt other industrialists to introduce a new round of technological innovation or other efficiencies so that prices could be dropped to induce more sales.

See also Business Cycles; Consumerism; Strikes; Technology.

Reference Mokyr, Joel, ed. *The Economics of the Industrial Revolution* (1985).

Professionalization

Professionalization was the process by which university-derived knowledge came to be defined and regulated by the professional associations and the state. The industrial revolution created an unprecedented demand for specialized forms of knowledge among engineers, accountants, and architects. The older professions of medicine and law increased their knowledge claims and public roles, carving out a strong position in industrial society through professionalization. Professional associations limited entry into job markets, but, unlike trade unions, professionals, because they were assumed to operate in the public interest, were allowed a considerable degree of self-regulation.

Early on, engineering emerged as one of the most important professions in industrialization. Civil engineers proved crucial to the building of the Erie Canal and other infrastructure projects. Because most universities in the first half of the nineteenth century offered only classical training (languages, religion, and philosophy), scientists and entrepreneurs urged the formation of universities that could train engineers to apply scientific principles to manufacturing. France and Germany already had polytechnic schools for mining and civil engineers. Before 1850 several technical universities were established in the United States, and the passage of the Morrill Act in 1862 offered substantial federal support (land grants) for universities that offered technical or agricultural training. In 1870 approximately one hundred engineers graduated from universities, and by 1914 over 4,000 graduates were joining the work force each year.

Engineering associations were formed relatively early: in England in 1818 and in the United States in 1852. Professional associations distinguished between university-trained mechanical engineers and the large numbers of mechanical engineers who were skilled workers with extensive experience in machine-tool shops. The professional associations helped make university training a prerequisite for entering into the managerial ranks of industrial corporations, and most "mechanics" remained foremen. By the early twentieth century, a new discipline of industrial engineering had begun to emerge that applied technical expertise to making the workplace more profitable.

See also Research and Development; Science; Scientific Management; Taylor, Frederick Winslow; Technology; Work Ethic.

References Layton, Edwin, Jr. *Revolt of the Engineers: Social Responsibility and the American Engineering Profession* (1986); Noble, David F. *America by Design: Science, Technology, and the Rise of Corporate Capitalism* (1977).

Professionals

Most preindustrial societies had a few groups that can be called professional, in that they were based on unusually extensive learning. In Europe, doctors, lawyers, and priests or ministers formed the "learned professions." Industrialization combined with political and scientific change altered the nature of the professions during the nineteenth century. Most older professions developed more specialized training, so that they could better serve the needs of an industrial society and also so that they could maintain prestige in an age increasingly dominated by business success. Advancing industrialization required new kinds of legal knowledge, for example, and more rigorous scientific training in medicine also made sense in the industrial context. Doctors played a major role in public health regulations that improved conditions in industrial cities. Generally, in Europe during the late nineteenth century and by the 1870s in the United States, the older professions had upgraded their educational achievements, formed new professional associations, and advocated careful licensing procedures to certify appropriate attainment. Along with these changes, a number of new professions were spawned by industrialization. Engineering became a profession as formal training improved and examinations and licensing were introduced. Accounting became a profession in the early twentieth century; architecture, too, emerged as a new professional field. The overall expansion of professions related closely to growth and redefinition in universities, the source of most professional training. University academics themselves became another profession.

A number of important job categories took on characteristics of a profession, but incompletely. Librarians, for example, required training, but access to the training was relatively easy, and no rigorous licensing procedures applied; the same held true for school teachers. Occupations of this sort, dominated by women, did not achieve full professional status by the late nineteenth and early twentieth century. Meanwhile, the popularity of the term "professional," as a badge of special training and expertise, expanded into industrial societies. Many occupations, including professional sports, picked up the label. In general, the growth and definition of modern professions follows the needs for specialized knowledge generated by industrial economies.

Professional success has not, however, always accompanied industrial expansion. Because professionals base their claims for status on knowledge rather than money, they can take a somewhat distinctive view of industrial economies. Moreover, the popularity of professions often lures more people into their ranks than an economy can easily support. "Overproduction" of professionals occurred in Europe at the end of the nineteenth century (over a third of the trained doctors in France, for example, could not find relevant work), as well as in industrializing India today. These factors can bring some professionals into opposition with industrial society, as they seek outlets in politics of protest or reform activities. Much of the socialist leadership around the world has come from the ranks of professionals. More recently, environmentalist causes gain greatly from professionals' support. Thus there remains a significant ambiguity in the relationship between modern professionals and ongoing industrialization.

See also Middle Class.

References Hatch, Nathan O., ed. *The Professions in American History* (1988); Larson, Magali S. *The Rise of Professionalism: A Sociological Analysis* (1977).

Profit

The desire to earn a profit—the money earned by a seller when prices exceed cost—is one of the strongest forces within capitalism and one that has profoundly shaped the development of the modern world economy and the industrial revolution. Yet industrial production is simply one way to earn a profit. Merchants, for example, circulate commodities (wool, cotton, or manufactured goods) to gain a profit, and although many merchants became (or financed) industrialists, merchants also relied on or indeed helped to create systems of slavery and other forms of coerced labor to supply raw materials for industrial production. Financiers played a crucial role in developing systems of factories in industrialized countries, but when markets for industrial goods become saturated (or industries become uncompetitive), bankers' desire for increased profits leads them to shift their investments into other forms of capital such as real estate or commodity speculation. The profit motive is a powerful and pitiless force that has been instrumental in building as well as destroying industry.

See also Deindustrialization; Finance Capital; Merchant Capital; Plantations; U.S. South.

Proletariat

See Industrial Workers.

Protectionism

Protectionism stresses high tariffs to protect one nation's goods by taxing imports. Debates over tariff policy accompanied every industrial revolution. Most early industrial societies were protectionist—that is, they sought to protect infant industry, to foster it against often better developed foreign competition. More established industrial societies typically press for freer trade, hoping that they can sell their products in foreign markets where there is less technologically sophisticated competition. Many of these societies also want lower tariffs on foods and raw materials, so that there will be less pressure for higher wages. Tariff debates frequently pit industrialists against other interests. In Britain during the early nineteenth century, factory owners wanted low tariffs, particularly on food, while aristocratic estate owners pressed for protection. At almost the same time, in the 1820s and 1830s, U.S. factory owners in the North urged tariffs to protect their industries against the more advanced British competition, while southern planters urged free trade so that they would not face retaliatory barriers in trying to sell their agricultural products, headed by cotton, abroad.

Through most of the nineteenth century, Britain, with its industrial lead, advocated low tariffs. (Ironically, British tariffs against Indian and other textile products in the eighteenth century had helped British factories get their start.) British liberals supported free trade from ideological conviction, and some continental liberals agreed. Free-trade movements first began within Britain, in attacks on high agricultural tariffs like the Corn Law. Free-trade advocates believed as a matter of principle that lower tariffs would cut prices for consumers and force producers to be maximally efficient. Some supporters of free trade simply wanted to improve their ability to export. Low tariffs in one's own country would help persuade other countries—potential markets—to cut their rates. After 1850 the British tried to negotiate freer trade with other countries, as in the Cobden-Chevalier treaty of 1860 with France.

As more countries began to industrialize in the late nineteenth century, tariffs tended to rise; most industrial nations, including the United States, raised their rates in the 1890s. Rates in France hit 15 percent on most industrial goods, and the United States and Russia (a new industrializer) went even higher. Britain abandoned its advocacy of free trade after World War I when its industries faced growing competition. High tariffs almost certainly reduced international commerce and exacerbated the economic problems of the 1920s and 1930s, impeding trade, protecting inefficiency, and worsening conditions in the Great Depression of the 1930s.

This example encouraged more free-trade efforts after World War II, often led by the United States. Free traders continue to believe that extensive commerce allows everyone to benefit from lower prices and the most productive economic specializations, advantages that outweigh damage to a few less competitive sectors. A series of negotiations and agreements, plus regional tariff reduction pacts such as the European Economic Community and, later, the North American Free Trade Association (NAFTA) have dotted the economic history of the second half of the twentieth century. In 1994 the U.S. government approved a new General Agreement on Trade and Tariffs (GATT) accord, designed to lower rates markedly around the world. At the same time, in the interest of protecting their factory sectors, many new industrializers, like South Korea, have hesitated to embrace free trade. Every industrial nation, including the United States, has certain products it seeks to protect either by outright tariffs or by other trade barriers. The debate continues, though the frankly protectionist climate of much early industrialization in the nineteenth century has definitely shifted.

See also Bretton Woods Agreement; Bülow Tariff; Calico Act; Laissez-faire; McKinley Tariff; Smoot-Hawley Tariff.

Reference Bowden, Witt, Michael Karpovich, and A. P. Usher. *An Economic History of Europe since 1750* (1937).

Protoindustrialization

This term was coined in 1972 by Franklin Mendels and has been elaborated by many socioeconomic historians, particularly in Germany. The term describes the rapid expansion of production between the sixteenth and eighteenth centuries in western and central Europe, where largely traditional methods were used in manufacturing but where market mechanisms increasingly came into play. Protoindustrialization is seen as a training ground for merchants and other directors in the process, who learned the kinds of business skills and capital accumulation later applied to industrialization per se. Workers loosened their ties to the land, becoming an incipient proletariat. Protoindustrial workers learned to take direction from strangers and to work for a wage, and they acquired new habits, such as consumerism and greater sexuality, that would expand when the working class encountered the outright factory system.

Protoindustrialization is also seen as a factor in eighteenth-century population growth, because people could earn at a relatively early age and not wait for inheritance of land. Thus sexual activity occurred earlier, with or without marriage. The protoindustrial concept has been applied to many other areas and periods as a description of the transition between traditional production and the novelty of industrialization. The theory has also been challenged, however, because it does not fit the facts for every region. In some cases, protoindustrialization actually delayed industrialization, and workers clung to home-based production instead of shifting to potentially more efficient factories. It is certainly clear that many protoindustrial regions lost ground to factory competition when workers and merchants proved unable to develop a factory system of their own. Hence the deindustrialization of western France and of many women workers in the early nineteenth century. The concept of protoindustrialization seems to have won considerable but far from complete acceptance, even when carefully applied, as providing a framework for developments that led up to the industrial period.

See also Causes of the Industrial Revolution; Deindustrialization; Domestic Manufacturing.

References Gullickson, Gay. *Spinners and Weavers of Auffray* (1986); Kriedte, Peter, Hans Medick, and Jurgen Schlumbohm. *Industrialization before Industrialization* (1981).

Prussia

See Germany.

Puddlers

Puddlers were highly skilled workers who refined iron after it came out of blast furnaces. Though a new category of workers in the nineteenth century, they were part of the aristocrats of labor whose relative privileges derived partly from their manual abilities to work iron but also from their ability to judge when the molten iron had sufficiently congealed. One puddler recalled that "none of us ever went to school and learned the chemistry of it [making iron] from books. We learned the trick by doing it, standing with our faces in the scorching heat while our hands puddled the metal in its glaring bath." Puddlers enjoyed a high degree of autonomy at work, which was codified in their union's elaborate work rules. Although industrialists frequently sought to circumvent puddlers' control over production, they were unsuccessful until the introduction of the Bessemer converter in the 1860s.

See also Workers' Control.

Reference Montgomery, David. *The Fall of the House of Labor: The Workplace, the State, and American Labor Activism, 1865–1925* (1987).

Pullman, George M. (1831–1897)

George Pullman established the Pullman Palace Car Company in 1867. Pullman sleeping cars were a common feature of train travel from the late nineteenth to the mid-twentieth century. Pullman wanted to provide his customers with a luxurious experience, and he employed only black workers as his porters to provide a sense of plantation-like service. Although the porter's costume was degrading, the position was, ironically, frequently the best job a black male could obtain; many porters were college graduates. The cars were manufactured (by native and immigrant whites) in the model community of Pullman, Illinois. One disgruntled worker reported that "we are born in a Pullman house, fed from the Pullman shop, taught in the Pullman school, catechized in the Pullman church, and when die we shall be buried in the Pullman cemetery and go to the Pullman hell." A wage cut in 1893 pushed workers to revolt; in 1894 Pullman workers struck, and railroad workers boycotted Pullman cars. Pullman convinced the federal government to place mail bags in their cars so that the boycott interfered with the delivery of the U.S. Mail. Confronted by company guards and federal troops, the strike quickly collapsed.

See also Paternalism; Railroads.

Racism

Racism is the belief that members of other races are inherently inferior. Historians have long been interested in the origins and influence of racism on the process of industrialization, vigorously debating whether the racism of Europeans had its roots in economic exploitation of African slaves or whether racialized slavery itself was a response to deep-rooted European values that associated "blackness" with negative qualities. One point of consensus in recent years has been that race is best understood as a social construct rather than a genetic or physiological "fact."

The racialization of slavery in the seventeenth century was a turning point in the history of racism. Whereas African workers had been treated similarly to European servants until that time, the codification of racial slavery meant that even impoverished Europeans were afforded preferential status as "whites," a concept that had to be invented for the occasion. In the nineteenth century, the colonialization of Asia and Africa by European empires and the industrialization of the United States reinforced Europeans' belief in their superiority over non-white races. The belief in the "natural" superiority of "whites" was further reinforced by the absolute and relative growth of European populations in the world and by technical and industrial superiority.

Even after the end of slavery, the ideology of whiteness legitimized the subordination of black workers in the United States, Latin America, South Africa, and European colonies. Although black slaves had held both skilled and unskilled positions in textile mills in the southern United States, blacks were largely barred from southern mills after emancipation. In fact, outside of the iron and steel industry, few blacks were allowed to operate machinery (although several black Americans became famous inventors). Whereas many workers from South and Eastern Europe also faced discrimination by employers, these stereotypes resulted more frequently in their being refused promotions than in their being refused employment. After World War II racism also divided the work force in Western Europe. Union movements in the United States and elsewhere have often been divided by racism, and some white unionists have even advocated racial exclusions.

See also Abolitionism; Black Workers; Dual Labor Markets; Ethnicity; Imperialism; Nationalism; Social Darwinism.

References Adas, Michael. *Machines as the Measure of Men: Science, Technology, and Ideologies of Western Dominance* (1989); Balibar, Étienne, and Immanuel Wallerstein. *Race, Nation, Class: Ambiguous Identities* (1991).

Railroads

Railroads played a major role in the "second" industrial revolution, creating dramatic changes in the ways that transportation, communication, markets, businesses, finance, and labor were organized. They were first launched in Britain around 1825. In 1830 the United States had 23 miles of railroad track; by 1890 it had over 150,000. Other industrializing countries, such as Germany, France, and Japan, were not far behind in developing their own national rail networks.

The speed and reliability of railroads (which unlike canals or rivers did not freeze over in wintertime) enabled producers to dramatically increase the volume and speed with which goods were shipped. Thanks to the railroad, postal rates fell dramatically in industrial countries during the mid-nineteenth century. This development was accompanied by the explosive growth of the telegraph system; together,

Workers repair Liberia's first railroad during the 1980s.

these two developments enabled the coordination of efficient safe shipments of goods by the railroads.

In the United States, railroads facilitated the marketing of grain, which could be shipped to ports and then exported to Europe. Rail networks encouraged both the development of national markets for consumer goods and the development of factories, in part because reliable deliveries of supplies allowed manufacturers to centralize their production and other activities. By the middle of the nineteenth century, railroads had themselves become major consumers of iron, and later in the century, of steel, coal, machinery, and labor. By the end of the century, railroads were the country's largest employers, and the railroad unions were among the strongest in the country.

Because railroads required enormous capital investments, they were an important arena for early investment bankers—much of the modern stock market had its beginnings in the raising of capital for new railroad firms. Because functioning railroads required the coordination of vast amounts of information, equipment, goods, and labor, these operations had a large impact on the development of modern corporate bureaucracies. Railroad companies were the most common model upon which national corporations modeled themselves.

See also Gould, Jay; Stephenson, George.

Reference Chandler, Alfred D., Jr. *The Railroads: The Nation's First Big Business* (1965).

Reconstruction

See Emancipation.

Refrigeration

Refrigeration technology married industry and agriculture in new ways. The expansion of meat production in the United States and Australia during the nineteenth century led to efforts to find ways to export more efficiently. Canned meats proved unsatisfactory for most products. T. S. Mort, a wool broker in Australia, began experiments with freezing meat in 1843, and in 1861 the first freezing plant was set up in Sydney. Regular supplies did not begin until 1875, and then several firms in the United States, Europe, and Australia perfected the techniques, all of which were based on ammonia compression. The first refrigerated ship was built in 1879. Regular shipments of frozen meat expanded steadily from the mid-1870s, particularly from North America, Australia, New Zealand, and Argentina. The result was a huge boost to commercial agriculture, while peasant farmers in Europe faced growing import competition.

See also Agriculture; Australia.

Religion

The relationship between religion and the industrial revolution is complex and varied. In most industrial societies, the importance of religion declines, but the rate of that decline varies greatly. The United States, one of the leading industrial societies by 1900, was much more religious than Britain or France, as measured by church attendance and polls of beliefs, a difference that has persisted in the twentieth century.

Religious affiliations play some role in causing aspects of the industrial revolution. Certain religious minorities turn to business innovation as a means of gaining status in societies that otherwise exclude them from power and to prove God's favor. Thus many entrepreneurs in Russia were Old Believers, members of a sect that separated from the mainstream of the Orthodox religion several centuries before. Certain religions may also encourage business life. The Weber thesis (Max Weber, German sociologist) argues that Protestantism promotes economic dynamism because people want to use worldly success to prove that they are saved (since God's will is preordained) and because a sober morality discourages expensive living and so enhances savings. This thesis cannot be carried too far in explaining entrepreneurial origins, but in certain cases, like Alsace in France, a disproportionate number of the most dynamic businessmen were certainly Protestant.

Industrialization can also promote a new religious fervor among the working class, where a separate, often rather emotional religion can provide comfort and community ties amid wrenching economic change. Many British workers converted to Methodism, a version of Protestantism created in the eighteenth century. Methodism gave them a sense of belonging separate from the more conventional faiths of employers. It also provided them with group cohesion and organizational experience; many early labor leaders were of Methodist background. For many immigrant workers in the United States, a fervent Catholicism played a similar role, which is one reason religion survived better in the United States than in some other industrial states. In another variant, the Japanese government (with some success) deliberately tried to revive Shintoism as a means of promoting national loyalty to ease the strains of industrialization. Employers in Europe often encouraged religion in hopes of contenting their workers with other-worldly solace, though this strategy did not always work.

Industrialization often weakened religion, however. Workers found big-city churches too strange and luxurious; they also noted that many established churches backed the employer class. Most socialist movements were hostile to religion. Middle-class people were less alienated from religion, but as their interest in consumer pleasures grew with their growing faith in science, their religious fervor often waned. Churches often tried to go along with this change. Mainstream Protestant sects in the

United States that had been hostile to consumer materialism in the 1830s were arguing by the 1870s that material pleasures were fully compatible with religious life. Similar trends entered the Reform current of Judaism. Either by outright abandonment of organized religious activity and belief, or by diluting the importance of religion, industrialization tended to cut religion back by the later nineteenth century. Western Europe and Japan became increasingly secular, though significant minorities of practicing faithful (Christians in Europe, Buddhists in Japan) remained. By the later twentieth century, continuing a trend visible since about 1850, only about 10 percent of the British population professed active religious commitment. After the revolution of 1917, the Soviet state actively repressed religion, though without full success.

By the late nineteenth century Christian churches in Europe and the United States made additional adjustments to industrial society beyond greater acceptance of consumer interests and, often, a reduced emphasis on hellfire and damnation. The tradition of charity gained new forms. The Salvation Army (founded in Britain in 1878) developed a new mission to the urban poor. Various churches ran settlement houses. Pope Leo XIII in 1891 issued the encyclical *Rerum novarum*, urging better treatment of workers, though attacking socialism. Important Catholic trade union movements arose in Germany, Belgium, and elsewhere—less aggressive and also smaller than socialist unions, they nevertheless pressed for reforms and participated in some strikes.

As religions revive in many less industrial areas of the world by the later twentieth century, the relationship of religion and industrialization remains complex. Islamic and Hindu fundamentalism, as well as the spread of Christianity and Islam in Africa and of evangelical Protestantism in Latin America, make it clear that religion remains a cultural force to be reckoned with.

See also Causes of the Industrial Revolution.

References Mcleod, Hugh. *Religion and the Working Class in Nineteenth-Century Britain* (1984); Tawney, R. W. *Religion and the Rise of Capitalism* (1962).

Research and Development

Research and development, or "R and D," refers to organized efforts by business or government to innovate in products and methods. Throughout the eighteenth and nineteenth centuries, many new manufacturing processes or products had been produced by brilliant individuals such as Richard Arkwright or Charles Goodyear. By the end of the nineteenth century, institutions that relied on a systematic scientific method rather than innovative individuals accounted for most of the new developments in science and technology. In 1900 few corporations underwrote research; by 1930 nearly 60 percent of the largest corporations in the United States had their own laboratories, almost 30 percent had cooperative arrangements with other companies or universities, and the remainder intended to begin a laboratory soon.

Germany pioneered in research and development, as chemical companies began to build laboratories with university researchers as early as the 1830s. Developments in the United States at first imitated the European example. Small research and development laboratories had been established by Thomas Alva Edison and Alexander Graham Bell in the late nineteenth century. However, research was expensive and only large corporations such as General Electric or American Telephone and Telegraph commanded the necessary financial and human resources for conducting both basic and applied research. A handful of companies, most of them in the electrical and petrochemical industries, employed one-third of all researchers in the United States. New products and production processes allowed these corporations and cartels to maintain a vast technological lead over their competitors— ensuring a near monopoly in such crucial areas as chemicals, telephones, radio, electrical equipment, and appliances.

During World War II the demands of large-scale military research (such as the project to build an atomic weapon) required new levels of collaboration among large corporations, the government, and universities. Wartime R&D produced significant new technologies such as atomic power, computers, and synthetic rubber, but the institutional relationships among military contractors, the government, and universities proved equally important in the long run. Throughout the Cold War era, the United States conducted an enormous amount of applied and especially basic research, although by the 1960s European and Japanese companies were spending more on basic research than their U.S. counterparts. Japanese companies proved more adept at marketing new technologies, particularly in the field of electronics.

See also Bell Laboratories; Military Industrial Complex; Science.

References Anderson, Alun M., and John Sigurdon. *Science and Technology in Japan* (1991); Hounshell, David A., and John K. Smith. *Science and Corporate Strategy: Du Pont R&D, 1902–1980* (1988); Noble, David F. *America by Design: Science, Technology and the Rise of Corporate Capitalism* (1979).

Research Laboratories

By the late nineteenth century, technological innovation or invention by the brilliant individual was displaced by cadres of university-trained technicians and scientists located within institutions devoted to the development of advanced technology that could be marketed. Even Thomas Edison and George Westinghouse, both extremely gifted inventors, developed corporate research laboratories that operated as "invention factories." Many German firms, in industries like chemicals, pioneered in corporate sponsorship of research operations. By the early twentieth century the technical expansion of the "second" industrial revolution relied on corporations' research laboratories. By World War II the complexity of technology was beginning to outstrip the resources of corporations, and government played an important role with private researchers and universities in developing such technologies like computers and nuclear power. During the Cold War this relationship accelerated and the military, universities, and corporations became increasingly intertwined.

See also Bell Laboratories; Military Industrial Complex; National Aeronautics and Space Administration.

Restriction of Output

One of workers' most important means of resistance to industrial employers has been to restrict output. Many new recruits to nineteenth- and twentieth-century factories were warned by established workers not to work too hard lest they help raise what was expected of everyone else. Simply by not working as hard, or equally important, by not working as smart, workers deny employers full potential productivity gains and therefore potential profits. From workers' perspective, the chief benefit of restricting output is that it does not entail as much risk as more confrontational methods such as strikes or petitions, and it is therefore possible for individual workers to employ this tactic. Many workers felt they had every right to maintain a traditional pace; they felt that employers simply took any extra effort for their own profit, often laying off workers in the process. Historians have observed that many workers, from slaves to secretaries, have used this tactic to their advantage and that much of the motivation for scientific management arose from managers' desire to circumvent workers' restriction of output.

The Industrial Workers of the World were great advocates of what they called soldiering or sabotage, which generally meant restricting output. The term sabotage derives from the French word sabot, or wooden shoe. Although some claim that French workers would throw a sabot into a machine as a protest, it is more likely that the term derived from the purportedly slow and clumsy work done by new workers, many of them peasants wearing sabots.

The IWW frequently used pictures of wooden shoes in their propaganda and many IWW members advocated more creative (or extreme) forms of sabotage. One IWW member wrote that if workers would merely work five minutes out of the day for the working class, for instance by snipping the bands off of bundles, thereby slowing the loading process, they could work the rest of the day for their employers without fear of unemployment.

Although time and motion studies and piece rates limit the effectiveness of restriction of output, many workers on repetitive jobs, even after their jobs have been made more efficient, have discovered new ways to increase their own productivity. Workers have frequently hidden these new short cuts in order to create breaks for themselves. One American autoworker in the 1980s found that by concentrating and not slowing down, he was able to work both his job and his neighbor's—although not for the full eight hours. By "doubling up," his work mate was able to sleep in a nearby storage room. Such extremes required not only the cooperation of his union but of his foreman as well. The worker had to carefully avoid doubling up when other foremen or time and motion men toured his plant, and when he was transferred to a new job, his new foreman forbade the practice.

Because the philosophy of scientific management has viewed workers as working best when given specific directions, another form of restricting output is to "work to rule." Under this strategy, workers only do exactly what their managers tell them to do. If they receive no instructions, or poorly worded instructions, unionists can make costly mistakes. Some unionists have observed that working to rule is simply an exaggerated form of what scientific managers themselves practice on an average working day. In the end, a rigid and inflexible manager may be the biggest saboteur of all.

See also Taylor, Frederick Winslow; Workers' Control.

Reference Montgomery, David. *Workers' Control in America: Studies in the History of Work, Technology, and Labor Struggles* (1979).

Retirement

No systematic idea of retirement existed before the industrial revolution. Many traditional workers and peasants hoped to be able to ease up in their later years, supported by younger family members, but actual patterns were diverse. Early industrialization worsened conditions for many older workers who were unable to keep up with the pace of factory labor. Older workers tended to suffer declining pay and increasing periods of unemployment. By the late nineteenth century many employers in the United States and Europe believed that only younger workers had the energy and learning capacity needed for industrial work, as belief in the debility of old age intensified. Various working-class movements, for their part, began to urge retirement funds and sometimes used mutual aid to provide benefits for older members. A few companies, like American Express, began to set up retirement funds in the 1870s, mainly for white-collar workers. Bismarck's social insurance laws in Germany, passed in the 1880s, included old-age insurance, and the legislation was widely copied. Benefits were low, however, and few workers qualified. It was the Great Depression of the 1930s that encouraged more systematic government attention to retirement, as many older workers suffered from unemployment, and the desire to trim the labor force to make room for the young spread widely. Most European countries, and the United States through the Social Security system, set up retirement insurance, which by the 1940s and 1950s began to encourage employers not just to permit retirement but often to require it as a means of trimming unwanted workers from their rosters. For their part, unions frequently demanded employer-paid pension schemes to supplement government plans. Other industrial societies, like Japan, also developed retirement systems, though standard ages ranged from fifty-five (Japan) to seventy (Scandinavia). Industrialization, in sum, complicated the work life of older workers; its later stages began to remove most older workers from the labor force (just as children had been removed earlier). While some workers resented compulsory retirement and suffered from the interruption in routines, most seemed to welcome it: pressures for earlier retirements developed in many industries, especially by blue-collar workers. Only at the end of the twentieth century did growing life expectancy and the cost of retirement programs bring some second thoughts about this industrial pattern.

See also State, Role of the.

References Graebner, William. *A History of Retirement* (1980); Hannah, Leslie. *Inventing Retirement* (1986).

Revolutions of 1848

Major revolutions broke out in many European countries during the winter and spring of 1848. Liberals sought more constitutional, parliamentary regimes, while nationalists in Italy, Germany, and Hungary worked for national unification or independence. Peasant unrest stirred in many countries. Urban workers played a vital role in the revolutions. They were roused by the impact of a severe depression (1846–1847), which had caused unemployment and rising food prices. Artisans in many areas sought to stem the advance of industrialization. Many German artisans asked for a return of the guild system, in order to protect established skills and values. Many French artisans and factory workers turned to utopian socialism, urging a new system of cooperation to replace the individualistic principles of industrial work and inequality among the classes. The 1848 revolutions saw the first entry of factory workers as significant components of popular protest, particularly in the Paris rising.

The 1848 revolutions largely failed, beaten down by the established governments. One reason for failure was growing middle-class fears that the working class was becoming too radical, and that social order was more important than continued revolutionary striving. Many radical leaders were arrested or exiled as the revolutions wound down in 1849. This loss set back the European labor movement and led to a period of repression, although those workers who emigrated to the United States often played a major role in the expansion of the labor movement there. Failure in 1848 marked the end of most visionary artisan risings in western and central Europe. As many artisans realized that they could not restore older work systems, they turned to more moderate unionism or (by the 1860s) joined new kinds of socialist movements. Partly because of the decline of traditional artisanal power, 1848–1849 marked the end of the revolutionary period in European history that had begun with the French Revolution of 1789. Later protest movements focused more explicitly on industrial conditions, although they were sometimes imbued with revolutionary rhetoric, and they operated in a different climate, with most middle-class people now opposed to revolution and with an increasingly effective state, flanked by larger police forces, also actively keeping protest within bounds. The revolutions of 1848, in other words, marked a boundary between preindustrial protest directed against some of the early signs of industrialization, and new kinds of action spurred by more advanced industrial forms.

See also Chartism; Franchise.

Reference Stearns, Peter N. *1848: The Tide of Revolutions* (1974).

Rhee, Syngman (1875–1965)

Syngman Rhee was the first President of the Republic of South Korea from 1948 until his ouster by military coup in 1961. Korea inherited from its Japanese colonizers a small textile industry and a system of agricultural taxation that shunted entrepreneurial activity into land speculation. Immediately after World War II Korea was divided into a communist North Korea and an anticommunist South Korea. After the invasion of South Korea by North Korea in 1950, a bitter war was fought until 1953 in which hundreds of thousands died.

The war made South Korea an important site of the Cold War, and Rhee garnered as much military aid and economic assistance as he could. By 1953 South Korea had the fourth largest army in the world outside of the Soviet bloc. Rhee's regime was notoriously corrupt, and development was further hindered by the fact that much of the advice of U.S. development officers was ill-suited to the needs of South Korea. For instance, Rhee's privatization of the banking system and encouragement of decentralized ownership of industry aided corruption and diverted investments away from strategic industries. (During Rhee's regime, the North Korean economy grew at a faster rate.) Because the United States made plentiful loans available for industrial concerns, the corrupt officials in the regime directed entrepreneurs toward industry. The military regime that ousted Rhee instituted tighter centralized control over the banking system and favored the creation of industrial cartels, but it continued to lobby for continued economic and military aid from the United States.

Reference Amsden, Alice. *Asia's Next Giant: South Korea and Late Industrialization* (1989).

Rockefeller, John D. (1837–1937)

John D. Rockefeller was one of the founders of the Standard Oil Company. He is also well known as the founder of the University of Chicago as well as of the philanthropic foundation that bears his name. The modern petroleum industry began in the oil fields of western Pennsylvania in the 1859; Rockefeller went into the refinery business in 1863 in the strategic location of Cleveland, Ohio. The market for oil was notoriously unstable during its early years, and the price per barrel fluctuated wildly. Rockefeller believed that the public needed to know his product was reliable and standardized, hence the choice of his company's name. Through Rockefeller's capacity for organization, planning, and deal making, Standard Oil garnered 90 percent of the market by 1880. Rockefeller used his monopoly to organize and standardize the entire U.S. market. Standard Oil retained its monopoly by using such tactics as railroad rebates, by which railroad companies paid Standard Oil part of the money paid to them by other companies. Such questionable tactics were perfectly legal at the time, although Rockefeller did not enjoy having his business practices exposed by muckraking journalists.

See also Interstate Commerce Commission.

Reference Yergin, Daniel. *The Prize: The Epic Conquest for Oil, Money, and Power* (1991).

Rubber

Uses of rubber were first discovered by Central and South American Indians, who used latex, the juice of the rubber tree, to make bouncing balls and to spread on bottles for waterproofing. European work on rubber began with experiments by French and English chemists in the eighteenth century; the discovery by Joseph Priestley that the material rubbed out marks led to the English word for the substance. British inventions advanced rubber processing. In 1823 Charles Macintosh made raincoats—macintoshes—with a rubber filler between layers of cloth. In 1839 Charles Goodyear, a Connecticut inventor, accidentally spilled a heated rubber-sulfur compound and discovered that it hardened without sticking or cracking in hot or cold weather. This process, called vulcanization, set the rubber industry in motion. Rubber could now be used for consumer products and industrial seals. In the 1870s growing demand led the British to cultivate rubber trees in Southeast Asia (for example, Malaysia, Vietnam, Sri Lanka), where huge, European-owned plantations developed and became the major source of world supply. Industrialization induced a huge change in rural labor in these areas. The invention of the automobile made rubber a big business. Work on synthetic rubber began in the 1920s and was perfected both in Germany and the United States by 1939. The U.S. government supported a crash campaign in synthetic rubber production in World War II—one of the great success stories of government sponsorship and emergency reaction—amid disruptions of supply due to Japanese conquests in Asia.

Reference Weinstein, Barbara. *The Amazon Rubber Boom, 1850–1920* (1983).

Ruling Class

The ruling class constitutes the social group or groups from which a society's power wielders are usually drawn—the leaders in government, the economy, and culture (religion, media). When the industrial revolution began, most societies had a fairly well-defined ruling class drawn from the upper ranks of the landowning aristocracy. In Europe (including Russia) and Japan, major government and military officials came from this group. The economy was dominated by the interests of big estate owners. Leading appointees to church positions in Europe came from aristocratic families or their nominees. In several places, such as France, the aristocracy had tightened its hold as a ruling class during the eighteenth century in response to challenges from the middle class and to internal population growth; more top positions were reserved for aristocratic families than had been true earlier. The United States had no aristocracy, but leading planter families in the South and traditional merchant families in the North provided the bulk of the ruling class prior to industrialization.

The industrial revolution did not change this traditional ruling class as rapidly as one might expect. Rising factory owners were content to leave a great deal of power in the hands of others, as long as industry was supported. Many early factory owners had only modest operations, and were in no position to challenge for entry to a ruling class. Even big business rivaled the wealth of the top landowners only gradually—only by 1850 in Britain did large factory owners and merchants match aristocratic wealth. The aristocracy retained great prestige aside from wealth, which made even successful factory owners somewhat deferential. The same held true in the United States, where old merchant families continued to dominate many urban elites well into the later part of the century. To be sure, voting rights expanded—in 1832 the British Reform Bill gave the middle class the vote—but the social origins of government leaders did not change much; the leaders simply became somewhat more sensitive to business interests, as in repealing the Corn Law.

By the late nineteenth century, a new ruling class did form in most industrial countries (including Japan, but not Russia, which tried to preserve traditional aristocratic power even as it industrialized). It consisted of a mixture of leading aristocrats and the most successful industrialists. This group now shared educational patterns, attending the same fashionable schools and universities. Intermarriage was common, as was compromise over economic policy. Leading government figures were drawn from this group, though aristocrats continued to dominate the military. Patterns were, again, somewhat different in the United States, where "Gilded Age" big businessmen had more exclusive power. In all industrial societies, talented individuals from lower social levels could rise into the ruling class on the basis of success in business or education. This new, merged ruling class persisted through World War II.

The failure of many industrial societies during the Great Depression and World War II prompted a substantial change in the ruling class after the mid-1940s. Many older big business families were shunted aside, sometimes because of fascist or collaborationist activities during World War II. The aristocracy faded, hit by new tax levels and the continued relative decline of agriculture. A new ruling class arose on the basis of managerial ability and educational achievements. Drawn mainly from middle-class ranks, it included a minority of educationally successful people from the working class. Training, more than ownership, now determined entry into the ruling class. Many people referred to the new ruling class as "technocrats" because of their emphasis on technical knowledge and their delight in planning. Newcomers were particularly successful in obtaining top positions in the increasingly powerful media, while church and military leadership continued to be more friendly to people with more traditional social credentials; some observers talked of "multiple elites" now running industrial societies, with somewhat different characteristics depending on sector (politics, media, unions, business, and so on). The increasing conversion of the most advanced industrial economies to service activities and the rise of the computer pushed this new ruling class toward increasing emphasis on technical and educational attainments and control of information.

References Dahrendorf, Ralf. *Class and Class Conflict in Industrial Society* (1959); Jaher, Frederic. *The Urban Establishment* (1982).

Russia and the Soviet Union

In the nineteenth century Russia had rich mineral deposits of coal and iron but lacked a vigorous class of merchants or artisans to fully exploit them. As a consequence, the role of the czarist state was particularly important, both in terms of its social reforms (such as the emancipation of the serfs) and of its sponsoring or subsidizing of industries. In the Crimean War of 1854–1855, Russia was defeated on its own doorstep by industrialized Western powers. The czar responded by freeing the serfs in 1861 (in large part to create a more flexible work force—a true working class) and by increasing the financial incentives to foreign entrepreneurs to set up factories in Russia. Serge Witte, Russia's Finance Minister, encouraged the growth of a railroad network, and by 1900 there were 35,000 miles of track. By the 1910s Russia was a major supplier of oil to Europe and had a large iron and steel industry, textile mills, and armament factories.

By the early twentieth century, industrialization was gaining steam, although the vast majority of the country (over 80 percent) were impoverished peasants, and the standard of living of the working class remained quite low. Over half of all industrial firms were foreign-owned. The political stability of the czarist regime was challenged in 1905 and then overthrown in 1917 by workers led by Lenin and his Bolshevik Party. With great difficulty the Bolshevik Party completed a unique industrial revolution in what was renamed the Union of Soviet Socialist Republics, or Soviet Union.

In 1928 Stalin launched the Soviet Union on a path toward a wholly state-run economy after a period of experimentation in the 1920s with a mix of private and state-run enterprises (the New Economic Policy). After 1928 heavy industry was favored (partly to defend the state from external attack) and production grew rapidly under a system of five-year plans in the 1930s. The state began to institute social welfare schemes for workers, including pensions, subsidized housing, and day care (to ease the burdens of working women so more of them could enter the work force). Just as standards of living were increasing, industrial production was shattered by the invasion by Nazi Germany. The Soviet Union's new factories (many of them built in the remote Ural mountains) allowed them to defeat the Nazis, but only after many cities were destroyed and 20 million people died.

The massive losses of World War II meant that Soviet society rebuilt slowly, particularly because many resources were directed toward the military during the Cold War. The state subsidized collective forms of consumption such as public transportation, public laundries, cultural institutions, and so on. Growth rates were high, about 6 percent a year. Half of all Russians now lived in cities, for the basic industrialization process had been completed. Beginning in the late 1950s, Nikita Khrushchev directed more production toward consumer goods, although heavy industry was still favored. However, workers' standards of living (particularly when compared to those of the Soviet Union's capitalist adversaries) remained low; workers' discontent with political repression and bread-and-butter issues resulted in a few strikes and widespread cynicism and restriction of output. (A common saying in the 1970s was that the state "pretends to pay us and we pretend to work.") By the 1980s Soviet society was in crisis, the economy was stagnating in the midst of massive military expenditures, and criticism of the government (particularly its inability to raise living standards) began to rise. By 1989 the political bonds of the Soviet Union began to unravel. Although promarket reformers gained control of Russia in 1991, industrial production and living standards for most people have plummeted.

See also Eastern Europe; Russian Revolution of 1917; Stakhanovites; Urbanization.

References Friedgut, Theodore H. *Life and Work in Russia's Donbass, 1860–1924* (1989); Hosking, Geoffrey. *The First Socialist Society: A History of the Soviet Union from Within* (1993).

Russian Revolution of 1917

Until 1917 most socialists believed that the first workers' revolution would take place in highly industrialized countries such as Germany, Austria, or France—certainly not in relatively backward Russia. Although there were many workers and large factories in Petrograd and Moscow, most of the country was comprised of impoverished, illiterate peasants. Indeed, even Lenin believed that Russia would only be the first country to embrace socialism and anticipated aid from revolutionary workers republics in Europe. Although several revolts occurred in Germany, Hungary, and Italy, they were temporary affairs; only in the mid-1920s did the Bolshevik Party accept the notion of "socialism in one country." The Russian revolution and the Soviet experiment in industrialization (without markets, unemployment, capitalists, entrepreneurs, or private banking or farming) provides a unique model of industrialization.

One of the classic latecomer industrializers, Imperial Russia in 1917 was still predominantly a rural, agricultural and underdeveloped country. Although many forces helped to produce its revolution, the nature of Russian industrialization and the organization of workers themselves played a crucial role. Industrial facilities in Russia tended to be large, and many owners were foreigners; thus workers had little opportunity to identify with their employers. Under the czar, workers were not free to form unions and there were no elections. Within clandestine organizations, workers proved receptive to socialist ideas. Without the social shock absorber of electoral politics, workers frequently made political as well as economic demands during their strikes and demonstrations. The czarist system was thrown into crisis by the strain of World War I. The requirements of prolonged modern war caused the relatively backward Russian economic system to unravel, while the incredibly harsh experiences of the war undermined many soldiers' faith in their government.

In February 1917, strikes and demonstrations by workers escalated into a revolution that attracted support from disgruntled soldiers, professionals, and even the Orthodox Church. Czar Nicholas abdicated, but councils (soviets) of workers and soldiers uneasily coexisted with parliamentary forms of government dominated by liberal members of the middle class. The provisional government refused to end the increasingly unpopular war, and by October the Bolsheviks seized power, promising to end the war and to give factories to the workers and land to the peasants. Once in power, the Bolshevik Party did end the war and conducted land reform; the party also moved decisively to consolidate its own power. Whether by design or in order to save the revolution from its myriad internal (nobles, priests, landlords) and external (western governments) enemies, workers' councils were gradually stripped of power and even socialist parties were banned.

After the chaotic period of "war communism," Lenin launched cautious market reforms, but by 1928 production of industrial and agricultural goods were still a fraction of what they had been in 1913—the result of world war, civil war, industrial upheaval, and mismanagement. In 1928

A Russian soldier (center) covers his ears as troops take aim during the 1917 Russian Revolution.

the Bolsheviks launched the five-year plans that reintroduced the quota system of production for most goods and instituted the brutal process of forced collectivization of agriculture. Although the Soviet Union was technically a workers' state, the Bolsheviks suppressed workers' soviets in the 1920s, and party leaders became far more privileged than those they supposedly represented. Under Stalin, millions of peasants, workers, and Bolsheviks were killed because they were considered direct or indirect threats to his rule. Although under capitalism the state had always played a large role in allocating productive resources and structuring markets, Stalin created a system in which the state completely took over the functions of entrepreneurs, capitalists, and markets. The system did provide workers some benefits: unemployment was abolished, and although workers were poor by Western standards, they eventually enjoyed free medical care, education, and housing.

Although there is a widespread tendency today to view the Soviet experiment as inevitably doomed, this assumption was certainly not generally held in the period between 1917 and the 1960s. The first successful workers' revolution gave hope to many nationalists and leftists around the world. Some Indian nationalists were encouraged by the success of the revolution against the czar. Many Americans feared or hoped that Seattle's general strike in 1919, in which the unions began to assume many of the powers of state, would emulate the soviet experiment. The very existence of the Soviet Union arguably increased the interest of Western governments and employers in shoring up workers' loyalty through social insurance schemes. Although both Hitler and Mussolini were vehemently anticommunist, both fascist leaders found it necessary to incorporate the rhetoric of socialism into their movements. Indeed, many observers felt that German, Italian, and Western elites tolerated fascism because they felt the alternative was socialist revolution.

Although its meaning is still bitterly contested by the left, right, and liberals, all agree that the Russian Revolution of 1917 was a major turning point in world history. For conservatives, this revolution proves that the insistence on egalitarianism inevitably leads to the prison camp, as well as indicating the superiority of an economy relatively free of state intervention. Liberals tend to be somewhat more sympathetic to the Bolsheviks' goals, though entirely disapproving of their means. Most leftists long ago developed their own harsh critiques of the Soviet Union, but many still find the ideal of a workers' republic appealing, and even the attempt by Stalin to launch his underdeveloped, agrarian nation into full industrialization earns their grudging respect. The impact of 1917 can be indirectly gauged by the significance that many people attach to 1989, the year that the Berlin Wall fell and the Soviet system collapsed.

See also Socialism.

Reference Mandel, David. *The Petrograd Workers and the Fall of the Old Regime: From the February Revolution to the July Days, 1917* (1983).

Saint Simon, Claude H. (1760–1825)

A French nobleman writing in the wake of the 1789 revolution and often called the founder of French socialism, Saint Simon's vision was actually more technocratic than socialist. He urged further industrialization as a means of progress, arguing that scientifically trained experts could devise more efficient production and eliminate idleness. His vision foreshadowed the beliefs of later engineers and state planners. Saint Simon's followers, however, in the 1830s and 1840s, began to argue that private property ownership was inconsistent with progress, and they joined the ranks of utopian socialists urging an alternative to capitalism. Saint Simon's views probably influenced Napoleon III, who took a more active role in economic planning and promoted technical innovation during the Second Empire (1852–1870).

See also Utopian Socialists.

Science

Europe's seventeenth-century scientific revolution was a vital backdrop to the later industrial revolution. During the scientific revolution, a variety of discoveries in physics (the understanding of gravity and planetary motion, synthesized by Isaac Newton) and in biology (the circulation of the blood) established that science could advance through a combination of experiment and mathematically based theory. This scientific method seemed to assure new knowledge, as against the relevance of traditional thinking. Scientific understanding began to advance over other forms of intellectual life, such as theology. Associated with the scientific revolution, most clearly in the thinking of Francis Bacon, was a contention that science could improve technology and better discipline the forces of nature.

Specific discoveries during the scientific revolution and the eighteenth century had direct relevance for industrialization. Better understanding of the behavior of gasses related to new work with steam. By the late eighteenth century, advances in chemistry, like Lavoisier's research on oxygen, prepared new industrial applications of chemistry. Scientific work with electricity and magnetism set the stage for invention of the telegraph.

Many early industrial inventors and some entrepreneurs had scientific training. The founder of the Du Pont firm in the United States, for example, had worked with Lavoisier. James Watt, though not formally trained in science, associated with scientists at the University of Glasgow and later did scientific research along with his technological focus.

Historians caution, however, against an oversimplified association of science with early industrialization and invention. Many inventors were artisan-tinkerers, with no scientific background. They used trial and error and their own manufacturing experience to come up with new methods. Formal scientific education was not widely available, either in Europe or the United States, until at least the 1830s. Most universities downplayed science in favor of philosophy and theology. Certainly many other factors besides science are necessary to account for technological advance.

The scientific revolution and the eighteenth-century Enlightenment, when scientific ideas were broadened and popularized, did help produce a new spirit of optimism and confidence that could inspire businessmen and political leaders beyond specific scientific findings. Benjamin Franklin expressed this spirit in 1790, when he wrote that progress gave promise of eradicating both disease and poverty—

and he worried that perhaps he had been born too soon. Optimism of this sort, widely discussed in the commercial and cultural associations many businessmen belonged to, contributed to a growing openness to change and innovation.

Science became more directly relevant to the industrial revolution by the 1830s. Training for engineers expanded, and it included applied science. Scientific research in German universities, in such areas as chemical fertilizers, had direct industrial relevance, and universities in other countries began to pick up this research approach. The nineteenth-century development of the oil industry depended on university-trained chemists and, later, geologists. British associations like the Royal Society played a vital role in research on electricity and chemistry, with many foreigners participating alongside British researchers. By the 1870s most inventors had engineering or scientific training, and corporations began to assemble formal research staffs to apply scientific knowledge and methods to the development of new techniques and products.

Regions seeking to industrialize late easily discerned the importance of science. Japanese visitors to the West in the 1860s and 1870s, including the educational reformer Yukichi Fukuzawa, urged that Japan adopt Western science in place of its Confucian approach to knowledge. Japanese scientific training expanded rapidly. Russia, especially in the Soviet period, also expanded scientific training and the role of science in education.

See also Causes of the Industrial Revolution; Engineering; Inventions; Research and Development.

Reference Musson, A. E., and Eric Robinson. *Science and Technology in the Industrial Revolution* (1969).

Scientific Management

Scientific Management (1911), by Frederick Winslow Taylor, outlines how to develop what one historian has termed "a technology of social production." Scientific managers sought to make the workplaces of large corporations more efficient and profitable by reducing the ability of workers to reduce output. Although Taylor was scientific management's chief publicist, the move toward applying the scientific method to the workplace also came from the increasing numbers of engineers in managerial positions. From the late nineteenth century until the 1920s, when management became a separate discipline, most discussion of managerial problems took place in engineering journals.

Scientific management sought to give managers unprecedented knowledge and control over the workplace. Rather than relying on the skill and initiative of skilled workers as they had done during the nineteenth century, managers sought to monopolize knowledge of the workplace through such means as time and motion studies. This reflected in part the exigencies of new forms of "continuous flow" technology such as the moving assembly line, but it also involved heightened levels of direct and indirect supervision. Workers were not simply watched but were offered incentives to produce—these new programs necessitated bureaucracies of accountants and clerical workers. The harsh pace of work frequently led to strikes or less obvious forms of sabotage, and after a government investigation in 1911 Taylorism was banned in the government shops of the United States. (This ban was lifted in 1949.)

By the 1920s scientific managers in the United States sought more humane ways to wring higher levels of production from workers. Many large corporations offered immigrant employees courses in English, opportunities to buy company stock, and sometimes subsidies to purchase a home. Industrial psychologists experimented with subtle ways to increase productivity such as piping music into work areas. Managers still supervised the workplace, but attempted (with some success) to induce workers to identify with their employers. The move toward "corporate welfare" was interrupted by the Great Depression of the 1930s and the unionization of many industries. Eventually, scientific managers found ways to use unions to help control workers—making the workplace more efficient. Scientific management continues to dominate the philosophies of many corporations.

See also Congress of Industrial Organizations; Restriction of Output; Workers' Control.

References Nelson, Daniel. *Managers and Workers: Origins of the New Factory System in the United States, 1880–1920* (1979); Noble, David F. *America by Design: Science, Technology, and the Rise of Corporate Capitalism* (1979).

"Second" Industrial Revolution

Many historians argue that between the late nineteenth and early twentieth centuries, a "second" industrial revolution occurred that built upon and then transformed earlier technological and organizational developments. Technological change in electrical equipment, petrochemicals, communications, and even steel increasingly required skills and resources beyond the scope of individual inventors and innovators; after the late nineteenth century, the centers of technological change were research laboratories and universities. Similarly, the dominant organizational form of business shifted from entrepreneurs to national corporations that were able to harness the massive financial, technical, scientific, and organizational resources required to develop, produce, market, and distribute industrial goods. Crucial skills were replaced by more automatic technologies such as riveting machines, which helped spur a larger labor movement.

See also Automobile; Bell Laboratories; Science.

Self-Help Literature

Samuel Smiles in Britain and Horatio Alger in the United States were classic authors of self-help literature during the mid-nineteenth century. The term "Horatio Alger story" came to mean a story about a self-made man. Alger, a clergyman, had titles like *Luck and Pluck*; Smiles featured *Character*, *Thrift*, and *Duty*. Smiles's and Alger's books sold widely, particularly to the middle class and artisanry, after the industrial revolution had begun, when people were eager to learn how to take advantage of new business opportunities. Smiles and Alger cited lots of rags-to-riches tales, with people whose hard work and diligence paid off in wealth despite a humble start. Personal qualities—the work ethic, honesty, savings, focus, and willpower—assured success in this vision, though the protagonist often took the precaution of marrying the boss's daughter. By implication, people who failed to rise lacked good personal qualities; the fault was their own. Smiles and Alger (and similar writers, including authors in France and Germany) undoubtedly fed the middle-class value system. Their approach also entered popular magazines, boys' stories, and primary-school readers. Writers like Smiles and Alger helped create powerful myths, particularly in the United States, about the degree of mobility available in the society and the number of business leaders who came from poor backgrounds. Both Smiles and Alger made considerable money from their writings, including books destined for young people. Interestingly, their popularity declined precipitously after the 1870s. By this point, the growing dominance of big business and the decline of the independent artisanry seemed to make this mobility message less relevant or realistic in industrial society. However, success-story values continued to be an important part of middle-class culture and social judgments well into the twentieth century.

See also Entrepreneurs, Origins of.

Reference Thernstrom, Stephan. *Poverty and Progress* (1964).

Semi-skilled Workers

Semi-skilled workers are probably the most common type of workers in factory industry, from the early industrial revolution onward. Unlike skilled workers, either in crafts or factories, the semi-skilled do not demand elaborate training. They typically operate a fairly small series of processes on a single-purpose machine like a mechanical loom or a lathe. They do, however, require a certain amount of training; people cannot be brought in off the street as unskilled operatives and perform their tasks successfully. In French textiles in the 1830s it was estimated that it took three to six months of training for a textile worker to become at all proficient and a year to reach full capacity. The existence of the category "semi-skilled" reflects the fact that most industrial operations require specialized knowledge or training but also that machines reduce the complexity of many formerly skilled tasks. The growing effort to break down complex tasks, which ultimately led to assembly-line operations, increased the number of semi-skilled workers in the factories.

Because the category was fairly new, and because by definition such workers lacked the bargaining power of their more skilled brethren, effective protest and formal organization by the semi-skilled was slow in coming. Many craft unions shunned them. As mass production spread, however, and as attempts to speed up semi-skilled work increased in the later nineteenth century, the semi-skilled came to dominate new forms of industrial unionism and the growing crescendo of strikes.

The stabilization of the size of the industrial working class in advanced industrial societies in the later twentieth century, with more advanced equipment and competition from new industrial areas, raises questions about the types of work available to the kinds of workers who once found semi-skilled employment.

See also Assembly Line; Working Class.

References Berlanstein, Lenard. *The Working People of Paris, 1870–1914* (1984); Evans, R. J., ed. *The German Working Class* (1982); Magraw, Roger. *A History of the French Working Class* (1992).

Serfs

Serfs are peasant farmers who work on a large estate (manor) in conditions between slavery and freedom. Under manorialism, serfs owe their landlords a portion of their produce and work service on the lords' land. They cannot legally leave the land. In return, landlords usually leave village agriculture undisturbed, provide some protection, and cannot evict serfs who fulfill their obligations. Serfdom is incompatible with industrialization, because it does not permit sufficient labor mobility; serfs who cannot leave their land cannot fill the ranks of factory workers. Manorialism declined in Western Europe from the later Middle Ages onward. Its early decline in Britain helps explain why this country had a particularly flexible labor force available for initial industrialization. Manorialism was fully abolished in much of western Europe in the French Revolution of 1789, in central Europe as a result of the 1848 revolutions. Russia, which developed a very harsh system of serfdom, sometimes used serf villages for manufacturing. Russians realized that they had to imitate Western Europe if they were to industrialize, and they enacted the Emancipation of the Serfs in 1861, thus permitting the spread of wage labor. Many Latin American peasants also worked in manorial conditions under colonialism and in the nineteenth century; here, too, land reforms, though incomplete, helped expand an industrial labor force.

See also Feudalism; Slavery.

Reference Blum, Jerome. *Lord and Peasant in Russia* (1961).

Sewing Machine

This device is a classic case of technology responding (if slowly) to need. As cloth output increased, the desirability of faster means of making clothing became obvious. But making sewing more automatic proved difficult. The first patented machine (1790) was invented by Thomas Saint, an Englishman. It passed thread automatically to a needle, while an awl made holes for the needle to pass through, but it was not practical. In 1830 a French inventor, Barthélemy Thimmonier, patented a machine for making soldiers' uniforms; the device was used, and indeed at one point angry workmen, out of their jobs, destroyed a number of machines. Other models were also developed before Elias Howe, an American, invented the type of machine now used (1846). Howe's machine carried thread to a needle while movements of an arm forced the needle through cloth. Subsequent inventions include a more automatic feed and Isaac Singer's foot-operated treadle and presser foot, the latter holding the fabric down on a feed plate.

Early machines were operated by human power, either in shops or at home. This device did not spark large factories, except for the manufacture of the machines themselves. The popularity of homemade clothing helped spur the growth of women's magazines containing patterns and dress designs. The Singer Sewing Machine Company first put an electric motor on the sewing machine in 1889, and sweatshop production of clothing spread rapidly thereafter. By this point sewing machines were also being applied to the manufacture of shoes, displacing many skilled cobblers and generating a growing number of shoe factories, with stitching done by semi-skilled workers, including many women.

See also Clothing; Inventions; Semi-skilled Workers.

Sexuality

Changes in sexual behavior predated the industrial revolution in places like Western Europe and Russia. Increased rural manufacturing allowed young people independent earnings and reduced community control over sexual behavior. Premarital sexual activity and rates of illegitimate births began to rise in the lower classes, beginning about 1780 in Western Europe and about 1880 in Russia. Industrialization fostered this trend. Young people moved into the cities, away from parental supervision. Single women had difficulty earning an adequate living, and urban prostitution increased rapidly. Male workers may have used sexuality to bolster their feelings of masculinity amid industrial jobs that deprived them of much sense of significance. Middle-class observers roundly criticized these trends of working-class sexuality. As middle-class standards relaxed and consumer values gained ground later in the nineteenth century, sexual pleasure began to seem more valid and important. Innovations such as vulcanized rubber (1840s) produced more reliable, cheaper means of birth control, decoupling sex and procreation. On balance, for a variety of reasons, industrialization promoted major changes in sexual behavior and enhanced the importance of sexual expression.

See also Women Workers.

Reference D'Emilio, John, and Estelle Freedman. *Intimate Matters: A History of Sexuality in America* (1989).

Sharecropping

Sharecropping is a system of labor organization in which laborers rent land from landowners and both receive "shares" of the crop at the end of the year. In theory the system is simple and fair, although in practice it was generally little better than the system of slavery that it replaced.

Sharecropping developed in the United States after the end of the American Civil War. In 1865 the South's economy was devastated, and it was unclear what would happen to several million former slaves or "freedmen" as they were called at the time. Most freedmen believed that the federal government should distribute land and the means to work it—a demand that boiled down to "forty acres and a mule." Former slaveowners generally succeeded in convincing the Northern army of occupation to favor property rights over the demands of freedmen for compensation for slavery. However, landowners generally lacked the means to pay freedmen wages, and freedmen refused to return to unfree labor. Sharecropping emerged as a compromise and spread throughout the cotton-growing regions of the South. Sharecropping was also common in southern Europe.

In practice, sharecropping generally degenerated into a form of semi-free labor through debt peonage. Landowners advanced sharecroppers seed, mules, supplies, and some food—all of which had to be repaid after the crops were harvested. Landowners frequently inflated the cost of what was advanced, and many illiterate farmers found themselves in a permanent cycle of debt. Of course, not all farmers were illiterate, but although some avoided the trap of debt, they were forced through lynchings or other terror tactics to stay another year. Many observers compared sharecropping in the United States to slavery, but sharecropping did in fact give black workers far greater control over their family and social lives than had been the case under bondage. It is a tribute to the resourcefulness of former slaves that by the end of the nineteenth century, several hundred thousand blacks had become landowners.

Many observers criticized the sharecropping system for retarding the development of industry in the South, for labor and capital remained tied to cotton production. The system of sharecropping began to break down in the period after World War I. Hundreds of thousands of white and black workers migrated to northern or southern cities during the 1910s during the Great Migration. Landowners resorted to desperate measures to retain their labor supply although sharecroppers were often able to maneuver their way to a factory job. During the 1930s the price of cotton plummeted and a blight of insects, the boll weevil, devastated much of the cotton crop. The New Deal government instituted price supports for agricultural commodities, which greatly eased the pressure for cotton farmers who owned their land. Farmers were given subsidies to take cotton out of production but as a rule refused to share the subsidy with their sharecroppers. In the late 1950s and 1960s, the sharecropping system was dealt a final blow when the mechanization of cotton picking eliminated the need for sharecroppers.

See also Black Workers.

References Jaynes, Gerald David. *Branches without Roots: Genesis of the Black Working Class in the American South, 1862–1882* (1986); Jones, Jacqueline. *The Dispossessed: America's Underclasses from the Civil War to the Present* (1992).

Sherman Anti-Trust Act

The Sherman Anti-Trust Act was passed by the U.S. Congress in 1890. It attempted to eliminate monopolies and penalize individuals who conspired to restrict trade. The law was intended to reduce the growing power of monopolies, such as John D. Rockefeller's Standard Oil Corporation. Many observers believed that the economic power of monopolistic corporations outstripped that of governments. In 1888, for instance, a single Boston-based railroad company had three times the number of employees and six times the revenues of the government of Massachusetts. In part because of its weak administrative enforcement and contradictory judicial interpretation, the law proved entirely ineffectual at preventing the merger movement of the early twentieth century, which created many monopolies and near monopolies. In fact, the first successful use of the Sherman Anti-Trust Act was directed against a union.

See also Interstate Commerce Commission; Laissez-faire.

Shibuzawa Eiichi (1840–1931)

An example of the Japanese industrialists who emanated from the growing ranks of commercial farmers, Shibuzawa, rural born, became a merchant and won a post in the Finance Ministry by backing the right side in Japan's 1860s conflicts that led to the establishment of the Meiji regime. In 1873 he made the so-called heavenly descent from government to private business, founding a bank and using depositors' money as capital for launching new industry. His first success was the Osaka Cotton Spinning Mill, which he started on a grand scale, because he was convinced that smaller units were uneconomical. He earned huge profits: the output of the company rose tenfold between 1896 and 1913. Shibuzawa expanded into cloth production, again sponsoring a massive growth in output. Shibuzawa exemplifies the links in Japan between government and private industry, but he made a lasting mark in the private sector, which dominated the growing textiles branch.

See also Japan; Mitsubishi.

Siemens

One of the great inventor-entrepreneur families of the industrial revolution, the Siemens family ultimately concentrated particularly on building Germany's huge electrical equipment industry. The family's industrial fortunes began with Werner Siemens, born in 1816 and trained in the army engineering school. Drawn to the new science of electricity, he won his first patent for using electricity in galvanizing metal in 1842; this process was sold to a Birmingham firm. Siemens invented improvements in telegraph wires and printing procedures, and his new company (with only three workers at first) produced equipment for new German railroads. Other family members joined as partners, and Siemens resigned from the army in 1849 to devote full time to the company. The company expanded steadily, selling equipment to Russia and the United States while maintaining close relations with a British subsidiary run by William Siemens. Siemens's procedures greatly improved the manufacture of steel (the Siemens-Martin process or open hearth). The main companies pioneered in laying underwater telegraph cables, laying a line from Ireland to the United States in 1874. Werner Siemens continued to apply his inventive genius, devising the electric dynamo by 1867 and advancing systems in electric lighting, the telephone, and electric elevators and trams. By 1914 the giant company employed 60,000 workers, rivaling Edison in creating the massive new electrical equipment industry.

Silk

This traditional luxury fabric had been commercially produced and exported for centuries; use of the silkworm was originally developed in China, which long remained a major source of world export. By the eighteenth century a considerable industry was located in Europe, particularly France and Italy, with many skilled artisans involved. Several early inventions were intended for silk—for example, a silk-throwing machine, devised in Italy and introduced into Britain by the Lombe brothers, for twisting cocoon filaments into thread. The Lombes set up a real factory, but silk was not readily mechanized. The threads broke easily, and complex silk designs required skilled handwork. Manual production of silk expanded among artisans in Lyons, France, for example, though again some factories developed by the 1840s. Japan seized silk export opportunities for the growing Western luxury market from the 1870s onward, taking over China's traditional role. During the 1870s the state introduced mechanical reeling machines, commonly powered by foot treadles, using machines devised in Europe. Equipment was simple and cheap, and small firms dominated the sector, depending on tens of thousands of low-paid female workers laboring in sweatshops. Thus silk was Japan's main means of earning foreign currency, and two-thirds of the product was exported. Japanese silk output expanded steadily; by 1923 production had expanded more than 50 times over the 1870 levels. With the 1920s artificial fibers like rayon and nylon began to cut into the silk market for products like women's stockings. Japanese industrialization weathered this strain, but the silk industry never fully recovered, a partial casualty of industrialization in the long run.

See also Synthetic Fabrics.

Skills

See Division of Labor.

Slater, Samuel (1768–1835)

Samuel Slater helped to found the textile industry in the United States. Born in England, Slater became a mechanic in Richard Arkwright's mill and learned how his system worked. Slater emigrated to the United States in 1789 in order to collect a bounty offered by the U.S. government for someone who could build a textile mill. Slater not only reconstructed Arkwright's designs from memory but succeeded in improving upon them in Pawtucket, Rhode Island.

Slavery

Slavery is a system of organizing labor in which some individuals are owned outright by others. Slavery has been an important method of accumulating surplus in many preindustrial societies, from ancient Greece and Rome to early modern Europe, Africa, and India. Before the conquest of the Americas, western European societies had a long history of unfree labor. Although serfdom had been reduced by the fifteenth century, forms of less than free labor still existed, largely in the form of bonded labor where servants or apprentices were bound over to a master for a period of several years. Early in the colonialization of the Americas, slavery became racialized, and Africans and African Americans became the largest group of unfree laborers. The enslavement of Africans in the plantation system provided many important crops for industrial production in Europe and the United States. Another important legacy of slavery was the enduring racial divisions it created between white and black workers.

By the seventeenth century, sugar production in the Caribbean was one of the most profitable ventures in the world. Conditions on sugar plantations were incredibly harsh; because so many slaves died, these slave societies required vast numbers of African slaves to replenish the labor supply. Caribbean slave societies were a social powder keg and slave revolts were a constant fear of the ruling class. The successful revolution in the British colonies in the late eighteenth century and the French Revolution inspired a revolution of slaves in Santo Domingo (Haiti). These "black Jacobins" succeeded in defending their revolution from their masters and the "revolutionary" French army. The revolution in Haiti reverberated throughout the Atlantic economy. The major reason why Napoleon was willing to sell the colony of Louisiana to the fledgling government of the United States was that France no longer required the foodstuffs that Louisiana had produced for Caribbean sugar planters.

Slavery in mainland North America was slower to develop into a plantation system. In the seventeenth century, numerous English bonded laborers (who had some legal rights) were used alongside African slaves. The status of African slaves was somewhat ambiguous, and some masters freed their slaves after several years of work. Slavery during this period was common in northern colonial seaports, and slaves were an important source of labor for artisans. The racial divide between slaves and Europeans was not fixed, and slaves and European workers cooperated in protests. During a revolt of slaves, servants, and workers in the mid-eighteenth century in New York City, one Irish seaman promised his comrades that he would "kill all the white people."

At this point, mainland North America was a society with slaves, but it was not a slave society. However, once tobacco, rice, indigo, and later cotton were discovered to be suitable crops for the southern colonies, the importance of slavery increased. As North America became a slave society, laws became harsher, and whites' racial attitudes began to harden. Slave masters succeeded in creating legal and cultural divisions between African slaves and British workers. Poor whites gained certain privileges over black slaves, earning what W. E. B. DuBois termed a "psychic wage." Many slaves took advantage of the American Revolution (1775–1783) and gained their freedom by fighting for the British, or less commonly, the rebel troops.

Slavery in the nineteenth century increased in the American South as the burgeoning textile mills of Britain and New England made slavery and cotton production more profitable. By the 1850s slaves were beginning to be used in southern coal mines, textile factories and iron mills. During this period, slavery in the North declined, although white workers and employers continued to marginalize black

This Virginia picture sketched in 1798 depicts an overseer standing casually as he watches two slaves. The original was ironically entitled "an overseer doing his duty."

workers by denying them access to factory or skilled work.

Although both Northern and Southern whites supported white supremacy, the social and cultural divisions between the slave and free labor systems was the largest factor leading to the American Civil War. The North initially desired to win the war without challenging slavery and returned runaway slaves to their masters. President Abraham Lincoln was convinced by abolitionists (and the difficulties of winning the war) that emancipating slaves would deny the South a major source of labor and provide much-needed troops for the Northern armies. "Freedmen" were a major factor in winning the war, although in the long run their freedom would remain problematic.

During the nineteenth century slavery was abolished in most societies, not just in the United States, though ironically it expanded for a time in Africa. Albeit industrialization could intensify slavery by demanding higher production of goods like cotton, in the long run slavery did not supply a sufficiently flexible or motivated labor force to meet industrial needs. Wage labor (sometimes miserably paid) was a more suitable instrument, with the added advantage of not requiring support when economic conditions deteriorated. New kinds of humanitarianism, developing first in industrial societies like Britain, also attacked slavery. In this context the Atlantic slave trade ended, followed soon by the slave societies in Brazil and Cuba.

See also Emancipation; Racism.

References Berlin, Ira. *Free at Last: A Documentary History of Slavery, Freedom, and the Civil War* (1992); Holt, Thomas C. *The Problem of Freedom: Race, Labor, and Politics in Jamaica and Britain, 1832–1938* (1992); Thornton, John. *Africa and Africans in the Making of the Atlantic World, 1400–1680* (1992).

Sloan, Alfred P. (1875–1966)

Alfred P. Sloan was instrumental in building General Motors into the world's largest manufacturing company and was an important influence on the development of the modern U.S. automobile market. Sloan was vice-president of the company in the 1910s, but in 1923 he became GM's president and in 1937 its chairman. Much of the credit for acquiring the elements that went into making GM goes to "Billy" Durant, who saw that GM could grow by acquiring different companies that made cars, car frames, auto parts, and even seemingly unrelated companies (Frigidaire, for instance). Sloan was less of an entrepreneur than a manager; he stabilized GM financially and helped establish its manufacturing divisions. In the mid-1920s, Sloan helped GM to best its main competitor, Ford, by offering consumers a wide choice of car models and accessories; GM customers could receive a loan from the carmaker and make monthly installments at a time when Henry Ford demanded cash. GM under Sloan introduced many technological innovations, but Sloan believed that even proven technologies should only be introduced slowly so that each year's model was slightly better than the previous year's.

Reference Flink, James. *The Automobile Age* (1988).

Smiles, Samuel (1812–1904)

See Self-Help Literature.

Smith, Adam (1723–1790)

Adam Smith was a Scottish economist who is best known for his 1776 work *An Inquiry into the Nature and Causes of the Wealth of Nations.* Smith articulated a comprehensive analysis of the origins and dynamics of capitalist economics—arguing in part that the profit motive and the discipline of the market helped to regulate the economic system. Entrepreneurs were important agents in meeting economic needs and setting competitive prices. Smith's approach was novel in the mercantilist period, when it was assumed that states should closely regulate trade. Smith also recognized the tendency of businessmen to attempt to circumvent the market by fixing prices through cartels. His work essentially founded economic liberalism and the discipline of economics.

See also Classical Economics.

Smoot-Hawley Tariff

The Smoot-Hawley Tariff was passed in 1930 by the United States. It raised the tariff in an attempt to combat the Great Depression of the 1930s by protecting domestic industries and products. It was passed over the objections of over 1,000 economists and many foreign governments who warned that it would raise prices for U.S. consumers, stifle U.S. exports, and lead to retaliatory measures by other governments. The subsequent loss of foreign markets and trade wars has been widely interpreted as intensifying the negative effects of the depression. In part to compensate for the loss of U.S. markets, Imperial Japan annexed Manchuria in 1931. Many believe that Smoot-Hawley was a contributing factor to World War II, and policymakers in the 1940s sought to build new international forums and institutions that would resolve trade disputes before they crippled trade or led to war among industrialized nations.

See also Bretton Woods Agreement.

Social Darwinism

Charles Darwin's theory that species evolve in part through a process of natural selection had an enormous impact on European and American societies. *Origin of Species* was published in 1859, and although the book was denounced by a few scientists, most proclaimed the work a breakthrough. A great deal of work done by other university-trained scientists had prepared the public for the idea of evolution—geologists, for example, showed that the earth had itself undergone a long process of shaping and reshaping itself. Darwin's writings were remarkably accessible to the intelligent reader and his ideas spread rapidly throughout Europe and North America. The term Social Darwinism describes the application of Darwin's theories to the social realm, and during the late nineteenth and early twentieth centuries was generally used to defend laissez-faire economic and social policies.

Social Darwinists argue that human societies naturally evolve through a ruthless competition among selfish individuals (or countries), each striving to protect their own interests and to dominate others. While brutal, the "struggle for existence" is understood by such thinkers as the only way that new and better ideas, technologies, or forms of social organization can emerge and displace outmoded ones. Social Darwinists argue that unfettered capitalism had encouraged British entrepreneurs to launch the industrial revolution. Thus the richest individuals in society were "naturally" the fittest and aiding the poor was interfering with the process of natural selection. This aspect of Social Darwinism spread particularly in the United States, sponsored by leaders like Andrew Carnegie. Social Darwinists also supported imperialism and often believed that "backward races" would either disappear over time or be "civilized" through contact with Europeans.

The Russian scientist and anarchist Peter Kropotkin felt compelled to refute the Social Darwinists in his study of Siberia, *Mutual Aid.* Kropotkin found that not only do weaker animals cooperate in order to survive (flocks of birds or herds of deer) but that even carnivorous animals survive through cooperation (raising their young, hunting in packs). Though Kropotkin's work was never as popular as Darwin's, Social Darwinism became, by the mid-twentieth century, a term of derision, although many of its tenets remain a fixture of popular conservative thought.

See also Racism; Science.

References Hofstadter, Richard. *Social Darwinism in American Thought, 1860–1915* (1944); Kropotkin, Petr Alekseevich. *Mutual Aid: A Factor of Evolution* (1989).

Social Democracy

See Socialism.

Social Insurance

Social insurance refers to measures taken by government to provide funds to workers struck by illness, accident, old age, or unemployment. These funds may be supported entirely or in part from tax revenues, or they may be supported by special contributions required of certain groups of employers and workers. Before the industrial revolution, most societies depended largely on families to tide people over, supplemented by guild funds, charity, and some local government resources. Industrialization so increased the scope of possible difficulties, by increasing the rate of accidents and making it harder for older workers to retain jobs, that possibilities of developing new kinds of programs were widely discussed. Even more important, urbanization drew workers away from community and extended family support and often put them in housing units where caring for disabled members became more difficult. Private programs of insurance or mutual aid developed in working-class organizations and among paternalistic companies beginning in the 1820s. By the 1870s the rise of working-class voting blocks and socialism put additional pressure on governments to deal with what was coming to be called, in Europe, the "social question."

Specific national social insurance measures were introduced by Chancellor Bismarck in Germany during the 1880s. They provided some income support for people afflicted with old age, sickness, or accidents, based on mixtures of tax funds and obligatory contributions. Many other nations followed this lead (Austria, Denmark) or developed other programs; Britain added the first unemployment insurance measure in 1911. These early programs did not apply to the majority of workers (heavy industry and male workers were favored) and provided rather low benefits. The impact of the depression spurred great extensions of social insurance programs, in most parts of Europe, Australia, Canada, and the United States (the New Deal). Scandinavian countries developed particularly extensive social insurance protection. Aid to the unemployed was greatly increased, along with new programs for older workers and retirees. The cause, as before, was the increasing misery evident in the wake of the depression and concern about growing political radicalism, including communism, in the working class. After World War II social insurance provisions were combined with other programs, such as national health coverage or benefits to families with numerous children, to build what was known as the welfare state. Welfare states used tax funds to provide basic material support for all sorts of problems that might push people into poverty.

See also Paternalism.

References Ashford, Douglas. *The Emergence of the Welfare States* (1986); Baldwin, Peter. *The Politics of Social Solidarity: Class Bases of the European Welfare State, 1875–1975* (1990); Flora, Peter, and Arnold Heidenheimer, eds. *The Development of the Welfare States in Europe and America* (1987).

Socialism

Socialism is a political theory or system of government designed to replace or modify capitalism and private property in the interest of greater economic equality. Since the early nineteenth century, socialists had argued that the incredible productive power unleashed by the industrial revolution should be placed under public control and used to fulfill social needs rather than the profit motive. During the late nineteenth century, revolutionary socialists such as Lenin called themselves social democrats, but after World War I the term was appropriated by far more moderate politicians and trade unionists. Social democracy generally refers to the reformist wing of the socialist movement that has been firmly committed to gradual reforms of capitalism via elections—revolutionary socialists are generally termed communists. Since the 1920s social democrats have formed governments throughout Europe, and their social welfare policies have been adopted by liberal and even conservative governments throughout the world.

During the late nineteenth and early twentieth centuries, the largest and best organized socialist party in the world was the German Social Democratic Party, which was rooted in the labor movement and, to a lesser extent, Marxism. Between 1878 and 1890, the Bismarck regime suppressed the German socialists, and Social Democrats' electoral successes were hindered by repression and the highly discriminatory method of voting in Prussia (where the number of votes was linked to the amount of taxes paid). Nonetheless, by 1890 the party had won the loyalty of 20 percent of the voters and had enrolled hundreds of thousands of workers in the party's unions or educational and leisure organizations. Though not all workers were socialists, and other classes provided some support, many workers believed deeply that socialist parties alone could end the exploitation of labor. Many of the goals of the party, such as universal suffrage for men and women, freedom of speech and assembly, and the eight-hour day, would not simply make existing society more democratic and tolerable for workers but would prepare the way for socialist revolution. Over time, however, the reformist means became the party's ends.

Throughout the late nineteenth century, the various social democratic parties were organized into the second Socialist International. The U.S. socialist movement was perhaps the weakest among industrialized countries, though a party did take root before World War I. Because social democrats' loyalties were to their international class (the working class or proletariat) and not their nation, social democrats often refused to support wars. For instance, the German Social Democrats opposed their government's war against the Paris Commune in 1871 and thereafter held to the slogan of "not a man, not a penny" for war. However, during World War I, every major socialist party succumbed to patriotism and supported their country's war efforts. (Oddly enough, the weak socialist parties in Italy and the United States did oppose the war.) When Lenin heard the news, he was so shocked that he believed the stories were capitalist propaganda. The war caused widespread

This 1897 German social-democratic print depicts the yearning for "The Sword of Intellect," the inscription around which reads "Knowledge is Power."

suffering among the working class, and at the end of the war, workers' revolts broke out in Germany, Hungary, and Italy (inspired in part by the 1917 Russian Revolution). In Germany the Social Democratic Party helped to suppress the rebellions, which helped to convince more radical workers to join the nascent communist parties in forming a new international that supported the Soviet Union. Thereafter, the Social Democrats participated in forming a government under the Weimar Republic and abandoned insurrection as a tactic.

During the 1920s the struggles between the social democratic parties and the new communist parties increasingly divided and weakened the left. Although social democratic governments were formed in Denmark in the 1920s, Sweden in 1932, and a "popular front" of liberals, socialists, and communists were elected in France in 1936, workers' divisions eased the rise of fascist governments in Italy, Germany, Spain, and throughout Eastern Europe. While the German Social Democrats opposed Hitler, they believed fascism would not fundamentally challenge their ability to come to power through the ballot box. (A slogan of the German Social Democrats was: "After Hitler, Our Turn.") However, under the Nazis, thousands of social democrats and communists were jailed or killed in concentration camps.

After World War II social democratic parties formed governments in England, Germany, France, and Scandinavia. Social democrats generally favored a large role for government in the economy and nationalized many industries. Social democrats also encouraged the state to assume a large role in meeting the social needs of its citizens and subsidized health care, education, unemployment benefits, and pensions. Unionization of the work force was encouraged. By the 1970s over 70 percent of Sweden's work force was unionized, and after 1951 German unions held between one-third and one-half of the seats on the board of directors of major corporations.

Although social democratic parties remain popular, the economic crisis in the world industrial system since the 1980s has led to higher unemployment and increased governmental deficits. Socialist governments in France, Spain, and elsewhere have instituted austerity plans similar to those undertaken by more conservative regimes.

See also Industrial Unions; State, Role of the.

References Fletcher, Roger, ed. *Bernstein to Brandt: A Short History of German Social Democracy* (1987); Przeworski, Adam. *Capitalism and Social Democracy* (1985).

Sony

Sony was formed in 1945 by Masura Ibuka as the Tokyo Telecommunications Laboratory (it adopted the trade name Sony in 1958). In its first year it had fewer than 40 employees; by 1975 the company employed over 20,000. Sony developed a reputation as a builder of compact, high-quality electronic equipment. Sony aggressively took advantage of the U.S. trade policy that sought to help stabilize the Japanese economy by allowing Japanese companies favorable access to the American market. By 1955 Sony had built the first all-transistor radio and by 1965 had developed the first home use video recorder. In the 1970s Sony became the first major Japanese company to develop a factory in the United States.

See also Honda Motor Company; Zaibatsus.

South

See United States South.

South Africa

The Dutch East India Company founded Capetown in the mid-seventeenth century as a supply site for its ships traveling between Europe and the lucrative commercial cities of Asia. For the next 200 years, white settler farmers (increasingly relying on African slaves) dominated the colonial economy, although they coexisted with nations of free African farmers and hunters. Throughout the nineteenth century, white settlers defeated the free Africans and took their lands; landless Africans would later form the bulk of South Africa's working class. In the mid-nineteenth century, British settlers (Britain had captured the Capetown colony in 1795) began to exploit the region's incredibly rich mineral resources, notably diamonds and gold. In order to work the mines, a modern transportation (rails and roads) and communication (telegraph and telephones) infrastructure was developed. The miners were a mix of skilled British workers and larger numbers of Africans employed in the less skilled and more dangerous tasks. Although South Africa did not begin to truly industrialize until the 1920s, the region's vast mineral wealth provided the financial surplus necessary to create the first industrialized country on the African continent.

Until the early twentieth century, the role of manufacturing was completely dwarfed by mining and agriculture. After the 1920s the government encouraged industrialization as a way to absorb the large numbers of poor white Afrikaners (descendants of Dutch settlers) who were entering the unskilled ranks of the working class after losing their farms to better capitalized farmers. As in other latecomer industrializers, the state played a major role in South Africa's industrialization effort. Beginning in the 1920s, the state began to assume control of the iron and steel industry, the railroads and the electrical system. This industrialization effort was given a boost by World War II, as the Western powers purchased many South African manufactured and mining products. By the 1980s South Africa was a modern economy that made steel, consumer goods, and high-quality armaments—including its own nuclear weapons.

The state also played a crucial role in regulating labor markets. Beginning in the 1920s, after demonstrations by white miners being displaced by Africans who earned far lower wages, the state encouraged a "civilized labor policy" that essentially preserved skilled and semi-skilled jobs for white workers. These policies hardened

Workers at a gold mine near Johannesburg, South Africa, reach the end of a shift. Critical in exploiting the country's rich mineral resources, South Africa's black working class also played an important role in overturning apartheid in the early 1990s.

after 1948, when the fascist National Party assumed power and instituted the now infamous policy of racial apartheid or separateness. The South African state created economically unviable "homelands" for blacks in the most impoverished 13 percent of the country. The National Party also tightened the pass laws that required blacks to obtain permits to live in the cities or mines; by the 1980s the vast majority of black men were migrant workers and their families lived in the rural "homelands."

Although unions of black workers were illegal, blacks formed such a large part of the working class that the apartheid regime proved unable to suppress their labor organizations—which by the early 1990s were instrumental organizations in overthrowing apartheid. Whether a democratic "New" South Africa can raise the living standards of the masses of black workers (many of whom are unemployed or underemployed) still remains to be seen.

See also Dual Labor Markets; Racism; Sub-Saharan Africa.

References Johnstone, Frederick A. *Class, Race, and Gold: A Study of Class Relations and Racial Discrimination in South Africa* (1976); Thompson, Leonard M. *A History of South Africa* (1990).

South Korea

South Korea is a classic latecomer industrializer, and today it is one of the world's foremost industrial countries. What makes the case of South Korea so interesting is the remarkable hurdles it had to overcome. Korea in the early nineteenth century was a quasi-feudal state whose weak government discouraged commerce. The Yi dynasty was too weak to resist foreign domination, which opened Korea to the world economy; Japan increasingly controlled Korea, annexing it outright in 1910. The Japanese encouraged economic development of Korea's coal and mineral resources; obviously, these policies benefited

Imperial Japan. By consent between the Soviet Union and the United States, Korea was divided after World War II, and 700,000 Japanese were repatriated. The Korean War (1950–1953) caused approximately 3 million casualties and massive damage to the country's industry and agriculture. The war was a watershed for the South, setting it on a path of military alliance with the United States, fierce anticommunism, and vigorous procapitalist industrial development.

South Korea possessed many of the attributes necessary for latecomer industrialization. It had an educated work force willing to work for low wages and large, diversified companies with efficient managers. Its state was strongly interventionist (in part seeking to compensate for the initial weakness of the upper and middle classes). The South Korean government encouraged the formation of "chaebol," or large holding companies similar to the Japanese zaibatsus. These companies are granted a variety of technical assistance and subsidies. However, the Korean government ruthlessly punishes companies whose efficiency flags; these firms are not bailed out, and their assets are generally turned over to other companies. Furthermore, the government strictly controls capital. It has nationalized the banking system and also regulates investment and profit taking. Like many latecomer modernizers, South Korea first developed light industries such as textiles (in the 1960s) but by the 1970s, chaebols were producing steel, ships, electronics, automobiles, and chemicals.

As an important ally in the Cold War, South Korea also benefited from U.S. government subsidies: first in the form of direct financial and technical aid through the U.S. Agency for International Development; later as directly purchased goods and services such as construction projects during the Vietnam War and access to the U.S. market for Korean producers.

Reference Amsden, Alice. *Asia's Next Giant: South Korea and Late Industrialization* (1989).

Soviet Union

See Russia and the Soviet Union.

Spain

As a nation, Spain long lagged in industrial development, and it remains one of the poorer nations in Western Europe. However, two regions experienced an industrial revolution fairly early. Industrialists in Catalonia, particularly in Barcelona, began to set up textile factories early in the nineteenth century, imitating Britain. A substantial factory labor force and an important working-class movement existed by the late nineteenth century, as peasants from other areas, particularly the south, immigrated in search of industrial work. A second industrial center arose around the port of Bilbao, where coal and iron resources were located. Industrialization in the nation as a whole lagged because of a weak merchant class and an inadequate infrastructure for transportation and banking; because of restrictive labor practices in agriculture, particularly on the great estates of the south where many workers were held through sharecropping arrangements; and because of political instability from the nineteenth century through the civil war of the 1930s. Competition from more advanced factory centers, particularly Britain, helped hold Spanish industry back, though Catalonian textiles competed favorably. The Spanish labor movement reflected distinctive conditions, including lack of a political voice; anarchism was widespread both among peasants and among workers in Catalonia until the repression of the Franco regime.

During the 1950s after a period of desperate recovery from the civil war, the Franco regime began to support greater industrialization. Even earlier, in 1941, the government had copied Italy by setting up the Institute for Industrial Reconstruction, using government funds to create firms or loan to private business, particularly in heavy industry and transportation. Workers were denied the right to strike or organize. In 1959 the government moved toward a more liberal policy, favorable to private enterprise, and in 1963 backed it with a national economic planning effort. By 1967 Spain had become an industrialized country. The percentage of workers in agriculture dropped from 49 percent in 1950 to 30 percent by 1967. Growth rates for the national economy, at 9–10 percent per year, were among the highest in the world. A large middle class arose, with increasing consumer expectations. Spain entered the European Common Market in the 1970s, a further step in solidifying industrialization, after the Franco regime was replaced by democracy, though Spain encountered new economic problems, including high unemployment in the late 1980s.

Reference Anderson, Charles W. *The Political Economy of Modern Spain* (1970).

Spinning Jenny

See Hargreaves, James.

Sports

The development of modern sports beginning in the mid-nineteenth century was directly related to industrialization. Britain led the way in standardizing rules for such traditional sports as soccer football and rugby. In the United States similar developments shaped baseball and American football. The importance of sports participation and spectatorship also increased, and professional teams were introduced in the 1860s. Sports provided physical release for people whose jobs were increasingly sedentary or governed by machines. Team loyalties, from tavern teams on up to big-city professional units, helped strangers gain community feeling, and spectatorship facilitated a release of emotion for people whose jobs often called for self-control. Sports also mirrored industrialization in their standardization, their emphasis on records and speed, the increasing specialization of different team positions, and the use of referees (like foremen) to regulate behavior. New industrial products like mass-produced rubber balls and urban transport systems facilitated the games and the huge stadiums that began to spring up in major centers. Sports, in other words, both contrasted with and paralleled industrialization, which accounts for their central importance in modern leisure. From initial centers, particularly Britain, modern sports spread rapidly around the world and were thus available in many societies just beginning the industrialization process.

See also Consumerism; Masculinity.

References Baker, William. *Sports in the Western World* (1988); Rader, Benjamin. *American Sports* (1990).

Springfield Armory

In the early nineteenth century, the Springfield (Massachusetts) Armory (which made weapons for the United States government) was crucial in developing and adapting machines and techniques for mechanized production that were later applied throughout the "American system" of manufacturing. Because the armory was a key government contractor (as well as being located in New England, then the geographical center of American industry), the factory was able to draw upon the expertise of many nearby innovators. Early mass production techniques were developed, such as ones that allowed machinists to turn gunbarrels from a master pattern. In 1842 Springfield produced the first mass-produced weapon with parts that were truly standardized and interchangeable. Many subsequent leaders of the U.S. arms and machine tool industry were trained in Springfield or other government armories.

See also Interchangeable Parts; Military Industrial Complex; State, Role of the.

Reference Pursell, Carroll W., Jr. *Technology in America: A History of Individuals and Ideas* (1981).

Stakhanovites

Stakhanovites were workers under Stalinist industrialization who met or exceeded their production quotas. Stakhanovites were given special privileges, such as increased food rations or better living quarters, as well as priority over shopfloor equipment. The phenomenon was named after a coal miner in the Donbass region, Aleksei Stakhanov, who on August 30, 1935, mined a record 105 tons of coals in a single shift. Stakhanov's achievement had been planned out well in advance by the state as a mechanism for achieving higher productivity and greater control over workers. Managers typically instituted higher production quotas after Stakhanovite workers had "proved" new levels of production were possible. This Stalinist innovation owed much to the zealously procapitalist theories of scientific management promulgated by Frederick Winslow Taylor. To understand why the first "workers' state" instituted what many trade unionists in the United States termed a speed up requires understanding the peculiar dynamics of industrialization in the Soviet Union.

The rapid increase of industrial production under Stalin's first five-year plan helped to create an acute shortage of raw materials, tools, and labor. Managers were ordered to meet quite ambitious quotas, but frequently they lacked the necessary equipment or raw materials; skilled workers were also in short supply during this period of rapid economic growth. Exacerbating the situation was the fact that in order to meet the state's ever-changing needs, or simply to create a public-relations stunt, certain plants were favored with goods and workers and therefore "overproduced" their quota. This factor simply created greater production bottlenecks, for raw materials, railroad rolling stock, or workers diverted toward a favored facility meant that others could not meet their quotas, thereby denying raw materials or finished goods to still other plants.

Although the most obvious goal of Stakhanovism was to increase the output of industry, the state also used Stakhanovism to increase its control over the working class. Typically, instituting Stakhanovism required shifting the best workers and equipment to one part of the plant. Many workers resisted the new quotas through a wide variety of individualistic strategies. Managers also sabotaged the Stakhanovite movement, often because Stakhanovites had wrecked machinery in their quest to exceed quotas. Stakhanovism did not result in dramatic increases in overall production. The chief social effect of Stakhanovism was to force workers into an acutely individualized scramble for survival under the harsh conditions of Stalinist industrialization.

See also Russia; Scientific Management; Stalinism; Taylor, Frederick Winslow; Workers' Control.

Reference Filtzer, Donald. *Soviet Workers and Stalinist Industrialization* (1986).

Stalinism

Stalinism generally refers to the cult of personality that arose around the "father of the peoples," Joseph Stalin (1879–1953). Stalinism also refers to the systems of political control and rapid state-run industrialization that Stalin advanced. Born Iosif Vissarionovich Dzhugashvili in a Georgian village that was part of the Russian Empire, Stalin joined the Bolshevik Party in 1898 and became a trade union organizer in the oil fields of Baku, activities that earned him several prison terms to Siberia; Stalin always escaped and threw himself back into revolutionary organizing. By the time of the 1917 Russian revolution, Stalin was a member of the Central Committee of the Bolsheviks, although during the revolution itself he stayed in the background, concentrating his efforts on organizing the Bolshevik Party itself.

Lenin maintained himself as leader of the Bolsheviks because of his indefatigible will, oratory power, sheer brilliance, and shrewd flexibility in guiding his party through the turmoil of war, revolution, counter-revolution, and civil war. Unlike Lenin, Stalin's intellect was crude and he was a mediocre orator; like Lenin, however, Stalin was a shrewd judge of power, particularly where it mattered most, that is, inside the Bolshevik Party. Appointed by Lenin as general secretary of the party, Stalin used his position to build a political machine that allowed him to maintain

Joseph Stalin (right) sits with Franklin Roosevelt (middle) and Winston Churchill (left) at the Yalta conference in 1945.

effective control over the party. By 1924, when Lenin died, Stalin had become leader of the Bolsheviks and gradually eliminated his rivals. By the end of the 1920s, the two main contenders for power, Leon Trotsky and N. I. Bukharin, had been exiled and marginalized.

By the time of his death in 1953, Stalin was undisputed leader of a major industrial country, and his rivals, as well as several million others, had been liquidated. The story of Stalin's rise to power and his murderous consolidation of control is intimately linked to how he shaped Russia into the world's first noncapitalist industrial power.

In the 1930s, Stalin initiated the five-year plans that sought a massive increase in Russia's heavy industry, in part to prepare for the eventuality of war, while simultaneously collectivizing agriculture. The latter policy resulted in a disastrous drop in agricultural production because kulaks and peasants resisted turning control over the land to the state, often by slaughtering livestock and destroying grain. In response, Stalin engineered the death and imprisonment of millions.

Stalin's industrial gambit was more successful, resulting in a dramatic increase in steel production, though at the cost of light industry. Even in heavy industry, workers and managers were given incentives to turn out poor quality goods, a feature that was to haunt Soviet industry for the next 60 years. In response to the problems of the five-year plans, Stalin carried out a hysterical search for spies, saboteurs, and counter-revolutionaries. Millions more, including nearly all of the original Bolshevik Party, were imprisoned or died in what came to be known as the Great Terror. Still, many Russians and foreign communists emphasized that Stalin had launched a successful industrialization effort in the midst of an incredibly hostile international climate.

Stalin left an important legacy for world industrialization. Russian society was completely transformed by Stalinism's policies of industrialization and police state rule. As neocolonies, Eastern Europe after World War II was directly influenced by the Stalinist model of industrial society. China was also influenced by Stalinism, although their Communist Party wished to develop consumer industries, in large part so that their population would realize an immediate rise in their standard of living. Several smaller countries, such as Vietnam and Cuba, also received Soviet technical assistance and trade, although Cuban revolutionaries in particular tried to make their state more flexible and democratic. Western leftists first looked to Stalin as a hero—as one observer said after a trip to Russia in the 1930s, "I have seen the future, and it works"—although later they would term the Soviet state "actually existing socialism" or, more ironically, state capitalism.

See also Russian Revolution of 1917.

References Filtzer, Donald. *Soviet Workers and Stalinist Industrialization* (1986); Medvedev, Roy Aleksandrovich. *Let History Judge: The Origins and Consequences of Stalinism* (1989).

Standard of Living

Standard of living refers to measurable material well-being: wages, consumption levels, and health conditions. Did material conditions improve or deteriorate for workers during the first decades of the industrial revolution? This question shaped a bitter debate during the 1950s and 1960s among historians dealing with the consequences of British industrialization. Historians friendly to capitalism argued that the great productive power of industrialization spread benefits to workers early on; their opponents, many of them Marxists, were bent on showing the miseries associated with the same period and process. Massive evidence was accumulated. On balance, it seems clear that industrialization cut clothing costs, allowing more purchases by the lower classes in this area. Housing deteriorated, as workers at least in the larger centers faced crowding, poor sanitation, and high rents. Food may have varied, with certain workers earning enough to improve their diets—by including more meat and better quality grains—while others fell back to inadequate nutritional levels. Health deteriorated in many working-class areas, though there were some exceptions. Neither side won a clearcut victory in the standard of living debate. It is clear that living standards were poor for most workers, and that in some categories of expenditure things got worse. It is also clear, however, that there was considerable variety. Skilled workers could do rather well, except in the periodic slumps. The worst conditions were suffered by former domestic workers, still in the countryside, who lost their jobs outright.

Living standards have been poor in many early industrial settings. Russian slums were miserable. As late as the 1960s, Japanese housing suffered in the crowded industrial cities, and many industries, like silk, depended on very low-wage labor. Early industrial revolutions did not all entail quite such clear deterioration, however, at least among factory workers. French industry, facing a labor shortage, may have offered slightly better conditions; German workers were poorly paid but their cities were somewhat better regulated than their chaotic British counterparts. Factory workers in the United States, including women, had reasonably good standards of living if only because labor was so scarce, though with the arrival of new Irish and other immigrants in the 1840s, deterioration set in.

There is no question that in the long run industrialization improved standards of living for the regions involved. Real wages tended to rise. In Britain, for example, the worst conditions began to ease after 1850. Diets improved, clothing and other factory products, from eating utensils to popular reading material, became more available, and even housing gained somewhat. The worst long-term hardships imposed by industrialization are probably not in living standards narrowly construed, but in the quality of work and community life, which in turn are more intangible and harder to measure. It is also true that considerable poverty persisted even into the late nineteenth century—by 1900 it was estimated that a third of all Britons were still at subsistence levels. It is true that material expectations tended to rise with industrialization, making many people feel deprived even when they had exceeded the sheer subsistence standard. Thus the standard of living question remains complex, in its association with ongoing industrialization and industrially based protest and discontent.

Reference Taylor, A. J. P., ed. *The Standard of Living in the Industrial Revolution* (1975).

Standard Oil Company

See Rockefeller, John D.

State, Role of the

The role of the state has been crucial in the successful industrialization of any particular country. Depending upon their policies, states can stifle industrialization (sometimes without meaning to) or step into the market and provide needed goods and services (such as infrastructure projects or the university system) that individual businesses cannot afford to provide. Not all of the interventions by states into the process of industrialization have been successful, but in all cases of latecomer industrialization, the state has played a major role.

While Adam Smith worried that Britain's mercantilist policies would stifle the initiative of eighteenth century entrepreneurs, governmental policies helped industrialists by opening up colonial markets for industrialists (such as India) and keeping labor prices low. However, other policies designed to aid industrialists, such as attempting to prevent the diffusion of British manufacturing technology abroad, proved less than fully successful. It is important to remember that industrialists were not the only powerful group to help shape state policies. Until the early nineteenth century, large-scale British farmers succeeded in keeping grain tariffs high, against the protests of workers and industrialists.

The rise of the industrial revolution made the British state, with its relatively small population, into a major military power. British naval prowess relied on better cannon and other military technology but also on the tight labor discipline on its warships. The economic and military power of the British Empire proved critical in besting the larger and more enthusiastic French armies in the Napoleonic Wars. Many European states (such as France, Germany, and Russia) began to encourage manufacturing, especially in armaments and the iron and steel industries, simply in order to retain their military strength in the face of rising British power.

Capitalism and the industrial system have long been part of a world system of trade, which has influenced the trajectory of any particular industrialization effort. Most latecomer industrializers have erected substantial tariff barriers to protect fledgling industries. Unchecked, the drive to protect domestic markets and industries can lead to devastating trade wars, and therefore states have played an important role in regulating international trade and finance. In the nineteenth century British power backed up the gold standard, which provided controls on the flow of investment capital and a check on business cycles. The breakdown of international controls on tariffs and trade after World War I contributed greatly to the global depression of the 1930s. In the 1940s the United States took the lead in establishing new international institutions that fostered free trade and provided investment capital to less industrialized countries.

Over the course of the twentieth century, the state has played an increasingly interventionist role. World War I was one cause of this development. Governments stepped in to control labor strife and to maximize production after industrialists proved unable or unwilling to coordinate an increasingly complex economy. A second reason was the Great Depression of the 1930s. In Western Europe and North America, new economic theories such as Keynesianism displaced laissez-faire economic practices, and states increasingly used unemployment insurance, payments to distressed farmers, and subsidies to industrialists to raise purchasing power and effect an economic recovery. These policies were the basis for the welfare state and formal economic planning, which became important features of most industrialized countries after World War II.

The extent of state intervention varied enormously. In extreme cases, as in the Soviet Union and Eastern Europe, the state has simply monopolized all economic activity. Although this approach to industrialization proved successful in its early phases, by the 1970s it was apparent to most observers that the Soviet Union had entered economic stagnation. Since 1978 China's communist state has decreased state control over the economy while maintaining tight political control. Outside of the military sector, the United States always had the least developed industrial policies—a fact that many have criticized as contributing to its problems in maintaining its industrial strength and living standards since 1970. In Japan and the Pacific Rim, the government established economic targets and rewarded or punished large companies accordingly in the decade after World War II. In South Korea, strict controls were placed on investments, profits, and the banking system to prevent capital from leaving the country.

See also Bretton Woods Agreement; Cold War; Combination Acts; Corn Laws; French Revolution; Import Substitution; Infrastructure; Krupp; Marshall Plan; Military Industrial Complex; Nationalism; Protectionism; Stalinism; World Bank.

Reference Henderson, William Otto. *The State and the Industrial Revolution in Prussia, 1740–1870* (1958).

Statute of Apprentices

This law was enacted in England in 1563. It restricted the exercise of the skilled crafts to a person who had apprenticed for seven years with an accredited master. This rule was a fairly standard kind of artisanal guild regulation, designed to protect established skills and limit competition in skilled urban manufacturing. British authorities began to be more flexible in administering the statute during the eighteenth century, allowing manufacturers to recruit less well trained workers and to abridge the apprenticeship period. This flexibility was crucial in permitting the expansion of the labor force and the technical innovation necessary in early British industrialization; it contrasted with more rigid guild enforcement on the European continent. Even British manufacturers found that the statute limited innovation, particularly in the wool industry, and it was finally repealed in 1813–1814. This repeal, part of the growing liberal current in English economic legislation, gave employers full freedom in hiring and firing. It also encouraged the gradual decline of formal apprenticeship in favor of ad hoc training for the semi-skilled workers increasingly needed in the factories.

See also Artisans; Laissez-faire; Liberalism; State, Role of the.

Steam Engine

Experiments on steam engines began in the seventeenth century. In 1690 Denis Patin devised an experimental engine with a piston that was forced through a cylinder by steam and forced back by the vacuum resulting from the condensation of the steam. About 1702 Thomas Newcomen developed an engine with a piston and cylinder, a separate boiler, hand-operated valves, and a lever beam for transmitting the power. After various improvements, this crude device was used extensively in Britain for pumping water out of mines. The main problem with the engine was that it was extremely inefficient in its use of fuel, which is one reason why it made sense to use it at a mine site, where the fuel was ready at hand, but not elsewhere.

James Watt, assigned the task of repairing a Newcomen engine at the University of Glasgow in 1763, was disturbed by the loss of three-fourths of the fuel by the condensing of the steam in the cylinder. In 1765 he hit upon the idea of a separate condensing chamber, and he took out a

An 1864 engraving of the Stephenson steam-locomotive factory's shop floor in Newcastle, England.

patent in 1769. Further experiments and the aid of various associates led Watt to work out an engine where the piston was forced through the cylinder in one direction only by steam, and the reverse movement was produced by the weight of the plunger. In 1782 Watt patented a "double acting" principle, using steam at both sides of the piston head; while one end of the cylinder received steam from the boiler, the other end discharged into the condenser, and vice versa. Later improvements by Watt included automatic control of the steam pressure by a governor. His first engines had no mode of transforming to-and-fro motion (the piston) into rotary motion for running machinery, but in 1781 he patented a system of gears (the sun-and-planet system) for transmitting the power from the piston. A more acceptable device came to be the crank and shaft for transforming the reciprocal or to-and-fro motion of the piston into rotary motion for operating machinery.

Watt's engines began to come into widespread use in the 1780s, by which time precision methods for making the double-acting cylinder had been developed by using John Wilkinson's boring machine (1774). Matthew Boulton became a partner to Watt, who had exhausted all his credit, in setting up a manufacturing plant. Engines were used not only for pumping water but also for running textile equipment and operating furnace blasts and forge hammers. Further use awaited the nineteenth-century era of machine tools and its application to transportation. The steam engine freed factories from having to operate near streams for water power. It allowed more powerful motors to be constructed, and it also greatly stimulated coal mining (for fuel) and metallurgy (for materials to make the engines). Its revolutionary significance was foreseen as early as 1787, when a writer declared that it would "change the appearance of the civilized world."

Steamboat

U.S. inventors played a particularly large role in applying the steam engine to water transportation, though the British effort was almost simultaneous. The work of John Fitch, in the later eighteenth century, was particularly crucial. The United States boasted a number of waterways that were difficult to utilize by sailing ships or a towpath; the Hudson River was a prime example. Hence Americans were eager to exploit the new inventions. Fitch, trained as a brass and silversmith, had failed in a number of land ventures. He became interested in steamship invention and produced the first example in 1785. On this base he obtained rights from several states for exclusive steamship trade on their waterways and secured financing from several Philadelphia businessmen. His first boat sailed the Delaware in 1787. Other boats followed, but a crash in 1792 ruined the business and drove Fitch into poverty. By 1793 American engineers had traveled widely enough in Europe for their work to be known, though again application was slow because Europe's inland rivers and canals could be addressed by other means. Still, England had 232 small steamers by 1827 and 924 by 1847.

Experiments on long-distance trips, using a combination of steam and sail, began in 1819, though the first effective seagoing steamship emerged only in 1838. Coal consumption remained high, though progressive improvements in engines made steamships more competitive. Americans, interestingly, lagged for a decade, putting their faith in dramatic new clipper ships. Use of steamships increased greatly after 1860, and soon the opening of new canals, like the Suez (1869), gave additional impetus to the development of faster ships capable of carrying larger cargoes.

See also Cunard; Fulton, Robert; Suez Canal.

Steel

See Iron and Steel Industry.

Stephenson, George (1781–1848)

Stephenson was the British inventor and entrepreneur most responsible for introducing the railroad. Work on the railroad was so complex that no one individual was a decisive inventor, and development work extended over at least four decades—but it was Stephenson who pulled the elements together in the first successful intercity rail line. Trained in clock making, where he learned much about mechanics, and also the inventor of a miner's safety lamp, Stephenson emerged as a force in railroad development in 1814, when he built a locomotive for a mine. Railroads had long been used in coal mines and some metallurgical plants, but Stephenson and others projected their use for more general transportation. He began producing locomotives at an engine works in the middle of the 1820s. While performance improved, early efforts were discouraging, and horses continued to be used to pull cars along rail lines. Along with engineer Timothy Hackworth, Stephenson improved locomotive design, particularly by increasing the heating surface in the boiler. The engine Royal George (1827) was the first locomotive to demonstrate real economy in operation, hauling coal between Stockdon and Darlington. After this success, Stephenson was able to persuade the Liverpool and Manchester company to rely exclusively on locomotives. Stephenson carefully analyzed the best track layout. His firm built the Rocket for a decisive contest in 1829, sponsored by the company's nervous backers, using a multitubular boiler initially patented in the United States (John Stevens, 1791). Two other locomotives broke down during the test run, but the Rocket passed all tests, and at speeds between thirteen and sixteen miles per hour easily beat the two horse-drawn teams also in the competition. The Liverpool-Manchester Railway opened in 1830, and the great age of railway development had begun.

See also Steam Engine; Watt, James.

Strikes

Strikes occur when workers withdraw their labor from an employer. Strikes have been recorded on ancient building projects, but with the industrial revolution transforming the work place and the role of the state, the character of strikes changed markedly.

In the early stages of the industrial revolution, workers were more likely to riot than to strike. Work regimes were harsh, and punishment for "insubordination" could be fatal—sailors who struck could be hung for mutiny. In fact, many shipboard strikes from the sixteenth to the eighteenth centuries ended up with sailors seizing their own ship and becoming pirates. Luddites were certainly attempting to redress their grievances over the conditions of their employment, but since unions or strikes were illegal, workers' protest took on insurrectionary features. After the 1830s until the 1850s, British workers were more likely to protest by joining the Chartist movement than through strikes. In the late nineteenth century unions became legal and strikes were viewed as a more disciplined and dignified form of protest than riots. British workers more often struck to enroll other workers in unions than just to gain wage increases.

Strikes in the United States were often far more violent than in Europe. Although workers could vote and unions were not illegal, employers often relied on police or private guards (such as the Pinkertons) to break strikes. Coal miners and hard-rock miners experienced particularly repressive conditions and often appeared on picket lines with rifles and shotguns. By the early twentieth century, even the conservative building-trades unions had resorted to hiring "goons" to battle employers' guards, and buildings that were put up with nonunion labor were sometimes dynamited.

At the end of the nineteenth century, the size and power of industrial corporations and cartels had grown and workers in different parts of the United States had common employers. As a result, national strikes began to occur. In 1877 a national strike of railroad workers spread along train lines to communities across the United States. The failure of that strike was due in large part to workers' lack of organization, and national union federations proved difficult to establish. For instance, in the 1880s, the Knights of Labor attempted to build a union open to all workers, but it was crushed by Jay Gould and other large employers.

Informal means of protest such as restricting output were common. Many skilled craft workers could engage in small work stoppages in order to pressure their foremen or employers to follow certain work rules. Because strikers often faced repression at the hands of police, vigilantes, or hired guards, the Industrial Workers of the World advocated different forms of "striking on the job" or sabotage. Rather than wrecking machines, IWW members advocated the "conscious withdrawal of efficiency," or "working to rule," whereby workers only do exactly what their foremen tell them to do. In Europe, strike rates by less-skilled workers such as dockers increased from the 1880s onward. Large union federations supported a rising tide of strikes until 1919, though goals increasingly focused on wage gains rather than on structural change. However, workers' strikes played a vital role in the 1905 and 1917 Russian revolutions, where workers' political goals were paramount.

In the United States, the IWW was destroyed by the FBI in the 1910s and the 1920s, but the IWW's tactics were nonetheless used to great effect in the 1930s by workers enrolled in the Congress of Industrial Organizations. In workplaces with moving assembly lines or other continuous production processes, a strike by even a few workers in one department could shut down an entire plant. In the mid-1930s, "sit down" strikes spread throughout the country as strikers realized it was easier to occupy factories than attempt to prevent strikebreakers from entering them. In 1934 Minneapolis truck drivers succeeded in shutting down decentralized trucking facilities by using another innovative tactic—"roving pickets" of

Picketing, such as this union picket in Tokyo, Japan, is just one of many tactics strikers utilize.

strikers in cars or trucks dispatched by radios.

While these new forms of strikes took advantage of changes in production and technology, they also relied on the fact that sympathetic governments often prevented employers from responding with violence. When governments were absolutely opposed to unions and strikes, as in the case of fascist and many "socialist" regimes, workers' forms of protest most commonly took individualized forms. Since the late 1960s in the United States, an increasingly hostile legal environment (in addition to changes brought on by "postindustrialism") have made strikes an increasingly rare phenomenon.

See also American Federation of Labor; Combination Acts; Great Strike of 1877; Industrial Unions; Monopoly Capitalism; Moral Economy; Restriction of Output; Stalinism.

References Brecher, Jeremy. *Strike!* (1972); Haimson, Leopold H., and Charles Tilly, eds. *Strikes, Wars, and Revolutions in an International Perspective: Strike Waves in the Late Nineteenth and Early Twentieth Centuries* (1989).

Structural Adjustment

See World Bank.

Sub-Saharan Africa

Although sub-Saharan Africa was not colonized until the 1880s, most scholars have emphasized the debilitating effects of colonialization and neocolonialism on the development of strong industrial economies in this region of the world. The first successful case of industrialization in sub-Saharan Africa occurred in South Africa, whose white rulers' ability to transform the country's mineral wealth into an industrial society was influenced in crucial ways by their preferential treatment at the hands of European powers. After the decolonization of the 1960s, black-led governments have had less success with industrialization, although oil-rich Nigeria has made significant progress. Both Nigeria and Zaire possess great natural wealth but have become victims of corrupt governments supported by military aid from Europe and the United States. The policies of international banking and development agencies are also an important barrier to industrialization.

See also Racism; World Bank.

References Davidson, Basil. *The Black Man's Burden: Africa and the Curse of the Nation-State* (1992); Rodney, Walter. *How Europe Underdeveloped Africa* (1981).

Subsidies

Direct and indirect subsidies—payments or grants to promote business—from governments have played an important role in all successful industrializations, with the possible exception of Britain in the late eighteenth century. In the mid-nineteenth century, developing the techniques, machines, and skills that made interchangeable parts a reality in factories in the United States was very much a product of the government's sponsorship of the Springfield Armory; furthermore, protective tariffs were crucial to the development of many industries in the United States. Railroad development was massively subsidized by large grants of government-owned land. Direct infusions of capital and monopoly markets were crucial to the successful industrialization of Japan in the late nineteenth century, and in the mid-twentieth century South Korea followed a similar path. Even Jashmed Tata, one of India's industrial leaders, who had to overcome the hostility of the Imperial British government, was saved from bankruptcy by government contracts in World War I and by a protective tariff in the 1920s. Subsidies alone are not sufficient for successful industrialization, as the case of post-1948 India makes clear, and the sheer expense of subsidizing unprofitable industries, as in the case of many steel industries in the 1980s, can force governments to abandon firms to the not-so-tender mercies of the marketplace.

See also Cold War; India.

Suez Canal

This great waterway, connecting the Indian Ocean through the Red Sea with the Mediterranean, was opened on November 17, 1869. Need for the canal resulted from rapidly increasing world trade, and it greatly shortened the route between Europe and Asia. The canal was built by a French company, using cheap Egyptian laborers, under the direction of the engineer Ferdinand de Lesseps and with the encouragement of the French government. Britain's superior merchant capacity and its vital interest in controlling routes to India prompted it to assert a growing role in Egypt, despite French resistance, and the British took over the canal in 1875. British control was finally removed by a new, independent Egyptian government in 1957, prompting a brief Anglo-French war against Egypt that was quickly abandoned. The canal remains a vital artery in international commerce.

See also Imperialism; Infrastructure.

Sugar

Sugar was an important plantation crop, first grown by European planters in the Azores and Canary Islands in the fifteenth century and then in the Caribbean and Brazil in the sixteenth century. Sugar was grown by gangs of slaves brought from Africa (approximately 7 million in the eighteenth century) and was extremely profitable: approximately two-thirds of France's overseas income in the eighteenth century derived from the sugar plantations of the Caribbean, and William Pitt estimated that sugar accounted for two-thirds of Britain's international commerce. Sugar was a luxury good until the fifteenth century, imported from Asia, but it became a mass consumption item in Europe by 1700. By the early nineteenth century, sugar was an increasing source of calories (if not nutrition) for the European working class. The plantation system (what later observers would term "factories in the field") was spread by imperial powers throughout the tropical world well into the twentieth century.

Reference Mintz, Sidney Wilfred. *Sweetness and Power: The Place of Sugar in Modern History* (1985).

Surplus Value

Surplus value is the term developed by Karl Marx to describe the financial surplus expropriated by employers of wage labor under capitalism. In Marx's analysis, because workers' labor power has the unique ability to create value, even employers who pay workers a fair wage receive the better end of the bargain. Employers accrue the surplus value that results from combining raw materials and tools with labor power—and they use this surplus value to increase their stocks of machinery, thereby enabling employers to lower their future production costs. Surplus value is broader than what neoclassical economists (those influenced by Adam Smith) term profit, for Marx includes rent, investment in machinery, and wages paid to nonproductive workers (e.g., supervisors, advertising) as part of surplus value.

See also Exploitation.

Reference Tucker, Robert C., ed. *The Marx-Engels Reader* (1978).

Syndicalism

Syndicalism was a late nineteenth-century political theory and a labor movement designed to replace capitalist industry and the state by a system of producer unions. Syndicalists sought not only to organize industrial unions, but to use them as a revolutionary vehicle to overthrow capitalism. Rather than rely on gradual political reforms as labor parties or social democrats advocated, syndicalists believed that workers could use their economic leverage to call general strikes that would ultimately bring society to a halt and then usher in a cooperative system of labor. Workers would also use their growing organization to coordinate the actual functioning of society, eventually making formal government unnecessary. Syndicalism (sometimes called anarchosyndicalism) was strongest in the late nineteenth and early twentieth centuries in countries with strong anarchist movements and large artisanal groups: France, Spain, Latin America.

French syndicalists were influenced in part by their country's revolutionary traditions, such as the French Revolution and the Paris Commune, which made them impatient with the gradual reforms advocated by middle-class reformers and socialists alike. In the late nineteenth century, French syndicalists were strong enough to organize a national federation of unions, the Confédération Générale du Travail, which conducted a major general strike for the radical goal of the eight-hour day in 1906. By 1914 general strikes, which syndicalists had once argued would usher in socialism, were settled by union leaders, with the support of most workers, for wage gains or political reforms.

In the case of Spain, whose parliamentary systems lagged behind those of France, Britain, or Germany, syndicalist unions retained their revolutionary outlook. Syndicalists in the countryside struck not only for better wages but for the redistribution of land. The decentralized organization of syndicalist unions proved quite resilient to periodic suppression by the Spanish government, and this prevented syndicalists from following their French brethren into a reformist stance. In the Spanish civil war (1936–1939) syndicalists in Barcelona organized the city's production and defense for over a year before being overwhelmed by better-armed communists and then fascist adversaries. Spanish, Portuguese, and Italian migrants to Latin America, particularly Argentina and

Brazil, had made anarchosyndicalism an influential force in workers' movements on that continent. Syndicalists formed the Brazilian federation of labor in 1906; in 1917 and 1919 syndicalists led general strikes they hoped would inaugurate a soviet revolution in their country. However, by the 1920s anarchosyndicalism was in decline as most workers chose either the path of reform or of communism.

The syndicalist union in the United States, the Industrial Workers of the World (IWW), was organized in 1905 with the cooperation of socialists and anarchists. The IWW opposed the conservative and craft-centered approach of the American Federation of Labor (AFL). IWW or "Wobbly" activists sought to organize workers whom the craft unions believed were "unorganizable"; the IWW helped to organize unions of timber workers and migrant farmworkers and led several strikes of eastern factory workers. By the 1920s the Wobblies had been destroyed, but the union's vision of organizing all industrial workers (though not the goal of revolution) was realized in the 1930s by the Congress of Industrial Organizations.

Reference Amdur, Kathryn E. *Syndicalist Legacy: Trade Unions and Politics in Two French Cities in the Era of World War I* (1986).

Synthetic Fabrics

Synthetic products—manufactured through manmade rather than natural chemical compounds—arose in the nineteenth century, thanks to advancing research in chemistry plus growing demand for more expensive natural products. Plastics thus substituted for wood. Synthetic fabrics were first developed by the French industrialist and chemist Hilaire Chardonnet, in 1885. The material, which he called artificial silk, was made from the cellulose fibers of wood or cotton. Various chemical processes reduced the fiber to a thick liquid, from which threads were made when forced through tiny holes in devices called spinnerets. Artificial silk was first made in the United States in 1910, and in 1924 it was named rayon (from shiny like the sun, hence ray, durable like cotton, hence -on). It became the most widely used fiber after cotton for clothing and decorator fabrics like drapery and upholstery.

Rayon competed actively with silk, causing problems for this industry, especially in Japan. Other synthetic products followed. Nylon, made from coal, water, and air (later, petroleum, natural gas, or animal byproducts would be substituted for coal), was first developed by chemists at the Du Pont company in the 1930s, following experiments with polymerization. This procedure formed larger molecules, resulting in stronger, more elastic fibers. After repeated refinements and experiments, stockings were first made from nylon in 1938. During World War II nylon replaced silk in the making of parachutes. Nylon is also used in industrial brushes and toothbrushes and for surgical thread. Other synthetic fibers were developed after World War II.

See also Artificial Silk Company; Chemical Industry; Plastics; Research and Development.

Takeoff

The takeoff concept is part of an effort to generalize about the stages of the industrial revolution. The takeoff is the period when traditional economic practices and beliefs are overcome, and growth becomes the "normal condition"—as in Britain (1783–1803), Japan (1875–1900), or Canada (1890–1914). New industries expand rapidly, investment increases, agriculture commercializes, and the new class of entrepreneurs expands. From this point, industrialization is assured. Economic historian W. W. Rostow used the takeoff concept as part of a model that not only generalized about past industrial revolutions but also predicted future economic progress. Thus he contended that India and China entered takeoff conditions in the 1950s, which meant their industrial revolutions would progress rather automatically. Other economic historians have objected to this model, and certainly its predictions, as being too rigid, not allowing for different characteristics of different societies and overdoing the amount and momentum of change in the early part of the industrialization process.

See also Development Theory.

Reference Rostow, W. W. *The Stages of Economic Growth* (1960).

Tariffs

See Protectionism.

Tata, Jamshed (1839–1904)

Jamshed Tata was the founder of the modern Indian steel industry. Born to a family of prosperous merchants, Tata made a sizable fortune outfitting English troops during the Abyssinia War of 1867–1868. He invested his profits in textile mills, which gave him valuable experience in running a factory. Tata dreamed of developing India's rich iron and coal resources and making India into a powerful, industrial nation. By the 1940s Tata steel mills were the largest in the British Empire and the twelfth largest in the world.

Beyond the sheer technical difficulties of locating the appropriate sources of raw material, Tata's most serious obstacle was the British government, which preferred to keep India as a consumer of British manufactured goods. Most of the capital for the Tata Iron and Steel Company (TISCO), founded in 1899, came from wealthy Indians. By 1907, relying on European and American technical personnel, TISCO constructed a modern mill in Jamshedpur (150 miles from Calcutta). The company might have failed, but World War I provided it with a boom market. The company ambitiously expanded in order to fulfill India's domestic market; by 1924 the company could produce 420,000 tons of steel a year. However, a worldwide glut of steel in the 1920s prevented TISCO from producing much more than half of its capacity and nearly ruined the company. TISCO was saved from dumping by European firms by a British protective tariff in 1924. The British government primarily sought to protect the Indian market for British mills but allowed TISCO to seize 30 percent of the market.

TISCO had always relied on Indians for their production workers, and despite paternalistic labor relations (the company provided hospitals, housing, and schools) there were several serious strikes in the 1920s. In 1921 TISCO established a technical institute and in 1937, a research and control laboratory. Beginning in the 1920s, TISCO began replacing foreign staff with Indian engineers, technicians, and skilled workers.

References Keenan, John L. *A Steel Man in India* (1943); Rothermund, Dietmar. *An Economic History of India: From Pre-Colonial Times to 1991* (1993); Tomlinson, B. R. *The Economy of Modern India, 1860–1970* (1993).

Taxation

Taxes are payments required by government. Most countries relied primarily on two forms of taxes before the industrial revolution: those on property and those on products. Britain, for example, combined property taxes (called hearth taxes, for each household) with taxes on imported goods and on products like alcohol. When more revenues were needed, as during the Napoleonic Wars, the government responded mainly by raising existing rates, though an income tax was briefly introduced. Prussia taxed landed property and goods, and so the pattern went.

The industrial revolution required governments to seek more revenue. Only in Britain and Norway, under the impact of nineteenth-century laissez-faire doctrines, did expenditures even temporarily go down. But there were no dramatic changes in tax categories. Taxation on property tended to go up; this allowed governments to tax businesses and also to increase levies on peasants to help raise capital for projects like railroad building. Except in Britain, which moved toward free trade, revenues from tariffs went up greatly. This was the main source of federal revenue in the United States during the nineteenth century. Some countries did increase sales taxes, particularly on special items like alcohol and tobacco (tobacco and matches were state monopolies in many European countries). In other words, taxation policies did not figure prominently in the industrial revolution except in the tariff category and in efforts to draw capital from rural residents by raising property rates.

This situation changed dramatically at the end of the nineteenth century. Government expenditures began to rise very rapidly because of welfare and school costs and, in Europe, accelerating military outlays. Industrial prosperity invited new taxes on incomes and corporations, which rapidly became the largest tax categories. The United States passed an income tax amendment in 1913; Canada adopted both income and corporate taxes in 1916. By 1920 the U.S. government was drawing over ten times more in income and other internal taxes than it was in customs revenue, even though the latter continued to rise. The industrial revolution, in sum, created needs and means that dramatically changed taxation categories, and these shifts formed a vital backdrop to the expansion of governments in industrial societies during the twentieth century.

See also Protectionism; State, Role of the.

Taylor, Frederick Winslow (1856–1915)

Frederick Winslow Taylor was an efficiency expert and one of the inventors of scientific management. Taylor was born to a professional family and was, from a very early age, an inveterate rule-maker. As one historian observed: "He was not a boy who took his ball home when he did not win the game. Instead, he made a practice of devising elaborate rules for the game so that, win or lose, his friends were playing on his terms." An illness prevented Taylor from attending college, and he entered a factory as an apprentice (where his illness mysteriously disappeared). At the age of 22, Taylor became a common laborer in the Midvale Steel Company (owned by a family friend) and proceeded to reorganize how the work was to be done by that firm's laborers.

Taylor's attempt to reorganize work was significant because, even in factories, managers relied heavily on the experience and innovation of workers. As one syndicalist remarked, "the bosses' brains are under the workman's cap." Taylor proceeded to try to reverse that relationship by rigorously studying workers and timing them with a stopwatch. Taylor then eliminated "wasted" motions or reorganized the workplace by giving workers shovels with longer handles. Workers were encouraged to follow Taylor's new piece-rate plans. In theory, both workers and the company would benefit; however, Taylor's plan had great appeal to managers because even in non-union factories, workers had ample opportunity to restrict output. Managers generally lowered piece rates over Taylor's objections. This fact, combined with Taylor's highly eccentric personality, often resulted in sabotage or strikes. For instance, prior to World War I, some French unionists struck in order to make efficiency experts work at the new pace that they had prescribed. Taylorism was expensive in the short run (in large part because of workers' resistance) but was often instituted during wartime labor shortages.

The significance of Taylor's schemes was that they allowed managers and not workers to control the pace of work—thus industrialists around the world eagerly applied "Taylorism" to their worksites. Because "Taylorism" increased output by rigorously scrutinizing workers and continuously subdividing work or reorganizing the workplace, it has become associated with the assembly line, although the system has been applied to other kinds of postindustrial work settings such as fast food restaurants or offices.

See also Fordism; Restriction of Output; Stakhanovites; Time and Motion Studies; Workers' Control.

References Merkle, Judith A. *Management and Ideology: The Legacy of the International Scientific Management Movement* (1980); Montgomery, David. *Workers' Control in America: Studies in the History of Work, Technology, and Labor Struggles* (1979).

Technocracy

In the early stages of the Great Depression of the 1930s, the technocracy movement argued that modern technology had made the established economic and political order obsolete. In the midst of mass unemployment, automation (or "technological unemployment") was accelerating and aggravating the problem of poverty. Technocrats proposed that engineers and others with technical knowledge, not businessmen and politicians, should run U.S. society. Their ideas were popular in 1933 and 1934 before being attacked as anticapitalist and antidemocratic. Embarrassing factual errors by zealous leaders of the technocratic movement, plus hostility to businessmen and disdain for political action, only compounded their problems. The movement declined with the success of the New Deal.

A technocrat is sometimes a term of derision for a technical bureaucrat and has been applied to people whose social status is based on their technical expertise. Examples of technocrats include the engineers and efficiency experts who monitored the time and motion studies of Frederick Winslow Taylor and the economists of MITI or Gosplan (the Soviet Union's planning agency). European economic planners after World War II or trained engineers and economists were often dubbed "technocrats."

Reference Akin, William E. *Technocracy and the American Dream: The Technocrat Movement, 1900–1941* (1977).

Technology

In the 1830s a French textile manufacturer decorated the previous week's most productive machine with a garland of flowers. The symbolism is apt: with industrialization, technology became more important in human life than it had been before. Technology did not, of course, originate with the industrial revolution. Hunting-gathering and agricultural societies had both introduced important new tools. But the industrial revolution elevated the significance of machines, in addition to making them far more complex and productive.

The essential definition of the industrial revolution is partly technological. It consisted of the application of new power sources to equipment and transportation and the development of more automatic mechanisms to make goods. In addition, industrialization meant recurrent technological change. The steam engine and early spinning and weaving equipment were soon upstaged by internal combustion and electrical motors and by vastly more complicated textile equipment, like the Northrop loom, which allowed a single worker to operate four to eight times as many looms as the early weaving frames. Machines themselves, initially made by hand, began by the later nineteenth cen-

Moorish women obtain computer training in Nouakchott, Mauritania.

tury to be made by other machines, guided by workers.

Although technology is always central to industrialization, it does not cause it. New economic needs, new ideas and educational networks, and new government policies have to exist before a society is motivated to develop or imitate advanced technology. This is why early industrialization, including an array of inventions, must be explained by other factors, and why some societies, though aware of advanced technology, cannot actually induce full industrialization.

Once launched, however, industrialization does raise questions about the impact of the greater importance of machinery. Many analysts would argue that the importance of human workers declines as expensive machines receive growing attention. Work pace is set by machines; by 1900 the leading entrepreneurs and engineers were trying to get workers to act as much like machines as possible, without spontaneous gestures or reactions. Even outside work life, machinery spreads. New forms of leisure by 1900 included the highly mechanical amusement parks, with their industrial-style ferris wheels and other rides, which were first introduced in the United States. Many artists began to use machine images, like the Italian Futurists. Soon thereafter, competition between machines, like automobile races, became a major spectator sport. Images of the human body became more mechanistic, and some interpreters argue that sexual activities also became more mechanical in industrial societies. Assessing the role of technology and its impact on the quality of personal and social life is one of the most challenging aspects of historical analysis applied to ongoing industrialization.

See also Work.

References Derry, T. K., and T. I. Williams. *A Short History of Technology* (1961); Giedion, S. *Mechanization Takes Command* (1948).

Telegraph

The telegraph revolutionized long-distance communication. It depended on basic discoveries in electricity. In 1820 Hans Oersted, a Danish scientist, showed how an electrical current can produce a magnetic field that can turn a compass needle. Five years later William Sturgeon invented the electric magnet. In 1837, using this knowledge, two British physicists, William Cooke and Charles Wheatstone, developed an electromagnetic telegraph: a wire sent an electrical current activating a magnetic field, causing a needle to point to a letter on a dial. The Cooke-Wheatstone telegraph was used in Britain until 1870. Also in 1837 the American Samuel Morse, using an improved electromagnet developed by the American physicist Joseph Henry, caused long-distance electric signals to activate a pen that marked paper; the marks could be varied to form a code. Developments the following year allowed the code to be translated into sounds, by a clicking bar pulled back and forth by a magnet activated by the transmitted electric current. The American telegraph was patented soon thereafter.

Newspapers began using the telegraph extensively to transmit breaking news. Railroads were also heavy users, in order to coordinate shipping and schedules. Military uses developed rapidly as well. Telegraph wires linked major U.S. cities by 1851, and in 1856 separate companies merged to form Western Union. Lines reached California in 1861. A transatlantic cable, a joint British-American venture, was laid in 1866. Later inventions, by Thomas Edison and Emile Baudot, allowed multiple messages to be sent simultaneously, and by 1900 telegraphic printing was being developed.

Telephone

The telephone is a device for electronically transmitting human speech between two points; it was invented in 1876 by Alexander Graham Bell. The invention of the telephone developed out of attempts to allow the telegraph system, which by the 1870s was becoming overburdened, to handle more traffic. The largest telegraph company, Western Union, disputed Bell's patents, but by 1879 Bell had won. By 1878 the first local network of telephones was established in New Haven, Connecticut; by 1884 New York's exchange was connected with Boston's. The telephone's electronic signal grew weaker with distance, but this technological hurdle was overcome in 1906 when Lee De Forest developed a method to boost the electrical signals. Calls had to be manually connected in telephone exchanges, first by men, then by young white women; although the technology for mechanical switching had developed in the 1820s, it was applied in the United States only in the 1920s. By 1915 phone traffic was carried across the United States, and by 1927 it was crossing the Atlantic Ocean. Telephone use expanded rapidly as the industry became a major commercial service. Farm families in the United States, for example, bought phones far more rapidly than the telephone company had expected. Expanding telephone systems also increased white-collar employment for such positions as switchboard operator.

See also Pink-Collar Workers.

Reference Fischer, Claude S. *America Calling: A Social History of the Telephone to 1940* (1992).

Temperance

Drinking was an important part of preindustrial culture, and many artisans and workers in the eighteenth century drank moderately throughout the working day. Temperance was a nineteenth- and twentieth-century movement that aimed at reducing or eliminating the consumption of alcohol throughout society. Many industrialists in Europe and the United States became early advocates of temperance because they recognized the productivity gains that could be realized from a sober work force—though many workers continued to drink on the job or enjoy drinking on Holy Monday. In the community, early temperance advocates tried to persuade individuals to "take the pledge" and abstain from drinking. Although many respectable workers took the pledge and many labor union leaders backed temperance campaigns, temperance proved unpopular among the increasingly urbanized working class for whom drinking was an important leisure activity. In the late nineteenth-century United States, Protestant middle-class reformers began to despair of "improving" an increasingly Catholic working class and advocated restrictions on the sale of alcohol that led to a national prohibition of the sale of alcohol by constitutional amendment in 1920—this effort was abandoned by 1933. Temperance efforts continued in industrial societies, as in the Soviet Union during the 1980s.

References Gusfield, Joseph R. *Symbolic Crusade: Status Politics and the American Temperance Movement* (1986); Harrison, Brian Howard. *Drink and the Victorians: The Temperance Question in England, 1815–1872* (1971); Rosenzweig, Roy. *Eight Hours for What We Will: Workers and Leisure in an Industrial City, 1870–1920* (1983).

Tesla, Nikola

See Alternating Current.

Textiles

The textiles industry, which produces thread and cloth, has been central to the industrial revolution from the outset. Consumption of textile products was rising in the eighteenth century, thanks to growing population, new consumer tastes, and export opportunities. This rise was a motivation to introduce new procedures to increase production and also to expand the labor force in protoindustrialization.

Hanks of viscose rayon are dyed at a Droylsden, England, textile factory in 1955.

Because of the easy manipulation of textile fibers, textile processes could be mechanized more easily than other consumer goods areas such as housing or even furnishings. New techniques in spinning and weaving, plus the introduction of factory production, thus quickly transformed key branches of textiles in Britain, New England, and western Europe. Factory workers in textiles long outnumbered their counterparts in other factory categories. Correspondingly, the industrialization of textiles had more impact on consumer habits than most other early industrial operations, creating new demand for colorful or stylish clothes and reducing old class barriers in dress. A "democratization of clothing" was widely noted during the early nineteenth century—and bemoaned by social conservatives. New retail outlets to handle textile sales were the basis of innovations such as department stores.

The industrialization of textiles actually reduced the labor force involved, because machines were so much more productive than traditional workers could be. Gradually, often painfully, traditional workers lost jobs not only in factory areas but in regions, like India or Latin America, open to European factory exports.

Because textile equipment is relatively cheap, compared to heavy industry, because textile companies are comparatively small (again in relation to heavy industry), and because cheap labor can make fledgling textile operations competitive, textile production has been a focus of many later industrializers, like Italy, Japan, and more recently Taiwan, Turkey, and India. Even though textile equipment became more elaborate and productive in the established industrial centers—the Northropp loom, for example, greatly increased per-worker weaving capacity in the late nineteenth century—it has been hard for older factory regions to keep up with the newcomers in textiles. Thus New England textile production began to migrate to the lower-wage South beginning in the late nineteenth century. More recently, Japanese textile industries have faded before Taiwanese competition, and U.S. and British textiles struggle. Textiles continue to be a dynamic but complex industrial sector.

See also Cotton; Linen; Silk; Wool.

Time

Most preindustrial work had been determined by natural phenomena, notably the seasons and the rising and setting of the sun. If a work day began at dawn, there was little need to regulate it further; people could decide what they wanted to do, when they wished to do it, in consultation perhaps with a small group of colleagues who were collaborating on a project. Of course, work was goaded by need—too much leisure could prevent the necessary output. And at specific seasons, like harvest time for peasants and farmers, December for coal miners and printers, requirements for production stepped up. Nevertheless, units of time within the day did not count for much.

Western Europe had developed exceptional skills in clock making, dating back to the Middle Ages. Religious rituals were performed by the clock—in monasteries, for example. Public clocks were a sign of a town's or a church's prosperity and began to spread as European wealth grew from the sixteenth century onward. There was a basis, in other words, for the application of clock time to other kinds of endeavor.

Linkage between work and the clock began to develop in the eighteenth century, at least in England. More and more people bought pocket watches. More people began to make appointments as part of their working day. The experience of clock time began to enter more aspects of life in the city. A similar development took place in the northeastern United States soon after 1800. Purchase of clocks and watches went up, apparently initially as a display of prosperity. People wanted these items as a badge of fashion and success. Gradually, they began to reckon their working days in terms of the clock, noting how many hours it took them to do something and often charging on this basis rather than simply for the task. From this it was a small move to timing workers, expecting them to show up at a certain hour and accomplish a certain amount per unit of time expended. This was a major change in the way work was conceived, difficult for many new workers to learn and a source of heightened pace and nervous tension. Time consciousness was also spread by the growth of railroads, with their strict time schedules.

Several developments, in this general context of new attention to clock time, definitively connected the clock to the industrialization process. The rise of factories separated work from home. No longer did workers wake each other up when it was time to get started, as in farmer or artisan households. Now it was necessary to start the factory at a certain hour and force workers to pay enough attention to the clock to get there promptly. (The factory whistle, a standard feature in most mill towns, provided workers with a vivid reminder.) The coordination required in factory work, with crews of workers necessary for each machine, also impelled use of the clock as a standardization device; everyone must show up together. Hence factories installed not only clocks but bells or whistles, to alert the neighborhood to the beginning of the working day. As gaslighting (and, later, electricity) allowed factories to operate at night, another link with the traditional timing of work was broken. Machines themselves ran quickly, which encouraged efforts to make workers think in terms of accomplishing quantities of work per hour. Pay systems increasingly shifted to a time base. If workers were paid by the product—what was called payment by the piece—they would be big gainers from the increased productivity of machines, because they could make units faster. But if workers were paid by the hour and expected to work hard each hour, a more productive machine would generate greater profits for the owners. Time-based pay, while it did not universally replace the piece rate for manufacturing workers, encouraged greater attention to the clock as a pace-setter for work.

Finally, factory owners themselves were frequently time addicts, convinced that economical use of time and pacing oneself by the clock were essential for economic success. Injunctions not to waste time became a standard part of the folk wisdom of the middle class, taught to children and enjoined on workers as well.

Adjusting to clock time as the framework for labor was one of the important developments in the work experience of early industrialization not only in western Europe but, later, in other societies as well. It constituted a big change in habits, making work perhaps less "natural" to human rhythms than it had been in preindustrial life. Other features of industrial societies conjoined to the new sense of time. School children were carefully taught time and regulated by the clock, as well as by a school's system of bells that mimicked the factory's system, so that they would not have to learn promptness and efficiency lessons from scratch in later life. Leisure began to be clock-regulated, with events starting "on time" and with speed records carefully kept—by the clock—and celebrated. Timeliness became an oft-repeated apology for fascism, for Mussolini was said to make Italy's trains run on time. The marriage of work and the clock constituted a fundamental change in the nature of life in a more industrial world.

See also Causes of the Industrial Revolution; Discipline; Education; Scientific Management; Work.

References Bruegel, Martin. "The Evolution of Time Consciousness in the Mid-Hudson Valley" (1995); Landes, David. *Revolution in Time: Clocks and the Making of the Modern World* (1983); Thompson, E. P. "Time, Industrial Work Discipline, and Capitalism" (1967).

Time and Motion Studies

Time and motion studies are an important aspect of scientific management. In the early twentieth century, efficiency experts such as Frederick Winslow Taylor argued that by closely studying how long it took workers to make the specific motions to complete their task, managers could radically improve productivity. After timing each of the workers' movements (later practitioners used slow-speed photographs to follow workers' movements) experts would try to eliminate wasted motions, either by redesigning the workplace, for instance by moving storage bins closer to lathe workers, further subdividing the task, or convincing workers to use new techniques, such as shovels with longer handles. Workers were frequently taken off hourly rates, where it was to their advantage to restrict production, and paid by a piece rate so as to give them an incentive. Piece rates were in turn set by the production achievement of the best workers. Workers resented not only the attempt to make them work without a break, but the fact that managers frequently lowered piece rates after the new quotas were achieved.

See also Division of Labor; Stakhanovites; Workers' Control.

References Garson, Barbara. *Electronic Sweatshop: How Computers Are Transforming the Office of the Future into the Factory of the Past* (1988); Meyer, Stephen. *The Five Dollar Day: Labor, Management, and Social Control in the Ford Motor Company, 1900–1921* (1981).

Tractors

Although small numbers of gasoline-powered tractors were produced in the early twentieth century, Henry Ford was the first to mass produce tractors in the 1910s. By 1927 Ford was producing 650,000 tractors a year—about half of the total in the United States. Tractors allowed farmers to plough and harvest far larger fields—particularly in grains and hay. Initially, farmers benefited, although overproduction led to a fall in the value of agricultural goods and contributed to the rapid depletion of the topsoil—problems that were partially addressed by the New Deal. In the 1920s and 1930s Stalin believed that tractors would help the newly collectivized farms in the Soviet Union to rapidly increase the amount of grain production—but the Soviet's mechanization of agriculture only began in earnest in the 1950s.

Reference Worster, Donald. *Dust Bowl: The Southern Plains in the 1930s* (1979).

Trusts

Trusts were an organizational device used in the United States to form larger business combinations. Cartels had not worked well in the United States. In the early form of trust, various companies joined, assigning voting rights in stocks to a central board of trustees, which could regulate individual policies on pricing, output, and so on. The Standard Oil Company used this voting trust form in 1882, and it was widely copied, but the courts soon held that the trust was illegal. Later trusts were holding companies, which acquired the majority of voting stocks in all companies involved. These new trusts included Standard Oil of New Jersey, United States Steel Company (1901), and International Harvester (1902). These trusts sought to monopolize much of the business in their industry, achieving not only economies of scale but above all manipulating prices paid for supplies and charged for goods, reducing competitive pressures. The U.S. government legislated against trusts, beginning with the Sherman Act of 1890, and several trusts were disbanded. But the development of highly centralized operations with large bureaucracies and great bargaining power continued.

See also Mergers.

Turkey

Scattered factories developed in Turkey in the late nineteenth century, particularly in industries like rugmaking where there was extensive foreign demand. Both foreign and Turkish businessmen participated. After Turkish independence in the 1920s, the reform-minded government worked hard to push industrialization. More secular education, new commercial laws, and other arrangements were designed to spur economic growth. But results came slowly, and Turkey was long regarded as a society where conscious policy had not paid off. Nevertheless, industry began to grow in the 1930s. State-sponsored roads and rails provided the best internal transportation network in the Middle East. State companies operated in textiles, chemicals, and mining. Turkish alliance with the West during the Cold War brought new foreign investments. A state-planning agency was set up in 1960 to coordinate policy, and private sector industries began to expand. Turkish textile production burgeoned, and an automobile industry developed. Turkey also promoted agricultural exports. By 1980 Turkey was by some measurements one of the most industrialized nations in the Middle East, second only to Israel. But Turkish per-capita income remained low; many workers, in a rapidly growing population, migrated to Western Europe in search of work; a full 49 percent of the labor force was still in agriculture. Whether Turkey was poised for a full industrial revolution remained debatable.

U

Underclass

In recent years journalists, social scientists, and politicians have called attention to a class of urban poor—the so-called underclass—who are purportedly socially isolated and economically marginalized. These individuals are frequently portrayed in the media as depraved hustlers, panhandlers, welfare queens, and drug addicts—in short, as people whose poverty is the result of social pathologies. However, historians have observed that contemporary policies toward the "underclass" are rooted in far older attitudes toward the poor.

Although industrialization did not create poverty, it did change the paths into poverty and the treatment wealthier people accorded poor people. In England, population growth, in tandem with the enclosure movement, helped to create a large class of landless laborers who worked when they could but who also relied on poor relief. Beginning in the seventeenth century, the rich began to view poverty as avoidable; they stigmatized those poor people who refused to work for the often inadequate wages and harsh conditions offered by employers. In England, Germany, and the Low Countries, the poor had to work (often in workhouses) in order to receive relief. Increasingly, the middle and upper classes analyzed the attitudes and behavior of the poor in order to make moral (and fiscal) distinctions between the "deserving" and "undeserving" poor. In the nineteenth century, most Marxists also drew distinctions between the virtuous proletariat or the laboring poor and the "Lumpenproletariat" whose marginality to the workplace and "vicious" habits made them socially undesirable (and allegedly politically reactionary). Attitudes toward the contemporary "underclass"—particularly the need on the part of richer people to make distinctions between deserving and undeserving poor—have developed from these earlier attitudes.

The creation of the contemporary "underclass" is rooted in the transformation of the urban industrial economy that has occurred over the last fifty years. Since the 1940s industrialists have reduced their reliance on laborers in large factories. In the United States the automobile facilitated the decentralization of factories and warehouses away from the inner cities. This process was accompanied by "white flight," as the white middle class (and later workers) avoided sharing their neighborhoods or schools with black workers. By the late 1960s older industrial cities had been progressively stripped of their economic vitality and fiscal viability. The urban riots of the 1960s were in the main a protest by younger black workers frustrated with being warehoused in urban wastelands.

The worst was yet to come: deindustrialization dealt industrial cities (and their residents) a final, crippling blow. The large factories built up during the last one hundred years of capital accumulation—the visible embodiment of the industrial revolution—were wiped out during the 1970s and 1980s. Deindustrialization eliminated many of the stable, unionized blue-collar jobs that had allowed black workers to support their families and send their children to college. Most postindustrial urban job markets simply failed to create jobs at comparable wages to the manufacturing sector. Similar developments occurred in Europe where immigrant workers, often people of color, were at risk for unstable employment and the pressures of urban slums.

When discussing the causes of poverty, however, many observers have ignored these structural economic shifts and have focused (as did earlier "experts") on the alleged moral failings of the poor. Politicians, journalists, and social scientists have focused attention on the "culture of poverty" among the urban poor. Alcoholism, drug taking, welfare "dependency," and the lack of dual-headed households have all been offered as causal explanations for the deepening crisis of urban poverty. Critics of this approach note that middle-class observers are notorious for isolating "pathological" behavior among the poor when it is a general phenomenon. For instance, drug abuse rates among middle-class white suburbanites are similar to those among poor inner-city blacks. However, drug laws against the sale and possession of "crack" cocaine (a drug used predominately by blacks) were far harsher than powder cocaine (favored by the white middle class). As a result of harsh and racially biased drug laws (and deteriorating economic conditions), young black males in the late 1980s were more likely to end up in prison than in college. In the increasingly harsh social and economic context of the postindustrial city, many members of the working class refused to accept the insecurity and frustration of low-wage jobs in the "secondary" labor market and dropped out of the labor force.

In the United States, and to some extent in Europe, the policies of government have either failed to alleviate or even helped to exacerbate the current problem of urban poverty. Since the 1970s city and county governments have fewer financial resources to counteract the increasing poverty of their residents. The public sector (which had become the avenue of upward mobility for many members of the black middle class) came under increasing pressure to "downsize." Throughout the 1980s and 1990s, the middle class (itself feeling the negative ripple effects of deindustrialization) supported drastically reducing federal antipoverty programs in order to break the "culture of welfare dependency." Federal subsidies have continued for suburban housing, education, and economic development, however, thus effectively exacerbating the effects of the dual labor markets.

See also Dual Labor Markets; Racism; Unemployment.

References Katz, Michael. *The Undeserving Poor: From the War on Poverty to the War on Welfare* (1989); Katz, Michael, ed. *The "Underclass" Debate: Views from History* (1993).

Underdevelopment.

See World Systems Theory.

Unemployment

The industrial revolution transformed the nature of work and unemployment. Although workers had long been subjected to being out of work and seeking employment, the term unemployment only came into popular usage in the United States during the 1870s. In Germany the term Arbeitslosigkeit or "the state of being without work" emerged in the 1890s. As one historian observed, however, "For workers, the problem came before the word."

Once workers had become dependent upon wage labor for survival, unemployment was a real misery that ravaged workers' savings and self-respect. Even during good years in the nineteenth century, approximately 5 percent of the U.S. work force was jobless, and during the Great Depression of the 1930s as many as 33 percent of all workers were looking for work. Ironically, layoffs in factories were often preceded by periods of feverish activity and mandatory overtime. Although by the 1890s unemployed U.S. workers agitated for greater state-sponsored relief or public works projects, politicians influenced by the philosophy of laissez-faire generally refused to intervene to aid the unemployed. Before the 1930s workers could only rely on their own savings or the charity of friends and family. (In 1916 Massachusetts was the first state in the United States to consider unemployment insurance but only enacted legislation in 1935—only the fifth state to do so.) Local governments and private charities were another source of support for the unemployed, but they were easily overwhelmed by severe economic downturns and adopted more restrictive guidelines. Many workers were forced to "tramp" in search of work—only to confront laws against tramps. Some commentators observe that the social system that made unemployment inevitable also made it illegal. In the nineteenth century national governments in industrial countries played a limited role in alleviating the effects of unemployment. Most national governments felt that it would exacerbate depressions if they funded public works projects or extended relief to the unemployed. Even during the severe depression of the 1890s, the federal government refused to fund public works projects. By the 1870s, however, local governments in industrial cities such as New York and Philadelphia launched public works projects, though with limited financial resources. In the late nineteenth century the German state was the first to institute social insurance policies for sick, injured, and retired workers (paid for by compulsory deductions from workers' wages), which provided workers some measure of security. The government did not provide unemployment insurance, although it did endeavor to help the jobless find employment (private employment agencies were sometimes referred to as "labor sharks" by trade unionists). The French government also created "labor exchanges" or bourses du travail.

In 1911 Britain created the world's first state-sponsored unemployment insurance program. During the 1920s approximately 12 percent of the British work force was unemployed and subsisted on government-subsidized housing, medical assistance, and cash relief. Britain's Labour Party gradually expanded benefits—which had the effect of blunting that country's notoriously sharp class tensions. In the 1920s unemployment was also a serious problem in the Soviet Union, but by the 1930s Stalin's crash industrialization program had created the only state with labor shortages. In the 1930s mass unemployment caused the rise of a welfare state in Scandinavia and a communist "popular front" government in France. In the 1920s and 1930s widespread unemployment aided the rise of fascist regimes in Italy, Germany, Japan, and much of Eastern Europe. Although the form of state intervention took many different forms, most governments began to take a measure of responsibility to alleviate unemployment.

The Great Depression hit the United States particularly hard, and unemployment was so widespread that it quickly overwhelmed the capacities of private charities and local relief. Many of the unemployed as well as private charities called on the federal government to intervene. In 1935 unemployment insurance (the monies were collected by the federal government but administered by the states) was created as part of the Social Security Act. The New Deal required work, however, from able-bodied people on relief. The Work Projects Administration provided work for nearly 2 million men and women on public works projects such as bridges, parks, and slum clearance. World War II moved most industrial countries' economies toward "full employment" (whereby all workers who wanted to work could find a job).

In the post–World War II or "Fordist" era, unemployment rates generally fell in industrialized countries; however, race and ethnicity played a large role in allocating unemployment. From the 1940s until the present, the rate of black unemployment in the United States has been two or three times higher than that of whites. Many European countries expelled foreign "guest workers" when unemployment became a problem. The policies of governments toward unemployment have differed widely. In the Soviet Union and Eastern Europe, workers were required to work—and the state was required to find them a job. In Japan and the United States, unemployment insurance has been of relatively short duration. In Western Europe, where socialist and labor parties and unions are stronger than in the United States, unemployed native-born workers could remain on unemployment for several years. During the 1980s young professionals in Germany and Sweden who were unable to find employment after college could receive unemployment benefits at 80 percent or more of their anticipated income. (Entry into professions and universities are more strictly regulated than in the United States.) By the late 1980s, however, unemployment in Europe was a chronic problem, and governments began to reduce benefits.

In thc post–World War II cra, thc problem of "underemployment" grew in severity. Underemployment is when workers or professionals are involuntarily employed part time in positions that do not allow them to make full use of their training, for instance, when a machinist or chemist is driving a cab. Although underemployment is growing in industrialized countries, the problem is particularly acute in developing countries (such as Mexico, India, or sub-Saharan Africa) that have developed a more educated work force but where industrialization has failed to "take off."

See also Keynesianism; Postindustrial Economies; Social Democracy; State, Role of the.

References Garraty, John A. *Unemployment in History: Economic Thought and Public Policy* (1978); Keyssar, Alexander. *Out of Work: The First Century of Unemployment in Massachusetts* (1986).

United Mine Workers

Founded in 1890, the United Mine Workers is an industrial union of coal miners in the United States. Unlike many unions at the time of its founding, the UMW allowed all workers who worked in or around the mines to join, regardless of their occupation, national origin, or color. By 1919, 400,000 miners belonged to the union, and there was widespread support among its members to nationalize the coal, railroad, and communications industries. The 1920s was a difficult period for the coal industry, however, and many employers refused to negotiate with the UMW; by 1932 only 100,000 members remained. Desperate conditions were a factor in driving the UMW to support the nascent CIO. After World War II automation eliminated many coal-mining jobs and heavily mechanized (and non-union) surface or strip mines outside the union's traditional stronghold of Appalachia reduced the union's membership. In the 1990s only 50,000 members remain in the UMW, although it remains one of the few unions capable of successfully conducting strikes in an increasingly hostile legal climate.

See also National Miners Union.

Reference Long, Priscilla. *Where the Sun Never Shines: A History of America's Bloody Coal Industry* (1989).

United States

The United States began the nineteenth century as a predominantly agricultural nation and by 1918 was the world's dominant industrial and financial power. The earliest phases of industrialization centered in New England. The region had abundant water power, a large number of entrepreneurs and, by the early nineteenth century, a large excess rural population. The textile industry was begun by Samuel Slater in the late eighteenth century and by the 1820s had spread throughout the region. In order to attract local farm women (who worked for wages a few years before marriage), industrialists had to prove that factory life could provide a morally uplifting environment. Early factories often took a paternalistic interest in the leisure time of their workers—a feature that some workers (or at least their families) appreciated and others resented and resisted. The efforts of the U.S. government to provide its own supply of armaments was important to the development of machine-building industries and modern factory management. The government also assisted industry by fostering mass education and subsidizing the building of roads, canals, and railroads. Early U.S. industrialization borrowed heavily from European, particularly British, businessmen and banks, and the nation was in debt until World War I. It depended heavily also on imported European technology.

The spread of industrialization throughout the North and Midwest and the creation of a working class was influenced by the reality and images of slavery. During the early nineteenth century, slavery in the North (which had been an important source of artisanal labor) was gradually eliminated. An important source of raw materials (and markets for finished products) for the textile and shoe factories were southern slave plantations. The growing political tensions between the North (which relied on free or wage labor) and the South (which had free laborers but was dominated by slavery) influenced the ideology of northern industrialists and workers alike. By the 1850s many northerners believed that the practice and spread of "free labor" was desirable and incompatible with slavery, a belief that helped precipitate the American Civil War. Although most workers subscribed to the dominant beliefs of white supremacy and helped to marginalize black workers, white workers feared becoming "wage slaves."

Throughout the middle and late nineteenth century, the rapid spread of railroads drove the industrialization process. New centers of heavy industry such as Pittsburgh and Chicago developed to make products for railroads. Railroads allowed the development of a national market for agricultural products and encouraged the industrialization of meatpacking and the processing of grain and other foods. New communication technologies, such as the telegraph, and more efficient managerial techniques were developed by railroad companies. Railroad companies even aided the standardization of time among different parts of the country.

The twentieth century was dominated by the rise of the automobile and industries such as petrochemicals and electrical equipment that relied on advances made by scientists based in universities or research laboratories. During World War I the federal government took an active role in coordinating industrial production, helping to allocate resources and labor and resolving patent disputes. As the economy became more complex, industrialists increasingly relied on government to resolve their disputes, coordinate production, open foreign markets, or subsidize their research. This tendency was well established by the 1920s, although the New Deal indicated that government would intervene on the behalf of labor as well as business.

See also Black Workers.

References Chandler, Alfred Dupont. *The Visible Hand: The Managerial Revolution in American Business* (1977); Gutman, Herbert George. *Work, Culture, and Society in Industrializing America: Essays in American Working-Class and Social History* (1976).

United States South

Until the 1860s the South was a supplier of raw materials to industrial regions, though not a major industrial producer in its own right. In the wake of the American Civil War, southern elites attempted to develop an industrial economy, the "New South," although production of cotton, tobacco, and other agricultural products continued to dominate its economy. The New South strategy was predicated on exploitation of the region's cheap labor as well as its rich supply of natural resources, such as timber, coal, and iron ore. By the beginning of the twentieth century, the South possessed numerous sawmills, textile mills, and tobacco processing factories, as well as a greatly expanded railroad network. Birmingham, Alabama, had become a major producer of coal and steel. Critics of the New South argue that the region remained a de facto colony of the North. Southern industry also often relied on low-cost labor and fierce anti-unionism, another source of criticism.

See also Emancipation; Neocolonialism; Slavery.

Reference Woodward, C. Vann. *Origins of the New South, 1877–1913* (1951).

University

Since the mid-nineteenth century, the university has played an important role in training individuals in the increasingly complex technical, scientific, and professional expertise necessary to manage modern corporations. Research universities first developed in Germany, where chemists, for example, developed products for industry and agriculture. Universities in

France as well as Germany also turned out increasing numbers of trained engineers and technicians. These features were gradually copied by the United States, England, and other societies as part of the ongoing industrialization effort. The first engineering programs in the United States (outside of West Point) were begun only in the 1850s, but university-based research developed quickly and provided crucial assistance in the development of electrical equipment, petrochemicals, electronics, and computers. The growth of the university system was given an enormous boost by government. In the 1860s the federal government of the United States spurred higher education by giving states "land grants" to help fund state university systems. University researchers often complemented the work done in private laboratories, and during the Cold War the federal government greatly expanded the scale of university-based technical and scientific research.

See also Research Laboratories.

Urbanization

Urbanization refers to the growth and development of extensive cities. Large cities predated the rise of the industrial form of production, although industrialization greatly facilitated the movement of masses of people into cities. In the late eighteenth century, most large cities in Europe were centers for government (London, Paris, St. Petersburg), although there was a steady growth in commercial cities (Liverpool, Amsterdam, Bristol) as a result of an increase in global trade. The growth of the factory system (see Protoindustrialization) drew many landless agricultural laborers to what had been relatively small cities (Manchester, Liège, or Lyons). During the nineteenth century, industrial cities throughout Europe, North America, and Japan mushroomed; by the early twentieth century, the majority of the British were urbanites and the populations of most industrializing countries were not far behind in reaching or passing the 50 percent urbanization mark.

A central feature of industrial cities was their rapid growth. In 1800 London had approximately 1 million residents and by the end of the century it had 5 million. Many cities expanded rapidly as labor-intensive factories, warehouses, docks, and offices attracted migrants from the countryside, many of whom were simultaneously becoming workers as they became urbanized. A symbiotic relationship emerged between the working-class experience and urban culture. Without the close social supervision of masters or merchants (as under the artisanal mode of production), working-class men and women developed their own institutions, culture, and political ideologies in their neighborhoods. Young working-class men and women developed distinctive styles of dress, courtship, and rituals that rankled the sensibilities of the middle class. More alarming were workers' protests, riots, and insurrections, such as the Paris Commune of 1871 that many feared (or hoped) was the harbinger of future trends.

Cities had always been crowded, dirty, and unhealthy places, but industrial cities added industrial pollution and rapid growth to the difficulties of urban life. However, industrialization eventually transformed cities' physical or "built" environment. Advances in transportation technology made cities more decentralized. Beginning in the 1830s horse-drawn streetcars enabled the upper and middle classes in the United States to withdraw to semi-rural suburbs—a process that accelerated with the advent of electric-powered streetcars in the late nineteenth century and automobiles in the early twentieth century. By the 1980s more Americans lived in suburbs than in cities. Throughout most of the world, however, it was the poor who commuted from the suburbs.

New technologies and organizational forms gradually transformed urban life. By the late nineteenth century most middle-class urbanites lived on paved streets, had indoor running water, and were connected to a sewage system—all of which meant that cities were becoming more healthy and livable places. Beginning in the early nineteenth century, cities also began to

The population of industrial cities, such as London, pictured here in 1905, quickly multiplied during the nineteenth century. Between 1800 and 1900, London's population grew from one million to five million.

provide improved social services such as professionalized fire and police departments that relied on new technologies (networks of water and telephones). Although industrial cities were notoriously biased against the poor, an increasing number of workers also began to receive better services. Furthermore, the expansion of city government provided a source of steady jobs for a few workers with personal or political connections to "boss" politicians. By the early nineteenth century mass-produced building supplies (nails, precut timber, and door and window frames) enabled workers in the United States to construct cheap frame or "balloon" style housing for themselves. European cities remained more compact but new products and work processes were used to construct apartment buildings and tenements. By the early twentieth century, many cities were building tall buildings (skyscrapers) in their downtown business district, using steel frames and incorporating new technologies such as elevators, telephones, and eventually air conditioning.

Industrial cities not only changed the built environment of the city but helped to transform the surrounding countryside as well. The explosive growth of cities relied on the countryside's raw materials in order to build its buildings and feed its population. Cities situated on transportation networks of canals, roads, and railroads became the trading centers for the countryside's mineral and agricultural wealth; in return, cities supplied farms, mines, and plantations with manufactured goods and capital. Labor migration patterns also followed these established flows of commodities. Although this relationship was most pronounced in colonial commercial cities (such as Lagos or Calcutta), it was also true for industrial cities such as Chicago or Philadelphia.

In the twentieth century there was an explosion of cities in developing countries (the "Third World"). One historian estimated that the urban population of Asia, Africa, and Latin America increased from 100 million in 1900 to over 1,000 million in 1985. Industrialization has pulled migrants to the cities with the promise of better jobs, housing, and education for their children, although "push" factors, such as the collapse of peasant agriculture, lack of alternative jobs, or social services in rural areas also were an important factor. The vast majority of these migrants work in the secondary labor market, and the vast numbers of these new workers overwhelm the capacity of most cities, even where the political will exists to extend basic social services such as running water, sewage, or electrical systems. As late as the 1960s many Japanese workers lived in substandard housing and lacked connections to water or sewer lines. Whereas the living standards in Japanese cities improved throughout the 1970s and 1980s, most new migrants to impoverished and rapidly expanding industrial cities such as São Paulo, Mexico City, or Cairo lack basic services. Whether industrializing cities will be able to replicate the successes of European, American, and Japanese cities is an open question. In the meantime, deindustrialization has decreased the economic vitality of center cities in the United States, and deteriorating water systems and health of residents has led to outbreaks of diseases once thought conquered.

See also Construction Industry; Infrastructure.

References Harvey, David. *The Urban Experience* (1989); Hohenberg, Paul, and Lynn Lees. *The Making of Urban Europe, 1000–1950* (1985); Mohl, Raymond A. *The New City: Urban America in the Industrial Age, 1860–1920* (1985).

USSR

See Russia.

Utopian Socialists

In contrast to "scientific" socialists (Marxists), who believed that socialism would only be realized after a thoroughgoing revolution, utopian socialists believed that an egalitarian society could be built generally through cooperative labor projects within existing society. Numerous utopian socialists emerged in the nineteenth century, often reacting against the brutality of the new factory regime. Problems frequently beset the attempted utopias. Although Robert Owen's New Lanark textile mills were both humane and commercially successful, his attempt to found the first "village of cooperation" in New Harmony, Indiana, failed due to problems in organizing production, finding incentives for work, and resolving questions about private property. However, many utopians remained excited by the prospect of building a society without poverty or class distinctions. Utopianism was a strong current among reformers into the twentieth century; for instance, both the Catholic Worker movement and Father Divine (who preached to black workers in the Great Depression) relied on utopianism. Many of the early Zionist colonists in what later became Israel formed successful agricultural communes that had strong utopian inspiration particularly in their early decades.

See also Saint Simon, Claude H.

References Berry, Brian J. L. *America's Utopian Experiments: Communal Havens from Long-Wave Crises* (1992); Heilbroner, Robert L. *The Worldly Philosophers: The Lives, Times, and Ideas of the Great Economic Thinkers* (1986).

Vanderbilt, Cornelius (1794–1877)
Cornelius Vanderbilt was a notorious "robber baron" who built his fortune in the steamship and railroad businesses. From the 1810s to the 1850s, "Commodore" Vanderbilt aggressively built a line of steamships and a simultaneous reputation for ruthlessness. When competitors attempted to take over his company, Vanderbilt replied: "Gentlemen, you have undertaken to cheat me. I will not sue you, for law takes too long. I will ruin you." In this instance, Vanderbilt was as good as his word. In the 1860s, with railroads threatening the viability of his steamships, the Commodore entered the railroad business. He was a master at gaining control by breaking his rivals and amassing riches by exploiting his newfound monopoly position or watering stock. Though he lost millions in financial struggles with Jay Gould over the Erie railroad, Vanderbilt remained one of the richest, if not the richest, man in the United States until the end of his life.

Reference Josephson, Matthew. *The Robber Barons: The Great American Capitalists, 1861–1901* (1934).

Wage Labor

Wage labor refers to work systems based on monetary pay, rather than other methods of support and control. Prior to the rise of capitalism and the industrial revolution, European laborers were not free, unencumbered workers who relied solely on wage labor for survival. Many workers were artisans whose wages and labor were regulated by the guild system. Most people who would later become workers were either peasants who had strong legal and emotional ties to specific pieces of land, or tenants or serfs who could not leave their manorial estates. Before the industrial revolution in England, many of the institutions that tied people to certain occupations (such as guilds) or to particular places (such as manorialism) were undermined or destroyed. Population growth in the eighteenth century increased the numbers of people without property who depended upon selling their labor for a wage.

Thus British industrial production arose in a situation where employers had greater flexibility to establish new work regimes and labor discipline than employers in other countries. Although there was widespread resistance to the harsh world of the early factory system, the repression by the state and institutions such as workhouses forced workers to accept the status quo. Standards of living were initially quite low, but the flexibility of the work force was a major factor in allowing the industrial revolution to succeed, turning Britain into an economic power and by the 1830s raising workers' living standards. Later in the nineteenth century, a similar process occurred in much of western Europe and the northern United States.

However, industrial production could occur in situations of less than free labor systems. Slavery had only been abolished in the northern United States in the early nineteenth century, well after the industrialization process had begun. Although the U.S. South was largely a producer of agricultural products, a nascent iron and steel industry and textile industry had arisen by the 1850s that relied on slaves as well as free workers. The economic and political conflict between North and South led to the American Civil War. Even after the period of emancipation and reconstruction, agricultural goods for industry (such as cotton) were produced by white and black sharecroppers. Industry in the South, notably textiles, continued to rely on highly repressive and paternalistic labor systems. Such institutions as company stores modified market-based wage labor by artificially controlling and requiring purchases at inflated prices so that workers could not get out of debt.

In general, industrialization seems to thrive more happily with wage labor than on less flexible arrangements like serfdom or slavery. Employers of wage labor do not have to support workers during slumps. Employers can pay low wages when workers are abundant and use wages to encourage skills acquisition or to divide workers. Industrialization has nonetheless often employed unfree labor—not only slaves but also groups of orphans bought by early English industrialists or women sold by husbands or fathers into sweatshop contracts in nineteenth-century Japan.

Some scholars have argued against the view of industrialization as a process that requires or creates free systems of wage labor (as it seems to have done for male workers in Britain and the northern United States). Instead, these scholars assert, industrialization has proved compatible with a variety of quasi-free labor systems. Russian industrialization relied on serfs as well as free workers, and under Stalinist industrialization, workers were not free to quit jobs. Industrialization does require a certain degree of flexibility from workers, and laborers cannot insist on working in certain occupations or remain committed to a particular place, thus they cannot be in guilds or remain peasants. However, the industrial system is often mediated through "sticky" institutions, such as families, unions, the state, or ethnicity, from which workers can expect resources in periods of economic crisis.

See also Dual Labor Markets; Enclosure Movement; Luddism; Working Class; World Systems Theory.

References Balibar, Étienne, and Immanuel Wallerstein. *Race, Nation, Class: Ambiguous Identities* (1991); Foner, Eric. *Free Soil, Free Labor, Free Men: The Ideology of the Republican Party before the Civil War* (1970).

Wagner Act

The Wagner Act (National Labor Relations Act) has been termed "the Magna Carta of the American Labor movement" because it made it much easier for U.S. workers to organize themselves into unions. Named after New York Senator Robert F. Wagner (1877–1953), the 1935 law assumed that workers and industrialists had fundamentally differing interests, but that their differences could be mediated by the state. The law built upon the National Industrial Recovery Act (1933), also written by Wagner, which protected workers' right to organize unions in the abstract but gave little concrete assistance. The Wagner Act gave the National Labor Relations Board (NLRB) the power to order employers to speedily conduct elections of its employees if a significant number of them indicated they wished to join or organize a union; the NLRB also barred company elections, the discharge of union organizers, and the refusal of either unions or employers to bargain in good faith. The Wagner Act greatly strengthened unions but was largely undone by the 1947 Taft-Hartley Act.

See also Congress of Industrial Organizations; Industrial Unions; State, Role of the.

Water Power

Water power was long used in water wheels to turn millstones. Massive wheels were placed in streams, with buckets that could catch the rapid current and turn the wheel. The wheel turned a crankshaft that could be connected, through gears, to other equipment. This method was widely used for early textile machinery, such as spinning mules and waterframe looms. Early textile factories spread along rivers, and for decades water power surpassed the use of steam engines in this industry. It was particularly important in industrializing areas like New England and France where coal was in short supply.

Beginning with Leonardo da Vinci, designers had worked on improvements in the water wheel, and some new types were installed in France and Italy in the early eighteenth century. The major advance, however, came in the 1820s and 1830s, primarily in France, where the turbine water wheel was introduced. This wheel had complex vanes fitted into a casing around the wheel; these curved passages reacted with the flow of water to greatly increase deficiency. The French engineer Burdin first used the term turbine in 1824, but his wheel had design defects. Another French engineer, Benoit Fourneyron, took up the problem and developed a series of turbine wheels; in 1832 he achieved a fifty-horsepower wheel used to power forge hammers in central France. The turbine was one of the great technical accomplishments of the nineteenth century, enabling greater use of water power throughout Europe and the United States. This in turn became the basis for using water to generate electricity—hydroelectric power—which could be distributed over long distances, freeing water-powered factories from the need to locate directly on riverways. Many later industrializers relied heavily on water power before they could afford many steam engines; almost half of Japanese manufacturing was water powered until 1890 (most of the rest still manual).

See also Hydroelectric Power.

Watt, James (1736–1819)
Watt, trained as an artisan producing precision equipment for scientists at the University of Glasgow, Scotland, was the inventor of the first steam engine usable for industry. Son of a Scottish shopkeeper and carpenter, he trained as a precision-instrument maker before taking his university post. He worked on a Newcomen engine in 1763, as part of his university assignment, and believed he could improve the utilization of fuel by adding a separate condensing chamber. He took out his first patent in 1769, and with the aid of several associates began to improve his engine further. He introduced a double-acting piston (patented in 1782) that was driven in both directions by steam, another major gain in efficiency. He also devised automatic control of the steam pressure by a governor and then in 1781 patented a system of gears for transmitting power from the piston to rotary equipment capable of running machinery. Watt also did scientific research in chemistry and metallurgy. Watt's inventions, though later perfected by others and commercially developed in collaboration with Matthew Boulton, provided the central technological basis for the industrial revolution, for they freed industry from the geographical and mechanical limitations of water power. It was he and Boulton who coined the term "horsepower". Watt's work, requiring a precision far beyond the capacity of traditional metal workers, also prompted the development of new skills in machine building. Watt was probably the single most important inventor of the industrial revolution; the power unit, the watt, was named in his honor. Watt also illustrates the connection between advancing scientific learning and technological innovation. Watt retired, a wealthy man, in 1800.

See also Machine Building.

Wedgwood, Josiah (1730–1795)
Wedgwood was born into a family of English potters. He was initially apprenticed to his brothers, but he took charge of a small establishment of his own at the age of twenty-one. He early showed a gift for technological innovation, also using earlier inventions relevant to potters. He began to expand his operations in partnership with other potters, who provided the capital. He set up his own sales agency in London in 1765 and built a new factory in the same year. Partnership with a Liverpool merchant, Thomas Benley, provided not only additional capital but a larger sales operation, including export capacity, and a knowledge of classical art that was to give particular distinction to Wedgwood pottery. Wedgwood developed both ordinary tableware and luxury, ornamental items; his firm expanded vertically, taking charge of raw materials markets through connections with various clay companies. Wedgwood reversed the normal subordination of manufacturers to merchants, setting up his own showrooms in various towns as well as extensive export facilities that guaranteed safe delivery. Mass-produced, carefully promoted chinaware fed into growing British consumerism, connecting it clearly to the early industrial period. Wedgwood operated on the basis of large sales, with low profit margins, instead of the more traditional high prices and limited output. Wedgwood was also an active paternalist, providing improved housing for his hundreds of workers. He was convinced that his work was responsible for "the most pleasing and rapid improvements," around his huge production complex, The Potteries; he also ended his career with extensive lands and a personal estate of about 240,000 pounds.

Welfare
See Social Insurance.

Wendel
The de Wendel family was one of a small number of pioneering metallurgical groups in France. The family had a background in traditional, charcoal-burning iron making in eastern France. In the

1780s, with government backing, a de Wendel set up the first iron-smelting operation using coke at the town of Le Creusot; his effort failed, though later another great industrial family, the Schneiders, revived it. François de Wendel began carefully copying British methods of coke-based smelting around 1818 in Lorraine, bringing in a number of skilled British workers (with whom he quickly grew dissatisfied because of what he termed their drunkenness and unreliability; here was a clear reason to develop a French labor force). His operation steadily expanded, particularly when he moved into railroad development as well. Producing 22,370 tons of pig iron in 1850, the firm boasted 134,470 just twenty years later, when it was making 12 percent of all French wrought iron and steel (a hint of the concentration of production in heavy industry). The company profited greatly from the Gilchrist-Thomas process in the 1870s, which allowed fuller use of Lorraine ore, even though many of its plants were now in Germany, and it continued to be a force in European industry until nationalization after World War II.

See also Carnegie, Andrew; Iron and Steel; Krupp.

Westinghouse, George (1846–1914)

George Westinghouse was an inventor and industrialist. In 1869 he invented the railroad airbrake, which allowed trains to stop quickly and safely. In 1886 he founded the Westinghouse Electrical Corporation, which in the 1880s and 1890s developed alternating current as the dominant source of electrical power. Alternating current enabled electricity to be transmitted further and allowed for much stronger electrical machines such as overhead cranes and printing presses, among others. By 1900, 25 million incandescent lamps using alternating current were in use in the United States, and 15,000 miles of electrical trolleys were in place. Under Westinghouse's guidance the corporation grew rapidly but became overextended (growing over thirty times larger its first four years). By 1908 bankers had forced Westinghouse to accept a marginal role in his company, and he soon resigned; the company that Westinghouse founded has continued to be a leader in the field of electrical equipment, playing a large role in the development of nuclear power.

White-Collar Workers

White-collar workers are the salaried stratum of the work force, such as bank employees or clerical workers in industrial, corporate, or governmental bureaucracies. White-collar workers generally earn more money than all but the best-paid blue-collar workers, and they often have better benefit systems. They enjoy far less prestige, income, and power, however, than middle-class professionals or managers. In terms of their position in the class hierarchy, most scholars argue that white-collar workers are lower-middle class and stress that although these workers share many similarities with manual workers, white-collar workers have often been at pains to distinguish themselves from blue-collar workers.

Clerical and other white-collar positions existed prior to the industrial revolution in commerce and government, but the numbers of white-collar workers increased dramatically in the late nineteenth century, when the organizational form of business became increasingly complex. They formed the fastest-growing employment category in western Europe from the 1870s onwards. The modern corporation required large numbers of clerks to process the paperwork, operators to work telegraph machines, and accountants to keep the books. By the 1890s white-collar workers comprised over 10 percent of the work force in the United States and Germany, and by 1940 that proportion had increased to 22 percent in Germany and 24 percent in North America. Women played an important role in this growing labor force because they were inexpensive and presumably docile, while also educated enough to handle calculations and record-keeping.

The growth of corporations may have increased the number of white-collar workers, but it also eroded the power and viability of small-scale entrepreneurial businesses that supported a sizable portion of the nineteenth-century middle class. Many white-collar workers had been drawn from the ranks of small business and were both suspicious of corporate leaders and unwilling to embrace trade-union or socialist movements. In the nineteenth century most white-collar workers had more education than manual workers, and, unlike laborers, the earnings of white-collar workers did not fall as they got older. Employers also deliberately drew social distinctions between salaried employees and hourly workers, trying also to limit the layoffs of white-collar workers. After 1911 the German government began to distinguish between salaried and hourly workers by means of pensions and other benefits. When employees were represented in company committees, white- and blue-collar workers had separate organizations.

During the 1920s the economic position of salaried employees in Germany and Italy deteriorated. While the organizations of white-collar workers became somewhat more radicalized, most clerical workers were not eager to join workers' organizations such as the Social Democratic Party. Instead, white-collar workers were radicalized to the right and disproportionately joined the fascist movement. In the United States, by contrast, many clerical workers and government employees joined industrial unions, some with ties to the Communist Party.

By the 1920s the line between white- and blue-collar workers was beginning to blur in the United States as more children from working-class families acquired the education to enter the world of white-collar work. Jobs nevertheless remained stratified within the world of office work, with the better positions going disproportionately to native-born white Protestants. Immigrant Jewish and Catholic women could become secretaries, telephone operators, and sales clerks, but black workers were barred from such positions. During the Great Depression of the 1930s and into the 1940s, communists and black protest organizations had some success at gaining jobs for black workers in the department stores and banks in ghettoes, but these jobs typically remained the exclusive preserve of whites.

After World War II the number of white-collar workers increased rapidly, and by the 1950s they began to outnumber production workers. Women made up an increasing proportion of the white-collar work force, although they were almost universally relegated to less-desirable positions. In the banking industry in the 1940s, women were generally typists, stenographers, and secretaries, being considered unsuitable for jobs as tellers, accountants, or managers. By the 1960s nearly all nonprofessional jobs in banks were filled by women. Blacks' protests against the hiring policies of corporations opened office work to African Americans after federal civil rights laws were passed in the mid-1960s.

Most white-collar positions were less affected by mechanization or automation than was factory work, but in the early twentieth century machines like typewriters and cash registers had changed skill requirements, and many employers tried to increase the pace and regimentation of work. Behavioral requirements, such as smiling at customers, were also emphasized. In the 1950s computers began to transform office work, eliminating many of the processing jobs once done by clerical workers. Although most companies did not lay off white-collar workers, computerization curtailed the demand for additional workers and/or limited workers' chances for advancement. Computers also exacerbated the division between highly skilled positions, such as computer programmers (who were overwhelmingly male) and low-skill, low-paid data-entry personnel (who were overwhelmingly female). Until the 1970s the incomes of white-collar workers had risen; over the last twenty years their incomes have stagnated in the United States. In the 1980s another wave of computerization and deindustrialization eliminated many white-collar positions.

See also Pink-Collar Workers; Professionalization.

References Kocka, Jürgen. *White Collar Workers in America, 1890–1940: A Social-Political History in International Perspective* (1980); Lockwood, David. *The Blackcoated Worker: A Study in Class Consciousness* (1958); McColloch, Mark. *White Collar Workers in Transition: The Boom Years, 1940–1970* (1983); Mills, C. Wright. *White Collar: The American Middle Classes* (1956).

Whitney, Eli (1765–1825)

Often hailed as the greatest American inventor of the early industrial revolution, Whitney was more a publicist than a creator. Along with others, he invented the cotton gin, which greatly aided cotton production and helped extend slavery in the cotton-growing regions of the South. Whitney was the son of a Massachusetts farmer. He early displayed mechanical aptitude, making a violin at age 12. He made hand-wrought nails during his teens, running his own business in the Revolutionary War. After teaching school to earn money, he attended Yale University, intending to pursue a legal career. Moving to Georgia for further training, he impressed his landlady with his mechanical talent, and she boasted to a group of cotton growers that he could solve their problem in making cotton profitable by devising a machine to clean it. By 1793 he had indeed invented the gin, which could clean cotton as fast as fifty people working by hand. He took out a patent and began making the machine in Connecticut. But his factory burned and others copied his device; though he ultimately won the patent case it had by then almost expired. In 1798 Whitney set up another factory to make muskets by a new method. Previously, guns had been handcrafted, but Whitney talked about tools and patterns to turn uniform parts, so that less-skilled workers could assemble the weapons (while using government grants to retire his other debts). He amazed an impatient government group by seemingly assembling guns from pieces chosen at random from piles of parts; recent studies suggest that the demonstration was rigged. It did at least promote the idea of interchangeable parts to be perfected by others. For Whitney himself, the arms factory at last made him rich.

See also Interchangeable Parts; Inventions.

Wilkinson, John (1728–1808)

A British businessman and inventor, Wilkinson developed new, powered boring machines capable of unprecedented precision. His first device, for boring cannon, greatly improved accuracy (1774). In 1776 he applied this machine by boring cylinders and condensers for Boulton and Watt. Wilkinson expanded his iron and steel manufacturing in other directions, one of those early industrialists capable of innovations in a number of specific areas. In 1776 he introduced the steam blast to the smelting of iron, using one of James Watt's steam engines, employing coke instead of charcoal; thereafter use of coke for smelting spread rapidly in Britain, which in turn greatly expanded the capacity for producing pig iron. In 1786 Wilkinson built a huge canal barge by using iron plates on a wood frame, one of the first examples of iron in shipbuilding; he also built the first cast-iron bridge in England.

See also Machine Building.

Witte, Sergei (Count) (1845–1915)

Russian minister of finance from 1892 to 1903, Witte played a major role in furthering Russian industrialization. He believed Russia must industrialize to remain economically self-sufficient, and he pressed forward in a period when many Russian leaders were opposed to further change. Witte used government guarantees and subsidies to foster new factories; he backed high tariffs to protect infant industry; and he actively promoted foreign investment, believing that the Russian government was strong enough to keep the foreigners in line. He also directed Russian railroad building and was responsible for the construction of the great trans-Siberian line (1892–1904).

See also State, Role of the.

Women

The industrial revolution often reduced the value of women's work, though many women were vital contributors to the industrial labor force. The impact of industrialization on women also depended on the precise economic and cultural conditions of each region.

Factory output directly competed, both in the domestic market and in production for the home, with many branches of manufacturing that had been dominated by women, such as spinning or food production. Because women had often done simpler manufacturing tasks than men, and because their work was often regarded as supplementary to the family production, they were particularly often displaced. Thus more women spinners than male weavers were affected in western Europe and the United States. As a result, many women had to seek nonmanufacturing jobs, like domestic service (the biggest urban employer of women) and even prostitution. There was also much outright unemployment for women, especially in the countryside. This effect of factory production affected nonindustrial societies as well; for example, tens of thousands of women textile workers in Latin America lost work under the spur of British factory import competition in the 1820s and 1830s. A similar competitive displacement occurred for many African women in the twentieth century. The result, in many areas, was a rebalancing of economic and family power, to women's disadvantage. Marriage became more important for women, for it was very hard to find work apart from family support.

Meanwhile, women played a vital role as early factory workers, particularly in light industries where machines reduced the strength requirements and where employers sought a docile, low-wage labor force. Late industrializers (Russia and Japan, for instance), with special needs for cheap labor, relied very heavily on women. Early Japanese textile factories were filled with women. The silk industry, also, depended on cheap women workers, often purchased in the countryside from their fathers or brothers and set to work in conditions of semi-servitude.

In the West, women workers during the industrial revolution were mainly young and unmarried. Middle-class women rarely held jobs at all, and married working-class women worked only occasionally, mainly in home-based tasks like laundry or boarding-house keeping. Only a minority, particularly in textile regions, continued to work in factories. By 1900 only about 20 percent of the manufacturing labor force was female in most Western countries, and much of this was in sweatshop industries like clothing rather than factories. Only a few urban groups, like African-American women or widows, commonly held jobs in adulthood. Starting in the 1840s, men argued that women's work contradicted family requirements and women's gentle nature; a middle-class ideology developed around the separation of women and most industrial work, and laws regulated women's hours to limit their activity. Women who did work changed jobs often and developed a different attitude to work from that of men. Though there were some important strikes by women workers, women's role in labor protest was limited, partly because women's commitments differed, partly because of male opposition. Women did, however, gain new family functions and moral authority during the industrial revolution, and historians argue over how much this compensated for the reduction of economic role.

Maturing industrial economies raised new job opportunities for women. Increasing mechanization reduced skill requirements and opened some crafts, like printing, against strenuous male opposition, and new light industries like chemicals and appliances had a large female contingent. The big opportunities occurred in white collar work and semi-professions like primary school teaching. Increasing numbers of middle-class women began to work around 1900, though no breakthrough for married women occurred (save in wartime) until the 1950s. A few early cases where women had been heavily involved in industry, like Japan, later pulled back, emphasizing domestic roles and offering exceptionally meager pay, often low piece rates rather than wages, to those women who did work. The Soviet Union, however, maintained high levels of women's employment as part of its ongoing industrialization.

The 1950s–1960s revolution in women's work in the West, which brought a majority of married women into the paid labor force, depended on a vast expansion of the service sector. Most of the industrial sector remained closed. At the same time, early industrial growth and the spread of production organized by multinational corporations in places like Latin America and the Caribbean relied heavily on women's work by the later twentieth century. Patterns of women's work and the results in terms of women's overall status remain varied and complex, as the impact of industrialization continues.

See also Feminism; Japan; Maquiladoras; Pink-Collar Workers; Women Industrial Workers.

References Afshar, Haleh, ed. *Women, Work, and Ideology in the Third World* (1985); Kessler-Harris, Alice. *Out to Work: A History of Wage-Earning Women in the United States* (1982); Tilly, Louise, and Joan Scott. *Women, Work, and Family* (1987).

Women Industrial Workers

Although many historians have portrayed the creation of the industrial work force as involving almost exclusively men, women have always played a significant role in manufacturing. Women comprised a significant portion of the work force in textile manufacturing, and many women worked as coal miners in the early stages of the industrial revolution. Partly at the urging of working-class men, many industrial jobs were reserved for males (especially skilled work), and the manufacturing fields with a large number of women workers—textiles, garment and hat making, and food and tobacco processing—were generally ill-paid.

Although women participated in early strikes, most craft unions sought to limit membership to men, arguing that employers should pay men a high enough wage to ensure that women could remain in the "domestic sphere." Albeit many male workers aspired to the roles described by the middle-class "cult of domesticity," the reality for most men was that the wages of their wives or at least their daughters was essential to the survival of the family. (Only a minority of wives continued factory work, although most earned money by work at home, such as laundering or keeping boarders.) If women made up only a small part of the union movement, they often proved to be fierce militants. In the late nineteenth century, the president of a boot and shoe union reported that "It is harder to induce women to compromise, they are likely to hold out to the bitter end to obtain exactly what they want."

Advancing mechanization gave new chances for women in chemical and electronics factories before 1900. The labor scarcities during World War I and World War II forced employers to hire women for numerous "nontraditional" manufacturing jobs in bomb factories, steel mills, and shipbuilding. Many women were forced to leave heavy industry after both wars, but in 1945 a significant number of women agitated to keep their jobs in automobile factories, arguing that the "hand that rocks the cradle can build tractors too." A large number of these women kept their jobs, although in other industries, such as steel mills, women were generally fired. After a twenty-year battle with their union and employers to eliminate lower pay for "women's jobs" (which were often as difficult as men's jobs) the autoworkers' union fought for women's rights in federal civil rights legislation. Since the 1950s women have gained jobs in construction and mining, though the industrial labor force continues to be disproportionately male outside the textile and appliance sectors. Women have played quite a large role in the industrial labor force of countries like Russia.

See also Housework; Women.

Reference Gabin, Nancy F. *Feminism in the Labor Movement: Women and the United Auto Workers, 1935–1975* (1990); Kessler-Harris, Alice. *Out to Work: A History of Wage-Earning Women in the United States* (1982).

A Czechoslovakian metal worker adjusts the machinery in a maintenance shop on a farming collective in 1987.

Wool

This fiber was, along with linen, a traditional fiber in the preindustrial manufacture of clothing in Europe. Like cotton, it was amenable to most of the early devices (spinning mules, frame looms) developed for mechanical spinning and weaving. Additional mechanical devices for combing wool were important early inventions. Thus the mechanization of wool proceeded rapidly in Britain by the 1780s and on the continent by the 1820s and 1830s. Wool cloth lost ground somewhat to the cheaper and more popular cotton, but it remained a major fabric in the industrial economy. Traditional wool producers did not, however, immediately give up. By accepting lower pay or working longer hours, and by exploiting family members as unpaid assistants, many domestic manufacturing operations in wool lasted into the late nineteenth century. Factory production of wool created vast new demand for raw material. Sheep growing continued in Europe, but businessmen scurried to negotiate for wool with herdsmen in Asia (in the Mosul region of Turkey, for example), and a vast export wool industry was established in Australia and New Zealand. The industrialization of wool thus affected the larger world economy.

Work

The industrial revolution had a tremendous impact on work. It changed its location by concentrating it in factories; it obviously exposed it to new kinds of machinery, to recurrent technological change, and to new levels of noise and safety hazards. It required workers to interact with relative strangers, with whom they had no family or community ties. The most significant changes brought about by industrialization were related, first, to the speed or pace of work, now set by machinery rather than human impulse. Opportunities to take informal breaks were reduced, and many workers began to complain of the toll industrial work exacted on their nerves. The application of clock time to the work process extended this new pace. A second crucial change occurred in the nature of supervision. Most people now worked their entire lives under the direction of others, rather than hoping (as most peasants and artisans had once done) for a period in which they would be their own master. Third, with growing specialization, increasing numbers of workers accomplished small stages of the production process, doing the same activities over and over again; they had less sense than traditional workers of the overall product. Highly skilled workers remained essential, but on average the training required for manufacturing work declined and semi-skilled workers became the norm.

On the whole, these new principles of industrial work—new pace, new supervision, and specialization—increased as industrialization advanced and factories became larger. Although these principles applied most extensively to factory workers, other kinds of workers were affected to some degree. Remaining artisans were subjected to a faster pace, greater supervision, and new specialization, for example. Office and sales workers also faced new equipment, new discipline, and an effort to speed the pace. New equipment in the later twentieth century, such as computers, has made the work of many twentieth-century professionals more flexible but has resulted in increasing regimentation of many clerical workers in airlines, post offices, and the like. Computers, for example, can be used to keep track of how much time office workers devote to record-keeping tasks.

At every stage of the industrialization process workers have attempted to modify features of the new work setting, either by formal protests (to reduce hours or allow greater worker voice over conditions) or by informal actions like taking unauthorized breaks, changing jobs simply to gain a bit of respite, and quietly defying new work rules. Over time, workers probably became somewhat more accustomed to basic features of industrial work—the shock was greatest for the first few generations exposed—but new equipment or new management techniques could still provoke shock, even by the twentieth century.

See also Alienation; Discipline; Time; Working Class.

Reference Joyce, Patrick, ed. *The Historical Meanings of Work* (1987).

Work Ethic

The view that work has intrinsic worth in addition to its material rewards has been an important ideological and moral belief that contributed to and was shaped by the industrial revolution. Since Max Weber's *The Protestant Ethic and the Spirit of Capitalism,* many scholars have highlighted the shifts in attitudes toward work that occurred roughly around the time of the Protestant Reformation. Between the fifteenth and seventeenth centuries, merchants and wealthier artisans increasingly viewed hard work and their level of wealth as an indication of their spiritual standing or moral stature, and this shift in attitude contributed to the rise of capitalism and then of the industrial revolution.

Many early industrialists valued hard work and eschewed leisure, both for themselves and their laborers. Although many artisans imbued their labor with moral as well as physical dimensions, it was difficult for poorly paid factory workers who labored twelve or fourteen hours a day to share this enthusiasm for work. For workers, "idleness" or unemployment was more a question of survival than of morality. Workers had their own work values, which included trying to set their own pace. From the eighteenth century onward, most workers supported the curtailment of the working day. However, many trade unionists argued that a shorter work day and better pay would encourage workers to work harder—the motto "a fair day's work for a fair day's wage" implicitly accepts the values of work ethic. The Industrial Workers of the World mocked respectable attitudes toward work when they sang songs with lyrics such as "Oh why don't you save all the money that you earn? / Well if I didn't eat, I'd have money to burn. / Hallelujah I'm a bum. . . ."

In the early nineteenth century, the valorization of labor was an important feature of middle-class and, to a lesser degree, working-class culture of the northern United States. Many northerners believed that through hard physical labor, workers could eventually own their own shop, farm, or store and they contrasted their own productivity to the "idleness" of the white southerners who allegedly preferred to let slaves labor. At least among farmers on the frontier, and to a lesser degree in industrial cities, upward mobility reached to the extent of owning a farm or shop. The rise of large-scale factories owned by corporations in the late nineteenth century demonstrated to the middle classes that wage labor was not a preliminary stage on the path to becoming a small-scale "producer" but a permanent condition (a fact that most urban workers already knew). Increasingly, members of the middle class were white-collar workers, managers, or members of bureaucratic institutions, and many of the ideological energies previously expended in extolling farming and shopkeeping went into professionalizing middle-class occupations (lawyers, doctors, engineers, and the like).

Maintaining a work ethic (or at least high productivity) was a constant problem for managers of the Soviet Union and other communist economies, including those of China and Eastern Europe. Once unemployment had been eliminated as a threat, factory workers had little incentive to work hard—indeed, some observers argue that the Soviet system's crisis of productivity was resolved by Stalin's creation of slave labor camps. Subsequent leaders eliminated the camps, although increasing productivity remained problematic.

Since the 1970s, the rise of aggressive export-oriented economies in Japan, South Korea, and Taiwan have caused U.S. observers to worry that Asian workers have a stronger work ethic. Certainly Asian workers and managers work longer hours and take fewer vacations than their Western counterparts, although this work regime is strongly encouraged by employers and the state, which provides few benefits for unemployed or retired workers. Ironically, since the 1980s, many Japanese intellectuals have begun to worry that the younger generation's obvious enjoyment of their leisure—a product of prosperity—may in turn threaten Japan's economic prowess.

Reference Rodgers, Daniel T. *The Work Ethic in Industrial America, 1850–1920* (1974).

Workers' Control

Industrialists have an interest in expanding output by subdividing labor, adding new machinery, or adapting new processes; employees rarely share their employers' enthusiasm for these innovations because changes frequently make work more repetitive and less interesting, and can result in lower earnings or the loss of their jobs. Workers' control is a term developed by historians to describe the formal and informal ways that workers have sought to control the workplace. Workers' control sometimes refers to informal strategies to restrict output, to union work rules, or to socialist or anarchist plans for workers to run not only the workplace but society as a whole.

Before the industrial revolution, many workers controlled their daily work patterns, and elements of this control persisted, particularly for skilled workers in early factories. Formal or informal workers' control efforts sought to counter growing employers' insistence on determining working conditions and discipline. Many nineteenth-century workers, particularly craftsmen, developed informal standards of conduct based on different values from those of industrialists or the middle class. For instance, workers typically worked at a far more leisurely pace than their employers desired. Workers' drinking on the job, or the slow pace of work (due to hangovers) on "Holy Monday," was a pattern even among the unskilled.

Many of workers' actions on the job or in the community suggest that mutualism—a desire to develop group support systems—as opposed to the more pronounced individualism of the middle class, was an important value of workers. The social solidarity of workmates was often the basis for self-help organizations that tried to ensure that individuals received some money if they were injured or fell sick. Although historians have also analyzed the ways that the social solidarity among workers within a trade can exclude or hold back other workers (the unskilled, women, blacks, or immigrants), the mutualistic ethic helped to make possible much of the trade union or socialist activity that was also a part of workers' control.

In the nineteenth century, many craft unions developed elaborate union work rules, primarily designed to guard against overproduction and maintain a reasonable pace of work. Workers were enjoined from such practices as running two machines; glass workers' unions wanted employers to close factories for the summer so that workers would not have to work in the debilitating heat of the furnaces. There was often a strong moral tone to these work rules, and unionists argued that their "manliness" required that individuals refuse to work under less generous conditions. Workers who defied the informal quotas established by the group could expect a fair degree of ostracism or even sabotage from their workmates. These were not simply preindustrial habits that survived into the modern era; iron rollers, glassblowers, or machinists all tried to maintain work rules. More recently, historians have begun to explore the implications for women of linking unionism to "manliness." Many "manly" unions in the United States, even those that espoused radical politics such as the machinists, also had a "Caucasian only" clause in their constitutions.

The conflict between employers and workers over who would control the workplace became more pronounced in the late nineteenth century. Employers began to assume a new level of control through scientific management. Instead of simply lengthening the work day, managers closely studied how workers completed their tasks, and then rearranged the process in order to make the workplace more productive. Often managers' strategies aimed at disrupting the social solidarity of workers by implementing piece-rate systems, which rewarded individual effort in exceeding quotas while slower workers were penalized. Many unionists rejected managers' views that workers worked best when closely supervised, and many coal miners often refused to work at all when managers were present. Because piece rates typically became less generous over time, managers frequently undermined their own authority and encouraged workers to take collective action in protest. In the early twentieth century, many unskilled factory workers engaged in spontaneous strikes against the arbitrary and heavy-handed management of their employers. In extreme cases, workers employed slowdowns, which is when an entire shop or department collectively and progressively restricts output. This is a difficult form of protest, because workers often find it hard to look like they are working hard, while actually working as slowly as possible.

Some historians have observed that the struggle over the workplace, combined with managers' belief that the workplace could be rationalized, allowed some workers to point to the irrationality of an industrial system that produced frequent layoffs, accidents, and depressions. Thus, workers' control was a slogan of radical workers within the American Federation of Labor during the early twentieth century. Radicals advocated that ordinary workers not only could resist the implementation of scientific management but could extend their strategies to run industry itself. Coal miners and railroad workers advocated nationalization of their industries, with workers assuming a high degree of responsibility for its management. Similar demands were made by syndicalist workers in Spain and Latin America. Radical socialists in Germany and Russia also advocated the idea that workers could manage the workplace through workers' councils (in Russia, soviets). A major workers' control movement developed in British industry after World War I.

The implementation of large union or party bureaucracies—for instance, the Congress of Industrial Organizations in the United States or the Bolshevik Party in the Soviet Union—displaced most of the energy directed toward workers' control. At least from workers' perspective, unions in the United States and Europe helped to make the industrial system more rational, reducing unemployment, increasing wages, and adding benefits. Unions also cost workers' direct control over the workplace, their organizations, and society. Sometimes wildcat (illegal) strikes, directed as much against unions as against employers, sought to return control to workers. But formal workers' control movements declined in the mid-twentieth century.

See also Scientific Management; Taylor, Frederick Winslow.

Reference Montgomery, David. *Workers' Control in America: Studies in the History of Work, Technology, and Labor Struggles* (1979).

Working Class

Workers are people who are dependent upon the sale of their labor power for their survival. The modern working class emerged out of the revolutionary changes that capitalism wrought first in Europe and then throughout the world after the fifteenth century—particularly after the industrial revolution began in Britain in the late eighteenth century. Although workers had existed in other historical periods, the number of workers dramatically increased after the industrial revolution, and their social and economic functions became central to the emerging industrial system to an unprecedented degree.

The creation of a European working class resulted in part from the breakdown of manorialism. In England, the rise of capitalist agriculture resulted in the enclosure movement, which along with rapid population growth created a class of landless laborers who could no longer survive as tenants on estates or by working subsistence plots of land as peasants. By the seventeenth and eighteenth centuries, many of these workers had found employment in rural industries. However, the rise of the factory system in the late eighteenth and early nineteenth century gradually destroyed the relative social and economic autonomy enjoyed by artisans in the rural industries and older urban trades. The early factory system was harsh, and many artisans and workers struggled vigorously to preserve the old order.

Harsh working conditions characterized mid-nineteenth-century factory systems. Large transmission belts rotate overhead as factory workers operate lathes in this 1865 woodcut.

Definitions of the modern working class vary. Some historians and sociologists define the class in terms of people who work with their hands for a wage, under managers or supervisors. Others see the working class in terms of self-conscious unity and shared problems of life. Ethnic and gender divisions, as well as gaps between artisans and factory operatives, often complicate this definition. In Europe and the United States, the spread of mechanization and factories made the self-definition of the working class clearer by 1900 than before.

As the factory system emerged in England in the late eighteenth and early nineteenth centuries, industrialists were able to convince the government to ignore or drop many of the traditional regulations on the workplace regarding wages and working conditions. Workers had few political rights, even within the emerging parliamentary forms of government in England, France, and the United States. Consequently, workers throughout the nineteenth century sought the right to vote, in part because they shared the democratic aspirations of the age, and in part to use government to reform the industrial system. By the 1830s, the property restrictions on voting were dropped for white males in the United States, although a similar process took much longer for European and Latin American workers. The extension of the franchise by the late nineteenth century contributed to the increasing power of the European and Latin American labor and social democratic parties responsible for many social welfare reforms. Governments continued to periodically repress workers' organizations in Japan, Latin America, and central, southern, and eastern Europe, but they were beginning to accommodate to make reforms by the late nineteenth century, leading many workers to believe in the efficacy of political parties and unions.

Although interrupted by the Great Depression of the 1930s and World War II, workers in Europe, Japan, and the United States experienced a dramatic rise in their standard of living between 1900 and the 1970s. Throughout the industrialized world, parliamentary democratic systems of government in which workers and unions could operate became firmly established. Although unions and voting were not free in the Soviet Union, the government paid considerable attention to workers' complaints. In capitalist countries the growing power of trade unions helped to improve wages for workers even in nonunionized companies. In the United States many workers were able to buy their own homes, purchase cars, and participate in the culture of consumerism.

Historians of black workers have emphasized that there are many different paths into the working class, and that while becoming workers was a step down for many European or European-American artisans and farmers, it was a step up for most former slaves and sharecroppers. Throughout the nineteenth century and much of the twentieth, free blacks in the United States and Latin America were generally blocked from becoming industrial workers and remained low-paid service workers. Black workers were technically free to vote after the 1860s, but, between the 1880s and the 1960s in the southern United States, terror was widely used to prevent blacks from voting in large numbers. Furthermore, blacks' subordinate position in urban labor markets made them particularly vulnerable to economic downturns. After World War II a significant number of Afro-Caribbeans, North Africans and residents of the Indian subcontinent migrated to Europe and entered the bottom of labor markets just before a period of massive unemployment. Historians are beginning to investigate the many paths into, and the diverse evolution of, the working class throughout the world.

See also Chartism; Dual Labor Markets; Emancipation; Industrial Workers; Internationals; Luddites; Marxism; Moral Economy; Protoindustrialization; Wage Labor; Women Industrial Workers.

References Chakrabarty, Dipesh. *Rethinking Working-Class History: Bengal 1890–1940* (1989); Montgomery, David. *The Fall of the House of Labor: The Workplace, the State, and American Labor Activism, 1865–1925* (1987); Trotter, Joe William. *Coal, Class, and Color: Blacks in Southern West Virginia, 1915–32* (1990).

World Bank

The International Bank for Reconstruction and Development (the World Bank) and the International Monetary Fund (IMF) were created in 1944 at the Bretton Woods Agreement. Both are semi-autonomous banking institutions that lend monies to governments seeking to increase the economic productivity of their countries. The World Bank is the world's most important development agency, and has an annual budget of over half a billion dollars. It makes direct loans of several billion dollars a year to various governments. The World Bank also exercises great influence within the private banking system and can help extend or deny capital to a debtor country. Working closely together, the World Bank offers loans of a longer duration (5–20 years) while IMF offers short-term loans (1–3 years in length).

Capital for both agencies is largely provided by creditor countries—and some critics have compared the agencies to "creditor cartels." In 1944 the United States was the world's largest lender, and its government has had great influence over both the World Bank and the IMF. Although some Eastern European countries were members of the World Bank in the 1940s and 1950s, the agency denied loans to countries that refused to participate in the Marshall Plan. During the late 1970s, the World Bank was prevented from making loans to Communist-led Vietnam (ironically, the head of the World Bank was then former U.S. Secretary of State and architect of the Vietnam war, Robert McNamara).

The objectives of the World Bank and the IMF have been to increase world trade and decrease the role of government in the economy. Many of the loans have gone to build highways and electric power systems (particularly power plants and hydroelectric dams), and other infrastructure projects. Critics of the bank charge that it encourages a neocolonialist form of economic development. In the 1960s Brazil received loans from the World Bank to expand its electrical power system, but had to purchase European and U.S. heavy electrical equipment rather than domestic products. Critics of the World Bank also charge that the environmental cost of these projects has been high. In the 1980s large loans were made to India to build hydroelectric and coal-fired power plants rather than smaller loans to improve the efficiency of electrical generators and distribution.

The World Bank has encouraged developing countries to focus on exports of raw materials such as timber or agricultural goods. In the early 1970s the cost of capital was cheap, and many countries were encouraged to take out loans. The prices for raw materials subsequently plunged (and much of the borrowed money was stolen or spent on military equipment), and many countries have had great difficulty repaying their loans. The cost for continued loans (and financial stability) has been "structural adjustment." Because the role of government is assumed to be inherently negative, debtor countries seeking additional loans are pressured to reduce tariffs and subsidies for food, housing, and education. Living standards (and, in some cases, overall economic output) have dropped, but their credit rating remains high. Critics have pointed out the irony that in all of the successful cases of industrialization since 1944 (South Korea and Taiwan, for example), local governments have followed a far different script from that advocated by the World Bank.

See also Finance Capital; World Systems Theory.

References Ayres, Robert C. *Banking on the Poor: The World Bank and World Poverty* (1983); Payer, Cheryl. *The World Bank: A Critical Analysis* (1982).

World Systems Theory

World systems theory offers an alternative to development theory; it is an attempt by contemporary Marxist scholars to understand how economic inequality between regions has developed and been sustained over the last several hundred years. Taking into account individual cultural and social institutions, world systems theory emphasizes how the world system of trade established in the sixteenth century has worked to accrue advantages to certain areas, particularly Western Europe, the United States, and Japan.

The development of European merchant capitalism in the fifteenth and sixteenth centuries transformed European agricultural production, making it more oriented toward profit and the market. For instance, in England, market-oriented farmers made into their own private property what had been common lands used by peasants for gathering of fuel and fodder. The enclosure movement allowed some farmers to supply the burgeoning market for wool and created a growing class of landless laborers (who bitterly remarked that "sheep ate men"). These capitalist values were carried to the Americas and influenced the creation of a plantation system that produced sugar, tobacco, cotton, and other products for consumption by European industries and workers. Rather than viewing these plantations as "preindustrial" (because they did not rely on wage labor but on racialized slave labor), some world systems theorists have argued that plantations were factories in the field—whose forms of labor discipline anticipated the work regime of the factory.

In Asia, the Portuguese (and later the Dutch) were able to use their superior ships and weaponry to dominate ocean-based trade but were too weak to conquer more than a few coastal cities. Therefore, whereas Europeans controlled the shipping of goods, production remained in the hands of Asians—giving them leverage over Europeans. It is important to note that until the mid-nineteenth century, preexisting Asian empires were often strong enough to limit trade and cultural contact with Europeans. The Japanese state limited the Dutch traders to one compound and successfully banned the use of firearms.

Although the European domination of global trade did not initially result in colonization of Africa and Asia, the new system of trade caused profound changes. West Africa had a long history of participation in trade with the Mediterranean, but the new dynamics of European-dominated trade transformed African society and societies. Those societies that formed a strong relationship with the new world system gained in power. For instance, the Portuguese sale of firearms to the Asante kingdom helped Portugal to become one of the premier "gunpowder empires" that conquered established kingdoms and "produced" slaves for the plantation system in the Americas.

The rise of industrial forms of production in Europe was grafted onto the global system of commercial capitalism. The industrial revolution gave European countries additional advantages over nonindustrialized regions in Africa and Asia. Beginning in the mid-eighteenth century, the East India Trading Company used new military technology to conquer much of the Indian subcontinent—a process largely complete by the mid-nineteenth century, when most of the Indian subcontinent was either directly or indirectly ruled by the British. In 1857, however, a mutiny of Indian mercenaries nearly destroyed the East India Company's rule, and the British Empire took over the subjugation of India. The British successfully deindustrialized Indian textile manufacturers, who had supplied much of the African market. India became a producer of raw materials such as cotton and opium that were exported to England and China, respectively.

By the late nineteenth century, European military technology had grown far more advanced than that of the rest of the world and allowed the British, French, and other European countries to overwhelm numerically superior empires throughout Africa and Asia. The Chinese empire was forced to accept a series of increasingly humiliating trade treaties that granted Europeans (and later Japanese) access to the Chinese market and privileges such as immunity from Chinese law and the right to print and circulate their own currency. Many Chinese found it particularly troubling that one of the imports that the British government insisted on exporting to China was opium. In two Opium Wars, the Europeans defended the opium trade against attempts by the Chinese to abolish it. Here was a case where Europeans used their superior military technology in order to extract a financial surplus by encouraging the drug addiction of thousands of Chinese.

Within the world systems framework, analysts distinguish between "core" (e.g., "metropolitan" industrial nations) and "peripheral" regions that produce raw materials (such as the U.S. South). There are also "external" economies, such as Russia or China in the eighteenth century, who are not fully integrated into the world market, though they have to compete with the increasing power of the core regions. It is important to realize that although regions that were drawn into the world market produced goods for the capitalist world market, not all regions were themselves capitalist. For instance, the rise of the world system resulted in a decline of manorialism in western Europe, but in Russia and eastern Europe a shift toward the market was accomplished by an intensified serfdom. Over time, the relationship of countries to the world system changes. For instance, throughout the course of the eighteenth and nineteenth centuries, China became an increasingly peripheral state while Japan became a core, industrialized country.

Even within "core" countries, certain regions can remain internal colonies and rely on more coercive labor systems. For instance, within the United States in the nineteenth and early twentieth centuries, the South remained a supplier of raw materials (cotton, timber, coal) for northern industries. The South did not rely primarily upon free or wage labor but on slavery and then sharecropping. Some scholars have argued that even once sharecroppers became part of the working class, they were ghettoized and remained an internal colony. Increasing industrial development and political independence in places like India, China, and Brazil make the applicability of the world economy theory increasingly complex in the later twentieth century.

See also Black Workers; Development Theory; Dual Labor Markets; Merchant Capital; Neocolonialism; Racism.

References Wallerstein, Immanuel. *The Modern World-System I: Capitalist Agriculture and the Origins of the European World-Economy in the Sixteenth Century* (1974); Wolf, Eric. *Europe and the People without History* (1982).

World War I

World War I (1914–1918) was an industrial war that demonstrated the destructive power of technological advances such as the machine gun, mustard gas, mechanized transportation (railroads and trucks), and warfare (tanks and airplanes). During the war governmental intervention in the economy proved crucial in the proper allocation of labor, raw material, and capital to meet war needs. In the United States the business community's attempt to meet wartime economic needs produced chaos, and industrial councils were soon created with members from business, labor, and government. Although, in the United States, this style of corporatism was abandoned almost as soon as the war was over, it served as a model for subsequent economic planning in Europe.

The economic consequences of the war were immense. By the war's end, the European "victors" (England, France, and Italy) had lost millions of adult men and were economically devastated. One-quarter of all British overseas capital and half that of France had been sacrificed to pay for the war. Russia and the losing nations suffered even greater losses, and the German, Austro-Hungarian, and the Ottoman (Turkey) empires were all destroyed. In 1920 European industrial production was roughly one-third to one-half of what it had been in 1913. The most profound consequences of the war was perhaps the 1917 Russian Revolution, the first instance when communists maintained power after a revolution.

After the war the center of global economic growth shifted from Europe to North America and, to a lesser extent, to Japan. In 1913, 43 percent of the world's production occurred in Europe, but ten years later that figure had dropped to 34 percent. The United States became the world's largest creditor country, and the withdrawal of European competitors from East Asia allowed Japan to capture greater market shares for its industrial goods and to acquire capital surpluses as well. Throughout Latin America, exports of raw materials increased and industrial production boomed as governments sought to replace European manufactured goods. However, much of Latin America's industrialization effort faltered during the 1920s, when cheaper foreign imports flooded its markets. Although the war stimulated jute, steel, and cotton manufacturing in India, the costs of the war (higher prices, loss of civilian markets) as well as the relatively early stage of Indian industrialization (there were few domestic producers of machinery) prevented this country from taking full advantage of the decline of European producers.

The incredibly high cost of the war (the best estimate puts its direct and indirect cost at 338 billion 1920 dollars) led Britain and France to impose harsh reparations on Germany—in part caused by the United States' demand that its allies fulfill their financial obligations. The inability of industrialized nations to create an equitable (or at least stable) peace eventually plunged the world into depression, fascism, and another bloody world war.

See also Great Depression (1930s).

Reference Hardach, Gerd. *The First World War, 1914–1918* (1977).

World War II

Prior to the outbreak of war, the German, Japanese, and Italian governments had all begun to intervene in the economy on a large scale in order to make their domestic economies more independent from international trade. In Germany and Japan, and

World War I witnessed the advent of fully mechanized instruments of combat, such as the machine gun, fired here in 1918 by a pair of American soldiers in France.

much less so in Italy, the government also began to reorganize the economy to meet the demands of war. Germany and Japan hoped that conquest would bring them reliable supplies of raw materials that would enable them to expand their domestic industrial economies. Thus, Germany viewed Eastern Europe and the Soviet Union as its future colonies and Japan looked to China and Southeast Asia for raw materials such as oil, iron ore, bauxite (to make aluminum), and coal.

Ironically, although Japan did quickly conquer vast areas that could have supplied it with raw materials, its merchant navy was soon devastated by the air and sea power of the United States—by late 1943 most ships carrying oil, iron ore, or other materials to Japan never arrived. The economic aims of Germany were frustrated by the "scorched earth" policy carried out by the Soviet Union (soldiers destroyed fields, mines, and factories as they retreated) as well as by the racism of the Nazi regime involving attacks on Jews and other nationalities and enforced labor recruitment, which caused economic chaos in Poland and occupied portions of Russia. However, German war production was bolstered by the seizure and collaboration of industrial firms in such occupied areas as France, Belgium, and Czechoslovakia. Occupied countries also provided tax revenues, foodstuffs, and workers to the Nazi war effort. The collaboration of French industrialists was particularly important; for instance, the French aircraft industry produced several thousand airplanes for Germany. Nevertheless, the inability of Germany to secure oil supplies in the Soviet Union or the

Middle East, together with Allied air raids, limited the effectiveness of the German military machine.

Although Britain was able to draw upon its colonies for supplies of raw materials and even finished products from India, South Africa, and Australia, the war destroyed Great Britain as an economic leader. The country lost too much of its work force and industries to be able to hold onto its colonies after the war; decolonization compounded Britain's inability to rebuild its industries or to recapture foreign markets. The devastation of Europe, Japan, and the Soviet Union left the United States the world's largest creditor and most advanced industrial producer. After a decade, however, most former industrial areas had bounced back. The war changed the world industrial map much less significantly than it rearranged its political boundaries.

See also Bretton Woods; Cold War; Fascism; World War I.

Reference Milward, Alan S. *War, Economy, and Society, 1939–1945* (1977).

Zaibatsus

Zaibatsus were Japanese holding companies; the literal translation is "financial clique." The growth of zaibatsus were encouraged by Meiji and subsequent Japanese governments. The relations between Japan's governing elite and zaibatsus were extremely close—one of the largest stockholders in the zaibatsus was the imperial family. By 1945 the four largest zaibatsus controlled about half of all investment capital and a third of heavy industry—one Japanese economist termed them "monopolies of capital." Zaibatsus were technically broken up during the military occupation of Japan by the United States after World War II. By the 1970s, however, former zaibatsus still controlled six of the seven largest commercial banks and almost 60 percent of the largest 300 industrial firms. The relationship between industry and finance remains extremely close, which eases economic planning and makes it extremely difficult for foreign companies or banks to acquire a controlling interest in a Japanese corporation.

See also Banking System; Finance Capital.

Zollverein

The Zollverein was an internal customs union in Germany. In the early nineteenth century, trade within Germany was hampered by the different tariffs and tolls of several hundred different governments. In 1818 Prussia dropped customs within its borders and in the 1820s advocated free trade with other German states. A rival customs union was established by other states, but by 1834 the two had merged. By 1888 all German cities and states had joined the Zollverein; trade was free within Germany, but high tariffs protected industry from international free trade.

Chronology

1563 English Statute of Apprentices requires guild regulation over skilled labor.

1600s–1750s Protoindustrialization.

1600s Beginning of plantation system in the Caribbean and spread of racialized slavery to the Americas; adoption in Europe of American crops such as corn and potatoes.

1601 English Poor Law authorizes local governments to provide relief to unemployed.

1619 English ironmakers begin to use coal instead of charcoal.

1694 Bank of England receives charter.

1702 Thomas Newcomen invents steam engine.

1721 Calico Act restricts imports of cloth to England.

1733 Flying shuttle invented in England by John Kay.

1750–1800 Rise of the factory system in England.

1757 East India Company begins to conquer India.

1769 Water frame invented by Richard Arkwright; James Watt patents his efficient steam engine.

1776 Adam Smith publishes *Wealth of Nations;* Matthew Boulton invents a steam engine suitable for industry.

1779 Samuel Crompton invents spinning mule.

1789–1791 French Revolution; manorialism abolished.

1790 National Bank of the United States established.

1791 Le Chapelier Law in France abolishes guilds and labor combinations.

1799–1815 Napoleonic Wars.

1790s Establishment of gold standard.

1793 Cotton gin invented by Eli Whitney.

1795 Britain wins Cape colony (South Africa) from Dutch.

Chronology

1799–1800 English Combination Acts prohibit strikes and unions.

1802 First English Factory Act limits work of pauper children to 12 hours a day.

1805–1840 Muhammed Ali begins attempt at industrialization of Egypt

1809 England suspends minimum wage.

1810s Luddite risings in England.

1813–1814 Repeal of English Statute of Apprentices

1815 British Corn Law raises tariffs on grains.

1817–1825 Construction of the Erie Canal.

1818 Prussia drops internal tariffs.

1819 Factory Act in England prohibits employers from hiring workers younger than 9, and children under 16 can only work 12 hours a day.

1820s Beginning of industrial revolution in Belgium, France, and New England; propertyless white males gain the vote in the United States; Prussia advocates Zollverein or customs union for Germany.

1830s Chartism in England; first department stores open in France; abolition of slavery in English colonies; charter for the Bank of the United States allowed to lapse.

1830 United States has 23 miles of railroad track; beginning of expansion of railroad system.

1832 Partial enfranchisement of British males.

1834 England passes harsh poor relief act.

1837 Telegraph developed in England by William Cooke and Charles Wheatstone and in the United States by William Morse.

1839–1842 Opium Wars in China.

1840s Beginning of industrial revolution in Germany.

1842 Springfield Armory in the United States begins to produce interchangeable parts for rifles; Chinese government forced to open ports to foreign trade.

1844 Rochdale Cooperative movement begins.

1846 Britain repeals Corn Laws.

1848 *Communist Manifesto* published by Karl Marx.

1848 Democratic revolutions attempted throughout Europe; manorialism abolished in most of central Europe.

1850s Crédit Mobilier helps to finance French railroad system; half of England lives in cities.

1851 First international industrial exposition in London (Crystal Palace); major U.S. cities connected by telegraph wires.

1854 Henry Bessemer invents Bessemer converter for steel-making.

1854–1856 Crimean War.

1858–1860 Second Opium Wars in China.

1861–1865 Civil War in United States.

1861–1867 Emancipation of slaves in the United States.

1861 Emancipation of the serfs in Russia; California connected to the eastern United States by telegraph wires.

1862 United States Morill Act provides federal land grants to universities that provide technical or agricultural training.

1864–1876 First Workingmen's International (collapses due to conflict between Marxists and anarchists).

1866 Transatlantic telegraph cable laid; sharecropping system begins in the U.S. South.

1867 English male workers receive the vote.

1868 Beginning of Meiji Era.

1869 Suez canal opens; formation of Knights of Labor.

1870s Rise of white-collar labor force; Sidney Thomas and Sidney Gilchrist develop process to use limestone to remove phosphorous from molten iron, which allows expansion of ironmaking in Germany.

1871 Paris Commune; English unions legalized.

1873–1877 Major depression.

1875 Japanese government gives Mitsubishi 11 steam ships in order to compete with Western companies.

1876 N. A. Otto produces first practical internal combustion motor; Alexander Graham Bell invents telephone.

1877 Railroad strike in the United States.

1879 First refrigerated ship built (eases transportation of meat and other foods).

1880s Bismarck suppresses German socialists, institutes limited welfare reforms.

1860s–1890s European powers colonize Africa in the "great scramble;" widespread adoption of open hearth in steelmaking; Populist movement (backlash against Populism disenfranchises nearly all blacks and most poor whites in southern United States).

1881 First coal-fired electrical power station established in England; hydroelectric plants set up in Niagara, New York.

1884 Knights of Labor successfully strike a railroad owned by Jay Gould, membership grows to several hundred thousand.

1886 Formation of the AFL.

1888 Zollverein (German custom's union) complete, internal tariffs dropped; Brazil abolishes slavery; Nikola Tesla sells alternating current motor to George Westinghouse; Jay Gould smashes railroad strike by Knights of Labor, membership begins to fall.

1890 Sherman Anti-Trust Act; United States has 150,000 miles of railroad track.

1892 Homestead Lockout.

1892–1904 Trans-Siberian Railroad built.

1894 Confédération Générale du Travail formed in France.

1895 Japan annexes Taiwan.

1897 Rudolf Diesel invents efficient internal combustion engine.

1898 Frontier in the United States closed; United States fights and wins war with Spain and gains several colonies.

1899–1920 Second Workingmen's International (collapses because nationalism during World War I overcomes internationalist principles).

1900s Taylorism and Scientific Management begin.

1900 Japanese Police Regulation Law makes it a crime to strike.

1901 Formation of U.S. Steel.

Chronology

1890s–1900s Many corporations and cartels formed.

1902 Restrictive Bülow Tariff instituted in Germany.

1904–1905 Russo-Japanese War.

1905 Failed revolution in Russia; formation of Industrial Workers of the World.

1906 First general strike in France, led by Confédération Générale du Travail; construction began on Panama Canal; syndicalists form Brazilian Federation of Labor.

1907 Jamshed Tata begins construction of steel mills in India.

1909 Price of Ford Model T is $900.

1910 Japan annexes Korea.

1910s–1920s Height of workers' control movement in industrialized countries; corporations seek to stem it by using Taylorism and scientific management.

1911 Britain passes the world's first state-run unemployment insurance system.

1914 Ford begins production of Model Ts in his River Rouge factory; price of Model T falls to $440; completion of Panama Canal.

1914–1918 World War I. By war's end, German, Austro-Hungarian, Russian, and Ottoman empires are fallen.

1915–1920s Great Migration in the United States.

1917 Russian Revolution.

1917–1921 Civil War in Soviet Union.

1919–1920 Attempted workers' revolutions in Germany, Austria, Hungary, and Italy.

1920s Fascists takes power in Italy; widespread adoption of radio; 12 percent of the British work force is unemployed.

1920s–1930s Industrialized countries abandon the gold standard.

1921 Major Japanese shipyard strike, union leaders arrested.

1921–1928 New Economic Policy in the Soviet Union.

1923 John Meynard Keynes writes *Tract on Monetary Reform*, a critique of the gold standard.

1924 United States limits immigration.

1925 Japan eases Police Regulation Law; Bell Laboratories established.

1926 British general strike.

1927 Transatlantic telephone cables laid; Ford Motor Company produces 650,000 tractors a year.

1928 Collectivization of Soviet agriculture, beginning of Stalinist industrialization (first five-year plan).

1929 Wall Street crash.

1930 Smoot-Hawley Tariff in the United States helps spark a trade war.

1930s Global depression.

1930s Purges in Soviet Union.

1931 Japan invades China.

1933 Hitler comes to power in Germany.

1935 Formation of Congress of Industrial Organizations (CIO); Wagner Act makes it easier to form unions in the United States.

1936 Sit-down strike by auto workers in Toledo.

1937 CIO wins contracts with U.S. Steel and General Motors.

1939–1945 World War II.

1944 Bretton Woods Agreement; formation of World Bank.

1945 Labour government in Britain begins nationalization of industry.

1945–1973 Global economic boom; suburbanization of working class in the United States; 40-hour workweek common.

1947 India gains independence; beginning of deconization in Asia and Africa; Marshall Plan begins in Europe; Taft-Hartley Act limits power of unions in the United States.

1948–1989 Cold War.

1949 Chinese Revolution; formation of Ministry of International Trade and Industry in Japan.

1950s Rapid increase of women in the labor force in Europe and the United States.

1951 First five-year plan in India.

1953 First (and last) five-year plan in China.

1957 Soviet Union launches Sputnik satellite.

1958 Formation of European Economic Community (Common Market)

1960s Beginning of Japanese export drive; industrialization in Pacific Rim, particularly South Korea, Singapore, Hong Kong, Taiwan.

1965 Beginning of maquiladora policy in Mexico.

1968 United States lands man on the moon.

1968–1972 Strikes and student demonstrations throughout the world.

1971 United States devalues dollar, ends convertibility of dollars into gold.

1973, 1979 OPEC raises prices of oil.

1974 Beginning of global depression.

mid-1970s onward Deindustrialization closes down much of the industrial base of advanced industrial countries.

1978 China begins to introduce market reforms.

1984 Explosion in chemical plant in Bhopal, India.

1989–1991 Collapse of Soviet Union.

1994 North American Free Trade Agreement.

Bibliography

Adas, Michael. *Machines as the Measure of Men: Science, Technology, and Ideologies of Western Dominance.* Ithaca, NY: Cornell University Press, 1989.

Afshar, Haleh, ed. *Women, Work, and Ideology in the Third World.* London: Tavistock, 1985.

Aikman, David. *Pacific Rim: Area of Change, Area of Opportunity.* Boston: Little, Brown, 1986.

Akamatsu, Paul. *Meiji 1868: Revolution and Counter-Revolution in Japan.* New York: Harper and Row, 1972.

Akin, William E. *Technocracy and the American Dream: The Technocrat Movement, 1900–1941.* Berkeley: University of California Press, 1977.

Amdur, Kathryn E. *Syndicalist Legacy: Trade Unions and Politics in Two French Cities in the Era of World War I.* Urbana: University of Illinois Press, 1986.

Amsden, Alice. *Asia's Next Giant: South Korea and Late Industrialization.* New York: Oxford University Press, 1989.

Anderson, Alun M., and John Sigurdon. *Science and Technology in Japan.* New York: Longman, 1991.

Anderson, Benedict. *Imagined Communities: Reflections on the Origins and Spread of Nationalism.* London: Verso, 1983.

Anderson, Charles W. *The Political Economy of Modern Spain.* Madison: University of Wisconsin Press, 1970.

Anderson, Perry. *Considerations on Western Marxism.* London: Verso, 1976.

Andreano, Ralph. *The Economic Impact of the American Civil War.* Cambridge, MA: Schenkman Publishing Company, 1962.

Ashford, Douglas. *The Emergence of the Welfare States.* Oxford, UK: Basil Blackwell, 1986.

Ashton, T. H., ed. *The Brenner Debate: Agrarian Class Structure and Economic Development in Preindustrial Europe.* Cambridge, UK: Cambridge University Press, 1954.

Avrich, Paul. *Anarchist Portraits.* Princeton, NJ: Princeton University Press, 1988.

Ayres, Robert C. *Banking on the Poor: The World Bank and World Poverty.* Cambridge, MA: MIT Press, 1983.

Baker, William. *Sports in the Western World.* Urbana: University of Illinois Press, 1988.

Baldwin, Peter. *The Politics of Social Solidarity: Class Bases of the European Welfare State, 1875–1975.* Cambridge, UK: Cambridge University Press, 1990.

Balibar, Étienne, and Immanuel Wallerstein. *Race, Nation, Class: Ambiguous Identities.*

London: Routledge, Chapman and Hall, 1991.

Bandarage, Asoka. *Colonialism in Sri Lanka: The Political Economy of the Kandyan Highlands, 1833–1886.* Berlin: Mouton, 1983.

Baran, P. A., and P. M. Sweezy. *Monopoly Capital: An Essay on the U.S. Economic and Social Order.* New York: Monthly Review, 1966.

Barnet, Richard J., and John Cavanaugh. *Global Dreams: Imperial Corporations and the New World Order.* New York: Simon and Schuster, 1994.

Barrett, James R. *Work and Community in the Jungle: Chicago's Packinghouse Workers, 1894–1922.* Urbana: University of Illinois Press, 1987.

Berg, Maxine. *The Age of Manufactures, 1700–1820.* Totowa, NJ: Barnes and Noble, 1985.

Berlanstein, Lenard. *The Working People of Paris, 1870–1914.* Baltimore: Johns Hopkins University Press, 1984.

Berlin, Ira. *Free at Last : A Documentary History of Slavery, Freedom, and the Civil War.* New York: New Press, 1992.

Bernstein, Irving. *Turbulent Years: A History of the American Worker.* Boston: Houghton-Mifflin, 1970.

Berry, Brian J. L. *America's Utopian Experiments: Communal Havens from Long-Wave Crises.* Hanover, NH: University Press of New England, 1992.

Black, Cyril E., et al. *The Modernization of Japan and Russia.* New York: Free Press, 1975.

Blackburn, Robin. *The Overthrow of Colonial Slavery, 1776–1848.* New York: Verso, 1988.

Bluestone, Barry, and Bennett Harrison. *The Deindustrialization of America: Plant Closings, Community Abandonment, and the Dismantling of Basic Industry.* New York: Basic, 1982.

Blum, Jerome. *Lord and Peasant in Russia.* Princeton, NJ: Princeton University Press, 1961.

Bodnar, John. *The Transplanted: A History of Immigrants in Urban America.* Bloomington: Indiana University Press, 1985.

Bowden, Witt, Michael Karpovich, and A. P. Usher. *An Economic History of Europe since 1750.* New York: American Book, 1937.

Braudel, Fernand. *The Wheels of Commerce.* New York: Harper and Row, 1979.

Braverman, Harry. *Labor and Monopoly Capital: The Degradation of Work in the Twentieth Century.* New York: Monthly Review, 1974.

Brecher, Jeremy. *Strike!* San Francisco: Straight Arrow Books, 1972.

Brett, E. A. *International Money and Capitalist Crisis: The Anatomy of Global Disintegration.* Boulder, CO: Westview, 1983.

Brimblecombe, Peter. *The Big Smoke: A History of Air Pollution in London.* London: Methuen, 1987.

Brody, David. *Steelworkers in America: The Nonunion Era.* Cambridge, MA: Harvard University Press, 1960.

Bruce, Robert V. *Alexander Graham Bell and the Conquest of Solitude.* Ithaca, NY: Cornell University Press, 1990.

Bruegel, Martin. "The Evolution of Time Consciousness in the Mid-Hudson Valley," *Journal of Social History* 20 (1995): 547–564.

Caldwell, John. *Theory of Fertility Decline.* London: Academic, 1983.

Cameron, Rondo. *France and the Economic Development of Europe, 1800–1914.* Princeton, NJ: Princeton University Press, 1961.

———. "The Industrial Revolution: A Misnomer," *History Teacher* 15 (1982): 337–384.

———. "The Industrial Revolution: Fact or Fiction?" *Contention* 4 (1994): 163–188.

Carnes, Mark, and Clyde Griffen, et al. *Meanings of Manhood.* Chicago: University of Chicago Press, 1990.

Carosso, Vincent P. *Investment Banking in America.* Cambridge, MA: Harvard University Press, 1970.

———. *The Morgans: Private International Bankers, 1854–1913.* Cambridge, MA: Harvard University Press, 1987.

Carr, J. C., and W. Taplin. *History of the British Steel Industry.* Cambridge, MA: Harvard University Press, 1962.

Chakrabarty, Dipesh. *Rethinking Working-Class History: Bengal 1890–1940.* Princeton, NJ: Princeton University Press, 1989.

Chandler, Alfred D., Jr. *Managerial Hierarchies.* Cambridge, MA: Harvard University Press, 1980.

———. *The Railroads: The Nation's First Big Business.* New York: Harcourt, Brace and World, 1965.

———. *The Visible Hand: The Managerial Revolution in American Business.* Cambridge, MA: Belknap, 1977.

Cipolla, Carlo, ed. *The Fontana Economic History of Europe.* 5 vols. London: Fontana, 1970.

Claudin, Fernando. *The Communist Movement: From Comintern to Cominform.* New York: Monthly Review, 1975.

Cline, William R. *International Monetary Reform and the Developing Countries.* Washington, DC: Brookings Institution, 1976.

Coale, Ansley, and Susan Watkins, eds. *The Decline of Fertility in Europe*. Princeton, NJ: Princeton University Press, 1986.

Cochran, Ben. *Welfare Capitalism—And After.* New York: Schocken, 1984.

Cohen, Lizabeth. *Making a New Deal: Industrial Workers in Chicago, 1919–1939.* New York: Cambridge University Press, 1990.

Collins, Robert M. *The Business Response to Keynes, 1929–1964.* New York: Columbia University Press, 1981.

Cortada, James W. *Before the Computer: IBM, NCR, Burroughs, and Remington Rand and the Industry They Created, 1865–1956.* Princeton, NJ: Princeton University Press, 1993.

Cowan, Ruth Schwarz. *More Work for Mother: The Ironies of Household Technology from the Open Hearth to the Microwave.* New York: Basic, 1983.

Cross, Gary. *Time and Money: The Making of Consumer Culture.* London and New York: Routledge, 1993.

Crouzet, François. *The First Industrialists: The Problem of Origins.* New York: Cambridge University Press, 1985.

D'Emilio, John, and Estelle Freedman. *Intimate Matters: A History of Sexuality in America*. New York: Harper and Row, 1989.

Dahrendorf, Ralf. *Class and Class Conflict in Industrial Society.* Stanford, CA: Stanford University Press, 1959.

Davidson, Basil. *The Black Man's Burden: Africa and the Curse of the Nation-State.* New York: Times, 1992.

Davis, Lance Edwin. "The Capital Markets and Industrial Concentration: The U.S. and U.K., A Comparative Study," *Economic History Review* 19 (1966): 255–272.

Deane, Phyllis. *The First Industrial Revolution.* Cambridge, UK: Cambridge University Press, 1969.

Denoun, Donald. *Settler Capitalism: The Dynamics of Dependent Development in the Southern Hemisphere.* New York: Oxford University Press, 1983.

Derry, Kingston, and T. I. Williams. *A Short History of Technology.* Oxford, UK: Oxford University Press, 1961.

di Ruggiero, Guido. *A History of European Liberalism.* London: Oxford University Press, 1927.

Dubinsky, Melvyn. *We Shall Be All: A History of the Industrial Workers of the World.* Chicago: Quadrangle, 1969.

Dublin, Thomas. *Women at Work: The Transformation of Work and Community in Lowell, Massachusetts, 1826–1860.* New York: Columbia University Press, 1979.

Dublin, Thomas, ed. *Farm to Factory: Women's Letters, 1830–1860.* New York: Columbia University Press, 1981.

Dziewanowski, M. K. *Poland in the Twentieth Century.* New York: Columbia University Press, 1971.

Eichengreen, Barry. *Golden Fetters: The Gold Standard and the Great Depression, 1919–1939.* New York: Oxford University Press, 1992.

Escobar, Arturo. *Encountering Development: The Making and Unmaking of the Third World.* Princeton, NJ: Princeton University Press, 1995.

Evans, R. J., ed. *The German Working Class.* London: Croom Helm, 1982.

Ewen, Elizabeth, and Stuart Ewen. *Captains of Consciousness: Mass Images and the Shaping of American Consumers.* New York: Oxford University Press, 1982.

Faemi, Khosrow, ed. *The Maquiladora Industry: Economic Solution or Problem?* New York: Praeger, 1990.

Feldman, Gerald D. *The Great Disorder: Politics, Economics, and Society in the German Inflation.* New York: Oxford University Press, 1993.

Feldman, Gerald D., and Klaus Tenfelde, eds. *Workers, Owners, and Politics in Coal Mining: An International Comparison of Industrial Relations.* Oxford, UK: Berg Publishing, 1990.

Fernandez-Kelly, Maria Patricia. *For We Are Sold, I and My People: Women and Industry in Mexico's Frontier.* Albany: State University of New York Press, 1984.

Filtzer, Donald. *Soviet Workers and Stalinist Industrialization.* London: Pluto, 1986.

Fink, Leon. *Workingmen's Democracy: The Knights of Labor and American Politics.* Urbana: University of Illinois Press, 1983.

Fischer, Claude S. *America Calling: A Social History of the Telephone to 1940.* Berkeley: University of California Press, 1992.

Fisher, Louis. *The Life of Lenin.* New York: Harper and Row, 1966.

Fitzpatrick, Sheila. *Stalin's Peasants: Resistance and Survival in the Russian Village after Collectivization.* New York: Oxford University Press, 1994.

Fitzpatrick, Sheila, Alexander Rabinowitch, and Richard Stites, eds. *Russia in the Era of NEP.* Bloomington: University of Indiana Press, 1991.

Fletcher, Roger, ed. *Bernstein to Brandt: A Short History of German Social Democracy.* London: Edward Arnold, 1987.

Flink, James J. *The Automobile Age.* Boston: MIT Press, 1988.

Flora, Peter, and Arnold Heidenheimer, eds. *The Development of the Welfare States in Europe and America.* New Brunswick, NJ: Transaction Books, 1987.

Foner, Eric. *Free Soil, Free Labor, Free Men: The Ideology of the Republican Party before the Civil War.* New York: Oxford University Press, 1970.

———. *Reconstruction: America's Unfinished Revolution, 1863–1877.* New York: Harper and Row, 1988.

Foner, Philip S. *The Great Labor Uprising of 1877.* New York: Monad Press, 1977.

Foster, Mark. *Henry J. Kaiser: Builder in the American West.* Austin: University of Texas Press, 1989.

Fox-Genovese, Elizabeth, and Eugene D. Genovese. *Fruits of Merchant Capital: Slavery and Bourgeois Property in the Rise and Expansion of Capitalism.* New York: Oxford University Press, 1983.

Frank, André Gunder. *Latin America: Underdevelopment or Revolution.* New York: Monthly Review, 1970.

Friedgut, Theodore H. *Life and Work in Russia's Donbass, 1860–1924.* Princeton, NJ: Princeton University Press, 1989.

Gabin, Nancy F. *Feminism in the Labor Movement: Women and the United Auto Workers, 1935–1975.* Ithaca, NY: Cornell University Press, 1990.

Garraty, John A. *Unemployment in History: Economic Thought and Public Policy.* New York: Harper and Row, 1978.

Garside, W. R., ed. *Capitalism in Crisis: International Responses to the Great Depression.* New York: St. Martin's Press, 1993.

Garson, Barbara. *Electronic Sweatshop: How Computers Are Transforming the Office of Tomorrow into the Factory of the Past.* New York: Simon and Schuster, 1988.

Geary, Dick. *European Labour Protest, 1848–1939.* New York: St. Martin's, 1981.

Geary, Dick, ed. *Labour and Socialist Movements in Europe before 1914.* Oxford, UK: Berg, 1989.

Gerschenkron, Alexander. *Bread and Democracy in Germany.* Berkeley: University of California Press, 1943.

———. *Economic Backwardness in Historical Perspective.* Cambridge, MA: Harvard University Press, 1962.

Ghosh, Suniti. *The Big Indian Bourgeoisie. Its*

Genesis, Growth and Character. Calcutta: Subarnarekha, 1985.

Giedion, S. *Mechanization Takes Command.* New York: Oxford University Press, 1948.

Goodwin, Albert, ed. *The American and French Revolutions.* Cambridge, UK: Cambridge University Press, 1965.

Goodwyn, Lawrence. *The Populist Moment: A Short History of the Agrarian Revolt in America.* New York: Oxford University Press, 1978.

Gordon, Andrew. *Labor and Imperial Democracy in Prewar Japan.* Berkeley: University of California Press, 1991.

Gordon, David M., Richard Edwards, and Michael Reich. *Segmented Work, Divided Workers: The Historical Transformation of Labor in the United States.* New York: Cambridge University Press, 1982.

Gordon, Linda, ed. *Women, the State, and Welfare.* Madison: University of Wisconsin Press, 1990.

Gosling, F. *Before Freud: Neurasthenia and the American Medical Community.* Urbana: University of Illinois Press, 1988.

Graebner, William. *A History of Retirement.* New Haven, CT: Yale University Press, 1980.

Graff, Harvey. *The Legacies of Literacy.* Bloomington: Indiana University Press, 1987.

Gramsci, Antonio. *Selections from the Prison Notebooks.* New York: International Press, 1971.

Grimal, Henri. *Decolonization: The British, French and Belgian Empires, 1919–1963.* Boulder, CO: Westview, 1978.

Gullickson, Gay. *Spinners and Weavers of Auffray.* New York: Cambridge University Press, 1986.

Gusfield, Joseph R. *Symbolic Crusade: Status Politics and the American Temperance Movement.* Urbana: University of Illinois Press, 1986.

Gutman, Herbert George. *Work, Culture, and Society in Industrializing America: Essays in American Working-Class and Social History.* New York: Knopf, 1976.

Habbakuk, H. J. *American and British Technology in the Nineteenth Century: The Search for Labor Saving Inventions.* Cambridge, UK: Cambridge University Press, 1962.

Haggard, Stephan, and Chung-in Moon, *Pacific Dynamics: The International Politics of Industrial Change.* Boulder, CO: Westview, 1989.

Haimson, Leopold H., and Charles Tilly, eds. *Strikes, Wars, and Revolutions in an International Perspective: Strike Waves in the Late Nineteenth and Early Twentieth Centuries.* New York: Cambridge University Press, 1989.

Hannah, Leslie. *Inventing Retirement.* Cambridge, UK: Cambridge University Press, 1986.

Hao, Yen-p'ing. *The Commercial Revolution in Nineteenth Century China: The Rise of the Sino-Western Mercantile Capitalism.* Berkeley: University of California Press, 1986.

Hardach, Gerd. *The First World War, 1914–1918.* Berkeley: University of California Press, 1977.

Harris, William Hamilton. *The Harder We Run: Black Workers since the Civil War.* New York: Oxford University Press, 1982.

Harrison, Bennett. *Lean and Mean: The Changing Landscape of Corporate Power in the Era of Flexibility.* New York: Basic, 1994.

Harrison, Bennett, and Barry Bluestone. *The Great U-Turn: Corporate Restructuring and the Polarizing of America.* New York: Basic, 1988.

Harrison, Brian Howard. *Drink and the Victorians: The Temperance Question in England, 1815–1872.* Pittsburgh, PA: University of Pittsburgh Press, 1971.

Hartwell, R. M., ed. *The Causes of the Industrial Revolution in England.* London: Methuen, 1967.

Harvey, David. *The Changing Landscape of Corporate Power in the Era of Flexibility.* New York: Basic, 1994.

———. *The Condition of Postmodernity: An Inquiry into the Origins of Cultural Change.* Oxford, UK: Blackwell, 1990.

———. *The Urban Experience.* Baltimore: Johns Hopkins University Press, 1989.

Hatch, Nathan O., ed. *The Professions in American History.* Notre Dame, IN: University of Notre Dame Press, 1988.

Haupt, Georges. *Aspects of International Socialism, 1871–1914: Essays.* New York: Columbia University Press, 1986.

Hawley, Ellis W. *The New Deal and the Problem of Monopoly.* Princeton, NJ: Princeton University Press, 1966.

Hays, Samuel. *Beauty, Health, and Permanance: Environmental Politics in the United States.* New York: Cambridge University Press, 1987.

———. *Conservation and the Gospel of Efficiency.* Cambridge, MA: Harvard University Press, 1959.

Heilbroner, Robert L. *The Worldly Philosophers: The Lives, Times, and Ideas of the Great Economic Thinkers.* New York: Simon and Schuster, 1986.

Henderson, William Otto. *The State and the Industrial Revolution in Prussia, 1740–1870.* Liverpool, UK: Liverpool University Press, 1958.

Heywood, Colin. *Childhood in Nineteenth-Century France.* Cambridge, UK: Cambridge University Press, 1988.

Hobsbawm, Eric. *The Age of Empire: 1875–1914.* New York: Vintage, 1987.

Hofstadter, Richard. *Social Darwinism in American Thought, 1860–1915.* Philadelphia: University of Pennsylvania Press, 1944.

Hohenberg, Paul, and Lynn Lees. *The Making of Urban Europe, 1000–1950.* Cambridge, MA: Harvard University Press, 1985.

Holt, Thomas C. *The Problem of Freedom: Race, Labor, and Politics in Jamaica and Britain, 1832–1938.* Baltimore: Johns Hopkins University Press, 1992.

Horn, Pamela. *The Rural World, 1780–1850: Social Change in the English Countryside.* New York: Oxford, 1981.

Hosking, Geoffrey. *The First Socialist Society: A History of the Soviet Union from Within.* Cambridge, MA: Harvard University Press, 1993.

Hounshell, David A. *From the American System to Mass Production, 1800–1932: The Development of Manufacturing Technology in the United States.* Baltimore: Johns Hopkins University Press, 1985.

Hounshell, David A., and John K. Smith. *Science and Corporate Strategy: Du Pont R&D, 1902–1980.* New York: Cambridge University Press, 1988.

Itoh, Makoto. *The World Economic Crisis and Japanese Capitalism.* New York: St. Martin's, 1990.

Jaher, Frederic. *The Urban Establishment.* Urbana: University of Illinois Press, 1982.

James, John A. *Money and Capital Markets in Postbellum America.* Princeton, NJ: Princeton University Press, 1978.

Jaynes, Gerald David. *Branches without Roots: Genesis of the Black Working Class in the American South, 1862–1882.* New York: Oxford University Press, 1986.

Johnson, Chalmers. *MITI and the Japanese Miracle: The Growth of Industrial Policy, 1925–1975.* Stanford, CA: Stanford University Press, 1982.

Johnstone, Frederick A. *Class, Race, and Gold: A Study of Class Relations and Racial Discrimination in South Africa.* Lanham, MD: University Press of America, 1976.

Jones, Jacqueline. *The Dispossessed: America's Underclasses from the Civil War to the Present.* New York: Basic, 1992.

Josephson, Matthew. *The Robber Barons: The Great American Capitalists, 1861–1901.* New York: Harcourt, Brace, 1934.

Joyce, Patrick. *Work, Society, and Politics: The Culture of the Factory.* New Brunswick, NJ: Rutgers University Press, 1980.

Joyce, Patrick, ed. *The Historical Meanings of Work.* New York: Oxford University Press, 1987.

Kaestle, Carl, et al. *Literacy in the United States.* New Haven, CT: Yale University Press, 1991.

Katz, Michael. *The Undeserving Poor: From the War on Poverty to the War on Welfare.* New York: Pantheon, 1989.

Katz, Michael, ed. *The "Underclass" Debate: Views from History*. Princeton, NJ: Princeton University Press, 1993.

Kaufman, Stuart Brace. *Samuel Gompers and the Origins of the American Federation of*

Labor, 1848–1896. Westport, CT: Greenwood, 1973.

Keen, Benjamin, and Mark Wasserman. *A Short History of Latin America.* Boston: Houghton Mifflin, 1984.

Keenan, John L. *A Steel Man in India.* New York: Duell, Sloan, and Pearce, 1943.

Kershaw, Ian. *The Nazi Dictatorship: Problem and Perspectives in Interpretation.* New York: Arnold, 1989.

Kessler-Harris, Alice. *Out to Work: A History of Wage-Earning Women in the United States.* New York: Oxford University Press, 1982.

Keyssar, Alexander. *Out of Work: The First Century of Unemployment in Massachusetts.* Cambridge, UK: Cambridge University Press, 1986.

Kindleberger, Charles P. *A Financial History of Western Europe.* London: Allen and Unwin, 1984.

Klein, Maury. *The Life and Legend of Jay Gould.* Baltimore: Johns Hopkins University Press, 1986.

Kocka, Jürgen. *White Collar Workers in America, 1890–1940: A Social-Political History in International Perspective.* London: Sage, 1980.

Koditschek, Theodore. *Class Formation and Urban Industrial Society: Bradford, 1750–1850.* New York: Cambridge University Press, 1990.

Kolko, Gabriel. *Railroads and Regulation, 1877–1916.* Princeton, NJ: Princeton University Press, 1965.

Kranzberg, M., and C. W. Pursell, Jr., eds. *Technology in Western Civilization. Vol. 2.* New York: Oxford University Press, 1977.

Krause, Paul. *The Battle for Homestead, 1880–1892: Politics, Culture, and Steel.* Pittsburgh, PA: University of Pittsburgh Press, 1992.

Kriedte, Peter, Hans Medick, and Jurgen Schlumbohm. *Industrialization before Industrialization.* New York: Cambridge University Press, 1981.

Kropotkin, Petr Alekseevich. *Mutual Aid: A Factor of Evolution.* Montreal: Black Rose Books, 1989.

Kudo, Akira, and Terushi Hara. *International Cartels in Business History.* Tokyo: University of Tokyo Press, 1992.

Landes, David. *Revolution in Time: Clocks and the Making of the Modern World.* Cambridge, MA: Harvard University Press, 1983.

———. *The Unbound Prometheus: Technical Change and Industrial Development in Western Europe.* Cambridge, UK: Cambridge University Press, 1969.

Laqueur, Walter, ed. *Fascism, A Reader's Guide: Analysis, Interpretations, Bibliography.* Berkeley: University of California Press, 1976.

Larson, Magali S. *The Rise of Professionalism: A Sociological Analysis.* Berkeley: University of California Press, 1977.

Layton, Edwin, Jr. *Revolt of the Engineers: Social Responsibility and the American Engineering Profession.* Baltimore: Johns Hopkins University Press, 1986.

Lefebvre, Georges. *The French Revolution.* New York: Columbia University Press, 1964.

Levy, Marion J., Jr. *Modernization and the Structure of Societies.* Princeton, NJ: Princeton University Press, 1966.

Lewis, Paul H. *The Crisis of Argentinean Capitalism.* Chapel Hill: University of North Carolina Press, 1990.

Lichtenstein, Nelson, and John Harris Howell. *Industrial Democracy in America: The Ambiguous Promise.* New York: Cambridge University Press, 1993.

Lichtenstein, Nelson, and Stephen Meyer, eds. *On the Line: Essays in the History of Auto Work.* Urbana: University of Illinois Press, 1989 (1971).

Lidtke, Vernon. *The Alternative Culture: Socialist Labor in Imperial Germany.* New York: Oxford University Press, 1985.

Lippit, Victor D. *The Economic Development of China.* Armonk, NY: M. E. Sharpe, 1987.

Litwack, Leon. *Been in the Storm So Long: The Aftermath of Slavery.* New York: Knopf, 1979.

Liu, Tessie. *The Weaver's Knot: The Contradictions of Class Struggle and Family Solidarity in Western France.* Ithaca, NY: Cornell University Press, 1994.

Lockwood, David. *The Blackcoated Worker: A Study in Class Consciousness.* London: Allen and Unwin, 1958.

Long, Priscilla. *Where the Sun Never Shines: A History of America's Bloody Coal Industry.* New York: Paragon, 1989.

Love, Joseph, and N. Jacobsen, eds. *Guiding the Invisible Hand. Economic Liberalism and the State in Latin American History.* New York: Praeger, 1988.

McColloch, Mark. *White Collar Workers in Transition: The Boom Years, 1940–1970.* Westport, CT: Greenwood, 1983.

McCurdy, Howard E. *Inside NASA: High Technology and Organizational Change in the U.S. Space Program.* Baltimore: Johns Hopkins University Press.

McLellan, David. *Karl Marx: His Life and Thought.* New York: Harper and Row, 1974.

Mcleod, Hugh. *Religion and the Working Class in Nineteenth-Century Britain.* London: Macmillan, 1984.

McWilliams, Carey. *Factories in the Field: The Story of Migratory Farm Labor in California.* Boston: Little, Brown and Company, 1939.

Magraw, Roger. *A History of the French Working Class.* 2 vols. London: Blackwell, 1992.

Mandel, David. *The Petrograd Workers and the Fall of the Old Regime: From the February Revolution to the July Days, 1917.* New York: St. Martin's, 1983.

Mandel, Ernest. *Long Waves in the History of Capitalism: The Marxist Interpretation.* Cambridge, UK: Cambridge University Press, 1978.

Marchand, Roland. *Advertising the U.S. Dream: Making Way for Modernity, 1920–1940.* Berkeley: University of California Press, 1985.

Markusen, Ann R., and Joel Yudken. *Dismantling the Cold War Economy.* New York: Basic, 1992.

Marx, Karl. *Capital: A Critical Analysis of Capitalist Production.* London: Penguin, 1976.

———. *Capital: A Critique of Political Economy.* New York: International Publishers, 1967.

Mathias, Peter. *The Transformation of England.* New York: Columbia University Press, 1979.

Medvedev, Roy Aleksandrovich. *Let History Judge: The Origins and Consequences of Stalinism.* New York: Columbia University Press, 1989.

Merkle, Judith A. *Management and Ideology: The Legacy of the International Scientific Management Movement.* Berkeley: University of California Press, 1980.

Meyer, Stephen. *The Five Dollar Day: Labor, Management, and Social Control in the Ford Motor Company, 1900–1921.* Albany: State University of New York Press, 1981.

Millard, Andre J. *Edison and the Business of Innovation.* Baltimore: Johns Hopkins University Press, 1990.

Miller, Joseph C. *Way of Death: Merchant Capitalism and the Angolan Slave Trade, 1730–1830.* Madison: University of Wisconsin Press, 1988.

Miller, Michael. *The Bon Marché: Bourgeois Culture and the Department Store, 1869–1920.* Princeton, NJ: Princeton University Press, 1981.

Mills, C. Wright. *White Collar: The American Middle Classes.* New York: Oxford University Press, 1956.

Milward, Alan S. *War, Economy, and Society, 1939–1945.* Berkeley: University of California Press, 1977.

Mintz, Sidney Wilfred. *Sweetness and Power: The Place of Sugar in Modern History.* New York: Viking, 1985.

Moch, Leslie. *Moving Europeans: Migration in Western Europe since 1650.* Bloomington: Indiana University Press, 1992.

Mohl, Raymond A. *The New City: Urban America in the Industrial Age, 1860–1920.* Arlington Heights, IL.: H. Davidson, 1985.

Mokyr, Joel *Industrialization in the Low Countries.* New Haven, CT: Yale University Press, 1978.

Mokyr, Joel, ed. *The Economics of the Industrial Revolution.* London: Allen and Unwin, 1985.

Montgomery, David. *The Fall of the House of Labor: The Workplace, the State, and American Labor Activism, 1865–1925.* Cambridge, UK: Cambridge University Press, 1987.

———. *Workers' Control in America: Studies in the History of Work, Technology, and Labor Struggles.* New York: Cambridge University Press, 1979.

Moss, Bernard. *Origins of the French Labor Movement.* Berkeley: University of California Press, 1976.

Musson, A. E. *Growth of British Industry.* New York: Oxford University Press, 1979.

Musson, A. E., and Eric Robinson. *Science and Technology in the Industrial Revolution.* Toronto: University of Toronto Press, 1969.

Nardinelli, Clark. *Child Labor and the Industrial Revolution.* Bloomington: Indiana University Press, 1990.

Nash, Gerald D. *The Great Depression and World War II: Organizing America, 1933–1945.* New York: St. Martin's, 1979.

Neeson, J. M. *Commoners, Common Right, and Social Change in England, 1700–1820.* Cambridge, UK: Cambridge University Press, 1993.

Nelson, Daniel. *Managers and Workers: Origins of the New Factory System in the United States, 1880–1920.* Madison: University of Wisconsin Press, 1975.

Noble, David F. *America by Design: Science, Technology and the Rise of Corporate Capitalism.* New York: Knopf, 1977.

———. *Forces of Production: A Social History of Automation.* New York: Alfred A. Knopf, 1984.

Norwood, Stephen H. *Labor's Flaming Youth: Telephone Operators and Worker Militancy.* Urbana: University of Illinois Press, 1990.

Nove, Alec. *An Economic History of the USSR, 1917–1991.* Harmondsworth, UK: Penguin, 1992.

Nurkse, Ragnald. *Problems of Capital Formation in Underdeveloped Countries.* Oxford, UK: Oxford University Press, 1953.

Pasdermaijan, Hrant. *The Department Store: Its Origins, Evolution, and Economics*. London: Routledge, 1954.

Patrick, Hugh, ed. *Japanese Industrialization and Its Social Consequences.* Berkeley: University of California Press, 1976.

Payer, Cheryl. *The World Bank: A Critical Analysis.* New York: Monthly Review, 1982.

Peralta-Ramos, Monica. *The Political Economy of Argentina: Power and Class since 1930.* Boulder, CO: Westview, 1992.

Philip, Taft. *The A.F. of L. in the Time of Gompers.* New York: Harper and Brothers, 1957.

Pilbeam, Pamela. *The Middle Classes in Europe, 1789–1914. France, Germany, Italy and Russia.* Chicago: Lyceum, 1990.

Pollard, Sidney. *The Genesis of Modern Management.* Cambridge, MA: Harvard University Press, 1965.

Preobrazhenskii, Evgenii Akekseevich. *The Crisis of Soviet Industrialization: Selected Essays.* White Plains, NY: M. E. Sharpe, 1979.

Przeworski, Adam. *Capitalism and Social Democracy.* New York: Cambridge University Press, 1985.

Pursell, Carroll W., Jr. *Technology in America: A History of Individuals and Ideas.* Boston: MIT Press, 1981.

Rachleff, Peter. *Black Labor in the South: Richmond, Virginia, 1865–1890.* Philadelphia: Temple University Press, 1984.

Rader, Benjamin. *American Sports.* Englewood Cliffs, NJ: Prentice-Hall, 1990.

Reich, Leonard S. *The Making of American Industrial Research: Science and Business at GE and Bell, 1876–1926.* New York: Cambridge University Press, 1985.

Rendell, Jane. *The Origins of Modern Feminism.* New York: Schocken Books, 1984.

Riskin, Carl. *China's Political Economy: The Quest for Development since 1949.* Oxford, UK: Oxford University Press, 1987.

Rock, Howard P. *Artisans of the New Republic: The Tradesmen of New York City in the Age of Jefferson.* New York: New York University Press, 1979.

Rodgers, Daniel T. *The Work Ethic in Industrial America, 1850–1920.* Chicago: University of Chicago Press, 1974.

Rodney, Walter. *How Europe Underdeveloped Africa*. Washington, D.C.: Howard University Press, 1981.

Roediger, David R., and Philip S. Foner. *Our Own Time: A History of American Labor and the Working Day.* New York: Verso, 1989.

Rosenzweig, Roy. *Eight Hours for What We Will: Workers and Leisure in an*

Industrializing City, 1870–1920. Cambridge, UK: Cambridge University Press, 1983.

Rosner, David, and Gerald Markowitz, eds. *Dying for Work: Workers' Health and Safety in Twentieth-Century America*. Bloomington: Indiana University Press, 1986.

Rostow, W. W. *The Stages of Economic Growth*. Cambridge, UK: Cambridge University Press, 1960.

Rothermund, Dietmar. *An Economic History of India: From Pre-Colonial Times to 1991*. London: Routledge, 1993.

Rozman, Gilbert, ed. *The Modernization of China*. New York: Free Press, 1980.

Rubinstein, W. D. *Men of Property: The Very Wealthy in Britain since the Industrial Revolution*. New Brunswick, NJ: Rutgers University Press, 1981.

Schaeffer, Robert K. *War in the World System*. Westport, CT: Greenwood, 1989.

Schor, Juliet B. *The Overworked American: The Unexpected Decline of Leisure*. New York: Basic, 1992.

Scott, Joan W. *Gender and the Politics of History*. New York: Columbia University Press, 1988.

———. *The Glassworkers of Carmaux*. Cambridge, MA: Harvard University Press, 1974.

Shanin, Teodor. *Peasants and Peasant Societies*. Oxford, UK: Basil Blackwell, 1987.

Shepard, Jon. *Automation and Alienation*. Cambridge, MA: MIT Press, 1971.

Sinclair, Upton. *The Jungle*. Memphis, TN: St. Lukes, 1988.

Skowronek, Stephen. *Building a New American State: The Expansion of National Administrative Capacity, 1877–1920*. New York: Cambridge University Press, 1982.

Smith, Thomas. *Political Change and Industrial Development in Japan: Governmental Enterprise, 1868–1880*. Stanford, CA: Stanford University Press, 1955.

Smith, Tony, ed. *The End of the European Empires: Decolonization after World War II*. Lexington, MA: Heath, 1975.

Spring, David. *European Landed Elites in the Nineteenth Century*. Baltimore: Johns Hopkins University Press, 1977.

Stearns, Peter N. *Be a Man: Males in Modern Society*. Rev. ed. New York: Holmes and Meier, 1990.

———. *1848: The Tide of Revolutions*. New York: Norton, 1974.

———. *The Industrial Revolution in World History*. Boulder, CO: Westview, 1993.

———. *Lives of Labor: Work in Maturing Industrial Society*. New York: Holmes and Meier, 1975.

———. *Paths to Authority*. Urbana: University of Illinois Press, 1978.

———. *Revolutionary Syndicalism and French Labor: A Cause without Rebels*. New Brunswick, NJ: Rutgers University Press, 1971.

Stearns, Peter N., and Herrick Chapman. *European Society in Upheaval: Social History since 1750*. 3d ed. New York: Macmillan, 1992.

Steinberg, Theodore. *Nature Incorporated: Industrialization and the Waters of New England*. Cambridge, UK: Cambridge University Press, 1951.

Sumiya, Mikio, and Koji Taira. *An Outline of Japanese Economic History, 1603–1940: Major Works and Research Findings*. Tokyo: University of Tokyo Press, 1979.

Sweezy, Paul M. *The Transition from Feudalism to Capitalism*. London: Verso, 1978.

Takaki, Ronald. *Strangers from a Different Shore: A History of Asian Americans*. New York: Penguin, 1989.

Tampke, J. *The People's Republics of Eastern Europe*. New York: St. Martin's, 1983.

Tawney, R. H. *Religion and the Rise of Capitalism*. Gloucester, MA: P. Smith, [1926] 1962.

Taylor, A. J. P., ed. *The Standard of Living in the Industrial Revolution*. London: Methuen, 1975.

Taylor, George Rogers. *The Transportation Revolution, 1815–1860*. Armonk, NY: M. E. Sharpe, 1977.

Tedlow, Richard S. *New and Improved: The Story of Mass Marketing in America*. New York: Basic, 1990.

Thernstrom, Stephan. *Poverty and Progress.* Cambridge, MA: Harvard University Press, 1964.

Thompson, E. P. *The Making of the English Working Class.* New York: Pantheon, 1963.

———. "The Moral Economy of the English Crowd," *Past and Present* 50 (1971): 76–136.

———. "Time, Industrial Work Discipline, and Capitalism," *Past and Present* 38 (1967): 56–97.

Thompson, Leonard M. *A History of South Africa.* New Haven, CT: Yale University Press, 1990.

Thompson, Roger C. *The Pacific Basin since 1945.* London: Longman, 1994.

Thornton, John. *Africa and Africans in the Making of the Atlantic World, 1400–1680.* New York: Cambridge University Press, 1992.

Tilly, Louise, and Joan Scott. *Women, Work, and Family.* New York: Methuen,1987.

Tomlins, Christopher L., and Andrew J. King, eds. *Labor Law in America: Historical and Critical Essays.* Baltimore: Johns Hopkins University Press, 1992.

Tomlinson, B. R. *The Economy of Modern India, 1860–1970.* New York: Cambridge University Press, 1993.

Torstendahl, Rolf. *Bureaucratisation in Northwestern Europe, 1880–1985.* London: Routledge, 1991.

Trattner, Walter. *Crusade for the Children: A History of the National Child Labor Committee and Child Labor Reform in America.* Chicago: Quadrangle, 1970.

Trotter, Joe William. *Coal, Class, and Color: Blacks in Southern West Virginia, 1915–32.* Urbana: University of Illinois Press, 1990.

Trotter, Joe William, ed. *The Great Migration in Historical Perspective: New Dimensions of Race, Class, and Gender.* Bloomington: University of Indiana Press, 1991.

Tucker, R. P., and J. F. Richards, eds. *Global Deforestation and the Nineteenth-Century World Economy.* Durham, NC: Duke University Press, 1983.

Tucker, Robert C. *The Marx-Engels Reader.* New York: W. W. Norton, 1978.

Turnbull, C. M. *A History of Singapore, 1819–1988.* 2d ed. New York: Oxford University Press, 1988.

Voss, Kim. *The Making of American Exceptionalism.* Ithaca, NY: Cornell University Press, 1993.

Wall, Joseph Frazier. *Andrew Carnegie.* Pittsburgh, PA: University of Pittsburgh Press, 1970.

Wallerstein, Immanuel. *The Modern World-System I: Capitalist Agriculture and the Origins of the European World-Economy in the Sixteenth Century.* San Diego, CA: Academic, 1974.

Warren, Kenneth. *The American Steel Industry, 1850–1970: A Geographical Interpretation.* Pittsburgh, PA: Pittsburgh University Press, 1973.

Way, Peter. *Common Labour: Workers and the Digging of North American Canals, 1780–1860.* Cambridge, UK: Cambridge University Press, 1993.

Weinstein, Barbara. *The Amazon Rubber Boom, 1850–1920.* Stanford, CA: Stanford University Press, 1983.

Weissbach, Lee. *Child Labor Reform in Nineteenth Century France.* Baton Rouge: Louisiana State University Press, 1989.

Wexler, Imanuel. *The Marshall Plan Revisited: The European Recovery Program in Economic Perspective.* Westport, CT: Greenwood, 1983.

Wiener, Martin. *English Culture and the Decline of the Industrial Spirit, 1850–1980.* Cambridge, UK: Cambridge University Press, 1981.

Williams, Eric. *Capitalism and Slavery.* Chapel Hill: University of North Carolina Press, 1944.

Williams, Rosalind. *Dream Worlds: Mass Consumption in Late Nineteenth Century France.* Berkeley: University of California Press, 1982.

Wilson, Charles. *Australia, 1788–1988: The Creation of a Nation.* New York: Barnes & Noble, 1987.

Wolf, Eric. *Europe and the People without History.* Berkeley: University of California Press, 1982.

Wolfe, Joel. *Working Women, Working Men: Sao Paulo and the Rise of Brazil's Industrial Working Class, 1900–1955*. Durham, NC: Duke University Press, 1993.

Woodward, C. Vann. *Origins of the New South, 1877–1913*. Baton Rouge: Louisiana State University Press, 1951.

Worster, Donald. *Dust Bowl: The Southern Plains in the 1930s*. New York: Oxford University Press, 1979.

Wergin, Daniel. *The Prize: The Epic Conquest for Oil, Money, and Power.* New York: Simon and Schuster, 1991.

Zaionchkovsky, Petr Andreevich. *The Abolition of Serfdom in Russia.* Gulf Breeze, FL: Academic International, 1978.

Zdatny, Steven. *The Politics of Survival: Artisans in Twentieth-Century France.* New York: Oxford University Press, 1990.

Illustration Credits

6 Courtesy of The Coca-Cola Company.
16 Courtesy of Courtaulds.
24 Library of Congress.
41 Library of Congress.
52 Library of Congress.
56 Boyer-Viollett.
58 From *The Crystal Palace Exhibition Illustrated Catalogue* (1851), courtesy of Dover Publications, Inc.
69 UPI/Bettmann.
77 The Bettmann Archive.
85 The Bettmann Archive.
88 Popperfoto/Archive Photo.
92 The Bettmann Archive.
96 Courtesy of Ford Motor Company, Photo Media.
97 Courtesy of Ford Motor Company, Photo Media.
107 Topham/The Image Works.
118 Library of Congress.
133 Ohio Historical Society.
136 AP/Wide World Photos.
157 The Bettmann Archive.
161 Courtesy of Sears, Roebuck Company.
170 Library of Congress.
177 Courtesy of Ford Motor Company, Photo Media.
184 The Bettmann Archive.
200 Corbis-Bettmann.
208 United Nations.
218 The Bettmann Archive.
229 Maryland Historical Society.
235 Cameramann/The Image Works.
239 The Bettmann Archive.
246 Popperfoto/Archive Photo.
254 Goodsmith/The Image Works.
256 Courtesy of Courtaulds.
267 The Bettmann Archive.
279 Eastcott/The Image Works.
284 The Bettmann Archive.
289 UPI/Bettmann.

Index

Page numbers in bold refer to main entries.

Index

(Continued from front flap)

Features of this user-friendly volume include a comprehensive introduction that places the industrial revolution in historical and social perspective, an extensive bibliography, a timeline that spans four centuries, and a subject index. The text is enhanced by more than 40 illustrations.

Peter N. Stearns is the Heinz Professor of History and Dean of the College of Humanities at Carnegie Mellon University. He is editor-in-chief of the *Journal of Social History* and author of the *Encyclopedia of Social History, The Industrial Revolution in World History,* and *World Civilization.*

John H. Hinshaw received his Ph.D. from Carnegie Mellon University. He has published numerous reviews and articles and is a contributor to the *Encyclopedia of Social History*. He also has been Program Director for Special Academic Projects at Carnegie Mellon and has taught at Bates College.